Baby, Let Me Follow You Down

ERIC VON SCHMIDT
(Books for Children)
COME FOR TO SING
THE YOUNG MAN WHO WOULDN'T HOE CORN
THE BALLAD OF BAD BEN BILGE
MR. CHRIS AND THE INSTANT ANIMALS

JIM ROONEY
BOSSMEN: BILL MONROE AND MUDDY WATERS

Baby, Let Me Follow You Down

The illustrated story of the Cambridge folk years

by Eric von Schmidt & Jim Rooney

Second Edition

University of Massachusetts Press

Amherst

TALKING HEADS

Page 18 Debbie Green; 22 Manny Greenhill; 24 Tony Saletan; 26 Clay Jackson; 28 Ethan Signer; 31 Bob Siggins; 47 Joan Baez; 49 Bob Neuwirth; 50 John Nagy; 58 Joan Baez; 65 Eric von Schmidt; 68 Leadbelly; 69 Eric von Schmidt; 75 Eric von Schmidt; 76 Rolf Cahn; 80 Rolf Cahn; 83 Bob Siggins' guitar; 84 Rolf Cahn; 92 Jim Rooney; 96 Bill Keith; 127 Maria Muldaur; 129 Jim Rooney; 136 Jackie Washington; 139 Joe Val; 142 Paul Rothchild; 144 Geoff Muldaur; 155 Jim Rooney; 156 Bill Keith; 162 Ralph Rinzler; 178 Maria & Geoff Muldaur; 189 Mississippi John Hurt; 189 Son House; 204 Mark Spoelstra; 206 Spider John Koerner; 208 Clarence White; 211 "Banana" Levinger; 215 Taj Mahal; 218 Jackie Washington; 220 Manny Greenhill; 222 Bob Neuwirth; 225 Mimi and Mama Joan Baez; 228 Clay Jackson; 232 Betsy Siggins; 236 Eric von Schmidt; 250 Joe Chambers; 274 Jim Field; 276 Tom Rush; 277 Chris Smither; 278 Dick Fariña; 280 Bob Dylan and Joan Baez; 287 Judy Collins and John Cooke; 290 Mel Lyman; 292 Fritz Richmond; 296 Bob Dylan; 301 Jim Rooney; 305 Bonnie Raitt

SONG TITLES

"Come All You Fair and Tender Ladies" (traditional); "Leavin' Home" as done by the Charles River Valley Boys, who learned it from Charlie Poole and the North Carolina Ramblers; "Sail Away, Ladies, Sail Away" as done by Uncle Dave Macon; "Black Is The Color" as done by John Jacob Niles; "Baby, Let Me Lay It On You" as done by Blind Boy Fuller; "We Shall Not Be Moved" as done by Mississippi John Hurt; "Overseas Stomp" as done by Will Shade of the Memphis Jug Band; "California to the New York Island" from "This Land Is Your Land," words and music by Woody Guthrie. TRO Music, copyright © 1956, 1958, 1970 Ludlow Music Inc., New York, N.Y. Used by permission; "Ocean of Diamonds" as done by Joe Val with Keith and Rooney. Written by Cliff Carnahan; "Nobody's Business" from "Champagne Don't Hurt Me, Baby" by Eric von Schmidt, copyright © 1963 Tru-Sound Music; "Foggy Mountain Top" as done by the Cortez Family; "Storybook Ball" as done by Jim Kweskin and the Jug Band. Written by Montgomery and Perry, Melrose Music; "Fixin' To Die" as done by Booker White; "Where Do You Come From? Where Do You Go?" from "Cotton-Eye Joe" (traditional); "Children of Darkness" by Richard Fariña, copyright © 1966 Warner Brothers Music. All rights reserved. Used by permission; "It's All Over Now, Baby Blue" by Bob Dylan, copyright © 1965, Warner Brothers Music. All rights reserved. Used by permission; "Got My Mojo Workin'" by McKinley Morganfield aka Muddy Waters; "Wet Birds Fly at Night" by Eric von Schmidt, copyright © 1970, 1972, 1978 Minglewood

CREDITS

Some of Bill Keith's remarks in "We Shall Not Be Moved" were recorded in an interview in England by Pete Frame; some of Geoff Muldaur's remarks in "Ocean of Diamonds," "Storybook Ball," and "Wet Birds Fly at Night" were recorded in an interview by Bob Kimmel; some of Phil Spiro's account describing the rediscovery of Son House in "Fixin' To Die" first appeared in *The Broadside*, vol. III, no. 11, July 22, 1964; Al Wilson's remarks at the end of "Fixin' To Die" appeared in an interview with Al by Pete Welding called "Just Those Five Notes" in *Rolling Stone*, Feb. 18, 1971; Joan Baez's remarks in "Sail Away, Ladies, Sail Away," "Children of Darkness," and "Wet Birds Fly At Night" appeared in *Daybreak* by Joan Baez, copyright © 1968 by Joan Baez. Used by permission of the Dial Press; Bob Dylan's remarks in "It's All Over Now, Baby Blue" reprinted from *Bob Dylan: An Intimate Biography* by Anthony Scaduto, copyright © 1971 by Anthony Scaduto. Used by permission of Grosset & Dunlap, Inc.

Cover design by Rebecca S. Neimark
Cover art copyright © 1979 by Eric von Schmidt

The University of Massachusetts Press edition is published by arrangement with Eric von Schmidt and James Rooney. Originally published 1979 by Anchor Press / Doubleday, Garden City, N.Y.
Copyright © 1979 by Eric von Schmidt and James Rooney
Preface to the second edition © 1994 by Eric von Schmidt and James Rooney
All rights reserved
Printed in the United States of America
LC 93–48172
ISBN 0–87023–925–2
Library of Congress Cataloging-in-Publication Data are available.
British Library Cataloguing in Publication data are available.

In honor of the fiftieth anniversary in 2008 of the founding of Club 47, all of the photographs in this book have been rescreened to achieve a higher quality of reproduction. This new edition was first printed in November 2007.

This one is for Caitlin and Megan. With love, from Papa.
It is also for John and Eileen Rooney. With love, from Jimmy.

The story of a book is not as important as the story in the book, so we will spare you that. Suffice it to say that it was no magic show. It was not done with mirrors. We worked hard, because we wanted to. And we were helped by a lot of people, because they wanted to.

You can't publish a book without a publisher, and it's hard to deal with a publisher without an editor. Bill Strachan took us at our word when we said we were serious, and if he ever doubted our abilities or lost faith, he kept it to himself and went out of his way to make it possible for us to write and produce the book in total freedom. Our thanks also to his secretary Gish Jen for keeping up with our mad rush to the deadline.

One of the most important elements in our story is the sound of each individual's voice. There are over sixty of them. We tried hard to talk to as many people in person as we could. Others we contacted by letter or phone. The time and the effort that they took to help us was a major incentive for us to be true to them. Our story is subjective, of course, but our conversations and communications gave much of the life to our story. They made it their story.

We were also fortunate to have the cooperation and help of the photographers whose work gives this story a visual dimension it never would have had otherwise. We have tried to credit as many of the photographs as we could. We must also thank some whose extra help made a big difference: Bob Aude, John Cooke, Charlie Frizzell, Steve Fenerjian, Charlie Sawyer, Rick Stafford, and Rick Sullo. They were there at the time, and they're still there.

Seeing so many people meant that we had to travel around a lot, and that meant staying somewhere and bringing our circus to somebody's house. In New York we stayed with Bob and Tori Freedman, Charlie Rothchild, and Peter von Schmidt; in Santa Monica with Mitch and Carol Greenhill; in Mill Valley with Debbie Andersen; in La Jolla with Bob Siggins; in Cambridge with Chance Browne and Darleen Wilson.

We did our best to gather up everyone's memorabilia along the way. Again, there were some who went above and beyond the call of whatever: John Cooke, Mimi Fariña, Manny Greenhill, Jim Kweskin and the Lyman Family, Byron Linardos, Peggy and Tex Logan, Betsy Schmidt, Bob Siggins, Phil Spiro, and Dick Waterman came through.

Although we have become better typists than we ever wanted to be, our skills pale in comparison to those of the ladies who have labored over our interview transcriptions and manuscripts: Judith Antares, Kayo Makita, and the girls at Girl Friday in Sarasota—Grace Cook, Debye Bernard, Susan Davis, Phyllis Russell, and Janet Startz. The book was set in type by Dick Roulston, Lynn Roulston, and Tamara Rodriguez at RW Roulston, Typographers, Sarasota, Florida. The cover photograph was taken by Mike Norton with the assistance of Bill Koplitz at the Michael Norton Studio, Tampa, Florida. Chuck Beck, Fred Hart, and Bob Simon at the RoMo Photo Shop on Siesta Key, Sarasota, provided us with first class service on a wide range of photographic needs. Pete Schmidt at Gan Eden in Sarasota was more than generous in letting us use his stat machine at all hours. Darleen Wilson helped with all sorts of things from transcribing interviews, to hunting down song lyrics, to adding just plain enthusiasm.

Our thanks to all of them.

This book was designed by Eric von Schmidt with a lot of help from his good friend Jim Rooney. The calligraphy, a little Elizabethan Zen, is by Paul Fowler. Thanks.

These people took the time to talk with us in person or by phone or communicated with us by letter: Debbie Andersen, Eric Andersen, Paul Arnoldi, David Barry, Dan Bump, Billy Burke, Rolf Cahn, Joe Chambers, Joyce Chopra, John Cooke, Earl Crabb, Owen DeLong, Mimi Fariña, Steve Fassett, Jim Field, Dave Frederickson, Vera Mae Frederickson, Charlie Frizzell, David Greenberg, Manny Greenhill, Mitch Greenhill, Peter Guralnick, Jill Henderson, Midge Huffman, Clay Jackson, Lynn Joiner, Robert L. Jones, Bill Keith, John Koerner, Barry Kornfeld, Jim Kweskin, Jack Landron, Carol Langstaff, "Banana" Levinger, Everett Alan Lilly, Byron Linardos, Tex Logan, Alice Macsorley, Don Macsorley, Taj Mahal, Buzz Marten, Susan Metzger, Geoff Muldaur, Maria Muldaur, John Nagy, Paul Nagy, Bob Neuwirth, Victor Oppenheimer, Bonnie Raitt, Fritz Richmond, Ralph Rinzler, Peter Robinson, Charlie Rothchild, Paul Rothchild, Peter Rowan, Tom Rush, Tony Saletan, Betsy Schmidt, John Sebastian, Bob Siggins, Ethan Signer, Chris Smither, Maynard Solomon, Phil Spiro, Mark Spoelstra, Rick Stafford, Moophy Sweezy, Nancy Sweezy, Joe Val, Helen von Schmidt, Dick Waterman, Roland White, Dave Wilson, Peter Wolf, and Dick Zaffron.

PREFACE TO THE SECOND EDITION

When we wrote this book in 1978, we were dealing with recollections that were still relatively fresh in our minds and in the minds of those we interviewed. Our sources were musicians, agents, producers, club managers, and the like, but they were also our friends. Everyone we talked with had the opportunity to say what was to be on or off the record. In the months that followed no one called and asked us to change anything they had told us. In fact, when we sometimes called people and asked if they really wanted a particular statement to be quoted, everyone said, "Yes. It happened. It's true. Print it." So, we did.

Now, it seems, we have slipped over an invisible but real boundary in time into the realm of "history." A whole generation has grown up in the thirty or more years since our story began. Many of them wonder what it was like "back then" in the fifties and sixties. We are very happy that this account, with the freshness and honesty of people's stories and the immediacy of the illustrations, will be available once again to help satisfy those who are curious about this period.

Although some of us suspected it then, there seems to be little doubt now that the time of our collective sojourn in Cambridge was a kind of generational watershed. We were searching for definition in our lives, and folk music was the vehicle we chose to help us in that search. Folk music in all its various forms, from Elizabethan ballads to Delta blues to Kentucky bluegrass to songs of social protest and personal discovery, brought us together in a community of our own making and led each of us to find a new path—a path that each could truly call his or her own.

The great majority of those involved in the folk music scene in Cambridge back then are still following the paths we found for ourselves. Many are still very much involved in music; others are in the arts, education, research, or social and community service. Folk music served to focus our energies on people themselves, their lives, and all the aspects of our common humanity, at a time when individuals seemed to be eclipsed by ever larger institutions. If there is anything we can take from our time together in Cambridge and pass on to those who will follow, it is that focus and the energy it generated in us.

Not long after the first edition of *Baby Let Me Follow You Down* was published, a friend of ours who had been directly involved in the folk music scene for many years said that it was the first book he had read on the subject that was *true*. That meant a lot to us. The book was true then and it still is.

Eric von Schmidt and Jim Rooney
October 1993

FOREWORD

This is the story of many people who happened to come together in Boston and Cambridge during the late fifties and early sixties, who became part of a musical community, and whose common bond was a rediscovery of the many basic forms of American folk music.

We came from many different backgrounds and many different places—places like Grand Island, Nebraska; Dedham, Massachusetts; Akron, Ohio; Kerrville, Texas; Westport, Connecticut; Los Angeles, California; Concord, New Hampshire; Grant's Pass, Oregon; New York, New York—wherever we were in the late forties and early fifties, "growing up," as they said then, during that flat pink and charcoal stretch of boredom known as the Eisenhower Years.

Education is the key to the American Dream. You go to grade school, you go to high school, you go to college. *At least.* Then you go on to have a career as a doctor, lawyer, teacher, businessman—something substantial and secure. You become a responsible member of society. So it was that most of us came to the Cambridge/Boston area in pursuit of a diploma. We certainly didn't come to participate in a musical scene. No scene existed.

However, music did exist in the lives of various individuals. Very often it had happened in an accidental, off-hand way. An uncle had given someone a ukelele; someone else heard a record somewhere; something came out of the radio one day and caught someone's ear; an older brother brought some records home from college. Each incident led each person to want to find out a little bit more. Maybe get an instrument or some more records. Get together with a friend or two and find out where to hear some more music like that. Share new information with each other. Have you heard Pete Seeger? Do you know where I can get some "folk" records? I heard this guy named Hank Williams. It's called hillbilly music. Wait 'til you hear this! It's the "San Francisco Bay Blues."

Listening to music and trying to play and sing a few songs started to become more important than whatever was going on in school. For some it became a passion that started to smoulder inside. It was at this point that certain individuals made a difference. Some were teachers, some were organizers, some were sources of energy, instigators, and others were simply talented, musically gifted.

So, where no scene had existed before, one came into being. What had been smouldering before burst into flames. Joan Baez was the most prominent member of a group whose numbers were growing daily, as were their abilities as musicians and performers. More important still was the fact that there was an audience for this music. People wanted to hear it. It filled some need that we all shared in common before we ever knew what it was. Whatever plans we might have had before were to be totally changed.

Come All You Fair & Tender Maidens

Don't you remember our days of courting,
When you'd lay your head upon my breast?
You could make me believe, by the falling of your arm,
That the sun rose in the west.

weet Innocence. None of us will ever be that innocent again. To the outsider, Boston and Cambridge often seem more like vast, sprawling towns than the huge cities that they really are. Back in the late fifties even the slums could look quaint if you weren't living there. The high-rises and Urban Renewal were still on the drawing boards. Politicians, city planners and architects were making their moves, but not much of it had become visible reality. Except for the twenty-five story John Hancock Building, the Boston cityscape still looked pretty much as it had a hundred years before and across the Charles River, in Cambridge, at Harvard University, Gropius was just beginning to play with his blocks.

The banks of the Charles up around the Larz Andersen Bridge were particularly idyllic. A spot where the "Cliffies" and their Harvard boyfriends could discuss the meaning of the latest Bergman film, worry about the bomb, and try not to notice the condoms floating down from a less lofty, but geographically higher, Watertown. Other less easily identifiable flotsam could almost seem, well — picturesque. Little bits of life in the raw.

And the politics. If you struck up a conversation with a native of either city that did not involve the Bruins or the Red Sox, you were assured that nowhere else on earth were there more corrupt city officials, more crooked police, more scoundrels on the dole, than right here in Cambridge and/or Boston. "May you be halfway into Heaven before the devil finds out you're dead" read the little plaque to be found in every little gift store in town. And one of the amazing things was that all this certifiable thievery seemed to be a constant source of civic pride! Mayor Curley, Honey Fitz, Joe Kennedy, and the rest were cult heroes. Even crime seemed picturesque. It is hardly surprising that many of the students arriving from more straitlaced parts of the country were quickly beguiled. The thought of such roguery added spice to the drab life in the gray and hallowed halls of erudition which dotted the area. In and around Boston were Boston University, Northeastern University, Emerson College, the Museum School, Tufts, Wellesley College, Boston College and more. Cambridge boasted Harvard, Radcliffe, and M.I.T., and a relatively new university, Brandeis, was starting out in

JOAN BAEZ (1958) Photographer unknown. Courtesy of Manny Greenhill.

Waltham. The usual sense of identity associated with "school spirit," the fraternities, the "Go, Team, Go!" sports trip was still strong in those days. Within all these institutions, however, there was a small group, a miniscule number, who simply couldn't get with it. They were looking elsewhere for stimulation and new phenomenon was occurring that would fulfill some of their needs. It was called the coffee house.

n the beginning there was Tulla's Coffee Grinder. That was it for coffee houses in Cambridge, circa 1957. Tulla's was one small, totally unpretentious room. It was crammed with small tables, many chairs, and the interior was on a level several feet lower than the sidewalk outside. The atmosphere was warm, womb-like, and it could get a little soggy when the cups were being washed and the coffee machine was in operation. It was run by a statuesque woman known simply as Tulla, and her husband. Tulla nearly always managed to look as serene as her husband looked worried. A talented young Harvard student, Dick Zaffron, sometimes played flamenco or classical guitar, but the music was not meant to intrude on the chess players, or interrupt the various conversations buzzing through the dim room. Classical records added to the ambience and cut down on the overhead. Tulla's was soon to become the spawning ground for a lot of the

Cambridge pickers, but it never did become a music club. That distinction was to fall to a failing antique store several blocks down the street.

If you walk down Mt. Auburn Street in the direction of Central Square today, you will notice a boat-like group of buildings looming before you. If you allow your gaze to drift upward you will be rewarded by a rare sight. Atop the building occupying the bow position is a huge green bird. Is it an Ibis? Is it a stork? Does it matter? These ornithological considerations are unimportant when you realize you have stumbled upon one of the little known wonders of the world, the Petrified Ship of Fools. It is the Harvard Lampoon Building. Amidships of this strange craft is a store called Cahaly's. Ralph Cahaly's. He was there in the fateful fall of '57, only a little closer to the bow. And if you had been there too you might have noticed Paula Kelly and Joyce Kalina a few steps down the street from Cahaly's little market, staring dreamily through the window of old Fournier's vacant antique store.

Music was not part of their dream. Certainly not folk music anyway. Cinema, poetry, perhaps, stimulating intellectual discussion, like Paris in the twenties...Joyce remembers the beginnings. **We had both graduated from Brandeis in 1957. I had a degree in comparative literature. I wanted to get into theater, and that didn't work out. I couldn't get a job. I met Paula who had got a job and was extremely unhappy, and we just both said, "The hell with it all! We'll start our own business. We won't work for anybody." There**

Two views of TULLA (c. 1959). Photographs by Stephen Fenerjian.

was a coffeeshop up the street called Tulla's. So we got the idea to open a coffeeshop, too. We wandered around looking at places. And we looked in the window at 47 Mt. Auburn Street.

It has been an antique store run by a man named Arnold Fournier, and he couldn't pay the rent and moved out. So we found out the landlord's name — Bertha Cohen — and we went to see her. She was a stereotype of the mad old miser. She was a little old scary lady whose office was in the basement of 999 Memorial Drive, and when you went down the steps there was an old-fashioned sign with a finger pointing that said, "OFFICE." She had a teeny little office, and an old secretary named Mrs. Cahill sat with her. They had these old-fashioned safes, and the rent checks were just lying strewn all over the place. She had a closet full of broken glass. I mean she was truly eccentric. She took to us, and she decided that we were going to be her proteges. At any rate, she signed a lease with us for $300.00 or so a month.

The girls managed to scrape up the $3,000 downpayment on the lease and talked endless numbers of people into extending them credit. Then they tackled the job of building a coffee house from scratch.

It was the most wonderful three or four months of my life. The place was just empty. There was no plumbing, no kitchen. We constructed walls. We made the little kitchen area. We painted. I had never done any carpentry in my life, and it is a terrific kick to find out that you can do it.

Paula had kept her job with the research firm to pay the original bills.

We were young. We were awfully naive, much more so than twenty-year-olds today. And we used to joke about it. Wouldn't it be fun to open up a coffee shop. And so we did it. We thought it would be a nice civilized sort of thing. Of course coffee shops in the European sense were not suited to America, particularly in 1957-58.

Both the girls were enchanted with things European. They had met in Brandeis after Joyce's junior year in Europe. Everything, it seemed, that was chic and sophisticated, that had any artistic value, was European. Americans were, let's face it, a bunch of klutzes. So the two of them labored nightly with buckets of paint and books on wiring. They strove to upgrade culture in Cambridge. They would get hysterics. They would get the giggles; but they would get it *done.*

They did, but somewhere along the line European ambience was given a back seat. The girls, splattered with KemTone and dizzy from attempting to solve the mysteries of electrical circuits, must have been an easy mark for a little talk, fast and sweet. Young jazz playing friends from Brandeis and Harvard took one look at that empty room, and had a collective bright idea. Hey, man, why be so snobby? Anyway Europeans dig jazz, don't they? What's wrong with an *American* coffee house? Jazz is *the* American art form, right? Not Dixie, but *progressive,* cool jazz, man. You want this place to be hip, right?

So when the club opened up on January 6, 1958, it was to the sound of the Steve Kuhn Trio, Steve on a newly purchased baby grand, Chuck Israels on bass, and Arnold Wise on drums. The menu read "47 mount auburn JAZZ coffee house." The Steve Kuhn Trio was soon to be followed by John and Paul Neves, Alan Dawson, Sam Rivers, Ken McIntyre, Tony Williams and others.

The menu of the Club Mt. Auburn 47 when it opened. Courtesy of Tillie Kalina.

The handwriting, however faint, was on the wall. It wasn't the wiring, the plumbing, or even the coffee that brought people in, it was the music. And it was the music that got them attention in the local press. John McLellan of the *Boston Traveler* mentioned them favorably. Father O'Connor, the "Jazz Priest," became a big supporter. In an interview with the *Harvard Crimson*, less than a week after the big opening, the glories of European culture had been all but forgotten.

"We are not trying to create a pseudo-European coffee house atmosphere," co-owner Paula Kelley explained. "This is an American coffee house; it is a place where one can relax, meet friends and listen to progressive jazz. We are not in business just to sell coffee."

"We have a relaxed natural atmosphere" the girls pointed out. "Nobody bothers anybody here."

Nobody but the Cambridge Police. Joyce was on hand when they arrived.

They came in very melodramatically, blew their whistles, and said, "This is a raid. The place is closed down." The problem was we didn't have a music license. And you had to be a private club to have one. It was all tied up with the old blue laws, and it was the reason why there was no music anywhere in Harvard Square. You couldn't have more than three stringed instruments and serve any kind of food or beverages. At the time, we also felt that they were after us because we hadn't paid anybody off. And they hit us with all sorts of violations. We didn't have two toilets. My favorite gossip was that we were running a call girl system with the Radcliffe girls.

Paula, born and bred in Boston, looks back on it now from a more worldly viewpoint.

I don't know... If we had opened a beer joint, we would have known enough to send a case of the best scotch to the local sergeant and what not. We probably never would have had any problems but we were a couple of dopey kids — that's how we got into it in the first place. We never would have signed all those leases and gotten ourselves into all those financial obligations otherwise.

Joyce remembers one particular individual with special distaste.

*PAULA KELLEY and JOYCE KALINA
do some light reading for the news
photographers covering the opening of the
Club Mt. Auburn 47. Courtesy of
Tillie Kalina.*

There was this nasty lieutenant who kept coming down — a little shrimp who would put his foot up on the table and tell us what we were doing wrong. He was clearly just waiting for some money. And we were reluctanct and naive. We didn't have the money, nor would we have paid him if we did. So we were closed down, which put us into debt from which we never recovered.

Through Paula being local Irish Catholic, we got in with a very good, tough Cambridge lawyer named Kennedy, and for next to nothing he got us this fancy non-profit educational charter just like Harvard! So we had to get ourselves a board of directors, and we were able to re-open as a private club, making people members at the door. This was four or five months later. And music, mostly jazz, was the main thing.

 fter reopening, the Club 47 initiated a film series and had some poetry readings as well. Audience response was not heartening. They were drifting deeper and deeper into debt and couldn't seem to come up with anything to stem the tide. Where in the first months they were thinking of expanding, now they were just trying to pay the rent. The police were pissed that they were once again in business, and the local youths, the "townies," were as hostile as ever. At this stage the curtains were not yet completed so that from outside both customer and performer seemed like so many mollies in a goldfish bowl. Billy Burke, who had been born in Somerville, and who had just spent a two-year hitch in the Marines, describes it:

I was working at a TV station, and I went over to meet these guys from North Cambridge to have a few drinks. So we're down in Teal Square, having a few drinks, and someone said, "Hey, let's go over and take a look at the beatniks." So we drove down to the Club 47, and we were standing outside on Mt. Auburn Street, peering in the window at the beatniks and thinking, "Jesus Christ! Aren't they just so fucking weird! Can anybody believe them? Oh, Jesus! And look at that son of a bitch!" So after awhile of that, we left and went back to our beers.

Around this time, another store opened up on Mt. Auburn Street. It was Cambridge's first discount record store, the Turntable, and it was right next door to Tulla's Coffee Grinder. It was managed by Byron Lord Linardos, and Byron was getting nervous. He couldn't get any straight answers from his boss on such routine questions as: How are the records ordered? Where are the records coming from? How are we going to keep an inventory? The reply was always: "Byron, baby, don't worry. We're going to make a killing." Then people started returning defective records. Lots of them. Byron really began to worry when he found out that all of the stock at the Turntable were returns that had gotten thrown off the truck, or "lost" at certain locations. He had been drinking a lot of coffee at Tulla's and was seriously considering getting out of the retail record business. Tulla liked him and when she and her husband left to spend the summer on Cape Cod they asked him to run the kitchen. Dick Zaffron would handle the music and he would attend to the rest. He remembers one particular night vividly. It was possibly Joan Baez's first appearance in Cambridge and was definitely unscheduled.

The Baez family came in one night, Dick was playing, and she started one of these "whoo-haa" things in the background, and it just went all over Cambridge. The place froze. Everybody was staring. What is this singing? That was the first time I heard her.

ebbie Green also has a very clear memory of Joan from that period. **The first or second day of school at B.U. we were all loaded into buses like cattle and driven to the outskirts of Boston, to a great big echo-y place with the entire freshman class — just thousands of people. Margie Gibbons was there with me. She was from Putney. We went in, and we all sat in the bleachers. It was Freshman orientation, and they were giving this big speech about football and all this stuff, and Margie and I weren't listening. We felt we were the only sane people in the whole world. We were saying, "My God, what is this? This is really too weird." And then they were passing out beanies. They were talking about life and things, and then they were passing out beanies...So we took the beanies, and we said, "Oh, God! Weirdness." We took the beanies and just held them, and we were looking around. Everyone's putting on their beanies. Somebody comes by and says, "You have to put on your beanie." I can't remember. I think we said, "No, we don't want to put on our beanies." And then we were horrified. "YOU HAVE TO PUT ON YOUR BEANIE." We looked around**

and out of, I don't know, two thousand people in this place there were only two other people in the entire place that didn't want to put on their beanies. It was Joanie and this guy Doug, her blond boyfriend sitting over in a corner on the floor. She looked kinda straight, but they were sitting on the floor. We were sitting on the floor too, and we didn't want to wear our beanies either, so that's how we communicated at first. And it turned out that Betsy Minot was in theater in the same class, and Jimmy Kweskin was in something there...Anyway, because we didn't wear our beanies, we kept getting fined and busted, so it turned out we had to sneak down the halls, and we had to pay fines, and we were rebels.

Debbie Green had started playing the guitar at the progressive Putney School in Vermont. Beanies were not her style. She remembers being miserable there, but enjoyed bopping into Greenwich Village while she was home on Staten Island during vacations. It was beatnik and black stocking time, and it was there she first heard Dave Van Ronk. Dave was only a few years older than Debbie, but he was already a good fingerpicker and one of the first white singers to get into heavy blues.

It just knocked me out. I mean he played all this rhythmic stuff, and he fingerpicked. And I asked, "How do you do that?" I went out with him for a while. I was a very tender young thing, and I did not need Dave Van Ronk, but I loved the way he played. That was my first guitar-player romance. I used to sit and learn, and I also really had a crush. I would watch him. I was so attuned to it that I would be able to get a whole thing. I actually learned to play guitar from him.

A chance to learn first-hand from someone like Van Ronk was unusual in those days. It's likely that Dave himself had painstakingly learned most of his songs and guitar riffs from records. In its earliest stages the folk revival was an urban phenomenon. Almost all the young people involved got their material from records. The most readily available were by the more commercially popular groups and performers — The Weavers, Burl Ives, Josh White, Harry Belafonte, Theo Bikel, Cynthia Gooding, Oscar Brand. A few labels — Folkways in particular — put out somewhat more esoteric fare including Woody Guthrie, Cisco Houston, Sonny Terry and Brownie McGhee, Andrew Rowan Summers, Bascom Lamar Lunceford, and many, many others. For the more adventuresome, there was the thrill of the hunt through racks of dusty

A DAY AT THE BEACH

DEBBIE GREEN evidently didn't mind a little sand in her guitar and took it along with her when she went to the beach with JOAN and MIMI BAEZ. We're not sure, but we think the fourth member of the quartet is MARGIE GIBBONS.

There can be little doubt that Joan is at the stage when she was watching Debbie's fingers very closely, trying to figure out chord positions. Considering the fact that she did her first recording a few months after these pictures were taken, we can assume that she was a very quick study, because her guitar playing was quite competent even at that early date. Photographer unknown. Courtesy of Mimi Baez.

78's — old Okeh, Bluebird, Brunswick, and Vocallion disks, each in its own manila sleeve. Also available, but only from Washington, D.C. or through a few college libraries, were the recordings from the Folksong Archives of the Library of Congress. Elektra Records was still a small outfit in Greenwich Village, its president,

Jac Holzman, delivering stock from the back of his Vespa. Riverside and Tradition were just starting out. Odetta was on the Tradition label and, though little known on the east coast, was to be a major influence in what was to come.

I got into records, and Odetta happened around then, and I learned. I learned stuff off records, then ended up spending a summer in New York and doing mostly playing, writing stuff, and going down to the Village and learning from Van Ronk.

For a pretty young thing already used to hanging out in the Village, Charlesgate Hall at B.U. was not much fun at all.

I had to be in at nine every night. And the only things that the girls could talk about was whether I'd had a nose job. I had a lot of books with me, and that was weird, too. It was like Never Never Land.

Not surprisingly, the perpetrators of the Great Beanie Rebellion of '58 became friends in a hurry. **We ended up in a car going someplace right after that freshman orientation. Joan knew two songs. One was "Donna Donna," and one was a rock and roll song, and I remember saying, "This voice is incredible!" She knew how to play two chords or something and was sitting in the back seat. I was really playing, you know, and she went, "Breeeeeng, yoing, yoing, yoing!"**

Joan was living with her parents just outside Cambridge in Belmont. Debbie was in Charlesgate Hall, but Margie Gibbons had scored an apartment, which soon became a focal point. **At Margie's we played all the time. And those two girls put more guys through more changes! I ended up just talking to these guys. They would sit and talk about how they'd just come along and had fallen into the pit. Dick Zaffron was one of those people. I don't know where he is now, but he was great. He was a good guitar player, too. He played very interesting arrangements. Picking. He was really good. So, we ended up sleepin' on Margie's floor a lot and Joanie would get in trouble because she'd stay out all night and she'd lie to her parents, and we'd cover up for her.**

Dick was a dashing fellow with the eyes of a satyr, and Margie's apartment was hard to resist. He had graduated from Harvard in June but was now considering a post-graduate course in freshpersons.

Born in Brooklyn, his entrance to the world of music had not been auspicious.

When I was twelve I insisted on taking some violin lessons. I took them for a year and never

9780385720250
+Thanks for shopping with us.
Kindest Regards, Customer Care

RETURNING GOODS

Please re-pack, in the original packaging if possible, and send back to us at the address below. **Caution!** Don't cover up the barcode (on original packaging) as it helps us to process your return.

We will email you when we have processed your return.

---✂--

PLEASE complete and include this section with your goods.

Your Name: _____

Your Order Number _____

Reason for return _____

Would you prefer: Refund ☐ or Replacement ☐?

(Please note, if we are unable to replace the item it will be refunded.)

Return to:

---✂--

PBS RETURNS
801 Penhorn Avenue
Unit 5
Secaucus
NJ 07094

practiced, and they were dreadful. I gave that up and after that it was really mostly LP records. The very first one my father got was a wonderful record by Tex Ritter called "Songs and Stories for Children." It was a great record. I must have been eleven or twelve and he sang things like "Billy the Kid," and there was a story about the Pony Express, "Froggie Went a Courtin'," and stuff like that.

Zaffron also listened to Oscar Brand's folksong program on WQXR and was soon a record buying fan of Josh White, Burl Ives, Richard Dyer-Bennett, and The Weavers. He also spent a good deal of time listening to an early Segovia record. Dick's brother, eight years older than he, got started on the guitar, and became so furious when the younger Zaffron messed with it that Dick was given a twelve dollar Stella. He later got a big Harmony, and on both guitars replaced the steel strings with nylon ones in order to sound more like Segovia and Richard Dyer-Bennett. By the time he arrived at Harvard he had come up the guitar ladder to an old Martin Classical, and even studied classical guitar in Boston for a while with Guy Simeone. He also learned some flamenco guitar and his playing thoroughly dazzled the three young Boston University Drama students. He was soon to be dazzled himself.

One of the songs I sang in Tulla's, which I had stolen from an old Josh White record, was "House of the Rising Sun," and Baez heard me play that, either at Tulla's or a party at Margie's. I can't remember, but what I do remember is the first time I ever heard her really sing was at Margie's. She picked up the guitar and played her version of my version of "House of the Rising Sun," and you can imagine what it was like. My jaw dropped open — astounded, astonished! It was marvelous! Extraordinary! Fantastic! And that was the first time I ever heard her sing.

"House of the Rising Sun" plays a capricious role in what had come before and what would follow. It touched several of the principal players in different ways. The song itself is something of a mystery. No one knows whether it is of white or black origin. It was collected first in Kentucky in 1937, yet it is about a whorehouse in New Orleans. Its tune is very close to the one Leadbelly used in "Black Girl," but he sings that in a major key, while "House of the Rising Sun" is in a minor. Wherever its roots may have been, it is always sung as a dirge, a slow and mournful song of warning.

Manuel Greenhill, who was to become Baez's manager, also had a record of Josh White playing the song. Manny's, however, was one of a kind. Josh had cut it himself on a portable disc cutter.

*I*n '42 I was working in Queens, building aircraft engines and a few of us chipped in and got Josh White to give us guitar lessons. He was accompanying Libby Holman at Cafe Society, and he'd come over and show us an E Chord and sing us a few songs. It was great. Then he'd make a little audio-disc to take when we each went into the Army. My disc had "The House of the Rising Sun" and "John Henry."

Greenhill's first real contact with the music of the Unions and the left wing groups occurred in the late thirties when he was in his teens, but for him there had been music from the very beginning.

My family was involved in music. My father was a "cappel meister" in Russia. He could play about a dozen instruments. The only kind of real family rapport that we had was through music. And there was an interest in folkloric music — Russian, Yiddish, and so on. And there was a lot of that kind of music connected with the various national groups in Brooklyn.

But the politicalizing of the thing is what brought me to this particular scene. I learned many songs, which I later learned were folk songs, like "Hold the Fort" and other Socialist labor songs. Woody Guthrie came around in '38 or '39, as did Pete Seeger. The Almanac Singers were the first organized group that I remember. They came to political rallies — mostly related to the Spanish Civil War.

Manny was a child of the Depression. He had worked in the shipyard, doing iron work, but most of the time he had been unemployed. He got into politics through the trade unions. An intense young man with a boxer's frame and lantern jaw, his face looked like it had been carved with an axe by a sculptor with more talent than time. He clearly wanted to right the wrongs of the world, and from his corner of the ring it looked like radical politics was the way to do it. To make it work you had to get your message to the People. With a capital "P." Theater and songs were assumed to be a relatively painless way.

I belonged to a group called the Flatbush Players. It later became more dignified and called itself the Flatbush Arts Theater and still later became

the American Youth Theater. They became the nucleus for a successful production called "Call Me Mister."

We did a lot of singing. One of our most successful things was a Marc Blitzstein opus called "The Cradle Will Rock." That was a singing play — "a play in music." I played the part of Mister Mister. The heavy. I had that look about me even then.

We did a lot of benefits, for Spain mostly. We would sing a lot of songs. Some Gershwin songs; stuff from "Porgy and Bess;" or "Strange Fruit" before Billie Holiday.

Each issue had its own momentum. About half of us were Communists. We had a lot of meetings, a lot of arguments, a lot of self-criticism, like the Chinese do today. We were a grassroots community group, very proud. We'd do shows wherever we could get a place.

So I cut my teeth on some of those things, but I had never thought of actually doing this for a living. The original motivation was political; but later when I started getting interested in songs for their own sake, I started to really get hooked on them. And that was a pattern followed by many of the people in that movement.

Then came World War II, aircraft factories, and the Josh White audio-disc. Greenhill spent three years in the Army. In 1946 he was back on the streets.

From '46 to '50, I did various things. Then I decided to make a complete change. A friend introduced me to the concept of selling advertising in foreign language newspapers. The idea was to go to a city which had a number of varied industrial and ethnic components. I looked at four cities and picked Boston. I never regretted it. I loved it. So I moved there and started the Foreign Language Press. By '58, I bought a house in Dorchester.

I would always find a little pocket of music wherever I was, and I began to connect with people in the Boston area. Bess Hawes lived in Cambridge. Peggy Seeger was going to Radcliffe. Tony Saletan started doing TV programs in 1956. He had studied music education for children at Harvard.

Opposite page:
MANNY GREENHILL waiting for Clifford Odets (c. 1960).
Photograph by Stephen Fenerjian.

nthony Saletan was born and bred in New York City. He remembers going to "Hootenannies" and "Wingdings," concerts sponsored by "People's Songs," where he heard Seeger, Lee Hayes, Woody Guthrie, and Josh White. Yet folk music was not young Saletan's first love:

I started playing piano as soon as I could reach up to the keyboard. My real love was boogie-woogie. I played by ear and I liked to improvise. My father took me to a rent party at Josh White's house, and Albert Ammons and Pete Johnson did four hand boogie-woogie that just amazed me. I would lie in my bed and invent improvisations in my head. I played out a lot of feeling that way. When President Roosevelt died I played the piano for hours.

My father was a dentist and Josh was one of his patients. He literally fixed Josh's teeth for a song. I remember him coming to the house. He'd play guitar and I'd play piano. He'd play the part about being ignorant about music, but when I'd ask a question about a chord he'd be right there with the proper name. He was a very smooth performer.

When Tony was fourteen, his father and Josh bought him a Martin guitar and he was off and picking. He found a five-string banjo in a pawnshop on Second Avenue, and by that time he had found an idol as well: Peter Seeger. His style, his taste, and especially his abilities as a song leader appealed to Tony who was very soon to be leading songs at summer camp himself.

When Saletan arrived at Harvard in 1950 the banjo and guitar went into the closet. This precaution was not followed by many of the Harvard pickers to follow, but it worked for Tony. After graduation he took his Master's in education at the University but was beginning to have some doubts about a future as a high school teacher. One day he ran into an old friend from high school who was practice teaching at the Harvard Demonstration Nursery School.

She asked me to come over with my guitar to sing and play for the kids. I did, and I really got interested in that. I enjoyed it in a way that opened me to the whole idea of using the kinds of songs that I loved with young children. I really liked the kids and I found that we could relate to each other through songs.

The following year Tony ended up with a part time job at the school, followed by a job at Tufts training teachers to perform music for young kids. He had found a niche for himself.

In about 1955, I went to the Swarthmore Folk Festival where I met Ellen and Irene Kossoy, Mike Seeger, Peggy Seeger, and Ralph Rinzler. Around that time a little group developed in Cambridge. Charles Seeger and his daughters, Penny, Barbara, and Peggy. Peggy was leading songs at the International Students Center on Friday nights and a bunch of us shared the song leadership. There was a similar group of people in Boston called "The Folk Arts Workshop," and when Pete Seeger came to Boston, that's where he'd sing. All of this was, of course, politically left, and the political motivation was as important as the musical for most people.

In 1955 the Public Television Station in Boston, WGBH-TV, was about to go on the air and they had no program for preschool kids. So they went out to Tufts and talked to Saletan. At first he thought they wanted someone to come in every couple of weeks and play a few songs. It turned out they wanted a host, so Tony and a senior at the school, Mary Lou Addams, took on the job. The show was called "Come and See" and ran for thirteen months.

Funds eventually ran out and so did Tony's enthusiasm for making his living with music. Save the music for fun and good times. He got a job as a social worker and counselor at Hecht House, a Jewish Community Center in Dorchester.

In the job description there was no mention of music. It involved working with the Golden Age Club and a teen-age group. But as the job wore on I found I was using music more and more. It really seemed to be the way I could communicate best.

Manny Greenhill and his wife Leona were active at Hecht House. We got to know each other and discovered that we knew a lot of the same people and shared an enthusiasm for folk music.

Manny remembers the meeting:

He was a student of Pete Seeger's, so we had things in common. We sang together at Jewish Community Centers, and I started arranging for him to sing at Bar Mitzvahs and weddings.

Greenhill and Saletan came from similar backgrounds, a left-wing milieu in which music was primarily an instrument for social improvement. More often than not it involved folk-dancing, song leading, and some good old fashioned propagandizing. Seeger was at the core of this world. It was a kind of an Us-Against-Them, Holier-Than-Thou world; a One-World-For-You-And-Me; a simple world splashed with primary colors in which "they" had no part;

THE BOSTON FOLK TRIO (left to right): JACKIE WASHINGTON, IRENE KOSSOY, and
TONY SALETAN, doing their best to look wholesome and educational. Publicity shot courtesy of
Manny Greenhill.

a sloganeering world whose rhetoric sometimes came dangerously close to being a mirror image of the rantings of the Right.

By the late fifties Manny was trying to cope with the change that seemed to be in the air. Manny the Radical now had a big house in Dorchester, with a garage and a big backyard, yet. The Depression, and even WW II, didn't mean anything to kids in their late teens, kids who were starting to pick up guitars, starting to sing.

Many of the younger performers coming up came out of what we called "The Silent Generation" and were apolitical. But they had something else going for them which related. They were a post-Kerouac group who were somewhat Bohemian in outlook and lifestyle. I looked at the broader picture, and they were part of a scene that was very important to me. I didn't know how that scene was going to develop. But whatever was happening, I wanted to find out.

Come all you fair and tender maidens,
Take warning how you court young men.
They're like the stars of a summer's morning,
They'll first appear, and then they're gone.

Leavin' Home

I'm going away, I'm going to stay, I'm never coming home.
You're gonna miss me, honey, in the days to come

lay Jackson was on his way to Harvard. He was from Kerrville, Texas, but he was no hillbilly. He liked Nat "King" Cole and could play the ukelele like Roy Smeck. His daddy listened to the Grand Old Opry, but Clay wouldn't. He sang with his sisters in churches and they were known as the Jackson Sisters — not the Jackson Sisters and Clay — just the Jackson Sisters. They were bigger than he was. Clay was leaving all that behind. He was headed to Cambridge, the sophisticated east.

Bob Siggins was headed east, too. He was coming from Grand Island, Nebraska, but he was no hillbilly either. He could play the bongos and "Ruby" on the chromatic harmonica. He was good at sports and with girls, but he was leaving all that behind to get a good education at Harvard.

Clay met Bob on the train:

He was the only guy on the train who had a knit tie on as narrow as mine. Except he was really smart. He had sort of a tweedy jacket with three buttons, and I had my one-button-at-the-waist robin's egg blue linen jacket. I thought, "Where'd he get that ugly three-button jacket?" I got up to Cambridge and about three days later I fell into a panic and went over to the Coop and got me a Harris tweed! Then we discovered we were living in the same dorm, and it was all downhill from there.

Eric Sackheim was definitely no hillbilly. He had grown up in New York City and was from a well-to-do family. But he loved hillbilly music — not the commercial stuff coming out of Nashville, but real, honest-to-goodness, old-time, down-to-earth hillbilly music: Uncle Dave Macon, Charlie Poole, Gid Tanner and the Skillet Lickers. He didn't leave this passion behind when he came to Harvard; he took a huge collection of records and tapes with him in boxes.

For the first year or so everybody played their cards pretty close to the vest. Occasionally Bob and Clay would take a break from their studies and play duets for chromatic harmonica and ukelele, but mostly it was work, work, work. In his sophomore year Bob roomed with Arthur Gilette, who had gone to the Putney School in Vermont, a hotbed of Seeger-style folk music. Bob borrowed a banjo from Arthur and started picking on it. Clay noticed a change in his friend.

Siggins first started getting the idea when he grew a mustache and a Van Dyke goatee and bought him a big black cloak which reached down to his ankles, and he'd go swooping around late at night. He was one of the first people of my group around Harvard that grew any hair. Then he decided to learn to play the banjo. And I thought, "Oh, God! He'll never learn anything." Then he went away, and he had a job that summer out in Nebraska working for the state agriculture department where he would drive around to various farms and make sure they

26

weren't using more water than they were supposed to. What he really did was to get in his car every morning and drive out into the woods and practice the banjo all day. So he came back next fall, and he could play the banjo. I wouldn't have believed it, but when he sets his mind to something he can really figure it out. And indeed he got really good.

When Bob returned to Cambridge in the fall of 1958 he started spending time at Tulla's. He got a job washing dishes, and in his spare time would sit around with whoever was there and play the banjo. One day Eric Sackheim came in and heard Bob playing:

He said to his friend, Henry Dane, who was a pretty good picker, too, "Gee, doesn't he sound like Charlie Poole?" I'd never heard of Charlie Poole, but Eric asked me if I'd like to help start a band.

 he fat was in the fire, but Bob wasn't the only one to feel the force of Sackheim's Hillbilly Ray. Ethan Signer was a graduate of Yale who had just landed in Cambridge to begin graduate studies in biophysics at M.I.T. He had already been exposed to "folk" music at Yale and knew how to sing a little and strum a guitar.

People had told me that when I got to Cambridge, I should check out the coffee houses. So I just went around. Tulla's was a good place for hanging out. At the time in Cambridge there were no bars with music. And college people weren't welcome in the old barrooms so it was coffee houses. I just showed up there one day with my guitar and met a bunch of people.

Playing with these people was a total revelation to me, because all I had known was that Leadbelly was this person who wrote nifty ditties like "Black Girl" which you would sing in sort of a romantic, sweet way, and I knew about Odetta and Alan Lomax. Then here was this guy, Eric Sackheim, who knew all these interesting songs that had interesting music, and I wound up being interested in all that stuff. And every so often a record would appear. I remember that Siggins had come into possession of this record by Obray Ramsay and George Pegram and some others. It was a treasure, and we took it back to his room and learned four songs from it, and we played those songs non-stop for about three weeks. I guess we drove everyone

crazy, but we were limited in what we could play. I was playing guitar then, and at these all-night sessions there were so many people playing guitar that it got to be out of the question. Siggins had an old mandolin, so one weekend I borrowed it and disappeared and learned where the notes were and tried to make it on that.

While Ethan and Bob and Eric were getting together at Tulla's, Clay was still holding out, hiding from the dread Hillbilly Ray in the library. He was only postponing the inevitable.

For about two years after I got to Harvard, I had been doing nothing but working. I went to class, spent my time in the library, and I was getting really sick of it, and I didn't quite know how sick of it I was getting. But I discovered in the Lamont Library that they had this room, the Woodbury Music and Poetry Listening Room, and they had a bunch of folk music records, and I just stumbled across somebody called Leadbelly. I guess I was really homesick, too; I didn't know that either, but I really was. So hearing this music suddenly came to mean more to me than anything in the world. I kept on spending the same amount of time in the library, but I spent it up there listening to records.

Then one day Bob and Eric and those guys were all playing, and I was sitting around the room, and they were trying to do "A Jewel Here on Earth" and none of them could sing the harmony, so I sang the harmony — that good old solid third — and they all went, "Wow! Hey!" One of my roommates, Paul D'Andrea from Belmont, Massachusetts, told me he had a guitar I could use out at his house, so we went out, and he had this old klud of a cedar guitar. It looked like it had cost a good twelve dollars new. It has a great big piece missing out of the back, and on the front it has embossed red cowboys on bucking horses. So I fooled with that for a while before I got a hold of that Stella and learned what pain can really be. The action was about half an inch high, and my fingers would be numb all the way up to the middle knuckle after about fifteen minutes. But I already knew music — chords and when to change them from the ukelele, so it wasn't that difficult to learn.

Before long, Clay was right down there with the rest of the budding young hillbillies at Tulla's. **We'd go up to Tulla's any time we could manage to. Any time you could find anybody who felt like they didn't want to work, we'd just go up there and sit around. It was really authentic as all shit there, dark, dank, and smoky. If you sat at the front table, you sat and looked out at people's knees**

Preceding page:
(left) CLAY JACKSON (c.1960)
Photographer unknown. Courtesy of
Mimi Farina.

(right) BOB SIGGINS (c.1962)
Photographer unknown. Courtesy of
Betsy Schmidt.

This page:
ETHAN SIGNER (c. 1960)
Photograph by Stephen Fenerjian.

going by. They had classical music on the record player, and people sat around and played chess and drank coffee and tea. Tulla really liked Siggins and said, "Sure, you boys can come in and bring your instruments." It was okay when there were just three or four. But when it got to be eight or ten or twelve of us in the winter when there was no ventilation, the air would just get so thick you could slice chunks of it. This was back before they had plastic heads for banjos and Siggins' head would just sink and sink and sink. The action would get lower, and the strings would get softer. He'd wipe it and hold matches under the head, and it was always out of tune. Mainly we would just play as fast as possible. He was frailing the banjo then. We'd do "Katy Kline" twelve times at top speed and laugh hysterically.

It was only a matter of time before all of this energy and music began to overflow the tiny confines of Tulla's. The first opportunity came when Eric Sackheim was asked to do a concert over in Boston. Ethan Signer recalls the famous event:

We played for Marcel Kistin and the Folk Song

Society of Greater Boston at the YMCA. Sackheim was a great folklorist at the time. He had a tape exchange going with some friends who sent him Library of Congress material. So he got invited to do this concert at the "Y," and he brought along Siggins and me. We had just been to New York to see the New Lost City Ramblers, and Eric said, "If they can do it, so can we," so we decided to do the show, and somebody said, "What are you going to call yourselves?" and Lynn Joiner had gotten a record by a group called the Laurel River Valley Boys, so he said jokingly, "Why don't you call yourselves the Charles River Valley Boys?" So we did, and it stuck.

  he horse was out of the barn for good. The Charles River Valley Boys were let loose on the world. Almost immediately they decided to strike again. This time the target was the Lowell House Dining Commons. The cast swelled to include nearly everyone who had ever picked anything ever at

Tulla's. In addition to Eric, Ethan, Bob, and Clay there was Fiddlin' John Provine, Bob Dees, Jim Conner, Johnny Shahn, and someone named Hollerin' Sam Fleishmann. Siggins sums up the magic of the day:

It was like a big musical gang bang. Eric brought all of his instruments. I had a couple by then. John Provine had a fiddle. He played guitar and banjo, too. Johnny Shahn was occasionally playing. Bob Dees. Ethan. Clay. There were about ten people, so we'd break up into groups of three or four, but some of our ensemble numbers were really great because we'd all be up there, playing as many different instruments as possible, all playing the same melody. It was terrific. The response from people was difficult to figure out. There were only thirty people or so, and they seemed a bit dumbfounded. We'd make jokes about there being more of us than them.

If some of the people there thought the show was strange, Mimi Baez didn't. She thought it was great.

I know precisely the moment when I got drawn into wanting to play folk music. I was thirteen. I got a call from Joanie who was at Harvard Square. I was at home and she said, "Get on a bus and get down here. There's a group here

I know you'd enjoy." It was the Charles River Valley Boys at Lowell House in one of their first times playing. I especially remember Clay. Every time he would do something I would look at Joanie, and we would both laugh.

By this time Siggins had moved up from being dishwasher at Tulla's to slinging hash at Tommy's Lunch down the street. His place was taken by Lynn Joiner whose place in history had been assured for naming the Charles River Valley Boys. Lynn was to further the cause in other ways through his affiliation with the Harvard radio station WHRB. He had become the producer of a show called "Balladeers." The host of the show was Bill Wood who was already a polished "folk" performer and leader of a popular assemblage called "The Raunch Hands." Bill's time was up, and Lynn needed a replacement. He started to use Eric and Bob and Ethan and Clay as "Balladeers," depending on who was free to do it. Lynn also started a show called "Old-Timey Music Time" as a result of a collecting trip to the South that he took with Peter Hoover, who was another member of Sackheim's hillbilly mafia. There already was a show on the air called "Hillbilly at Harvard," so they were ahead of the game there. It seems that the station had been founded by a bunch of veterans in the forties who liked hillbilly music. The current show was hosted by a fellow named Ken Gilchrist, and he had nothing but old 78's to play. He gave way to "Uncle Ed" Simpson, who was being supplied with more up-to-date country records by Brian "Sinc" Sinclair, a closet hillbilly-phile. Before it was over, these boys had three solid hours on Saturday morning. First Lynn Joiner and Mike

(left) THE CHARLES RIVER VALLEY BOYS at sea. (c.1960) (left to right) JON SHAHN, BOB SIGGINS, ETHAN SIGNER, and FIDDLIN' JOHN PROVINE. Photographer unknown. Courtesy of Bob Siggins.

Eisenstadt, a Classics student, did "Saturday Morning Jamboree," which was old-timey and bluegrass music. Then "Uncle Ed" came on with hard-core country, followed by Spike Milligan and Peter Sellers with "The Goon Show." It was a natural.

By the fall of 1959 the Charles River Valley Boys were becoming a legend in their own time — at least in the Charles River Valley. The Boys' fame soon spread to Boston, and they made a few forays. Things were a little different over there, as Siggins was quick to notice.

Sackheim had a car, so we'd drive over to Boston to the Cafe Yana. We thought that was the funniest. Everyone was going, "Hi, man." They were super cool. Probably smoking dope.

Then there was the Golden Vanity, which Eric called "The Bold Inanity." For Eric, this was pretty thin, because he'd already been into the scene in New York. But we did do a gig there.

Of course, Boston people felt that people in Cambridge were strange too. Betsy Minot was waitressing at the Golden Vanity when the River Boys arrived.

We were devoted to the Boston side of folk music. We thought that the Harvard/Cambridge side was very elite — very snotty. We all thought of ourselves as "Townies." We were doing our best to be beat. It was when the Charles River Valley Boys came to the Vanity that we started to think that those people in Cambridge might be okay after all. They came over and played and I thought, "Is that what Cambridge is all about? I think I'll try it out." Bob and I hit it off right away. The Charles River Valley Boys made it clear to us that we could make it over to Cambridge and back alive.

There was no question about it — playing music was definitely changing people's lives. Betsy and Bob showed that the Charles River could bring people together as well as keep them apart. Clay's studies came to a complete halt as a result of his new obsession. He decided to bust out entirely and go to California to work in the oil fields for a while. Ethan was totally amazed by the ease with which he had been drawn into this musical maelstrom.

Before I came up to Cambridge, I didn't really consider myself as someone who played music. So when I got to Cambridge one of the things that impressed me was that you could just pick up an instrument and go out and play. Find other people who could play. A lot of my involvement with Appalachian music came out of that because it was something that was so accessible. And the scene was interesting to me in that our expectations were so small. Nobody was really

thinking about performing very much. We played for ourselves and for people who would listen but with no commercial thoughts in mind. We used to play at parties a lot and usually in the kitchen. We would look forward to and get up for parties the way we would do now for a gig. There would be that point in a party when we would get out the instruments and get into the kitchen, and you could talk to the people who were listening to you.

Gradually it all seemed to go up a level about the time the River Boys started to get more formalized and we started doing these little concerts around Harvard and then when we started going to Boston to play. That's when we began to get some sort of repertoire and performing style. Eric had already had a group before he got to Harvard, so he sort of knew what he was doing. The rest of us just happened to fall into it mainly because it was so much fun.

here was no question in anyone's mind that Sackheim was single-handedly responsible for turning all of these young men into lifetime lovers of rural American music, white and black. There were different categories and styles. The River Boys were playing mostly "Old-Timey" string band music as performed by such artists as Gid Tanner and the Skillet Lickers, The Fruit Jar Drinkers, The Stoneman Family, and Uncle Dave Macon. But Sackheim's interests really covered the whole range of early country or "hillbilly" music, ballads, instrumentals, as well as the whole world of "country blues" and black string bands and jug bands. In the course of teaching the River Boys songs he exposed them to all of his sources. In addition to his own tapes which he made on trips to the South, he also made them aware of Library of Congress recordings and records available through companies such as Riverside and Folkways, which had put out the "Anthology of American Folk Music," a great collection of the best of all this music compiled by Harry Smith. The Anthology included performances by people such as Mississippi John Hurt, Clarence Ashley, and Dick Boggs, all of whom were to be rediscovered alive and well within a few years time. In his way Eric was a one-man folk revival. Siggins marvelled at the way he turned his enthusiasm into a field of study:

He had the best record collection of anybody I'd ever known. He was fortunate enough to have enough money to just go buy whatever he saw. He just bought every blues record that was made,

CLAY JACKSON and ETHAN SIGNER picking and singing for all the friends and neighbors out in radioland. MIKE EISENSTADT strums along on banjo. Photograph by Stephen Fenerjian.

THE CHARLES RIVER VALLEY BOYS go to an "Orgy." (c. 1960) (left to right) BOB DEES, BOB SIGGINS, ELLEN JAMESON, FIDDLIN' JOHN PROVINE, and ETHAN SIGNER. Photographer unknown. Courtesy of Betsy Schmidt.

and just about every country record as well. So I learned it all from him.

Eric was the first person I knew who took little trips South and taped people. That was one of the sources of his great collection. He had real tapes of people that you only heard about ten years later. Funky, funky people. He knew them all. He called Estil Ball "Slimy Estil." He was a real greaser. He taped him in 1956. Eric wrote his thesis at Harvard on folk music. He created a whole department at Harvard because he didn't know where he was supposed to be, and they didn't, either. Some kind of language studies. He wrote his thesis on folk music and got a "summa cum laude" because there was no one else in the department. He was a very clever guy.

Betsy loved him too:

Eric Sackheim was crazy, but smart. Funny. Really quick. He could play anything. Mostly he played banjo and mandolin. He introduced me to old-time music. He had a scungy, disgusting apartment in Cambridge. He kept a dead cat in his ice box.

oon it was Orgy time in Dudley Gulch, home of WHRB. During exam time the station would run marathons of different kinds of music. The live folk orgy was an all-night affair that provided the River Boys one last chance to infect the airwaves with their music. Clay had returned from the oil fields, having deposited his hard earned money in New Orleans before he returned. Only fantasies of "meals of undercooked pork and potatoes mashed with water" sustained him until he made it back to the Lowell House dining room. The reality soon wore thin, however, and he was out of school again and in with Ethan living in a house on Columbia Street. He could no longer be a "Balladeer," however, and turned the show over to a young undergraduate who could do all of Josh White's runs named Tom Rush.

So Clay and Bob and Ethan and Eric got together to play down at the Orgy, and everyone had a great time. It was going to be one of their last good times together, because Eric had been awarded a Fulbright to go to Japan. Bob wasn't sure what he was going to do (He and Betsy were getting pretty hot and heavy), but he was thinking about going to medical school. Clay was starting to worry about the draft. All of a sudden everything was about to change. Lynn Joiner was not about to see all of this music scatter to the four winds without making some attempt to record it.

We did a marathon taping session with the Charles River Valley Boys for about a week after school ended in 1960. I recorded them as well as I could for that time. There was some great stuff there of Eric Sackheim, and Clay did an inspired version of "Waiting for a Train." Eric Sackheim did a very forceful "Train 45" on the banjo. He was an amazing musician.

Lynn never regretted making those recordings. Eric Sackheim did indeed go to Japan where he remains to this day. He has published a collection of blues words called *The Blues Line* with drawings by Jon Shahn, one of the many who played along with the River Boys and later one of the members of the Mother Bay State Entertainers, along with Siggins, Clay, and fiddler Bob Mamis. He has also published books of poetry translations and translations of songs. They have titles such as *The Silent Firefly* and *The Silent Zero, In Search of Sound.* Nor has Sackheim's humor been drowned out by the sound of one hand clapping. He has formed a group of Japanese bluegrass musicians called The Carolina Tar Heel Rattlers.

Siggins and Betsy got married in October and went to Europe to spend her inheritance. Clay was not far behind, having been 4-F'd, and soon it was pickin' time again. This time in Rome.
For about two months in Rome, Siggins and I would go play at this great tourist trap nightclub in Trastevere. It was a huge underground place with about six or eight interconnected caverns. So we'd go there and get free meals and then just stroll around from room to room and play. We'd play "Oh, Susannah" for some drunk Americans and they'd say, "God damn! I'm so glad to hear something from America!" They'd have a pile of funny money there and pick out a 5,000 lire note about as big as a bedsheet and say, "Here, have

one of these big green ones! Har, har, har." So we made pretty good money playing there.

That year it seemed that half of Cambridge was criss-crossing the Continent. John Cooke was an undergraduate at Harvard who had been hanging around the folk scene trying to find a place for himself. He showed up in Rome, and everybody took turns giving him a hard time. He wanted to learn how to play and asked Bob and Clay to help him. Bob told him, "John, you have to realize that we don't care if you learn to play or not." It was a moment of Satori for John, who from that moment determined to teach himself to play.

Betsy wasn't about to be a mother to John either:
He was gross. I hit him a lot. He was real fussy about his Italian and what fork you ate with.

Eventually he left for Spain, while Clay went to Florence, and Bob and Betsy eventually made their way to England via Copenhagen. By the summertime Clay was in England, too, playing with an excellent English banjo player named Peter Stanley. Ethan got a month off and flew over, and before anyone knew it, it was Charles River Valley time again. Siggins had met someone named Red Sullivan.
Red Sullivan was a wild Irishman. He'd walk at about ninety miles an hour all over London, with us carrying our shit, trying to keep up running

Below:
THE CHARLES RIVER VALLEY BOYS *in a rare appearance at the Club Mt. Auburn 47 (c. 1960). (left to right)* BOB SIGGINS, ERIC SACKHEIM, ETHAN SIGNER, *and* CLAY JACKSON. *Photograph by John Cooke.*

THE CHARLES RIVER VALLEY BOYS at Dobell's Record Shop in London (1961). (left to right) BOB SIGGINS, CLAY JACKSON, and ETHAN SIGNER. A case of Guiness awaits the thirsty pickers in the back room. Photographer unknown. Courtesy of Bob Siggins.

behind him. He knew when all of the clubs closed and when all of the theaters opened and closed. He had it down. He'd tell us to just play three songs and get out. He had a little spiel, he'd pass the hat. He knew exactly when to pack it up. It was pretty neat. We did that for about a month.

Red talked to Doug Dobell, who had a small record shop specializing in folk music, and convinced him to let the boys do some recording in the basement of the store. They did about ten or twelve numbers. Then they took some of those and some from the WHRB tapes and put a record together. It was called "Bringin' in The Georgia Mail," the first record of the now internationally famous and popular Charles River Valley Boys. For their efforts they received about seven pounds and a case of Guiness Stout. The Hillbillies from Harvard had done good.

When the winter winds begin to blow, the ground is covered up with snow,
You'll think about the way you're gonna wish me back, your lovin' man.
You're gonna miss me, honey, in the day they say's to come.

Sail Away, Ladies, Sail Away

If ever I get my new house done,
Sail away, ladies, sail away.
I'll give my old one to my son.
Sail away, ladies, sail away.

Club 47 was having money problems. Progressive jazz wasn't quite the draw that Paula Kelley and Joyce Kalina had hoped. Even the films Joyce was able to get with their new non-profit charter from the Museum of Modern Art's catalog weren't bringing in the customers. Byron Linardos up at Tulla's had been helpful: he had shown them how to make Café Viennese. But he couldn't show them how to make money. Joyce remembers this frustrating period.

We were barely breaking even. People would sit all night drinking their coffee. It was a dollar to get in. All the business was on the weekend, and maybe some on Wednesday. The rest of the week was dead.

One night this fellow named Peter Robinson came in and introduced himself and said he was a friend of this young female singer — a folk singer. We said we weren't interested, that we had jazz. And he said, "She's really very, very good, and I think you ought to listen to her. We kept saying, "We're not interested." So he finally arranged to rent the place on a Monday night to show us that she could do it. He said, "She has a

following, and you'll see that it will be worth it to you."

Peter Robinson, a good friend of the Baez family, set things up, and pretty much ran the show. He had heard Joan sing with a shy and personable Harvard senior, Bill Wood.

He and Joanie shared it, because I didn't feel that it was fair to impose on her the full load of holding down an evening. I stood behind the kitchen and told each one when to go out, when to come back, and all that.

Joan's mother came, as did some family friends who had been alerted for the occasion, and Bill Wood's Harvard buddies. Even at this early stage there were a number of young people, mostly males, who were firmly under her spell. She was comfortable playing with Bill. He was the current "Balladeer" on WHRB at Harvard. If her repertoire was minuscule, her guitar playing was delicate and assured, and her voice soared as if some glorious bird was set free in the room.

Peter Robinson remembers another person in the room that night, a nightclub owner from Chicago named Al Grossman. Al was shortly to become Albert and manage just about every major performer of the period. At that time, he managed Odetta and a young singer named Bob Gibson. Grossman had the idea that Gibson and

JOAN BAEZ at the Club Mt. Auburn 47 (c. 1960).
Photograph by Stephen Fenerjian.

Baez would make a hell of a duo. So after the performance he approached Robinson and said he would be interested in having Joan come to Chicago and sing with Gibson at his club, the Gate of Horn.

Robinson remembers Grossman unflatteringly.

He looked like a pelican, the way he strutted about, and I remember Joanie and I making fun to each other because of that. I don't remember if he approached me directly, but I think he did. I passed the message on to her in Bill Wood's hearing and Bill said very diffidently, "Did he say anything about my singing, about me?" And I said, "Bill, no, he didn't."

Such conversations take place quickly and are delivered and received in low and controlled tones. The audience had loved every bit of it. Paula and Joyce were delighted. Next week it

would be their turn to do the hiring, and at fifteen bucks a night it was a pretty good deal.

It is nothing short of incredible that this girl, just barely eighteen years old, had come so far in so short a time. Since the fall of '58 she had been devouring the songs and arrangements of the people around her. Debbie Green, Dick Zaffron, and another Cambridge singer, Ted Alevizos, found their material Baezized at an alarming rate. These singers were also becoming aware of the fact that once Joan focused her laser beam on a song, it then sounded as if she were the source not they. To their dismay they found that they were in danger of becoming pale imitations of themselves.

Alevizos was at that time Assistant Chief of Circulation and Stacks at Harvard's Widner Library. A graduate of Columbia and Marquette Universities, he had also put in some time at

Julliard as a Special Student of Voice and was one of the few people who could come close to her vocal pyrotechnics. As close as he could come musically, no one could match her relentless drive.

It is remarkable, too, that only a few months before her debut in a rented hall, Joan was just starting to perform before any kind of world at Tulla's, the Salamander, and the Cafe Yana. Soon Debbie was performing here and there, sometimes as a solo and sometimes with Dick or Joan. She remembers one early fiasco at the Cafe Yana, a coffee shop on Beacon Street in Boston. **I used to get five dollars. I don't know whether there was a microphone or not. I think maybe there wasn't. Joanie and I got the giggles and laughed for an entire half hour, with no exaggeration. We were giggly, silly little girls. We had no business performing.**

Above:
JOAN BAEZ and DEBBIE GREEN
being "silly little girls." (c.1961) Photograph by Stephen Fenerjian.
Opposite:
"Table for Three?" ALBERT GROSSMAN (in white jacket) discussing something or other at the 1959 Newport Folk Festival. Photographer unknown. Courtesy of Festival Productions.

hether they had any business performing or not, they were. And if the show was not a musical milestone it was purely a visual treat. Those were grey and serious days, and there, folks, for the first time on any stage: That Pan-like and diminutive devil himself, Dick Zaffron! Give 'em a rasgado Dick (applause). All right! And here ladies and gentlemen, direct from the Big Apple (with a brief detour to old Pinko Putney) that Willowy Wonder of the World of Folk, the Girl with the Botticelli Beauty and the Beeeutiful Bod, Miss DEB-BIE GREEN! Hit 'em with an A minor 7th, baby. (applause) Well all right! A class act folks! And last but not least, folks, by way of Baghdad, Belmont, and Boston U! That Raven Haired Queen of the Nile, the gal with the million dollar smile, that Virginal Vamp, the kid with the STYLE! Let's hear it for little JOAN-KNEE BUY-EZZZZ! (thunderous applause)

Of course that wasn't quite the way it was. Dick wasn't quite as impressed with his own playing as were most others at the time — pitting yourself against a Segovia record is not the best way to build confidence. Debbie was only beginning to have an awareness of her svelte and photogenic beauty. She worried a lot about her teeth and a few stubborn pounds of baby fat. As far as Joan was concerned, she felt just flat-out ugly. Dark-skinned, flat-chested, nose too big, a whole catalog of teenage woe. Her hands and feet were the exception. She knew she had pretty hands and feet.

Those who remember her during that period remember those slender lovely feet. She had much to learn about music, about the world, about herself, but she already knew about bare feet. Any self-respecting Virginal Princess singing softly into the ear of the Unicorn while she braided its flaxen mane must herself be unshod. Her feet must lightly touch the tapestry of profane earth, the mingling of plants, flowers, and small animals. And further than that, at the risk of inciting mythological riot, letting loose the wild eroticism of primitive gods, let her have *naked* feet!

Joan always seemed to arrive wearing sandals or flats. But at a certain moment, the right moment, the ritual moment, she would *strip them off!* And so, everyone at that party or more likely, at that concert would be symbolically freed by the Virgin Princess whose wanton toes now caressed the pagan soil while her voice soared to celestial heights. Certainly a powerful undercurrent of sexuality was present from the first. And for those who chose to see her more as a dark and angularly graceful Queen of the Nile, the coal black hair, the sexy "Little Egypt" moves, with an occasional thrilling flash of white teeth framed by the pinkest of lips — well, the naked feet worked with that image too. In fact, she must have been bedeviled by images: what her devoted Quaker parents hoped and imagined she might be; what the many young men who were attracted to her like moths to a flame considered her to be; what she, herself, thought or imagined. It was a very difficult time for Joanie Baez. But if one accepts the fact that to a certain degree all performers are self-created, certainly Joan Baez built her persona from the ground up.

If Joan imagined her dark beauty to exist only in the eye of her beholders, it would not be long before these rapt beholders would have something of undeniable beauty to stick in their ears. Only eight months after those unscheduled notes in Tulla's Coffee Grinder she would be slipping off her sandals to feel the impartial carpet of her first recording studio.

Manny Greenhill had become something of a local promoter. The meeting four years before with Tony Saletan had rekindled memories of the good old folksings in New York, so why the hell not do something up here in Boston. "Just for a gas," as Manny remembers. One thing led to another: A couple of things at the Commander Hotel in Cambridge; a three-concert series at Boston's Jordan Hall that included Josh White, Seeger, and local talent led by Saletan. Soon he

had an interview show on WXHR called "Meet the Folksingers" to be followed by a program on WGBH, "The Sounds of Folk Music," using Pete Seeger's "Goofing Off Suite" as a theme song. Finally in 1958 he took another tentative step away from selling space in ethnic newspapers. He formed Folklore Productions and ran it out of his office at the Foreign Language Press. In early 1959 he received an unexpected call from a man named Lemuel Wells.

He had watched what was going on in the Club 47 and elsewhere. He had done a recording on his "Veritas" label of the minister of the Park Street Church and wanted to do a folk record. So I said, "Let's pick three people and see if they want to do it."

I originally selected Tony Saletan, Joan Baez, and Bill Wood. Because Tony was going to Asia on a government tour, we got Ted Alevizos who sang those wonderful Greek songs. Lem asked me if I'd write the notes for it, and he also wanted to use my mailing list. He did the mailing in my home. That's when my real acquaintance with Peter Robinson and Joan Baez began.

There were really only two recording studios in Boston at that time. One, Ace Recordings, was located in downtown Boston. It had a big ad in the yellow pages, a huge glass window fronting the control room, overweight men smoking cigars and red lights that flashed on when the tape was "rolling" — the stereotype of a fifties "Ya Wanna Be A Star?" mono recording studio. The other, Fassett Recordings, was located on Beacon Hill and was housed in a handsome five-story row building built in the eighteenth century. It really was a house. The studio itself was an afterthought. Steve Fassett had already made contact with some of the Cambridge folksingers. He had recorded an album with Bill Wood and his group from Harvard, the Raunchhands. They had played together as students, and realizing that graduation would be the end of their collective raunch, they all chipped in and got Fassett to record them. Then he got a call from Lem Wells.

I was contacted by Lemuel Wells. He was a black, well-trained in publicity. He had the idea of recording Dr. Theodore Parker Ferris of Trinity Church, the leading Episcopalian minister in the city of Boston. So they came here, and Wells published the record. That was my first introduction to Lem Wells. And it was he who put "Folk Singers 'Round Harvard Square" together. Peter Robinson came to all the sessions. Lem didn't. Peter, I guess, was like a father to the whole group.

Fassett was quite right about Peter's relationship to Joan. He had not only become an instant advocate of her musical talents, but had gone so far as to suggest to her father that she leave B.U. and make singing her profession.

Robinson was in a unique position to take this stand since he was a colleague of her father and a friend of the family. Albert Baez is a physicist and had come up the academic ladder step by difficult step. Born in Mexico, he sweated hard for his Ph.D. and felt that his three girls, Pauline, Joan, and Mimi would relish as a gift the education for which he had to struggle. That was not the case. If Joan's father was blind to Joan's dislike of College, Peter certainly was not.

Peter Robinson was and is a technical illus-trator whose real love is landscape painting. Thwarted in his own art by the need to make a living, he no doubt took a vicarious thrill in nurturing this budding young talent in its first purity and innocence. He had married a close friend of Joan's mother and knew the Baez family in California when the oldest daughter, Pauline, was just a baby. He always felt Joan to be artistic and took her on sketching trips when she was twelve.

In the fall of 1958, Peter decided to move his family east and, from October to December, was living at the Baez house in Belmont while he looked for one of his own. It was here that he first realized what Joanie's real gift was. The occasion was a small party for some of Al Baez's co-

JOAN BAEZ playing her guitar at home in Belmont. (c. 1959) Photograph by Rick Stafford.

workers — not academic types, but "a hot shot director from New York" and other members of his sound and film crew.

They were all invited to Al's, and they were all sitting around that magnificent living room drinking drinks and eating little stuff, and Joanie wandered into the room in that sort of vague, gamin, unorganized way that she had and sat down in a corner. Nobody spoke to her because she was only a kid, and all these fellows continued to brag, mutually, about their skills or whatever the hell they did, and over the course of the next fifteen minutes or so she sat and listened. She listened for a long time and started picking at her guitar vaguely and quietly. Unobtrusively and unnoticed, she started tuning it up. The way she was sitting there caught my eye. I was extremely fond of her, so when she came in I took notice of the fact that nobody noticed her.

Soon she began humming to herself, and pretty soon after that she was singing in a voice that hardly carried across the room. In fact, it really didn't. But I noticed almost immediately that when she opened her mouth, the guy sitting next to her stopped talking and listened. And that sort of spreading listening quieted the whole room! And, by God, for the next half hour or hour, or however long it was, she sang. It was the most arresting performance, because it started with no introduction, no nothing.

You know, Al is something of a performer himself, in the way he presents himself in public. He plays the piano, and he's always been the center of attention in every way at any sort of gathering of which he is a part. I think it really took him aback. Not that he'd not been taken aback previously, but here were all these hard-bitten, goddamned New Yorkers, and they were listening to his bloody daughter!

Above:
Rick Stafford's photograph of JOAN BAEZ and Eric von Schmidt's poster using the photograph to announce the summer program at the Club Mt. Auburn 47 (1959).

Following page:
PETE SEEGER and JOAN BAEZ all alone as they wait to go on. Photograph by John Cooke.

ecording at Steve Fassett's was a unique experience. Steve was burrowed mole-like in the basement with his big Ampex, while the "studio" was located on the second floor in a sparsely furnished but elegant nineteenth century room. The sole communication between Fassett in the basement and the artist on the second floor was through the one omnidirectional mike which was being used for the recording. If one disembodied voice was not enough, another occasionally came from the Terra Incognita above the studio: Steve's wife Agatha would inquire in the rich accents of Hungarian nobility, "Steeef, hav da cots been fed?" Steve was actually glimpsed from time to time; the well-fed cats loved to curl up in the guitar cases and were in constant view, but the majestic Agatha never appeared.

I remember Joan Baez came over one afternoon. She liked to be barefoot. It was a beautiful spring day. She had a boyfriend then. He was rather sullen. I didn't think he added much to the occasion. When she listened down here with the other musicians and with Peter Robinson, I remember she made a note "sounds constipated." She was very forthright about the quality of her work. She was patient. She had this soaring range. And at that time she used her full dynamic range when recording. The original tape has all that. I made a copy with eight or ten db compression done backwards, but still the radio stations complained about the levels. It was really one of the unique qualities of her style.

Shortly after the "Folksingers 'Round Harvard Square" album was recorded, a poster appeared on telephone poles and store windows around Harvard Square. It pictured an intense young girl in full song emerging from a background of forest-green ink. It announced to anyone who could decipher the caligraphy that the Club Mt. Auburn 47 "A private club open to summer students" was presenting "A NEW SUMMER PROGRAM/tuesdays/An Evening of Folk Music with JOAN BAEZ/thursday-saturday/PROGRESSIVE JAZZ." The snappy drawing of the drum set that had dominated the menu when the Club had opened had been replaced by this girl picking a guitar. The tide had turned. Progressive jazz was regressing. Joan was becoming the headliner. Joan *was* the headliner. Paula Kelley

remembers the audiences who were starting to pack the 47 on Tuesday nights.

The audiences were worshipful of Joan. They were never worshipful of anyone else. They were not knowledgeable about folk music. Joanie just happened to be a personality with a nice voice as far as they were concerned — it had nothing to do with folk music. After a period of time there really were a lot of folk buffs around, and I think that the Club did educate them to become folk buffs.

As much as Joan may have desired the adulation she was suddenly receiving, it was extremely difficult to cope with once it arrived. Today, when teenagers and even pre-teen kids are a gigantic chunk of the record buying public, it is not uncommon to be a "Superstar" at a much earlier age. But this was 1959 and Joan at eighteen was not singing "Earth Angel." She was emerging from a self-tormented childhood directly into the unblinking spotlight of an art form still largely associated with adult values. She was a young girl singing songs of deep knowledge drawn from life's experiences, while her own life was a tangle of fears and uncertainties. She was singing songs of wisdom she could only partially comprehend.

All of this pressure was bound to take its toll. Debbie Green:

Dick Zaffron, Joanie, and I were supposed to play a dormitory on the corner of Plympton Street. I got sick and was in no shape to play, and was to be taken home, but I really wanted to see the concert. Joanie did a number. She sang all the songs — you know how you have a certain list of ones you really like to do — all my arrangements, and when she finished all the good ones, she maneuvered Zaffron into introducing me, and there I was in the audience. I remember coming up. No capo was available. It was awful . . .

Paula Kelley:

The only mankind that was acceptable was the mankind, like her, who shared her ideals and who shared her way of life. Joyce and I never knew Joan personally. She was not an easy person to know. She was not friendly.

Joyce Kalina:

Joan could be very difficult, very arrogant, rude, hysterical — she had stage-fright half the time. She used to go out in the alley and throw up, she was so scared. Her boyfriend at the time was driving her crazy. She was always running out in the back.

oan battled her demons in the dark. The unknown fear. It could swarm in her mind at any second and she was terrified of it. When she sang of strange metamorphoses, of anguished maidens in distress, she was singing straight from her heart.

By the age of five the fears were so solid that I had already become a genius at running away from them, and running like that is a hard habit to break. Mother nursed me through terror from that early age until I moved out of the house at nineteen. Perhaps the blows of adolescence made junior high and early high school the roughest time.

The major part of my childhood was spent in fighting off terror of things which don't exist, and I don't think my father understood that kind of fear. The overriding and most terrifying bogeyman of my life, which has been with me since my earliest memories, and remains faithfully with me, though now it seldom puts me out of commission, has been a fear of vomiting.

It has used up and wasted and blackened many hours of my life. But my father never had a notion of what I was talking about when I cried and shook and said, "You know . . . It's that thing again . . ." While I was in junior high school and even high school, I was still going to my parents bedroom, sometimes five nights a week, and climbing in their bed, all hot and cold and shaking, pleading for Mother to say the key sentences which would begin to send the fear away.

Come along, boys, and don't you cry.
Sail away, ladies, sail away.
You'll be an angel, by and by.
Sail away, ladies, sail away.

Black Is the Color

Black is the color of my true love's hair.
Her lips are something wondrous fair,
The prettiest feet and the daintiest hands,
I love the grass on where she stands.

oston was some serious street business going on. Going to Cambridge was like free lunch after Boston. You could get killed in Boston. There's no walking around after dark with your eyes closed in Boston. It gave rise to a slightly different cultural outlook.

Bobby Neuwirth didn't take long to find his way around when he hit Boston. Neuwirth came from Ohio to go to the Boston Museum School of Fine Arts.

Don't forget Shelly. Shelly and Norman. Shelly Cohen and Norman Kumin and this girl named Gabby had the first beatnik coffee shop in the Boston University area — the Cafe Yana, right next to the railroad tracks on Beacon Street. When it first started off, the Cafe Yana was really a hot place. It was the other axis from Cambridge. Everybody who came from the other side of the river used to play there.

When I first got there I only knew artists, and, through them, the South End street people — Walter and "Doc" and "Blinky" — all guys that bet the pooches. They were pals with a guy named Ronnie Vial. Ronnie had an apartment right next to the Cafe Yana with a bunch of Irish guys who worked as attendants in the cuckoo house. So I started hanging out over there. It was a little more straight than Cambridge. Cambridge was a little academic, sort of Europeanish. We were a little closer to the Boston streets. It was an art and painter crowd. There were Boston University chicks and B.U., Mass School of Art, and Museum School painters all hanging out.

At first the kind of music that was around was very academic, folky, Elizabethan ballads. Fred Basler was connected with the Mass. School of Art, and he'd come to the Yana to sing that stuff. That's how the painters got involved. Debbie Green was sort of tentatively strumming away on a little, brown-faced Martin guitar. She and Betsy Minot were very tight. They were both theater majors at B.U. and used to wear little checked, gingham shirts. They were fairly attractive, young, long-haired Bohemian girls. Looked like easy touches, you know.

Neuwirth liked action. If there wasn't any he'd make it or find it. The Yana had it all. Some music, some pretty girls, and whatever was going on next door.

For other, more innocent souls, it was the music that brought them in the door. For them finding a place in Boston where you could sing and play and listen to folk songs was like a dream come true.

Portrait of The Artist as a Young NEUWIRTH. Photograph by John Cooke.

ohn Nagy had just discovered Pete Seeger. He had actually met him while visiting his brother Paul out at Oberlin College in Ohio. John's father was a violinist with the Boston Symphony Orchestra, and John had been studying cello for thirteen years, but when he got back to Newton he had a banjo, not a cello, on his knee.

I came home and desperately tried to find a banjo. I got one from a kid in school. It had a short neck. I took it over to Fritz Richmond's, who went to high school with me, and we felt that we could lengthen the neck. So we did it. It wasn't really a success, but it got us started. The nature of the five-string banjo fascinated me. I'd never heard one before or seen one. I tried to figure out how he got that sound — the basic strum (up with the finger, brush over with the thumb). It sounded like he was hitting one string with a finger and then taking four fingers very fast and ending with the thumb.

John had another friend from high school who knew something about music and how to play the guitar. His name was John Marten, but everyone called him Buzz.

I had an uncle who played guitar. He came through one time, and my father bought a little twelve dollar guitar for him to play on. Before he left he showed me the three chords to the key of D. I played everything in "D" for about two years. Eventually I branched out to the other keys. I never liked rock and roll that much. Growing up in Newton I either listened to classical music or country music whenever I could find it. I listened to WWVA at night. Bluegrass almost made me wet my pants the first time I heard it.

Buzz was obviously ready to be Seegerized, and the occasion was not long in coming.

Pete Seeger came to Jordan Hall and Buzzy and I went in. We sat down front and watched every move his fingers made. We were off and running. I got on the banjo. He got on the guitar. I finally found a good banjo. Buzzy's father lent me the twenty-five dollars to buy it. My own folks had nothing to do with it. I went into my room for days to practice with my Pete Seeger records and his instruction book.

There was no question about it. This Seeger stuff was a force to be reckoned with. There was almost a sense of inevitability about it once it got started.

Within two weeks I went into the Cafe Yana. It was almost magic the way it happened. I was walking across the street from my house with my banjo. A car pulled up. It was another freak who played the banjo. He knew about the Cafe Yana. He told me about it, and I couldn't believe it — a place in Boston that had this folk music! That night I got my banjo and put it in a paper bag and went in there. Fred Basler was playing guitar. I asked if I could play, and they said, "sure." I did the songs I had just learned. About nine songs. And the people liked it. Here I was playing on a stage for these people on an instrument with which I was very unfamiliar and in an environment which was completely new to me. I was a very conservative, laid-back, shy cellist. I really didn't know how to respond to it but I was thrilled with it. And they offered me a job a couple of nights a week.

John raced home and got hold of Buzz. They immediately started to learn some more songs off their Weavers records. John got hold of a Stella six-string guitar and took it over to Fritz's basement to convert it into a twelve-string. Both Buzz and John wanted Fritz to get in on the act for which they even had a name — "The Hoppers." (Fritz's name was John, too. Three Johns. A little attempt at humor.)

Buzzy did songs, I did songs, and we did some together. Fritz didn't play anything, and we had to get him in somehow. He is one of the most innovative people I've ever known. He came up with the washtub. We got one at Sears. He experimented with different tubs, different string, and cable. He really made a science out of it.

Our playing together was the beginning of Fritz starting to come out of himself. He had been very shy and socially uninvolved until then. He really went out there once he got going.

Fritz was definitely not alone. Lots of other people were starting to get going, too. The Yana soon became the center of a swarm. John's brother Paul and his friend David Gurness started to play. They took an apartment upstairs with another friend of theirs who was just getting into Seeger and Woody Guthrie, Robert L. Jones. Jones had grown up in nearby West Roxbury and was in his second year at B.U. Soon his sister Helen arrived from Iowa where she had been going to school and moved in. Betsy Minot started waitressing and going out with John. Her friend, Debbie Green, started singing there. Of course, John, Buzz, and Fritz were playing, too, and they started attracting other budding young

pickers from B.U. Jim Kweskin and his friend
Teddy Bernstein started coming in. They'd sit
right down front the way Buzzy and John had for
Pete Seeger and watch their fingers and write
down the words to the songs. It was the blind
leading the blind. Nobody knew that much, but
they were willing to share what they did know.
Through it all Fred Basler kept up his ballads and
singalongs. Soon they were all joined by a refugee
from Antioch College who had also fallen under
Pete Seeger's spell. His name was Peter Lenz. If
Pete Seeger himself had walked through the door
he might have wondered if he was needed any
more. One more "Wimoweh" might have been
one too many.

Above:
JIM KWESKIN and BUZZ
MARTEN playing and singing their
hearts out. (c.1961) Photograph by
Stephen Fenerjian.

Like some kind of erratic Northeast storm, the Yana scene went through many changes over the next months. Betsy and Debbie moved out of their dorm and into an apartment on Beacon Hill. John Nagy moved in until his parents decided that it was time for John to enlist.

It was decided that if I were to get into the army it would help to straighten me out. It put an end to what would have been a natural development. It would have only been a matter of time before I would have played out all the copying and really have started to develop. I did commute a lot from Fort Devens. Buzzy got better. Jim Kweskin was blowing a comb with tissue paper and learning how to fingerpick. Fritz had to go into the army too. Eventually he went to Korea and I went to Europe. I was gone for a year and a half, and in that time the whole scene had exploded. Joan Baez could barely play when I left. She was already a star when I came back. Kweskin was on his own. Tom Rush was coming on. And I was still playing Pete Seeger music.

When John moved out, Neuwirth didn't waste any time, and soon his boots were under Betsy's bed. Geno Foreman started to come over. He knew Debbie from Putney and was really living the life, running between Boston and Cambridge and New York, jazzing, jiving, scoring, picking, grinning. He and Neuwirth became good buddies. Betsy was fighting an uphill battle.

Debbie was into sleeping all day and staying up all night. A lot. Finally she got mono and had to go home. By the summer it was clear that neither Debbie nor Joan Baez were going back to B.U. I switched to the Museum School because Neuwirth thought it would be a good idea. I got an apartment alone with him on Beacon Street near the Yana. Sandy Bull lived downstairs. There were always a whole lot of weirdos around. I was into wearing black then. I think a "black outfit" was on my freshman clothing list. It was a real serious time. We hadn't graduated to cowboy boots yet.

A little further on down the street, Buzzy had moved in with Kweskin and Teddy Bernstein. He was doing his best to stay ahead of his students. **I latched onto a Chet Atkins record and a Merle Travis record, and those were the two guys who really did it for me. By that time I was so tired of the Weavers' music that I never could listen to it again, but it did get us going and playing which was the main thing.**

Jim Kweskin's life had changed considerably as a result of starting to play.

It was so exciting, going to coffeehouses every night, hearing a new song for the first time, copying down the words, learning a new chord progression, figuring out a blues lick. My whole life was filled with discovery. I discovered there was another way to live. I got turned on to marijuana. Soon I was playing English and Appalachian ballads at the small time Boston coffeehouses.

Above the Yana, Robert L. Jones was quietly learning a lot of ballads from David Gurness and Woody Guthrie songs from records. He and his

sister Helen and Gurness discovered another coffeehouse over on Huntington Avenue called The Salamander. They heard Dick Zaffron there, and one night he brought up Joan Baez who sang some Odetta songs. They also got into going over to the YMCA on Huntington Avenue for concerts put on by the Folksong Society of Greater Boston. They were meeting more and more people who shared their enthusiasm for folk music. The circle was widening.

y the fall of 1959 the scene at the Yana had changed. Brawls and street business were starting to find their way into the Cafe. So when Freddy Basler and Peter Lenz heard of a space on the other side of the tracks on a street behind B.U. they decided to investigate. It turned out to be available, and they decided to open a place of their own, called "The Golden Vanity" after one of Fred's favorite ballads. The Vanity would not only feature local performers, but would also bring in many of the artists who had become prominent in the folk movement which had built up around Pete Seeger — people like Guy Carawan, Sonny Terry and Brownie McGhee, Oscar Brand, and Theo Bikel. It was a big step forward for the Boston folk community. Freddy and Peter enlisted the help of just about everyone who had been involved at the Yana.

Neuwirth came over and took one look at all

the space upstairs and saw what any artist would see — a loft. Freddy understood and let him have it. Soon the place was echoing to the sound of hammers and saws. From her vantage point at the luncheonette next door Alice Foreman watched them come and go, bringing in lumber and wallboard and barrels which were going to be used for tables and chairs. On breaks they'd come

(far left) FRITZ RICHMOND playing his very first washtub bass. John Nagy carried this picture in his wallet all the time he was in the army to give him strength. (c. 1958)

(center left) MARCEL KISTIN, organizer of the Folksong Society of Greater Boston, thoughtfully puffs his pipe as he listens to Paul Nagy (with guitar) and others play and sing. Decor is by the YMCA. Betsy Minot is the girl on the right who is all ears. (c.1959). Photographer unknown. Courtesy of Manny Greenhill.

(center right) BETSY MINOT displaying her famous profile to advantge. Taken at the Golden Vanity. (c.1960) Photograph by Alan Klein.

(far right) FRED BASLER testing out the acoustics of his new club, The Golden Vanity. (1959) Photographer unknown.

in and have a cup of coffee and talk to her about their new club.

As it happened, the Vanity wasn't the only new folk club getting ready to open. Across town Manny Greenhill had plans of his own.

George Wein had run Storyville as an excellent jazz club and had the idea for a folk club. He and Albert Grossman had already done the first Newport Folk Festival which was a success, and I had been involved with him on that. We were talking about the Festival one day and he said, "I've got this room downstairs where Mahogany Hall used to be. Why don't we do something with it?" I said that I didn't know anything about running a club, but he had a woman in mind to run it named Terri Turner. I came up with the name "The Ballad Room" and got Eric von Schmidt to do the logo — a banjo and guitar — and I used some paintings of his in the room. I found out later that George had never made any money with Storyville, but I thought it was a good idea. It lasted less than one season. Terri was running it Storyville style — bartenders in red jackets, a maitre d', cover, minimum — just the wrong kind of thing for the college kids who didn't care for the nightclub atmosphere. They were starting to go to the coffeehouses. Of course, it didn't help that the Golden Vanity opened at about the same time. Peter Lenz would come in and make his negotiations with the same artists I was having as soon as they got off the stage! It's great to be naive! You can get away with a lot.

A lot, perhaps, but not everything. Peter wanted to have Sonny Terry and Brownie McGhee for his opening night, which was a Sunday. They were to play a concert for Manny at Jordan Hall the night before. Reluctantly, Manny agreed. Then Peter changed his mind and wanted to open with them on Friday night, before they were to play the concert. Manny pointed out to Peter that their contract forbade that, so Peter called Eric von Schmidt and asked him if he would play with Sonny.

Would I play with Sonny? Does God make honky-tonk angels? Was Leadbelly the King of the twelve-string guitar players of the world?

So at last all was in readiness for the maiden voyage of the Golden Vanity with music by Sonny and von Schmidt. Eric couldn't help but be impressed by the decor when he arrived.

The place was rigged up like a nightmare catered by Herman Melville. The tables were huge barrels. Nets were hung all over the place. A ship's wheel was hung behind the stage and some sort of phony weathervane was overhead. You expected the guy at the door to be wearing a yellow slicker.

Eric went upstairs, unpacked his guitar and two bottles of gin and introduced himself to Sonny. **It was a great thrill for me. Sonny was one of my musical heroes. It just blew my mind that I was actually going to play with someone who I'd never seen, but had heard for years on records.**

Soon it was time to go on. Downstairs the place was packed. Eric was starting to work on the gin to calm himself down. Freddy and Peter came up to get them. Sonny asked for his money. They said that they had a check. Sonny said that he needed money — M-O-N-E-Y. Cash. Before he went on. Freddy and Peter went back downstairs and in a few minutes they were back. They counted it out to Eric who, in turn, placed each bill in Sonny's hand telling him what it was. When they got to one hundred Sonny said, "Let's go."

The Vanity was a coffeehouse, but you never would have known it that night. By the middle of the evening Eric and Sonny were feeling no pain. Back in the kitchen Neuwirth and Jones were starting to get behind on the dishes.

Neuwirth and I were getting slowly juiced. The place was pretty well stocked and had a lot of dishes. We couldn't get any hot water, so we decided, "Fuck this. Let's sit down and get juiced and enjoy the music and when all the dishes come we'll get a huge stack and do them all at once," which is what we did. Unfortunately, the dishes got stacked up a little more than we thought, and we had had a little bit too much to drink, so when we finally got started we didn't know what we were doing and were dropping things all over the place.

Upstairs Eric had just tossed an empty gin bottle out the window onto the street below, narrowly missing some of the patrons who were still trying to get in to catch the third set. It was a toss-up as to whether Eric was going to lead Sonny or Sonny was going to lead Eric back down to cap off the evening. When it was all over Neuwirth and Jones got ten bucks cash for their efforts. Eric got a twenty dollar check for his which he promptly misplaced. When he did find it weeks later, it bounced. It didn't matter though. He'd played with Sonny Terry, and the Golden Vanity had been launched.

The Vanity brought to five the number of places with folk music in Boston. The others were

ERIC VON SCHMIDT and SONNY TERRY "one night only" at the opening of the Golden Vanity (1959).
Photographer unknown.

the Turk's Head over on Charles Street, where Paul Nagy and David Gurness were starting to play; The Salamander on Huntington where Dick Zaffron, Joan Baez, and now Tom Rush occasionally appeared; the Cafe Yana, which still had many of the old crew — Buzz Marten, Robert L. Jones, and the rapidly improving Jim Kweskin; and the Ballad Room, which was bringing "name" artists like Oscar Brand, The Tarriers, and Brother John Sellers. Occasionally the Ballad Room would have some of the younger, local artists like Eric von Schmidt and Joan Baez. As a result of the proliferation of clubs, the audience began to grow. Many people who had never heard of folk music before found themselves listening to it for the first time, often more by accident than by design — but by the second or

third time they found themselves being drawn into what was becoming the "folk world."

 illy Burke was still working at WHDH-TV as a film editor, and he was making time with a girl named Elaine. **This girl was a hairdresser and really beautiful. Together we really looked like the Coca-Cola kids. One night we were going out to this new club that had opened called the Ballad Room. We were going to see Oscar Brand, and this girl, Joan Baez, was the opening act. So I went in with this girl, and we sat down, and we're sitting there having our drinks, really feeling very slick and**

JOAN BAEZ at the Golden Vanity (1960). Photograph by Charles Frizzell.

together here at this new club that had just opened in town. This girl walked in with long, black hair — sort of stringy, black hair — no shoes, and got up on the stage. I'm saying to myself, "Jesus! Fuckin' beatniks!"

Then she started singing, and it just blew me away. Really knocked me out. Elaine said something to me about something in the middle of one of Joan's songs, and I turned to her and said, "Can't you be quiet until she finishes?" That was the beginning of the end of us. Elaine and I separated soon after that. It happened sort of slowly, with me calling up and saying, "I won't be able to come over," because I'd read in the paper that this Joan Baez was appearing at the Golden Vanity or the Club Mt. Auburn 47. So I started

taking nights and going into the clubs.

Neuwirth told me that he remembers that I used to come in wearing a freshly laundered sweatshirt. I had three sweatshirts. I really wanted to let myself start breaking down, but my whole upbringing and the Marine Corps pulled the other way.

Donald Macsorley was another who, like Billy, had stumbled into this scene by accident.
I was from South Boston and had never heard of folk music. I met this girl while I was pumping gas, and she brought me into the Golden Vanity one night. Suddenly I became aware that there was this world that I knew nothing about. All the girls seemed mysterious. And you knew that something else was happening upstairs or

downstairs or wherever. What was there for the paying audience wasn't the whole thing. The people on the inside were a scene in themselves. They sort of tolerated the audience, but they really thought they were fools — because they paid to get in. Nobody who was anybody paid to get in. But the music struck a chord — especially when I heard Joan Baez do something like *Mary Hamilton*. The Irish-English traditional music began to really appeal to me. All of it just sucked me in. It was handy to B.U., where I was going to school, so I started to go over there a lot. I wound up washing dishes a couple of nights a week, and that was my ticket into that world.

The way you learned to play the guitar was to start on the fringes at a party and gradually work your way into the center as your confidence increased. Eventually you would be accepted as one of the group. That was the nice thing about the folk scene: Once you were in it, the musical exchange with other people was an education, and it was also fun. Being involved with this scene helped me break out of the parochial world I grew up in in South Boston. It made me aware that something else was out there.

Jill Henderson grew up far from the streets of Boston in nearby Belmont.

Growing up I really didn't know anybody who wasn't white, Anglo-Saxon Episcopal until I went to college. During the Depression, my family was not depressed. My grandfather had done very well in law in Boston, so my mother was in Paris at a time when a lot of people here were in soup kitchens. Maybe that had a lot to do with why I later got interested in the music of people like Woody Guthrie. I just didn't know about that side of life. While she was in Paris, my mother used to frequent a club called "Bricktop's," where Josephine Baker played, and she became close friends with Bricktop, which was pretty daring for a girl with her background. So I had an interest in Black music from her.

All of this was in the back of my mind when I came back from college in 1958. I was starting to become fascinated by people from different parts of the country, different backgrounds, and different religions. Through my brother I began to discover the folk clubs. We were sharing an apartment on Beacon Hill and we first went to the Turk's Head which was the only coffee house on Charles Street at the time. Then we discovered the Cafe Yana. I walked in one night and someone was playing "Twelve Gates to the City" on a twelve-string guitar. I had never heard

one and just fell in love with the sound. I knew the words to the song — don't ask me how or why — and I started to sing along. As a result, people started to talk to me, and so I began going there regularly and got to know everyone. When there was too much else going on over there besides music, I shifted over to the Golden Vanity and then to the Club 47.

It was like being caught up in a wave. The minute I heard that twelve-string guitar I just wanted to know everything I could about everyone's music. And I could see it happen to other people. In the daytime I was working as a secretary at the M.I.T. Instrumentation Lab. The people I knew at work were straight, but they liked music too. I'd tell them about the Vanity of the 47 and three months later they'd suddenly be wearing dungarees, reading books, and buying records. I knew it was tumbling.

However it was happening, folk music was bringing people together in more ways than one. Robert L. Jones celebrated Valentine's Day 1960 by going into the army, but others were observing the holiday in the more traditional manner. Soon songs like "Kisses Sweeter Than Wine," "Careless Love," and ultimately, "What'll We Do With The Baby-O" began to take on new meaning to many of the pickers and singers around the Vanity. Peter Lenz's affair with another man's wife led to such dramatic scenes that Peter had to relinquish his role in the club to a no less randy but more discreet Carl Bowers. Don Macsorley was distracted from his dishwashing chores by the beautiful Alice Foreman, who had left her post at the luncheonette to become a waitress at the Vanity. Eric von Schmidt showed up even when he was not playing to discuss current events with Helen Jones. Betsy Minot went across the river a lot to listen to Uncle Dave Macon records with Bob Siggins. Even the jaded Neuwirth couldn't resist one of Cupid's little darts:

When I lived at the Golden Vanity, Mimi Baez and a friend of hers from high school used to come over and clean my pad and sometimes do my ironing! They were only fourteen and were so cute! I took Mimi on her first date to a gallery opening. It was a trip just to do that. They had just done my laundry and cleaned my pad and were waiting for Joan, who was downstairs negotiating for a job. They heard Brice Marden and me talking about going to a gallery opening and obviously wanted to go, so we took them. It was so innocent I loved it.

I f everyone else had but one admirer, Joan Baez had hundreds. As the year progressed, her following was swelling on both sides of the river. Led by Geno Foreman, she had acquired a band of would-be bikers who would show up at the 47 or the Vanity whenever she played. There was David Barry, Cy Koch, Todd Stuart, David Piper, Tom Goodwin, and John Cooke. Some went to Harvard, some just hung around. They were all pretty well off and were heavy into blues, jazz, movies, and machines. Not your ordinary machines, but Vincents and Shadows and Super Rockets. It became a thing to ride a bike into the Vanity or the 47 while Joan was singing and let her rev the bike up, being real cool about it all. Eat your hearts out, all your Baez-crazed college boys! She was the Rebel Queen and wouldn't look at you.

When it came time for the Newport Folk Festival that year, it was decided they would bring Joan down in style. The year before she had been Bob Gibson's guest, and she was almost totally unknown to the audience. This year she had been invited as a featured performer, and her appearance was going to be a triumph. John Stein was a friend of Tom Goodwin from Yale who had been coming up regularly to see Joan perform. John didn't have a bike, he was a bit too elegant for that. He had a hearse. What could be better than to bring Joan to Newport in a hearse complete with motorcycle escort! And so it happened. Buoyed by the loyalty of her friends and secure in the knowledge that she already had many fans out in the audience, Joan went on stage.

Her performance that night was the highlight of the evening whether you knew her or not. There was something about her voice as it floated out on the night air, singing these beautiful strange songs that left you speechless. She was so young and looked so vulnerable in a simple dress and her bare feet, but her voice had power in it to chill you to the bone. There was no denying that she was a star. She was riding the crest of a new wave of folk music that was building in Cambridge and Boston that was growing larger by the day. Bob Neuwirth came to Boston looking for action, and he'd found it. For life.

I watched it go from the living room to ten dollars a night paid engagements, which consisted of sitting around with a cup of expresso watching somebody in a workshirt sing a folksong. I watched it move to a stage, watching little Joan Baez get up in her pinafore and sing a folksong, watching her make ten dollars a night. Once she made fifteen dollars and thought it was immoral, which it was. It went from there to larger places like the Golden Vanity, where Peter Lenz and Freddy Basler booked people in for fifty dollars a night. Sometimes you had to make reservations on the weekends to sit around barrels and drink swill. Then it went from clubs to real showbusiness.

Cambridge and Boston was a great melting pot of cultural things. Because it was an academic center it brought people from so many different places who had all sorts of interests. Some people were interested in mountain music, some people were interested in blues, some people were interested in bluegrass, and a lot of people became interested in it all. All of this became the source of Joan's material. The fact that Joan came out of all these and became the best known was important because she went on to influence a generation.

I love my love and well she knows.
I love the grass whereon she goes,
And if my love no more I see,
My life will quickly fade away.

Baby, Let Me Lay it on You

I'll get you a brand new suit,
I'll slit your throat to boot.
I'll do anything in this godalmighty world,
Just to let me lay it on you.

o genuine beatniks resent pseudo-beatniks? Such a question might seem the concern of psychologists, the subject for a Doctoral thesis, a study funded by the government. But questions such as this, even in a "City of Scholars" such as Cambridge, are not always academic. All social observers do not wear tweed jackets and conduct their inquiries behind ivy covered walls. Some of them wear dark blue suits and carry .38 caliber pistols. If one is to believe an article entitled "Police Eye Beatnik Imposters" in Boston's *Record American,* the question was of real concern to at least one group involved in behavioral studies: the Cambridge Police.

An influx of pseudo-beatniks in the Harvard Sq. area has created police concern, alarmed staid Cantabridgians and prestige conscious college faculties... Since the close of the Harvard and Radcliffe academic year, police have members of "The Unwashed" society under constant surveillance.

An eatery is the center for the gathering of

these peculiars who, while trying to give the impression of college students, actually are 17 to 30... They gather late at night and in the early morning hours over coffee, exhibiting their Castro beards, short-haired women sport near masculine dress.

A local police sergeant has been watching conditions at a unique club in the area where so-called beatniks and other characters gather nightly... Intellectual types mingle with the others to the beat of string music and "folk songs." ...In some instances the guests are under the influence of more than the music, the sergeant found, not to overlook his suspicion of the presence of narcotic users.

The article, printed under the by-line of the "Cambridge Rambler," didn't mention any names but all concerned parties knew sure as hell which "eatery" and what "club." The eatery was the Hayes-Bickford. The club was the 47. Joyce Kalina and Paula Kelley were learning things that were not included in the curriculum at Brandeis: They were learning that the police had delicate sensibilities and long memories. The cops had closed the club in 1958 with the dramatic flourishes of a million dollar dope bust, and here was the same

joint back in operation. It was an affront to their sense of purpose. At least the Club 47 wasn't right in the middle of Harvard Square (which would have constituted a constant aggravating *visual* offense in the first degree). Whereas and Heretofore the God Damned Hayes-Bickford *was!*

Located on the corner of Holyoke Street, just past where Massachusetts Avenue makes its end run around the Harvard Yard, it squatted only two blocks away from an endless succession of Irish and Italian cops who have forever stood guard on the Square. This was *the* visible presence of law enforcement in Harvard Square. During the day Dr. Jekyll dined at the Bickford on his mashed potatoes and overdone roast beef, with student, shopgirl, and scholar alike. Massive indigestion is not a matter for police concern.

But when the full moon rose high above Harvard Square, and the bats in Lowell House rose in tremulous response to the beat of stringed music resounding from the hell holes along Mt. Auburn Street, the policemen guarding Harvard Square began to experience a rising, a mounting, an *inflamed* sense of concern. For they knew in their hearts that Dr. Jekyll would be returning—returning in the terrible visage of Mr. Hyde, his face smeared with a ghastly slather of mashed potatoes, grease-laden gravy dripping from his brutish chin. A pseudo-beatnik! After a hard evening of raping virgins, despoiling widows, and shooting up junk, the Bick was just the place that a bastard like that would go.

Robert Siggins was by this time totally addicted to the five-string banjo. Through the trickery of the sinister Sackheim, he was a hopeless slave to old-timey music. It was in this degraded state that he, Siggins, entered the aforementioned eatery.

The fried-egg special was it. Half an English muffin, a piece of bacon, and an egg. Clay Jackson called it a "Splayed Egg Facial." Worst coffee in the world. People were falling in and out of that place. It was like Gertrude Stein's without the host.

I spent a New Year's Eve there. I figured it would be real destitute, but it was terrific. A guy showed up out of nowhere. I'd never seen him before, and he organized the whole place. He had the whole place going. He did this phony interview show. He had us doing trains in our chairs, scooting all around. I was the caboose. I almost fell off the chair, laughing.

The Bick wasn't just a music hangout. Henry Geldzahler, who's now the head of the Museum of Modern Art, hung out there; Chuck Wein, who's a big movie guy now; and Eric Sackheim, of course.

Further observations by the Cambridge Rambler on the lifestyle of the Pseudo-Beatniks revealed the following:

They would convey the idea of learning, they are students of Cambridge institutions, riding motor scooters and cycles in tandem and carrying books on psychology, etc. which some can't even read. Police, who have been observing the conditions closely, upon questioning these loiterers find they come from Greater Boston communities... In many instances they are unable to give a sound reason for their presence... Some from Roxbury and Jamaica Plains have been found to have police records. Investigation has also shown that some of these "intellectual morons" have moved into the city bag and baggage... In one building alone, three short-haired women and seven bearded imitators reside, on different floors... Neighbors have complained of peculiar actions and noisy scooters day and night.

Why this sudden influx of intellectual morons, bearded imitators, and short-haired women? Close the Bick! Shut the Club! hollered the cops. But it was too late. The Pied Pipers had come to town.

Folk music represents many things to many people. The American Left had for years tried to make it their own. Fortunately it didn't work. When the Kingston Trio hit the charts, folk music, or at least their up-tempo brand of it, became public property. Together with the Limeliters, the Chad Mitchell Trio, and the Brothers Four, they opened up a vast audience for a more ethnic approach. Folk music was, is, and always will be public property.

The pickers and singers around Cambridge and Boston at that time were not into politics of any variety. Three of them — Geno Foreman, Eric von Schmidt, and Rolf Cahn, the Pied Pipers of Cambridge — definitely were not. Collectively they represented something that all students long for: Freedom. And the music that they

played and the way they played it embodied that same freedom. It said "come away, you can be free, you can be alive, you can be you." And the student pickers sitting in their dormitories staring blankly at tomorrow's lesson began hearing that song in their heads and began to wonder if *that* might just be the real lesson.

Almost everyone remembers their first meeting with Geno. He entered a room with the delicacy of a bazooka shell. Clay Jackson was sitting in the Bick.

Geno just walked in. When he was in his friend-making mood he'd just walk up to anybody's table and start talking, and within fifteen minutes not only would he have learned each one's personality, he would have talked the whole group into some activity. He'd say, "All right, we've got it figured out. We're just gonna drive down to the harbor and catch a fish. Now who's got a car?" Then he'd say, "Hey! You got a car, man, let me borrow it for fifteen minutes, I'll be right back." Woooosh, gone like a flash. Suddenly, the guy would say, "Good God! I just loaned my car to this madman." And he'd sit there chewing his fingernails. "Should I call the cops? This crazy person has taken my car!" About half an hour later Geno would roar up, come in, "Wow!" You know he'd have a fish and all kinds of good stuff, and he would have made a connection somewhere. He probably drove to Dorchester and sold a couple of ounces to a man in a pool hall, — you know, that kind of shit — and he was fourteen. And that was just warming up.

He kept getting kicked out of schools, so his parents had sent him to some kind of academy out in Concord or someplace like that. He stayed there about two weeks and then came in and started hanging around the Square. He was the first cat that I ever knew that ever brought grass to Harvard Square. In about 1957, I guess. He'd have to show people how to roll it, and tell them what it was.

Geno was probably a couple of years older than fourteen, but his life had been a full-tilt-boogie for years. The son of Clark Foreman, a well-known civil rights lawyer, Geno was a one-man army at war with the Establishment, with Authority, with Squares, and with his own tendencies to self-destruct.

Joan Baez had fallen under his spell. Shy and aloof herself, she found his honesty, energy, and exuberance irresistible. Bob Neuwirth remembers his introduction to Foreman at the Club 47. **Joan kept telling me, "You've got to meet Geno. Wait 'til you meet Geno." Then it was, "Geno's in Europe." "Geno's coming." Geno had been coming for six months. One night, she was on stage at the 47. The door flew open. It was the middle of the winter. This guy clomped through, wearing giant wide-wale corduroys, a turtleneck sweater, no socks, some kind of crazy, zonked-out, European goat-herder boots — typical Parisian left-bank attire. He just clomped through and stopped her in the middle of a song. It had already got to the point where she had a hushed, reverential audience, and her clarity and purity shone through. Geno put an end to that and caused her to crack up on the spot. There was nothing she could do except to get him on the stage.**

She was going out with Michael New. Michael New and Geno were European hustling friends. Geno was structurally very heavy and a strong influence on Joan.

eter Rowan was just about Geno's age when he first heard him play at Tulla's Coffee Grinder. Peter grew up west of Boston in Wayland and had been given a plastic ukelele when he was twelve. He played it "until the frets were worn out." Three years later he got hold of a 45 of Elvis Presley singing "I'm Left, You're Right, She's Gone," and so was he. Soon after that he and some school buddies had put together a band called "The Cupids."

We started playing for record hops all over the Boston area. To be barely sixteen and be doing

JOAN BAEZ. Photograph by Jerry Lewis.

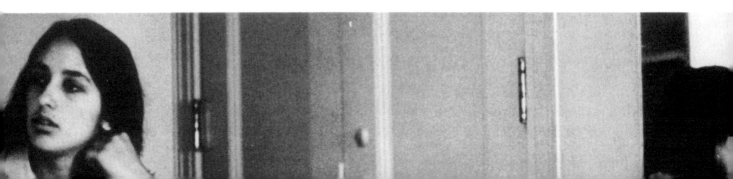

this was great. One night we were coming back through Cambridge, and one of the guys who was older than me asked if I'd like to stop and get some coffee. I said, "I dunno, are there girls there?" He said, "I don't know. It's a real different kind of place."

So we went into Tulla's. There was this conga player beating in one corner and someone else in another corner. The whole room was a stage. People were drinking coffee and moving their heads up and down. I couldn't believe it. It was summertime, and everyone was just hanging out. When they stopped playing jazz for a minute along comes this guy Geno Foreman. He had fingerpicks sharp as knives on his fingers. He tore up someone's guitar with them. He was unbelievable. He just shredded the soundhole with those fingerpicks. This was my first introduction to what Soul was — where you went beyond. I got to know Geno, and I realized he really was out there. He came in one night and told me he'd been out looking for "squares." I asked him what he did when he found one. He said he'd lit a cherry bomb and threw it through the guy's window and drove on. I'd led a pretty sheltered life and here was this guy into student guerilla warfare! Geno would play "Keep on Truckin' Mama" four or five times a night. Man, that was racy stuff.

Geno was interested in black music, especially blues. He searched out old Blind Boy Fuller records, learned them, and then speeded his versions up. At that time everything, even music, was done at top velocity. Jackson recalls it.
The thing is at that age he had this unbelievable energy that he channeled into activity. Like moving around and driving cars and buying and selling. Then, when he got into music, when he actually started playing music, he started channeling all his energy into that. He affected people by being around them. It was his attitude toward being alive. He didn't stand still and pull the world toward him. He ran forward at top speed, so that to be around him changed the way you thought and understood and felt.

Neuwirth:
All of this strongly influenced Joan. It certainly influenced Dylan. Between Von Schmidt and Baez and the ease with which you could be a guitarist without having to watch out for having your guitar stolen nightly — as opposed to New York — it was very impressive to a lot of people. You could be loose in Cambridge and not have your head kicked in. I'm living proof of that.

Cambridge may have been a piece of cake compared to New York but as Eric von Schmidt found out it is possible to get your lumps just about anywhere. Eric had moved to Cambridge in 1957 after spending a year in Italy on a Fulbright Painting Grant.

One evening in the summer of '61 he was crossing Brattle Square with a bag of artichokes and a belly full of martinis when a young fellow wearing a warm-up jacket and driving a souped up roadster barrelled up to him doing about sixty and slammed on the brakes several feet away. The car's lights were not on. Von Schmidt, in an extremely mellow mood, walked around to the driver's side and suggested that the lad turn on his lights, take things a little more easy, enjoy life, and have an artichoke. At which point he found himself being swept along at an uncomfortably high velocity, his arm locked in the grip of the young driver. Standing fully upright all the while, he was wondering how long it would take his leather soles to wear through when the kid slammed the car into second and Eric slammed into the pavement.

 here was nobody else in the square and those artichokes rolled soundlessly all over the place. It was like a camera shot from a Hitchcock movie. A real low angle shot. When I got up to pick up the artichokes I realized I had a broken rib. I got mad as hell and chased after the car hoping he'd get hung up at a stoplight at Boylston and Mt. Auburn. But the son of a bitch was long gone.

A friend of mine, Joe Berk, insisted that I go up with him to Mt. Auburn Hospital to get an X-ray taken. I told him "What the hell do I do with a fucking picture of my broken rib?" But he dragged me up there, and they took my picture, gave me an Ace bandage, and sent me a bill for twenty damned bucks.

When I got back to my apartment, I just kept getting madder and madder. They didn't give me any pain killer at the damn hospital, so I prescribed about a half a glass of gin for myself. When I couldn't stand it any longer, I stormed down to the Club 47. I might have even gone to the Harvard radio station too, I don't remember.

I went up to whoever it was when he finished his song — I think it was Jim Kweskin — and said, "Could I borrow your guitar, man? I got to sing a song real bad." So I took the guitar and sat down because I was hurting pretty bad, and mad as a hornet. Jackie Washington was there that night and remembers the first verse going:

Well, he really rocked me, but I did not die,
Yes, he really rocked me, oh yes, but I did not die.
And the only thing I want to know — is why?

Well, it broke everybody up. I was so pissed. What I really wanted to get was a lynch mob together, form a posse, call out the vigilantes. So I kept making up verse after verse, alerting everybody to this guy, the color of his car, what letter was on the warm-up jacket. But it was all so bizarre it came out mostly funny. I must have gone on for ten or fifteen minutes. Then I asked everybody to keep an eye out for the son of a bitch and let me know if they saw him. Then I went back home and zonked out.

The next day there was a knock on the door and it was Bad Bill Henderson. He liked to think of himself as the unofficial bouncer at the 47. He said, "We think we know who the guy is. Do you want me to break his leg or what?" I said, "What the hell are you talking about?" He looked kind of hurt and said, "The guy that busted your rib!" It was really strange, because I had sung it all out. I still had a cracked rib, but I had gotten all the bad shit out. It was just gone. Gone into Henderson. That was a little bit scary. I told him, "Thanks, but forget it." I think he was a little disappointed.

Eric von Schmidt grew up in Westport, Connecticut. From the first, music had a certain wonder and mystery.

The first song I learned to sing was "My Country 'Tis of Thee." I must have been about five or six. I thought the last line was "Lev-vree-dom-bree." I always sang it that way and no one ever said anything. I thought it meant something in French.

Eric's first instrument was a harmonica "out of a Christmas stocking, or given to me when I was sick," and a ukelele given to him by his aunt when he was in his middle teens. His parents had tried a more formal approach to music with his older brother.

My folks hired a piano teacher for my brother when he was about nine. It didn't last long. Pete was tone deaf, and the piano teacher, it turned out, liked to play with little boys, piano or no

piano. So I didn't get any lessons. Didn't want 'em either, back then. My father was a painter and illustrator, and a few years later I picked up some boogie-woogie licks from one of his models. I attempted to carry the idea of a walking bass over to my uke without a hell of a lot of success.

I was an avid radio listener. The Lucky Strike Hit Parade was a big favorite. It was fascinating to find out which songs had risen or fallen in the magical Top Ten in the Nation! I thought the people at Lucky Strike were really wonderful to put on such a swell program. Sold American! I was also a big fan of the Grand Ole Opry. I was forbidden to listen to the program because it didn't come on the air until 11:00 p.m., so I would hide the radio under the covers and enjoy it all the more because it was illegal. It kind of faded in and out and it was also suffocating, but well worth the risk of death or discovery to hear the Duke of Paducah say, "I'm going back to the wagon folks, these shoes are killin' me!"

I think my first attempts at writing lyrics were around ten or eleven. I didn't have friends my own age then and my brother's friends were all three years older than me. They started coming back from prep school singing these great songs. They were called "dirty songs," and you never heard them on the radio. They had a special kind of magic. There were lots of them, but the best was considered to be the "Ring-Dang-Doo."

In order to be accepted I had become a Court Jester. I had the good fortune of seeing many Charlie Chaplin films at an early age, and I used to fall down a flight of stairs for laughs. I enjoyed it. So when the dirty songs came along, I learned them as fast as I could. The trouble was that my brother's friends were lazy. I would get some verses here and some there because no single one knew them all. "The Ring-Dang-Doo" was the longest and even after pestering everybody there still seemed to me to be gaps in the narrative line. So I made up three verses. Like the last line of "My Country 'Tis of Thee" — nobody knew the difference — they thought it was great.

on Schmidt didn't follow these early heroes to Exeter, Tabor, or Loomis. He went to Staples High School in Westport. By this time he had friends his own age, and girls his own age had become very interesting, too. But the academic part of school was not making much sense.

I was beginning to hate school. I wanted to be an illustrator like my father and you didn't need a college degree for that. And I was already damned good. I'd been working in his studio since I was a little kid. We were at a point where he would paint a little bit on one of my pictures and I would paint a little bit on his.

Then one day, it was on a Sunday, I was by myself out in the studio, painting a poster for the Senior Football Dance, and I heard this incredible voice coming right out of the radio. I couldn't believe it. It was honey-smooth, but had the bite of a buzz-saw cutting through a cement block. It was Leadbelly "live." And it changed my life.

By the time the fifteen-minute program came on the air the following week, Eric had found an album of 78's—"Negro Sinful Songs as sung by Leadbelly"—on the Musicraft label and was mad to get a guitar. Self-respecting small town music stores seldom carried guitars in the late forties, at least not in New England. They sold band instruments, pianos, and organs. Real instruments. Guitars were picked up in hock shops and Westport didn't have one. His father located one by calling the desk clerk at the local YMCA. It was a little Gibson with a raised top and a sound hole. It cost fifty dollars. The muffled sound of Leadbelly songs—"Good Night, Irene," "Yellow Gal," "De Kalb Blues"—played over and over, came from the Von Schmidt basement. In Eric's class at Staples High was a girl who looked very much like a Petty Girl from the *Esquire* centerfold. Her name was Irene Rojas. She was much more interesting than any of the subjects, and another good reason for learning "Good Night, Irene."

When the third Sunday came along Von Schmidt was crushed. No Leadbelly. He had left for Europe on a concert tour. There was no one in town who gave lessons, but Eric realized that the Revelation Chord Book revealed guitar chords as well as ones for the ukelele. Leadbelly's self-appointed disciple struggled on.

I listened to the records over and over and tried to learn all the songs. I tried to sound as much like him as I could. It never entered my head that because he was a black man from Texas and I was a white kid from Connecticut there was anything odd about it at all. He was my favorite singer and that was it.

There was another kid in my class who was into learning the guitar too. His name was Paul Richard, but he was known as Shakey. We were soon into Guthrie, Burl Ives, Josh White, Sonny and Brownie, Richard Dyer-Bennett, and John Jacob Niles. We loved them all. We played together a lot. We certainly weren't very good but no one else was doing it, so we were something of a novelty. We played some songs on a dinky little radio station in Norwalk. We also played at a Methodist Church. We sang "Jesse James" and forgot the words. Then we tried our big instrumental number, "Along the Navajo Trail," and blew that, too. We were awful. Nobody clapped. We found out later that nobody claps for anybody — even for Fred Waring and his Pennsylvanians — in a Methodist Church.

We passed chord diagrams back and forth to each other in homeroom and were always talking about Leadbelly. One day this guy with big round eyes called the "Owl" said that he thought this must be the same guy he passed every day walking back from the school bus out in Wilton. We told him he was full of shit. He said, "Well he's a real black guy with white hair, and he sits out on his porch and plays this big green guitar with lots of strings, and screw you guys, too."

That December my folks gave me an early Christmas present, "Close your eyes, hold out your hands." I guess it was about the greatest present I ever got. It was a book. "Negro Folk Songs as sung by Leadbelly." There were the words to all those songs I'd been trying to figure out for months! It had some text, too, but it was the words, the words! I'd always figured he'd sang "I'll get you in my dreams" but it was actually "I'll guess you in my dreams," which was some kind of Texas/Louisiana hip talk for "I guess I'll be with you." It was like figuring out the Rosetta Stone, like deciphering the Dead Sea Scrolls.

The next day they announced on the 5 o'clock news that Huddie Ledbetter, known as Leadbelly, had just died in Bellevue Hospital. He had become ill on his European tour. He was survived by his wife, the former Martha Promise of Wilton, Connecticut. Wilton, Connecticut? Martha Promise? It hit me that another one of his songs I'd learned from another album I'd gotten hold of by then had the lines in it:

> Julie Ann Johnson, Oh Lord,
> I'm going to leave you, Oh Lord.
> Gonna marry Marthy, Oh Lord,
> Marry Marthy Promise, Oh Lord.

I grabbed the book and started going through the text back to front, and there it was. Leadbelly had married Martha Promise in a Civil Ceremony and had been living right up there in Wilton about ten miles away. I learned right then that folk songs were about real things, real people. That was what gave them the power they had. But it was a damned sad way to learn. The Owl had been right all along.

At that time the legal drinking age was twenty-one in Connecticut, but we had all phoneyed up our draft cards by the time we were fifteen or sixteen. And we knew which liquor stores had poor lighting and didn't ask questions. Our favorite was Greasy Caleezy. He was always getting busted for selling booze on Sunday out the backdoor of his house, and we loved him for it. We felt a kinship and imagined ourselves all to be outlaws in that stuffy little New England town.

And that was a big appeal of the music, too. The shit on the jukeboxes and the radio was "It was Just a Saturday Dance, That's All That It Was (But Oh What It Meant To Me)," "Symphony of Love," "A Rose Must Remain in the Sun and the Rain (For Its Lovely Promise to Come True)". Jeeeeeezus! No wonder we lusted after songs of thievery, mayhem, and fornication. Those pop songs of the late forties were the worst, man, and you never heard a guitar note in there anywhere. Alvino Rey, Les Paul, that was it. They had guitars in those big bands but you never heard them. It was on about the same level of importance as a triangle.

 he Westport pickers kept at it. Eric heard Josh White at the Illustrators Club in New York and got to play Josh's Guitar. Shakey met a kid in Washington Square called Xerxes, later to be called Buck Elliott, then Jack, then Ramblin' Jack Elliott. Through Jack, Eric met Woody Guthrie, and also played on Oscar Brand's folkmusic program, and then they met Tom Paley, and on and on, each meeting a chance to sing and play and share their devotion and excitement. Von Schmidt also stumbled onto

Below:
ERIC VON SCHMIDT (1951) Portrait of a Young Artist About to be Drafted. The guitar is a Harmony Sovereign, stripped and painted with blue ski-lacquer. A painting of Leadbelly was on the back. Photograph by Russell O. Kuhner.

Following Page:
(top) RAMBLIN' JACK ELLIOTT giving an inpromptu performance at the Berkeley Folk Festival in 1959. Courtesy of Manny Greenhill.

(bottom) THE WESTPORT PICKERS (left to right) (standing) Steve Skidmore, Bob Lamdon, Bobby McMahon, Joe Piccorillo. (sitting) Dan Harvey, Paul "Shakey" Richard, "Doc" Doubleday, Dave (?), Eric von Schmidt. Doc Doubleday worked at the Westport "Y." He was a saintly man who could pick the hell out of "I'm Looking Over a Four Leaf Clover" on either banjo or mandolin. When the going got rough he would just turn down his hearing aid, smile his wonderful smile, and keep on picking. Photograph by Jean Foard.

two very fine collections of folksongs by John and Alan Lomax and because he couldn't read music, started making up tunes to songs that he particularly fancied. Many of the songs in the Lomax books were listed as having been recorded by the "Folk Song Archives of the Library of Congress."

I didn't know what that was all about so driving up from Florida in the spring of 1950 I thought I'd check it out. It was a couple of little rooms buried under these tons of marble, back there in the bowels of this gigantic building. And it was like finding buried treasure. You could sit all day and listen to these funky records, and they really had good notes and the words and everything. Because I couldn't read music, the song books just whetted my appetite. Hearing the actual songs was a feast. The records were expensive, but I came away with "Wasn't That a Mighty Storm," "He Was a Friend of Mine," "Ain't No Grave Can Hold My Body Down," and a bunch of others.

I met my first folklorist that summer. A friend of mine, Marshall Bolden, and I decided to take a painting trip through the west. His family lived in Clarksdale, Mississippi, so we thought we'd start out from there. Marshall had an aunt, I think it was his aunt, that was into preserving folksongs, and he wanted me to meet her.

When I got down there I played "Irene" for her on my new twelve-string. My big number. She wasn't impressed at all. She said I was leaving out lots of chords that should be in there. Minors and augmenteds, and all kinds of shit. Then she sang some black kids play-party songs and did the little dances that went along with them.

Mary Mack, dressed in Black
Silver buttons up and down her back.
(tap shuffle, tap shuffle, tap, tap, tap)

After what she'd said about my song I was hoping she'd be a dud. But it was delightful, no doubt about it. Prim, straightlaced, and looking me straight in the eye, she had the beat just right. I was very impressed.

So I asked her if she knew, or had heard of Bosie Sturdevant who had sung "Ain't No Grave Can Hold My Body Down," one of the greatest spirituals recorded — recorded right there in Clarksdale for the Library of Congress. It wasn't a cutting contest, I just wanted to get to hear the guy. "No." Well, were there any blues singers in Clarksdale? "No." Was there any place I could hear any Negro music in Clarksdale? "No." And that was that. Only later did I find out that

Clarksdale, Mississippi, was the Delta Blues Capital of the world.

It was my introduction to the tightassed world of the folklorists of that period. Little kids sang "folk music." The rest of it was "nigger music." The less said about that the better.

Another convention of the period was that if you were not going to college, or getting some kind of degree, you were assumed to have a natural aptitude for marching up and down and shooting at Commies. On July 14, 1952, von Schmidt found himself in a position to learn some work songs first hand:

Ain't no use in lookin' down,
(One, two, three, four)
Ain't no discharge on the ground.
(one, two, three, four)

He was stationed at Fort Myer, Virginia, and was soon going to Washington, D.C. to sing and play guitar at boogies on P Street off DuPont Circle. **It was pre-Presely, but the handwriting was on the wall, on the ceiling, on the sidewalk. I even learned "Ain't Nothing But A Hound Dog" from a little blond girl, Peggy, who learned it from a Big Mama Thornton record. We were raising the roof with that in the summer of '53, right there in the nation's capitol.**

Opposite:
CPL. VON SCHMIDT, USA. (1953) playing the "P. Street Blues." Photograph by Tom Shoemaker.

ne night on CQ duty Eric read *The Doors of Perception* by Aldous Huxley. It was all about a drug called mescaline, which was the chemical equivalent of a *plant*. The plant was called Peyote.

When I got out of the army, I just wanted to be *free* for a while. I'd shaved off my beard the night before I went in and I let it grow again the day I got out. I let my hair grow, too, which was a little extravagant for those days. I went down to Florida and I met this couple, Peter and Jean Krohn, and their three kids. They were peyote people. It was even legal then. You just sent five bucks to Moore's Orchid Farm in Laredo, Texas, and they sent you back anywhere from fifty to one-hundred-and-fifty buttons. It had some kind of government agricultural stamp right on the box. I found out years later that the CIA was getting it from the same place. We would get totally blasted. It was very kind, loving — no bad trips. There was no paranoia.

I ended up building two boats with Peter Krohn, which he designed. He drew the plans on a paper bag and a half-framing plan on an old piece of plywood. I just did whatever he did, and near the end put in my own little things. I called my boat the "John Hurt," after an old bluesman I admired. I figured he was dead. We thought all those old guys were dead. I guess we figured they were real old when they recorded those things back in the thirties. Seems kind of dumb when you think about it now.

I applied for a Fulbright Scholarship right after I got out of the army. I didn't think I'd get it, but I did, so I decided to sail the "John Hurt" to Connecticut and leave it there while I was in Italy. She was a twenty-six foot cat-ketch with a sprite rig and I was single-handing her. It was a great sail, but I ran into some trouble off of Melbourne on the east coast of Florida. Got hung up on a little coquina shell reef and damn near drowned getting her off. So the "John Hurt" stayed in Florida. Late one evening driving in Italy a tune just appeared in my head. It was the tune that later became the "Gulf Coast Blues," which was partly about the same experience. I'd been writing songs now and then since about 1951. The first one was a kind of "down, derry, down" kind of thing. It was the only way I could get Little Connie to rhyme with Waterbury.

Italy was great. I brought my five-string banjo hoping I could learn to play "Molly and Tenbrooks" like Earl Scruggs. I never made it but that fifth string sure drove the Italians up the wall. After a year and a half of "mio cuore, bella amore" I loved blues and folk music more than ever. Just before I left I played a couple of times at Bricktop's in Rome. She loved blues and wanted to hire me, but it was time to move on.

When I got back, I moved to Cambridge in the summer of '57 hoping to get enough paintings together for a show. A lovely girl I'd met in Italy was up there and through her I met Bill Keough, and another guy, Lou Dorfman. They were both sometimes jazz musicians. I played my first job with Billy at a place called Packie's Bar and Grille in East Cambridge. They even had an M.C. The guy asked me what my name was, and I guess he couldn't believe it, so he asked Bill, too. Just before we start to play he says "...and with us tonight on guitar we have a very warm personality, a little hand, folks, for...Richard Vaughn!" We didn't exactly tear 'em up down at Packie's. Later I played once at Tulla's with Dorfman's Dixieland-type band. Things were very lean and I was down to doing just about anything for anything. I was singing the blues all right but mostly into my beat-up old Wollensack tape machine.

Somehow or other I started meeting people real fast — people who were very much into the kind of music I was doing. It sort of just happened. I think Geno might have been the first. I think maybe he'd heard about me from Jack Elliott. Anyway, he found out where I lived and just came banging on the door. There was nothing shy about Geno. When he found out that I had a Jesse Fuller record he went ape. He usually had about half a joint and I usually had some wine. Geno could fingerpick like a mother. We'd play all day. We knew different stuff and we'd show each other. He had learned, "Baby, Let Me Lay It On You" off a Blind Boy Fuller '78 record and he taught me that. I taught him "I Love Traveling" and we once played that son of a bitch for about four hours straight. We started out playing it on two guitars in my apartment and ended up playing it on two pianos at Betsy Minot's mother's house in Concord. We never stopped once. He was a fucking dynamo. I remember once he came blasting in the door describing how he had the hots for Joan Baez and had been driving a motorcycle all over her folks lawn out in Belmont, hollering for her to come on out and let him eat her pussy! Oh, man! He was something else! I thought he was a lot older, but I guess he was only about fifteen then. I think I met him in '58 when I was twenty-seven and I figured him to be in his early twenties.

I guess it was through Geno that the Harvard

guys started coming up to the place. Peter Hoover and Eric Sackheim were both old-time music crazies. We'd play, listen to old records, bullshit. Sackheim was interested in my Fulbright, too; he was thinking about getting one. I'd also scored a trip to the Orient to do a picture for the Air Force earlier that year and he wanted to know about that. They were interesting guys — appreciative, knowledgeable, and usually thirsty. My apartment was half a block from Harvard Square, so they were up there quite a bit. The action was heavy on rainy days.

They said they played down at Tulla's sometimes with a bunch of other guys and why didn't I come down and sit in? Coffee wasn't my idea of a real drink, so it took a while to get down there. When I did it was a lot of fun. All the guys

who were in the process of becoming the Charles River Valley Boys were sitting around singing and picking their asses off.

Another night Peter Hoover came up and said "Rolf Cahn is playing down there" and why not go down and jam with him. I'd heard of Rolf. He had a record out on Folkways which was a big deal at the time, so I thought, "Sure, let's see what's happening." We hit it right off, knew all kinds of songs we could do together. He had a real crisp attack in his guitar playing, lots of treble, and I had developed a loose and goosey sound, heavy on the bass, so we sounded pretty good together. As I remember he asked me to be on his next Folkways album right there in Tulla's. Well all right! Just goes to show it's good to get out of the house once in a while.

ROLF CAHN and ERIC VON SCHMIDT (c. 1959)
Rehearsing in Rolf's elegant apartment on Dana Street. Photograph by Rick Stafford.

hrough Rolf I met Manny Greenhill. He ran the Foreign Language Press down on Federal Street in Boston. Rolf told him about my graphic work and guitar picking and he called me up to do a flyer for a Seeger concert he was putting on. Later I did a poster for a summer program with Joan Baez and progressive jazz groups for a club I hadn't heard of, Club Mt. Auburn 47.

That fall Manny called up again and asked if I wanted to audition at the Club 47. Joan Baez, it seems, had split with her boyfriend, Michael New, to Trinidad, and Bill Woods was gone, too. They were looking for replacements. Manny had never even heard me, he was just going by what Rolf said. My guitar was in pretty bad shape so I borrowed Peter Hoover's and went down. It was set up so that I would play between sets of the jazz group that was playing there that night. I think it was Sam Rivers. I was pretty nervous. The people at Bricktop's in Rome had been mostly juiced out Americans a long way from home. Here was a bunch of people who had come to hear progressive jazz, drinking *coffee*. I played all the jazzy stuff I knew, all of it New Orleans Dixieland. "Buddy Bolden," "Sister Kate," "Whinnin' Boy," "Nobody Knows You When You're Down and Out," that kind of thing. Everybody seemed to like it, including Manny, Joyce, and Paula. I was hired to split the bill the following week. Manny lent me the money to buy a guitar so I wouldn't have to borrow Peter Hoover's. It was the Big Time, man.

I alternated sets with Debbie Green. I fell in love with her immediately. I was not alone. It seemed very easy to fall in love in those days. She did ballads and I did a little bit of everything. We were paid ten bucks apiece. One night she was sitting up there in that bright red debutante-type dress singing a very beautiful ballad, "Silkie," when something strange began to happen. At first I thought the mike was feeding back. Then I realized that the feedback was in *harmony*.

Joan Baez was back from the Islands. It was my introduction to the Baez Blitz. Debbie was not amused, but the audience ate it up.

My apartment became Action Central. It wasn't the best way to get a lot of work done, but I met a lot of nice people. Dylan came up once. It was Huck Finn hat time, before he made his first record. Robert L. Jones had met him down at the first Indian Neck Folk Festival. He and Jim Kweskin and Neuwirth and Dylan had sung Woody Guthrie, Hank Williams, and Jimmie

Rodgers songs all day long. Dylan looked Jones up when he got to Cambridge. We played croquet out at Robert L's and Dylan was absolutely the worst player I have ever seen. He was having a ball, giggling like mad. A little spastic gnome. He could not connect the mallet with the ball! We went driving around looking for people to join the party, playing harmonica duets all the time. When we got to my apartment he wasn't much interested in playing; he wanted to listen. So I played "He Was A Friend Of Mine," "Wasn't That A Mighty Storm," "Baby, Let Me Lay It On You," "Acne," and a couple of others. It was something the way he was soaking up material in those days — like a sponge and a half. Later somebody said, "Hey, Bob's put one of your songs on his album. They were talking about "Baby, Let Me Follow You Down" which had a spoken introduction saying he first heard it from me "...in the green fields of Harvard University." The tune was the same, and the chords were real pretty, but they weren't the same. I don't know if he changed them or if he'd heard a different version from Van Ronk. He also did Van Ronk's version of "House of the Rising Sun" on that record which pissed Dave off. They weren't getting along at the time of those sessions. The label on the record lists "R. Von Schmidt" as the composer but Witmark had copyrighted it under Dylan's name. I figured it was a good plug for me, so what the hell.

The next time I saw Bob he said, "Hey man, that's your song" or something like that. And sure enough, a little later I got a contract signed by him listing us as co-composers. It was to become effective when I signed it. I called Manny Greenhill and explained the situation to him. He said, "Whatever you do, don't distort the facts, because you could get into trouble." So I wrote Witmark and gave them the "facts," but explained that if we co-wrote the moment I signed the contract, then we co-wrote it when the record was released and royalties should start from there. Geno wasn't around at the time, and I figured I could split them with him at a later date. They wrote back a nice note thanking me for my trouble and saying that I was quite right, I didn't have a claim to the song, and they were honoring a "prior copyright." I figured they were talking about Blind Boy Fuller's heirs or something, but they were talking about Dylan's copyright. Apparently they turned around with the "facts" I had supplied them and used them to void *that* copyright. Sorry Bob. A postscript to all of this is that my ex-mentor, Manny Greenhill, now claims that the song was written by Reverend Gary Davis. Well, that's showbiz.

BOB DYLAN (1961). Photograph by Stephen Fenerjian.

Yes, a strange element has invaded the quaint, quiet and tranquil City of Scholars, but their presence by no means is unobserved by the public, authorities, and true scholars.

The situation could explode and it is the wish of some that it would before the return of the regular students who, unfortunately, are falsely discredited by the actions of the out-of-towners.

True, our educational institutions have their share of beatniks and they will be in evidence when the colleges reopen, gathering at times in the same restaurant and possibly the same club... But, the genuine Beatniks dislike very much to be mistaken for them.

The situation, as described by the ever-vigilant "Cambridge Rambler," didn't explode. If there was any revolution going on, it was a musical one, and everyone was too busy making music to read the *Boston Record/American.*

The tune might be the same, but each piper has his own way of playing it. If Geno Foreman was set in motion by impulse, and Eric von Schmidt preferred the mountain to come to him, Rolf Cahn quite logically desired them both at the same time.

When Adolf Hitler started rounding up Jews in the Thirties, Rolf and his parents quite logically left Germany. After settling in one of the toughest neighborhoods in Detroit, Rolf quite logically learned to box and soon could beat the shit out of anybody on the block. When World War II came along, Rolf was quite logically right in the thick of it. Von Schmidt remembers Rolf discussing the war. **Rolf doesn't talk about it much, but he was in some heavy shit in WW II. Parachuting behind the German lines, setting up roadblocks and machine gun positions — the works. And he spoke of the tremendous high of it, pulling the trigger. I'm sure it had a massive effect on what came later. When I first met him he was into karate and started teaching me, too, at the Cambridge YMCA. The idea of our going to Germany and finishing up the job appealed to him. What a dynamic duo, the Prussian Jew and the Jewish Prussian. BAM! Zap! Sayonara! But at a certain point he realized killing people wasn't the answer. He learned everything there was to know about the martial arts — all very logical, step by step — then his heart took over, and he just turned it all around and tried to figure a way to use it, so** that people could be gentle. Rolf's heart is always at war with his head, and it almost always wins.

When Cahn went back to Detroit after the army he enlisted in a new cause.
We were all young, aspiring Communists — highly motivated, bright-eyed, bushy-tailed. This organizer decided our branch needed money, so he organized a hootenanny. That was the first time we'd heard the word. It was a concert, sort of left-wingy, and it made money. I didn't know anything about this music. It just knocked me over. It's hard now to give words to what pulls you into music, what part of your instinct is drawn to it. In the worst sense, in that paradise where the Freudians would be bopping around, one would be drawn into this music in order to immigrate to a deeper America. You understand, everybody wants to immigrate to another America. But there was another feeling, and it was in the tone colors, in the melodies, in the chords. It wasn't that much in the lyrics, but the lyrics had a wonderful force of their own.

Anyway, I got into playing the guitar. My old lady, Barbara, who later became Barbara Dane, showed me things, then Bernie Asbell did. We considered ourselves isolated. There wasn't any problem finding someone to play the guitar in Detroit, especially if you had illusions about having any kind of contact with black people, but we were so self-ghettoized by that old Stalinesque rhetoric that we took forever to learn that simple shit.
We were very serious, very young Communists. We sang very heavy, not quite charming, political songs. Our heroes were Woody Guthrie, Pete Seeger, Huddie Ledbetter. Even then, hundreds of little Woody Guthries were running around. Did you know that? That early, and it was beginning to be a pain in the ass to listen to your fifteenth Woody Guthrie that week. There was a desperation about them—all Brooklynesque, heavy footed. And I was in another reimmigration—which was just as absurd—which was that this was indeed a deeper "America" than I had lived or experienced, and that I could get into those feelings and shadings through this music. That was very instinctive, it wasn't formulated.

What *was* formulated was a highly rhetoric-ridden, rhetoric-beleaguered, tightass, conservative, classical music. Looking back on it, I realize how conservative we were. If Maybelle Carter missed her timing by two beats, you didn't ever think of what made it musical or what gave it the experience.

ROLF CAHN. Rolf von Rhetoric, the Prussian Jew, debating with himself. Photograph by Stephen Fenerjian.

ahn's reimmigration to America led him to California and a parting of the ways with the Communist party. By this time he had progressed on the guitar to the point where he was teaching both flamenco and folk styles. But his influence had gone far beyond teaching. He was a force in San Francisco and by the time he reached Berkeley he was an eminence.

I was in a stranger place than most people. It was bad enough to be living the strange contradictions within the Party's semantic. Because all you had at the bottom of this whole thing was some kind of feeling that the relation to the music somehow made a whole lot of sense. But we didn't know where! I know more about Child Ballads, and grownup ballads, all that crap! I was teaching at universities! I mean, it's hilarious. People say "Where is it at?" and all you do is just babble this self-verifying rhetoric.

So in the middle of this I opened the Blind Lemon in Berkeley. Opening night was a concert of K.C. Douglas, Larry Moore, Odetta, and me — it was sold out. It was the hub of the folk music community, but for me it was a heavy disaster. Nobody's fault, just the wrong idea. Then I ran into Molly Scott and that was the end of that.

Rolf had been having a bad time of it in Berkeley. It was a time of separation — the Party, Barbara, the Blind Lemon, and worst of all, the tragic drowning of his two-year-old son, Paul David. His disillusionment was eased by meeting Molly Scott, a young folksinger both bright and beautiful. But Molly had her own life to lead. This was one separation Rolf couldn't take.

At the end of that summer of '58 she decided she was going back to Smith College. Not staying with *me*. So off she goes, three thousand miles away. Immense psycho-drama! I get into my Buick and drive across country to Northampton to be with Molly Scott. Got myself a place in between Cambridge and her in that big awful town, Worcester. I could teach around Harvard Square. I could teach in Northampton. I was teaching not just the Smithies, but also the Amherst bunch. The fellow that ended up playing with Bill Monroe — Bill Keith — was studying guitar with me.

This was in the winter of 1959, and my child had just died. My head's gone, and I'm bopping

back and forth between these three towns. In Worcester, Molly and I have a place with two totally mad, old landladies to whom we are the biggest thing since the circus came to town. For them, Molly and I came straight out of a television screen . . . and they came straight out of a television screen for us. The Amherst people, and the Smith people, those women at Smith, they came straight out of some *weird* television screen. So the guys in Cambridge had a wonderful freshness that just stunned me. The Child Ballads would really bounce off them. They were *listening* instead of wondering which variant of Child Ballad eighty-four they were deflowering. I was teaching at the YMCA in Cambridge — just teaching the guitar and playing around. Life was very simple.

It was a very magical time. I just floated on the magic. I was a little leery of not being a visiting eminence. You have an immense edge if you're a visiting eminence. I carefully nurtured my visiting rabbi thing because the magic I was getting was too valuable to take a chance "mit," so I was very careful to keep that in balance. And

it worked. Teaching always pulled me out of the fire.

Until Rolf came there really weren't any teachers of folk or blues guitar styles around Cambridge. And he could teach flamenco as well. Foreman and Von Schmidt played by a combination of ear, instinct, and energy, and although they could show someone how *they* played a particular song, the person would have to have real ability to be able to play it.

Eminence, rabbi, guru, whatever, Rolf could be intense and volatile, or tender and calming. Like most good teachers, he was always searching and learning himself. When he left Worcester and lived for a while with Manny Greenhill, he started giving lessons to the Greenhill's sixteen-year-old son, Mitchell.

Rolf came and stayed with us for a long time. I think part of the deal was for him to give me guitar lessons. Then when he moved to Cambridge, I would go over there once a week. I was really faithful about studying. He would take me through various blues people and analyze solos. He would write them out in tab-lature and put them on tape, and I'd go home and work my ass off. He was a very good teacher for me at the time. I learned to hear something and figure out how it was played.

Then a time came when I had to forget all the analysis and just play the blues. He got me talking about my stupid adolescent love life, expressing my emotions, and playing blues. That was another step. One time he played at the "Y" and asked me to back him up. I considered that a great honor.

Above:
(left) MOLLY SCOTT singing at the Indian Neck Folk Festival. (1961) Photograph by Stephen Fenerjian.
(right) MITCHELL GREENHILL discovering the joys of singing to himself in his room at home in Dorchester. (1956) Photograph by Manny Greenhill.

olf had moved from Manny's house in Dorchester to an apartment on Dana Street, not far from Harvard Square. It was a basement apartment painted yellow, a vague and unsatisfactory substitute for sunlight, a cheery Cro-Magnon cave furnished by the Goodwill. Rolf couldn't have cared less. When he wasn't giving lessons on the guitar, he was taking them in karate. He dragged Von Schmidt down to test his mettle. If they were going to de-nazify Germany doublehandedly they would have to get their act together.

Through Greenhill's connection with Marcel Kisten, an amiable lawyer who was running the Folksong Society of Greater Boston at the Huntington Avenue YMCA, Rolf set up a lecture series with "live demonstration, recordings, tapes, and guest performers." The course went from "The European Ballad and its American Descendants," through Flamenco (I & II), African Music and the Western World, Negro Spirituals, the Blues, White Folk Music in the United States, and ended up some seven months later with The Aesthetics of Folk Music. Rolf Cahn was firmly entrenched as the resident Rabbi at the YMCA.

Rolf was hustling on the club scene, too. Eminency does not pay the bills. When Manny Greenhill opened the Ballad Room in October Cahn split the bill with Bud and Travis, a popular Kingston-Trio-type duo. The dressing room was a barber shop with three or four functioning barber's chairs and an impressive wall length mirror. Unfortunately, not many months had passed before the performers warming up could count more reflected figures than paying customers.

There were several good reasons for this. One was that the drinking age in Massachusetts was twenty-one. Another was that the crowd of folks out on the town who were willing to get clipped with both a cover charge and a minimum were there to be damn well *entertained, cha cha cha.* Students, who were the real audience for folkmusic at the time, considered the boozy/floozy ambience of a cocktail lounge a big commercial hype. In addition, an attractive alternative had appeared — the Golden Vanity.

Run by young people for other young people, and anybody *else* who loved folk music, the owners, Freddie Basler and Peter Lenz enjoyed their turn on the stage. It abounded in newfound enthusiasm and lacked the snobbery that Club Mt. Auburn 47 served up along with the Cafe Annisette Royale.

Calm, lover of milkmaids, pursuer of beauty, dispenser of Talmudic truth, prestidigitator to the folk folks was soon playing at *both.*

You have to give each other magic, which is a very frail commodity. If you're royalty you depend on the fact that everybody's going to give you magic. If you're an aristocrat, then you give magic or you fail to give magic; you do not have to be in the center of the stage. But if you *are* in the center of the stage, then you have to just indiscriminately throw magic around. Magic is then a very important commodity. It gave that particular energy crackle that came out of Cambridge. There was no question that you could go to the Club 47 and get some and give some. And you could go to Von Schmidt's little place in Harvard Square...

I don't know whether these things are self-generating, but it really turned out to be true.

The women! I can always tell whether a community has it or doesn't have it. Just see whether it attracts beautiful women. It is a pure barometer. It's a very strange thing. Women seem to have a sense of that energy, and also I think that they need men who are a challenge. I'm sorry if it crashes into Women's Liberation. Maybe it doesn't. It may not be that paradoxical.

Paradoxical or not, the Visiting Rabbi was once again about to throw off his tallis and pick up the pipes of Pan. Debbie Green had come to hear him play.

She came to the dressing room at the Golden Vanity. We made some music, and that was the end of that. She was going to be running around Europe at that time, so we made arrangements to meet in Spain. We met in Barcelona.

Once in France, Debbie discovered some previously undetected flaws in her traveling companion.

I was in Paris, done in by a Harvard, latent-fag, sadistic, fraternity-kid, smartass. I ended up in Spain with Rolf. He was studying flamenco. I spent the rest of the summer there.

They had some rough times at first. Rolf had taken one too many karate trips to the "Y."

I had taken that bad fall and done some sparring. My neck was totally out of gear and paralyzing my left side. Poor Deb had to nurse me through this horror show.

Debbie remembers that it was quite a show. **We lived with the nuns in the hospital. He would freak the nuns out. He thought he was dying for sure and he would scream at these nuns. He would wear this black leather coat around — his stormtrooper coat. He was just a lunatic. People stared at us. It was so extreme I think I got over** worrying what you look like, or seeming absurd to others.

Debbie had been freaked out herself the summer before at the first Newport Folk Festival. Bob Gibson had invited Joanie. By then it was just amazing. George Wein had given her a rented car. We ended up driving around in a convertible! She was going to play with Bob Gibson! Afterwards there was this formal dinner in the old dining room of the Viking Hotel. Albert Grossman was there. It was the first Newport and they were there deciding how to do the next one.

There was a piano in the middle of the room and there was a buffet banquet happening and I thought, "My goodness!" It was really the Big Time! It was utterly astounding. Here were all those people whose records I had bought. Odetta and Cynthia Gooding were there; Seeger was there. Memphis Slim was sitting near the piano. He went over to it and started playing some boogie-woogie number. And Joanie and I were there. She was a shy, young thing just like me, but all of a sudden she started doing her little boogie dance. Her boogie dance was one of those things she'd learned by watching something. It

was a little step — she could probably still do it — and I looked, and there's this hushed silence in the whole room, and Cynthia Gooding turned around and said to me in that funny little voice, "Who is *that?*" And it was horrifying to me. I mean I was amazed she could do that. I didn't have anything like that in me.

Joan's appearance with Gibson on the Newport stage was equally impressive. At that time she had no manager. Peter Robinson knew he was out of his depth. Manny Greenhill got her a job that summer opening a concert for John Jacob Niles at the University of Massachusetts, but this was pretty small potatoes for someone with the obvious potential of Joan Baez. Albert Grossman had bigger things in mind when he offered Joan his services. After her triumphal debut, the next step was a record, which meant a record contract, which was something Albert knew about. Albert is a high roller and he figured that Columbia, which was a gigantic force in the industry at that time, was the place to go. Columbia's line was, "Here's what we can do for *you.*" Joan was turned off by the lavish trappings and the big money talk. Her style was the broken water cooler and the proletarian clutter of Vanguard Records. Van-

BOB GIBSON and JOAN BAEZ. Duet at the 1959 Newport Folk Festival. Photograph by Lawrence N. Shustak. Courtesy of Manny Greenhill.

TED ALEVIZOS, ROLF CAHN, and MANNY GREENHILL (1961) Photograph by Stephen Fenerjian.

guard was small and was quick to acknowledge what *she* could do for them. It was also very much in their favor that they had signed the Weavers when no other record company would touch them because of Pete Seeger's problems with the House Un-American Activities Committee. All of it struck a responsive chord.

Not surprisingly, Manny was pulling for Vanguard, too.

Albert Grossman was involved with Joan to the extent of doing the original negotiations for the first Vanguard record. He was trying to get her on Columbia. We had meetings with him and Milt Okun. I had no official capacity at that time. I was just getting her jobs. She would come to my office and talk about this, that, and the other thing, and she would ask me what I thought. I think I was responsible more than any other individual for getting her on Vanguard just by virtue of influencing her. But Albert actually negotiated the contract, which was strange because of her feelings about Albert, which were very negative. But at that time, there just weren't that many people who could do that kind of thing.

Vanguard was using the top-floor ballroom of the Manhattan Towers Hotel, a huge space with a control room at one end. Maynard Solomon, who, along with his brother, Seymour, owned and ran the company, produced the sessions, using Fred Hellerman of the Weavers as a second guitarist on six of the thirteen songs. Joan had learned most of them from Debbie Green who had, of course, learned them from a variety of sources. She sang "Donna, Donna," the song Debbie remembered from the time of the Great Beanie Rebellion, but chose not to include the rock 'n' roll song. There were also two Carter Family songs, a Mexican song (translated into English on the liner by John Cooke of the Charles River Valley Boys), a Bahamian lullaby, seven ballads, and "House of the Rising Sun." The cover had the same Rick Stafford photograph that Von Schmidt had used for the 47 poster, and vermilion type announcing "JOAN BAEZ."

Joan had come a long way in a short time, but she was still without a manager. The Baez family were impressed with the jobs Manny had gotten for Joan and trusted him.

The actual management thing came about in the late spring of '60 when Al Baez got a job in California for two years. Joanie wasn't going to be going with them. Before they left, they invited me and my wife, Leona, to the house one late spring evening, and that's when I was asked to take over. Joan was sitting there and didn't say a word. I was talking to the parents, and I said, "Sure. I'd be honored to. I'd be very happy to, but

I'd like to hear her say something." She just nodded, and Al said, "Well, do you have a paper to draw up?" and I said, "At the moment, the way these things stand, I think a handshake will do." I gathered later that that was the smartest thing I could have done. We never had a written contract until '66.

The record contract for Vanguard was for one album, and they had an option for a second one. She thought the option was up to her, which was typical of the way she thought. She has never accepted that it means anything else.

It was a big summer for the Cambridge pickers in Europe. In addition to Rolf and Debbie, Betsy and Bob Siggins and Clay Jackson were in Italy. While Bob and Clay were singing for their pasta in Rome, Geno Foreman and Bob Neuwirth were working the Boulevards of Paris.

Rolf managed to find a neurologist to patch him up, and he and Debbie left Madrid for Mallaga, and then Granada. Debbie had enrolled at N.Y.U. for the fall term, and Rolf once again lost his love to the groves of academe. He headed back to Cambridge in mid-fall to check out the scene and do the Folkways record with Von Schmidt. By this time Eric had married one of the pretty waitresses at the Golden Vanity, Helen Jones, and was now playing solo at both the Vanity and the Club 47. Rolf got an apartment on Windsor Street in Cambridge, and they started working regularly as a duo. Rolf was not particularly happy with his first Folkways album. He felt Moe Asch had been careless with the mastering and hoped to have more control of things the second time around.

Peter Robinson was still working as Art Director with Al Baez out in Watertown. He had tried his hand at an experimental film of Joan's younger sister, Mimi, for which Rolf had improvised a sound track. The film didn't quite come off, but Peter suggested that Rolf use the facilities for making the record with Eric. It was made in two evening sessions of about three hours apiece. Eric had recorded a tape of songs for the Lamont Library at Harvard at Steve Fassett's studio in Boston, but this was the real thing. After years of listening to Folkways records he was actually going to be making one.

I don't remember that we even had a list of songs. We just winged it. Peter Robinson was sitting up with the engineer. We'd ask him, "How'd it sound?" and that was about it. I'd brought along a

bottle of gin and a bottle of tonic. We just had ourselves a little party. We had to take our shoes off because we made so much noise tapping. The only difference between recording and playing a gig at the Club 47 was we didn't have any shoes on.

The record contract with Folkways was not untypical of the period. Rolf and Eric were paid an advance of $150, but not in cash. They were to receive seventy-five records at the distributor's cost of $2.00 apiece. The list price for Folkways was high at the time, but they were solidly packaged and included notes and, often, lyrics. They went for about five bucks. Cahn and Von Schmidt were to split fifty cents on the list price of each album sold, so that after three-hundred records were sold (not including the seventy-five given them which would have been considered as promotional copies) they would have repaid the advance and were then due fifty cents per record sold. The record was released in late spring of 1961 and is still in print, and Rolf and Eric have yet to see their first royalty check. Von Schmidt has since had other dealings with Folkways as a graphics artist.

What can you do with a guy like Moe? Once I wrote him, trying to collect seventy-five bucks

SPECIAL ADVANCE SALE PRICE! $4.25 *New Folkways Release*

ROLF CAHN & ERIC VON SCHMIDT

NOBODY KNOWS YOU WHEN YOU'RE DOWN & OUT
GRIZZLY BEAR   POOR LAZARUS   COLUMBUS STOCKADE   WHO'S THAT YONDER
YOU GOT TO HURRY   MAKE ME A PALLET   2.19 BLUES   BUDDY BOLDEN BLUES
FRANKIE & ALBERT   HE WAS A FRIEND OF MINE   WASN'T THAT A MIGHTY STORM

Make checks payable to MINGLEWOOD ENTERPRISES, 26 Boylston St., Cambridge 38, Mass.

NAME

ADDRESS

CITY   ZONE   STATE

Available late May / No C.O.D.'S

he owed me on a record jacket I did for Mark Spoelstra. Mark was a buddy, so I did it, but I needed the bucks, too. So after about eight months had gone by, I finally wrote him: "Dear Moe, You call yourself a friend to the artist, when, in fact, you're screwing them, blah, blah, blah..." — that kind of shit. Well that got him pissed. He just annotated my letter in red ballpoint pen. He circled the "Moe" and in a little red scrawl wrote, "Moses to you," then went on to tell me how much he'd done for Mark, got him out of jail, blah, blah, blah. No check. Then I noticed that he'd addressed it to Eric "Van" Schmidt. So I annotated that with "von to you," annotated his annotations and sent the whole damn thing back to him. He paid me about a month later.

"Moses to you" Asch is a bit of a goniff, but it's hard not to love him a little bit, too. He put out all those great records. Through those records he became our father. There's that old Jewish joke where the father puts his little son on the kitchen table and says, "Sonny, jump into your father's arms." The kid jumps and the father lets him fall right on his face. Then he tells the kid, "So that's to show you don't even trust your own father too far."

 olf Cahn was in his element that spring. Jim Kweskin, Teddy Bernstein, Mitch Greenhill, and Jackie Washington became his eager students. None was more eager or devoted than Debbie Green.

Rolf was teaching all of these people. He was the professor. He would rap and he'd pace, and he was fascinating. He knew all kinds of shit. He would give a lesson, and all the kids would sit around. We had great, wonderful times in that kitchen.

Taking it from the kitchen to the stage was the next step.

That was when we started this thing of getting people to get on the stage and play. I don't know if I got the idea from Rolf, but I started promoting it. Rolf and Eric and I started getting a lot of people up there. Fritz, Jackie Washington, Kweskin. I remember getting Kweskin up there because he had not imagined being on a stage before. They were all learning avidly, madly picking. We started to get everyone on the stage; we said, "Come on, you can do it. It's so pretty! Oh, come on!" It was great. Then the crowds started really happening.

DEBBIE GREEN and ROLF CAHN. Tete a tete on Windsor Street. Photograph by Stephen Fenerjian.

ROLF & STUDENTS & FRIENDS & LOVERS, (1961) (top left) ROLF in the kitchen with DEBBIE, pickin' on the old guitar. TEDDY BERNSTEIN is taking notes. (top right) TEDDY BERNSTEIN, GORDIE EDWARDS, and JIM KWESKIN getting their feet wet at the Club 47. (middle left) ROLF CAHN smoking kazoo; JIM KWESKIN exhaling; DEBBIE GREEN inhaling.

(middle right) ROLF CAHN relaxing, MITCH GREENHILL tearing it up; ERIC VON SCHMIDT taking it easy. (bottom left) FRITZ RICHMOND playing some Mozart; ROLF CAHN playing some Villa-Lobos; ERIC VON SCHMIDT playing some Wagner; DEBBIE GREEN playing some Debussy. A class act. (bottom right) ROLF CAHN staring; JACKIE WASHINGTON charming; ERIC VON SCHMIDT wheezing.

All photographs by Stephen Fenjerian.

BOB NEUWIRTH *having a great time. He looks like he is about to bite off the neck of his banjo. His cigarette is out, but his clip-on shades are an indication of savoir-faire to come. An historic glimpse of Bob Dylan's right knee has been cropped out of this photograph, which is by Stephen Fenerjian.*

Opposite:
'ROUND THE CLOCK MUSIC AT INDIAN NECK, 1961.
(top left) JIM KWESKIN *and* BUZZ MARTEN.
(top right) BOB DYLAN, MARK SPOELSTRA, *and* BOB NEUWIRTH.
(bottom left) JUDY COLLINS.
(bottom right) REV. GARY DAVIS.
Photographs by Stephen Fenerjian.

For Jim Kweskin going over to the 47 after playing at the Yana was a big step up musically. As a kid growing up in Stamford, Connecticut, he had listened to a lot of New Orleans Jazz. He was playing music now, but he still wasn't playing the music he loved most — the jazz of the twenties and thirties.

The first night I ever went to the Club 47, Eric von Schmidt was playing. He was a scruffy looking guy with a big black beard, and he came out on stage, picked up his guitar and sang Jelly Roll Morton's "Buddy Bolden's Blues." I completely flipped out. There it was, just what I'd been looking for. He was actually singing an old-time jazz song with a guitar like a folksinger. IT COULD BE DONE! My life was completely changed. I spent the next two years learning how to three-finger-pick ragtime on the guitar. I soon discovered Jesse Fuller and learned his "San Francisco Bay Blues," Mississippi John Hurt's "Frankie" and "Spike Driver Blues," and Pink Anderson's "I Got Mine" and "He's In The Jailhouse Now." I started playing at the Club 47's hootenannies hoping I was good enough to become a part of the tight clique of professional musicians and their entourage. But it wasn't my music that finally got me a real job there — I had an affair with Paula.

The excitement generated by everybody learning and jamming together really came to a head at the Indian Neck Folk Festival. The Festival was the idea of the folk crowd at Yale. They hired an old resort hotel for the weekend, laid in a supply of beer, and put out the word to the pickers in Cambridge and New York that there was going to be a bash, and that was it. Everybody got to meet everybody all at once. Bob Neuwirth never forgot one of the people he met that weekend.

I met Bob Dylan at the first Indian Neck Folk Festival in May 1961. It was when I was in New York and I went there with Sandy Bull. People came up from New York, and people came down from Cambridge, and there was a big meeting around the beer barrel. Wow! It was intense!

I remember running into Dylan because he was the only other guy with a harmonica holder around his neck. I remember standing around the beer barrel, and Kweskin and Robert L. Jones and I were singing some Woody Guthrie song. Bob came up and he started playing along with it, and he had another Woody song, and it went from then until dark — obscure Woody Guthrie and Hank Williams songs. It never came apart after that between Dylan and me. Laughed all day. Laughed *so* hard. That was when Dylan used to get on stage and talk a lot. He'd do more talking than playing. And he was really great. I told him at Indian Neck that he should really come up to Cambridge.

CRUISING TIME AT INDIAN NECK, 1961.
Photographs by Stephen Fenerjian. The Indian Neck
Folk Festivals deserve more space than we can give them
here. It was a wonderful idea. Free lodging, free food, and
free beer for the folksingers and for anyone else
lucky enough to be invited. The early Festivals were
held at an old clapboard Victorian hotel called
the Montowesi.

Nighttime. Most of the pickers are picked out, but
everyone is hanging in, cruising, wondering what to do
next and who to do it with. In the upper left of the top
photograph we find BUZZ MARTEN eagerly listening
to something that JIM KWESKIN is telling him.
SALLY SCHOENFELD is listening, too. Then we have
PAULA KELLEY talking very confidentially to the man
in the dark glasses. ROBERT L. JONES, in the zip-up
jacket, is looking at the girl with the dark hair, while
BOB DYLAN looks at no one in particular. In the
foreground, MANNY and MITCH GREENHILL are
still trying to listen to the music.

Panning back, we can catch a little bit more of the scene
in the bottom photograph. BOB DYLAN still seems to
be alone with his harmonica rack on. MOLLY SCOTT,
in the pigtails, is giving someone the eye. CHARLIE
ROTHCHILD, in the V-neck, is giving Molly Scott
the eye. ROBERT L. JONES is also trying to make
eye contact with someone. Some people down in
front, like BOB YELLIN and MANNY GREENHILL,
are still listening, but are hardly on the edge of their
chairs. Most people seem to be nodding out, yawning,
or packing up, like WINNIE WINSTON, with his
banjo case. The man from the New York Times,
ROBERT SHELTON (adjusting his dark glasses), is
having a quiet chuckle, but most are too tired to
laugh. Even PAULA KELLEY has found a seat
(right rear) under the glazed gaze of
CAROLYN HESTER. It looks like these boys
and girls have just about played
themselves out.

Following Page:
(top) JOAN BAEZ in California. Photograph by
Jim Marshall. Courtesy of Manny Greenhill.

(bottom) CAROLYN HESTER and DICK
FARIÑA at the Club 47. (1961) Photograph by
Stephen Fenerjian.

When Dylan got up, Neuwirth brought him over to the 47, but he didn't fare as well as Kweskin.

Joan was playing at the club at about the time it was becoming a non-jazz club. I took Dylan over there and afterwards he said, "I'd like to get a job here." This was when they had those big plate glass windows, and people could look in and see you on stage. So we went back to see Paula, but she didn't want to hire anyone.

Paula Kelley recalls the encounter well.

I vividly remember Bob Dylan coming in as a really scrawny, shabby kid. He's the only person I've ever seen with green teeth. Singing in between sets for nothing and then going out and saying that he'd sang at the Club 47. It's so funny now to look back.

Rolf and Debbie were spending that summer on Martha's Vineyard and got to know Carolyn Hester and her husband, Richard Fariña. Carolyn was a folksinger from Texas, and Dick was a talented young man who sang, wrote poetry, and was working on a novel. Born in Brooklyn, Dick had gone to college at Cornell and as an English major had been in Vladimir Nabokov's classes. The two despised each other. Fariña's heros were Ernest Hemingway and Dylan Thomas. Where Nabokov was content to spin a web of fantasy in his fiction, Dick, the Realist/Romantic, chose it for a way of life. Rolf was impressed with Carolyn and thought Dick a bit out there.

He was afraid the English were going to avenge themselves because he'd blown up a torpedo boat in Ireland. He was always carrying a .38 around. He thought the Protestants were going to bump him off. I couldn't believe it. He was half Cuban and half Irish. I'm as paranoid as most, but there was no way anyone could pop you on Martha's Vineyard.

Rolf suggested to Eric and Helen that they go to hear Carolyn. The Von Schmidts were in the process of moving. They wanted space. Eric's graphic work was going very well, and he was doing a series of filmstrip illustrations for the United Church of Christ that would provide a fair income over the coming year and perhaps more. Eric was getting tired of the northern winters and was beginning to feel a southern longing. They decided to pack up and go to the Islands.

Just as we were getting ready to go to St. Vincent's, I met Carolyn Hester and Dick Fariña. She was playing at the Club 47, and Dick did a couple of things with her. "Johnny's Gone to Hilo" was beautiful. Bob Dylan was there and

sang his "Bear Mountain Picnic" song. It was a talking blues and funny as hell. The next day we all went out to Revere Beach for a picnic. We just goofed off, talked about this and that. Dylan as usual had the jiggles, didn't say much. We brought along some punch and got pretty mellow. Dick told me that he was a poet and was writing a novel. He wanted me to illustrate the novel. Just about everybody you met in Harvard Square was either a poet or writing a novel, so I didn't pay much attention to it, but I said, "Sure, You write the novel, send it down to the Islands, and I'll illustrate it." At the same time there seemed something different about him. Underneath all the kidding you sensed a real determination.

By this time the Club 47 Mt. Auburn was becoming *the* place to play in the northeast and many young performers who had been playing regularly at various other coffee houses in Boston were knocking on the door. Tom Rush, Geoff Muldaur, Jackie Washington, Bill Keith and Jim Rooney, Zola, Paul Arnoldi, Dayle Stanley, and Mitch Greenhill were all feeling their oats.

At the same time the Pied Pipers were pulling up stakes. Geno had been the first to go. Rolf had decided to give Berkeley another try, and Debbie was going to try it with him. Eric and his family were getting on a boat — not the "John Hurt" this time, but a Dutch freighter named the "Osisis," and heading south to the island of St. Vincent in the British West Indies.

Most important, the key figure in the folk revival movement — Joan Baez — was heading west to live in California.

By late fall they all were gone. No sooner had they left, than the Cambridge Police decided the beatnik imposters had blackened the name of the genuine beatniks long enough. They closed the Club 47 down again.

I'll buy you a brand new car,
Don't want you to go very far.
I'll do anything in this godalmighty world,
Just to let me lay it on you.

We Shall Not Be Moved

We're sanctified and holy, we shall not be moved,
Sanctified and holy, we shall not be moved.
Just like a tree planted by the water, we shall not be moved.

im Rooney had done it. He had moved across the river to Cambridge. **The very first day I moved to Cambridge I met Eric von Schmidt.** I was standing on the street talking to Ted Alevizos when Eric came along. I had seen him play and had been wanting to meet him. Ted introduced us, and Eric said that he'd be showing some Chaplin films that night up at his apartment, and that I'd be welcome. So I went over, and Bob and Betsy Siggins were there. They'd just got back from Europe. I'd met Bob before down at Tulla's, and I had run into Betsy a couple of times at the Golden Vanity and at Newport. I definitely remembered her mouth and her legs. The next day Bob and Betsy came by my place at Dana Street in their MG, and that was the beginning of the end for me. That party went on for days and years.

One night a few weeks later, Jim was riding his bicycle down to the Club 47. He was going to talk to Paula and Victor about letting him and Bill Keith play on a "Sing Out for SANE" hootenany the following Monday night. It wasn't that Jim and Bill were all that excited about banning the bomb or whatever SANE was all about; they really wanted to sing on the hoot because they thought that if they did well, they'd get hired to play regularly. Gig now; save the world later.

As I came around the corner I could see that something was up. There was a police car there and people were milling around. I rode up to the door and saw that it was padlocked! Paula was there but seemed in a daze. I couldn't believe it, and immediately began to get pissed. I was determined to find out what was going on. There was obviously no point in talking to the patrolmen. They never knew anything. So I wheeled over to an unmarked car where the man in charge was. I started having a conversation with him. The upshot of the conversation was that if I didn't get my ass on my bicycle and out of there, I would be taking a trip downtown. Of course, being a man of my convictions, I turned and got the hell out of there.

What a blow! Jim and Bill had been hovering on the edge of the folk scene for over a year. Here they were, finally living in Cambridge, ready to get into it, and the Club had been closed. Who knows? Maybe it was part of some great plan to keep Jim on the straight and narrow. For years he had been resisting the pull of music and trying to maintain an academic career.

JIM ROONEY (c. 1962). Photographer unknown. Courtesy of Betsy Schmidt.

My folks thought that education was it. I was going to get the best education I could get. The Dedham schools where I grew up were no good. I went to them through the seventh grade and then switched to the Roxbury Latin School in West Roxbury. It was rough. Five years of Latin, algebra, calculus, history, Greek. Definitely a change. I finally got my head above water around the ninth grade, but at the same time I discovered the wonderful world of hillbilly music. My buddy Dick Curley told me about this show on WCOP called "The Hayloft Jamboree." It was the funniest thing he'd ever heard. They played crazy songs like "The Gal Who Invented Kissin'," and the people had funny names like Ferlin Husky and Webb Pierce. There was even a group called Lester Flatt and Earl Scruggs and the Foggy Mountain Boys.

It sounded like a "Lil' Abner" of the air, and that night I went home and tuned in. Everything Dick had told me was true. The disc jockey's name was Nelson Bragg. He had a real downeast accent and called himself "The Merry Mayor of Milo, Maine." He was funny, the songs were funny, and I started listening every night. One night I tuned in a little early and out jumped something new. It was a voice with a thick southern drawl:

"All right, friends and neighbors, that's about all the time we have on this go 'round. This is your old buddy, Everett Lilly, speaking for brother Bea Lilly, little Don Stover, Tex Logan, and all the Confederate Mountaineers saying, 'If the creeks don't rise, and the good Lord's willin',' we'll be back with you same time, same station, tomorrow night." Then a fiddle and a banjo raced along until Nelson Bragg cut in with a station break.

That was it for me. I was a goner. I started listening every night. Gradually I started sorting out the music. I loved the Confederate Mountaineers with their lonesome harmonies, their songs about the mountains, and the sound of the banjo, mandolin, and fiddle. Curley and I started following them around to "Jamboree" shows at Symphony Hall and the Hillbilly Ranch in Boston. The night my brother John graduated from Harvard in 1953 we went to see them at the Mohawk Ranch. We were fans in the worst way. I also was totally taken by the singing of Hank Williams. He moved me in a way the others didn't. He was no joke. He was for real. Soon I got a ukelele from my Uncle Jim and then a plywood guitar. I sang for my friends and relatives, all of whom thought I would soon grow out of it. No such luck.

One day I was listening to a "live" Jamboree broadcast and heard two girls trying to sing.

They were awful. I said to myself, "I'm as good as they are. Maybe I'll go in there and try out for the show." The next Saturday I put my guitar in its little canvas case, took a bus and a trolley into Boston, and walked into WCOP. I asked who I should talk to to try out, and was introduced to a sharp looking guy with slicked-back hair who was wearing a sports jacket with pointy shoulders. His name was Aubrey Mayhew. He took me into a studio. I unsnapped my guitar case and put my guitar on and started to sing. Who knows what? I must have been something to look at — a skinny, red-headed kid playing a little plywood guitar, left-handed and upside down, doing his best to sound like Hank Williams. Finally, Aburey said, "How'd you like to be on the radio this afternoon?"

So I became a Hillbilly star. My friends at school started to call me "Tex." Every weekend I'd go in and play on the Jamboree. I got some powder blue pants and a flashy shirt and even signed autographs. I was assigned to a band from Torrington, Connecticut — Cappy Paxton and the Trailsmen. Cappy was a nice guy. He had been a boxer and decided there must be an easier way. So he did baggy-pants and polka-dot country comedy, sang, played rhythm guitar, and fronted the band. He had a singer — Jackie Russell, "the boy with the golden voice"; a steel player — Ronnie Lee, "king of the pedal steel guitar"; and a kid a year or so older than me who played bass.

The year closed with a big show at the Mechanics Building headlined by Hank Thompson and his Brazos Valley Boys. I had never seen such a big band. They arrived in a bus. They had twin electric fiddles and trumpets! This was definitely the big time! My own spot was a little less than the big time, but I was grateful to be there under any circumstances. I dressed up in overalls and sang "Honky Tonk Blues," while Cappy did a barbershop comedy sketch. After the show I was talking with our bass player. We'd become friends, and he said, "You're good. Why don't you come with us full time?"

"I can't. I'm going to school."

"Quit school."

"I can't. I've got to go to school.

He might as well have asked me to go to the moon. It was inconceivable to me that I could just quit school and play music full time. It went against everything my parents had worked for. It would have meant leaving home and breaking with my family. At the age of sixteen in 1954 I was not ready for that. As it turned out, it was all academic anyway. By the following fall Aubrey Mayhew had left town and gone back where he came from. I was left to sing and play for myself. My mother was relieved.

Cast of the WCOP "Hayloft Jamboree" (c.1953) The star of the show, ELTON BRITT, is standing to the left of center in the fringed shirt with his arm outstretched. On his immediate right is BUZZ BUSBY and on his left in the matching outfit is JACK "COWBOY" CLEMENT, who later went on to fame and fortune in Memphis and Nashville. JOE VAL, looking quite young, is under the "O" in "Jamboree." JIM ROONEY joined the show a few months after this picture was taken. Photographer unknown. Courtesy of Jack Clement.

ill Keith's mother had worried about him a bit, too. Like his father and brother before him, Bill had gone to Exeter and then to Amherst College in western Massachusetts. Something wasn't clicking, though, and Bill didn't seem too happy. That was soon to change, though in a way she could not have predicted.

There came a significant turning point: I was idly looking over the bulletin board one morning when I saw an ad — "Banjo For Sale — $15.00." I had just run across a record by the Weavers on the floor of somebody's room in the dorm and was getting interested in the Seeger style of banjo, so I went over to check this banjo out. It was a 5-string in miserable repair. I'd played tenor banjo in a dixieland band called "The Merry Morticians" at home in Brockton and in another group at Exeter called "The Sow Seven," so the five-string was new to me. I bought it, got a copy of Pete Seeger's instruction manual, and set to work.

In the section at the back, where he talked about the Scruggs style, Seeger recommended various records to exemplify the technique. I got hold of one or two and was devastated by the difference between Scruggs' and Seeger's own playing in The Weavers. Hearing Scruggs' banjo rippling and ringing out sent me headlong into trying to play the same way. And just after I started getting into this I met Jim Rooney. He had learned a lot of Flatt and Scruggs tunes from the Lilly Brothers back in his "Hayloft Jamboree" days in Boston, so we just started getting together a lot.

By 1959 we had begun to get into the folk scene down in Cambridge and Boston. Tom West and John Scott were classmates of mine who were taking a year off. We went to visit them in Cambridge. They were living in a typical run-down Cambridge student apartment on Elmer Street near Putnam Avenue. Davy Gude, who we all knew from living on Martha's Vineyard in the summertime, was staying there, too. While we were sitting around talking and playing, Davy came in with a girl he had been doing some singing with. That was the first time we met Joan Baez. We just spent the afternoon singing and playing and showing each other all the songs we had been learning. Davy showed me one instrumental thing for the banjo. Later, back at Amherst, I was fooling with it, and Jim said that he thought the changes would work for a song he'd found in Carl Sandburg's "American Songbag" called "One Morning In May." He changed it into a waltz and we came up with a melody that I played on the autoharp, which I was starting to learn as well. It became one of our most popular songs and was later recorded by James Taylor on his "One Man Dog" album. Our first and only hit.

We met Manny Greenhill in the spring of 1960. With his help we organized the Connecticut Valley Folklore Society with the purpose of putting Odetta on in concert at the University of Massachusetts which was also in Amherst. He got a few representatives from each of the colleges in the area. One of the people from UMass was Beverly Ste. Marie. Another turned out to be Taj Majal. As a result of meeting Manny, Jim and I got our first paying gig at "The Ballad Room" in Boston. It was a big deal for us at the time. We opened for a blues singer named Charlotte Daniels. If it hadn't been for our folks and a few friends we would have been playing for the bartender and the chairs. At the end of our first number there was a smattering of applause, and then from the back of the room came this great big voice saying, "Now that's real toe-tappin' music!" It was Odetta, and that made us feel great.

I had another year to go at Amherst, and Jim went to Harvard to do graduate work in Classics, so we didn't get too many chances to play. What we did was mainly through Manny. We did a concert for his series at the "Y" and one over at Agassiz Theater in Cambridge for the Harvard-Radcliffe Liberal Union. Probably the most exciting was one we did with Joan Baez up at the Dartmouth Winter Carnival. We were getting paid two-hundred bucks, which was crazy to begin with. The concert was at 10:30 on a Saturday morning. We couldn't imagine anyone getting up at that hour — especially during Winter Carnival. We spent the night with our friends Sterling and Sue Klinck playing music and drinking home brew. When we woke up there was a blizzard going on. We were sure that the concert would be a bust. We got over to the hall and got together with Joan so we could do "Banks of the Ohio" and a couple of others with her at the end. When we went upstairs to go on we couldn't believe it. You couldn't have put another person in there sideways. We went out and did our set and couldn't believe the response, but that was nothing compared to what they did for Joan. After every song they'd stamp and

(top) THE CONFEDERATE
MOUNTAINEERS
(foreground, BEA LILLY
and DON STOVER;
background, EVERETT
LILLY and TEX LOGAN)
Photographer unknown.
Courtesy of Tex and Peggy
Logan.

(bottom) WINNIE
WINSTON and BILL
KEITH performing some
sleight of hand at the 1961
Indian Neck Folk Festival.
Photograph by Stephen
Fenerjian.

Following Page:
(top) JIM ROONEY prac-
ticing his pear-shaped tones
with BILL KEITH (1962)
Photograph by
Eric von Schmidt.
(bottom) KEITH &
ROONEY in their television
debut over WWLP "high
atop Springfield Mountain"
in Springfield, Mass. The
day before this historic
broadcast, Bill fell and broke
his banjo neck. A little
Elmer's and a lot of luck kept
it all together, which
probably explains Bill's extra
big smile. (1960) Photo-
graph courtesy of Bill Keith.

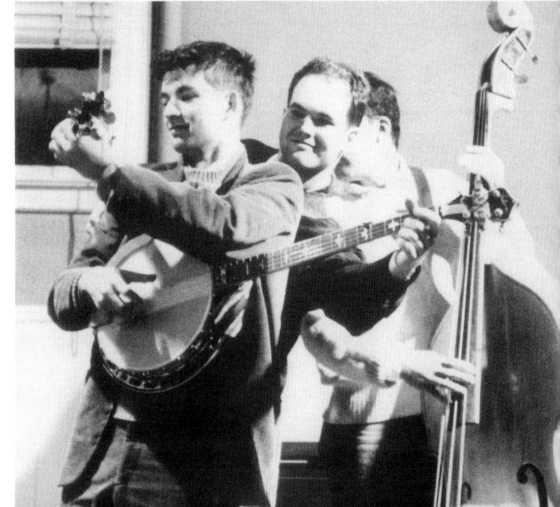

whistle and applaud as if it was the end of the world. I guess that's when we realized how big a star she was going to be. It was phenomenal.

That summer Manny got us jobs up at the Cafe Lena in Saratoga Springs and at a place called the Purple Onion in Toronto. It was our first trip "on the road." Lena's was great. We met Uncle Dave Macon's nephew up there. He'd come in every night drunk as a skunk and shout out requests. After every number he'd say, "Never heard it better, boys." We got to see all the great old mansions up there, and we began to like the idea of getting paid to go play in interesting places. Toronto was great, too, except for the club and the accommodations. The club was about ten feet wide and eighty feet long. You played to the wall. We did a lot of twisting and turning. They put us up upstairs in a little room with one bed which we both slept in — or tried to. There was a guy next door who loved Jimmy Smith all night long at top volume. But we got around town a lot. The folk scene was starting to happen there. Ian and Sylvia came down and sat in, and we got to meet a lot of the local pickers.

That summer we also made a trip down to Asheville, North Carolina, and Galax, Virginia to hit the festivals there. We were really getting into meeting pickers everywhere. I just wanted to find out as much as I could and play as much as possible. I still wasn't thinking about music as a career, though. I was probably going to go to business school, which was a pattern in my family. My first concern, though, was dealing with my military obligation. Vietnam was starting to happen, and I had to take precautions about the service. Through Jim's classmate Dan Bump I found out about a special Air Force hospital unit in Boston. You had to do two months basic training in San Antonio, but you wound up in Boston, which looked like a perfect setup for me to get into the Cambridge scene, which was really starting to percolate.

he Cambridge folk world was going to have to wait a bit longer to hear Keith and Rooney because of the closing of the 47, but the closing did have the positive effect of bringing the entire folk community together in a way it had never been before. Meetings were held, benefits were organized, lawyers were hired. Most importantly, the performers in the community began to realize that they had a stake in the 47's survival. Because of the success of Joan Baez, Eric von Schmidt and Rolf Cahn, the Club was becoming known as the center of the burgeoning Cambridge scene. Keith and Rooney weren't the only ones out of a place to play. Bob Siggins was forming the Charles River Valley Boys with Ethan Signer and John Cooke; Tom Rush wanted to make the 47 a weekly gig, as did Jackie Washington and Mitch Greenhill. And there was the added factor of the stupidity of it all. The idea that the police could actually come in and close down a place mainly because they didn't like the looks of the people going in there or the kind of music being played was something that no one believed would happen. It was enough to make you mad — to make you a radical, if being a radical meant that you'd fight for your right to play what you wanted and look the way you wanted. Was singing songs a crime? Was wearing Levis or tights a public menace? Could you be put out of business if you were opposed to nuclear testing? None of this was news to someone like Manny Greenhill, but it was to most of the young performers and their audience. They began to realize how much this musical scene meant to them, and they were not about to let anyone take it away without a fight.

Tom Rush put the word out over his 'Balladeers' show on WHRB at Harvard. Phil Spiro and Dave Wilson did the same over WTBS at M.I.T. The SANE people put together a concert at Kresge Auditorium at M.I.T. The Yana put on a benefit hoot and so did the Unicorn, Boston's newest coffee house. Suddenly it seemed that everyone was playing all the time. They weren't getting paid, but it didn't matter. The Hoots gave everybody a chance to see each other, hear each other, and play with each other, and showed the audience what a wide variety of music was being played by all the various artists. There was Siggins' great old-time banjo, Robert L. Jones with his dry wit and haunting Guthrie ballads, Mitch

Greenhill's phenomenal guitar picking, Rooney's Hank Williams songs, Rush's understated humor and blues, Jackie Washington's devastating monologues and soulful singing, Bill Keith's unbelievable Scruggs picking. It was all there and more. The second wave was gathering strength.

One of the most successful hoots was at the Unicorn on Boylston Street in Boston. Jim Rooney had never been there. He'd heard about it from Jones, who started to run hoots there.

The place was packed, and we were all having a good time. At some point I started to go into the kitchen to get something to drink and this guy told me to get out.

"But I'm a performer."

"I don't care who you are. Get out of the kitchen!" I was pissed. Who did this guy think he was? Here I was doing a benefit, and he was yelling at me to get out of his kitchen. I asked Jones who this asshole was.

"Oh, that's Byron. Don't mind him. He's a good guy. He's just got a thing about people going into his kitchen.

When Byron was working at Tulla's he had been approached by the owners of a fancy European style coffee house on Boston's fashionable Newbury Street called the Cafe Florian. It seemed like a good thing to do, so he ran that for a while.

ome time after that I got together with George Papado-poulos. He was teaching at Went-worth Institute, and was always looking to keep as many things in the fire as possible. He'd be half of anything — you guys do the work. My father's advice to me was never to go in partnership — ever. It was in the back of my head all the time I dealt with George. And, of course, my father's advice was right.

We must have met at the Cafe Florian, and what he had in mind was for me to run a coffeehouse. We were walking down Boylston Street, talking about the future of the Prudential Center, and we saw this "For Rent" sign, and there was this little stairway that went down in the middle of this big wide sidewalk. So we walked down, and there were three stores. The third store was an office with a name on the door: Max Bernstein. He was a very sweet old Jewish gentleman. He was impressed by us and rented one of the places for thirty-five dollars a month! It never went up too much. George song-and-danced him with a story about a share of the profits. Of course, there never

were any profits. That was one of the things between George and me. I really liked the man, and he was never getting a cent out of the place. We were just using him.

So we walked in. There were plaster walls. We took a crowbar to one corner and saw there were bricks behind there. So we spent a week taking down all the plaster. That gave us brick walls. The kitchen consisted of a pipe that came in through the wall. We stuck a spigot on the thing. That gave us cold water. We got an electric hot plate. Hence — coffee time! The beginning of a coffeehouse. We opened just like that. No advertising. One day a guitar floated down the stairs. I don't remember inviting anyone to come in and play. A flamenco guitarist was the first thing I remember putting on in the corner. It just progressed slowly from there.

The first time I saw Tom Rush's name was on a poster that Gene Cluster had done for the Club 47 benefit. That's where I first heard him, and after that I started having him regularly. Robert L. Jones started running hootnenannies there and spreading the word, and, while the 47 was closed, we took up a lot of the slack.

It was January when the 47 case finally came to trial. The trial was held in the pits of East Cambridge in the Middlesex Superior Court. Everything about the place reeked of old-time politics. The halls were filled with a motley mixture of defendants and their families, most of whom looked pretty down, and courthouse lawyers who stood around with their hands in their pockets or their arms thrown over somebody's shoulder talking deals or the races. Paula's ethereal beauty looked very out of place in the dingy surroundings of the high-ceilinged courtroom, and the group of supporters from the 47, with the exception of Manny Greenhill, were unacquainted with the cold, hard facts of courtroom life. Perry Mason was about as close as they'd ever been to the real thing.

Perry would have been proud of Gerry Gillerman, the lawyer for the defense. Gillerman had been down this road before fighting civil rights cases and set out immediately to discredit the main witness for the prosecution, Lieutenant Francis Barry, who had gone into the club in plain clothes one night and testified that, despite its status as a private club, as far as he could tell from watching the door, anyone who wanted to could come in whether they had a membership card or not. The assistant district attorney Efthemios J. Bentas contended that the Club should have

BYRON LORD LINARDOS Photograph by Charles Frizzell.

obtained an entertainment license because "Anyone can present a dollar and is allowed to go in." Bentas argued further that even though the Club was chartered as a "non-profit educational institution" it was really offering entertainment pure and simple. "We've seen no evidence that the Sam Rivers jazz combo was educating anyone into anything."

Gillerman lost no time in getting at Lieutenant Barry. At one point he strode over to where Paula was sitting ever so demurely in the defendant's chair. As Barry peered from the witness stand, Gillerman turned his back, showed a card to Paula, and mumbled something to her. Then he turned to Barry and told him to tell the court exactly what he had just seen and heard. He also reminded Barry that he had already said that the music was loud and pointed out that there was a post between the desk at the door and where he said he had been sitting. That was it for poor Lieutenant Barry.

Paula's turn to shine came when Gillerman skillfully led her through a recital of the 47's cultural virtues. By the time she was through expounding on the Club's film series, the experimental theater, the art gallery, the jazz, the folk music and the poetry, Harvard was starting to look like a poor second to the 47 as a source of cultural uplift to the deprived Cambridge community. Duly impressed, the Judge waived the testimony of a group of musicologists and academicians who were also ready to extoll the Club's virtues. He then gave the Club a slap on the wrist, finding it guilty of "unlicensed exhibition." He imposed a five dollar fine and made an informal suggestion that it shape up and act in more strict accordance with the membership procedures outlined in its by-laws and generally keep its nose clean. End of trial. Court is adjourned.

PAULA KELLEY "I swear to God, your Honor." Photograph by Stephen Fenerjian.

he taste of victory was sweet. Everyone was all smiles. Paula received kudos for her performance on the stand. Gillerman accepted his thanks and congratulations with modest pleasure and left to fight the good fight in yet another courtroom. As word of the victory spread through the folk community there were many mini-celebrations in kitchens and living rooms around Boston and Cambridge. Suddenly the Club had become "ours." "We" had gotten together, and "we" had helped save it. Paula suddenly sensed more than the winter chill in the air.

At that point in time folk music had suddenly become "in." There were a lot of people who wanted to be in on the Club. It was well known then. It was known way outside the geographical area of Cambridge and Boston. And there were a lot of people who wanted a finger in the pie. One way to get it was to be friendly with me during the period before the trial and during the trial and then as soon as the trial was over to try and move in. It was okay with me because I was ready to move out. Things had changed. The ambience was gone. It was becoming a business. It hadn't started out that way. It had been part of the whole student kick. It was never a business. It was just a fun thing to do.

For Paula the fun time was clearly over. The celebrations gave way to a seemingly endless series of meetings. Victor Oppenheimer found himself in the uncomfortable position of being Paula's best friend and also wanting the Club to continue on a sound basis.

We had been good friends. Paula and I wrote a movie scenario together. They asked me to be on the board of directors and then to be President with Paula as Treasurer when Joyce left. During the time of the trouble we got a number of strong people on the board. I asked Manny Greenhill, and then there were two law school students, Fred Greenman and Bob O'Neill, who did a lot of the spade work for the trial. Betsy Siggins asked to become involved since she was close to the musicians side of things. They were upset with the way Paula was running things, and said that if she continued to set policy and be Treasurer they would leave the Board which would have meant the end of the Club, because there was a large debt which had been accumulating that she had no way to pay off without a lot of help. So she remained a Director in name, but the spirit was gone, and she just stopped coming around. It seemed at the time that it was the right thing to do, but ever since it happened it's left a bad taste in my mouth.

And Paula? She discovered that she was perhaps more talented as a writer of technical manuals than as a club owner, and went on her way.

That was a passing phase of our lives. It was something that Joyce and I enjoyed, but it was not a way of life for either of us. Maybe because neither of us were musicians. It was a fun thing to do as a kid, but there comes a time . . .

We're on our way to heaven, we shall not be moved.
We're on our way to heaven, we shall not be moved.
Just like a tree planted by the water, we shall not be moved.

Overseas Stomp

I know they're gonna write to me,
When they get way 'cross the sea,
Every chance, when the "Washington" lands in France.

We are soon to evacuate these states. There is an irridescent fluid at the base of America's spine called Apathyum. It ignores hydraulic physics and rises easily away from gravity, creeping upwards past the Indolencia gland into the red, white & blue matter of the brain where it works fast on the motor lobes affecting physical areas of creativity, such as the fingers which might poise a brush; then on the occipital cortex where it produces in the eyes a stare which is often mistaken for Objectivity, Sprezzatura and the like. Finally it makes synaptic connection with the butt, encouraging a condition known as Lardassia, the symptoms of which are a strange, almost magnetic attraction between the cheeks of the posterior and the surface against which they rest.

The disease is said to be contagious. I have taken some special shots derived from an aged and fermented liquid which has no medical name, spread some fresh deer blood under my eyes, eaten the livers of three mountain quail, and killed a Madison Avenue fag by screaming in his ear. I am purged.

Richard Fariña had just returned from a hunting trip in Oregon, crossing the continent, meeting Hemingway, Vance Bourjaily, Philip Roth, finally to connect with his wife Carolyn Hester in New York City. Fariña diagnosed America's ills, and decided to leave the country — London, Paris, and possibly St. Vincent.

Geno Foreman had led the parade. Among those to follow was Tom Rush. Tom had taken over the "Balladeer" program at Harvard where Clay Jackson had become a non-student, but he was extremely shy about performing.

I started going over to the Golden Vanity looking for people to play on the show. I'd go in on a Hoot night with an empty guitar case because they'd let you in free if you walked in with a guitar (or a guitar case, as it turned out). One night they ran out of performers, so I had to play. I was a little embarrassed and had to borrow somebody's guitar, but I did two or three numbers. About a week later Carl Bowers called and asked me if I could come down and play for someone who was sick. So I was a substitute folkie for a while. That eventually developed into a regular night at ten bucks a shot.

The summer after my freshman year, I went to Europe with a buddy and did a lot of street singing

RICHARD FARIÑA Photograph by Dan Kramer.

in France which helped me a lot. We got to Paris and were dying of boredom. We didn't know what to do. Museums didn't really have much appeal. I ran into these two guys street singing and fell in with them and really enjoyed it — playing for people, trying to entertain people — especially people who didn't understand a word you were saying. It was quite a challenge. It really whetted my appetite for performing, so that when I got back I was ready to go out and play in public.

Bob Neuwirth was having something of a revelation that summer, too. After hanging out with Bob Dylan at the Indian Neck Folk Festival, and casing the Cambridge scene, he found himself drifting away from painting.

I sort of stopped making art and started playing the guitar and singing to make money to live, and I couldn't believe that anybody would pay you to sing hillbilly songs.

That realization was to mean a lot to Neuwirth in the years to come, when singing his little hillbilly songs often made the difference between eating and not.

In Europe, Geno and I got into street singing. Tom Rush was over there. Jack Elliott and Alex Campbell, some English guys, the Bennett Brothers. Geno held the record. He made ninety bucks in one day.

Clay Jackson hung out with Geno, too, and from his description it's not hard to see why Foreman held the record.

He was one of these kids who had more energy than he could ever have time on earth to do with. Just walking down the street with him was utterly exhausting. He was tall, and he had long legs and walked just as fast as he possibly could, talking at the top of his lungs and waving both arms. In about three blocks you'd be totally out of breath. This white kid in Paris. And the kind of music he was playing there. He was the last of the black, crazy blues players, the last of the Robert Johnsons, the last of the Blind who*ever*. He was playing that kind of blues music, and it was that strong, it was that great.

Being a white/crazy black blues singer on the streets of Paris involved a lifestyle that was both

Sunday, Paris, June

← Portrait of the artist suffering incurable condition known to Western Medicine as "Pagewatch" Comes from watching pages. Symptoms generally take the form of tremens, vapours, deleriums, conversations with the wall, catatonic stare, excessive & offensive farting, rottenmouth, atrophied asshole, palpitations, runs, hot flashes, insomnia, unrequired erections, inflammation of the postate, & giggle-fits. Common to writers & painters. Perpetual Ease seems to be the only permanent cure. Temporary relief secured through teaspoonfuls of Gordon's Gin laced with equal parts Schweppes, spray from the rind of an unripe lemon.

Above:
LETTER FROM RICHARD FARIÑA. *The first page of a letter sent to Eric von Schmidt shortly before Dick and Mimi left Paris in 1963. The pages he had been watching, and would continue to watch for two more long years, were those of his novel in progress,* Been Down So Long It Looks Like Up to Me. *Courtesy of Eric von Schmidt.*

Opposite:
TOM RUSH *as "The Balladeer" with guest* ERIC VON SCHMIDT. *A piece of vest is all you can see of the elusive* GENO FOREMAN. DAVID GREENBERG's *head is to the right of Tom's.* BRAD MEYER *is the man at the door giving the "stand-by" notice. The usual crew of bright, young, energetic Harvard students is in attendance. Photograph by Stephen Fenerjian.*

reckless and self-destructive. This was the image he had created for himself, but there was more to it than that. There were indications that he also realized that it might also be self-*defeating*, limiting in terms of what he longed to accomplish musically. The child of freedom who fought discipline from the cradle was beginning to feel the need of it. His streetsinging buddy Neuwirth was with him on his first quest for order.

eno decided to apply to the State Conservatory of Music in Berlin. I was thinking of maybe studying art in Berlin, too. He arrived for his exam. It was a magnificent place. Marble hallways and marble pillars. Busts of the "three B's." He had his guitar slung over his shoulder on a string. We'd been up all night and we looked pretty sleazy.

The first thing you do is to have a little examination of your chosen instrument. People were going into this little room and little piccolo solos and violin pieces would come trickling through the door. Then they called Geno's name: "Herr Foreman." He goes through the door with his guitar. The first thing you hear is "Memphis Boogie," Jesse Fuller style. Then the door opens, and Geno is grinning this toothless grin and says, "Let's go upstairs." The next step was a piano exam. Who was going to tell him he didn't know how to play blues guitar? Piano might be another matter.

Upstairs there was a long hallway. People were sitting on these benches reading Brahms' scores and chuckling over the grace notes! There were about five rooms where they were giving the piano exams. People were trying not to notice us. They were all very middle class and well dressed, trying to look their best. Finally they called him. He gave me his guitar to hold and went in. You could hear faint traces of Chopin coming from one of the rooms. Suddenly you heard "DA DA DA DA DA!" It was "Memphis Boogie" again on the piano and it was great! Everyone dropped their scores. It was loud, rolling down this great hall. Then there was a silence. The next thing you hear is "Memphis Boogie" coming through the door again with Geno singing! He had happened to run into a guy who was a total blues fan who could not believe his good fortune at having picked Herr Foreman. So Geno became an honored entrant. We went back to Paris to get some money, but Betsy had got married or something. We were flat broke and cold, and we never made it back. I've still got clothes in the laundry there.

That fall Betsy Minot married Bob Siggins in her grandmother's wedding gown. The society column announced that Mr. Siggins would be continuing "his education with research in Europe." Betsy remembers spending Christmas in Berlin with Geno.

Smoking dope. Geno was playing music and being real obnoxious and trying to get arrested a lot. We went into East Berlin with him. On the way back into West Berlin there was something wrong with the insurance papers. That was okay with Geno because he wanted to tangle with the cops. After that we went back to Rome.

Refugees from the Cambridge folk community were zig-zagging all over Europe in the years '60 to '63. Whether it was a moveable feast or a staggering famine depended on the time and place, and the locomotions were usually haphazard. A few had a definite purpose, but for most it was a time to ramble, to taste freedom, to come and go when they pleased, to get in touch with themselves. It was not a guided tour. It wasn't lived for the memories, it was lived for the moment. Life was a river at spring flood.

Clay was all over the place: with Bob and Betsy in Rome and in London to record with the Charles River Valley Boys; from Paris down through Spain on Cooke's motorcycle to score some grass from Geno in Tangier; with an English banjo player, Peter Stanley, playing in Italy, England, and Germany.

In Germany we were playing for American enlisted men. Most of them were rednecks, so I'd come on real down-home. We wore cowboy hats and boots and string ties. We got by great, and they really liked us, except that Peter was absolutely forbidden to utter a word because he had a near-Cockney accent, and the minute he'd have opened his mouth on stage he'd have been dead. So we had a routine. I'd insult him and make fun of him on stage, he'd get redder and redder, and after the show was over he'd beat the shit out of me. We made a lot of money at it, but the American occupation scene was so horrible we got out.

Jackson had met Stanley in Florence after being adopted by a pair of inept Italian gangsters.
These were two guys that had been in the Italian underground and after the war they just kind of never came out. One of them was a guy called Nanni; he was about five foot two, and looked exactly like a weasel with slicked back, grey hair and a long pointy nose. He would steal plaster of Paris madonnas and broken clock-radios, and would leave them in our closet until he got a chance to dispose of them. He could never dispose of them because nobody wanted them.

He'd walk in, roll his large protruding eyes which were set rather close on each side of that nose of his, pull out both pants pockets to show they were completely empty, and say, "Clake! No money in pocket!"

After the River Boys' sessions in London, Clay got together with Geno in Paris.

He'd gotten very saint-like and very quiet, and he moved as little as possible. He smoked a lot of grass and occasionally he'd been known to snort a little heroin but he refused to take the needle. Sometimes I'd wake up about 10:30 or 11:00 in the morning and I'd realize I'd already been listening to music for an hour. He'd be sitting there playing Thelonious Monk on the guitar, playing something like "Blue Monk," note by note perfect; very quietly, but perfect. He'd always been very undisciplined on guitar, but toward the end he was playing the finest jazz, country, old-time country blues — just the finest stuff you ever heard. He never had much of a voice, but he had such sheer will and desire that he finally got what little voice he had to where it started getting really funky and good — gravelly and rough and just great.

The Von Schmidts had been looking for a Caribbean paradise; the Island of St. Vincent wasn't it.

Helen didn't like it much. After a couple of months she took Caitlin and left. She just went home, and it was rough. I painted a lot, worked hard at the commercial jobs, drank a bunch of rum punches. I began singing in the evenings. All alone, you know. And I'd be singing with tears coming down. Be half juiced, and I'd hit on a line that would let loose all the pain. Tears would pour down, and then I'd feel better. Then I started writing some of those verses down. It helped a lot. It was a way to get through it.

The people on that island were really great. Norma who cooked and worked for us and her brother Sonny and her mother and her mother's sister. They would come and sing every now and then. They sang Anglican hymns, man. That's all they sang, except for Norma's mother who would also sing, "Where Is My Wandering Boy Tonight?" It would break your heart. I showed Norma how to work the tape machine and when I played some of the tapes after I'd got back she had put on a song that I didn't know anything about — "Goodbye Mr. von Schmidt, goodbye, I don't know when I'll ever see you again. Goodbye, Mr. von Schmidt, goodbye."

Von Schmidt received the first chapter of Fariña's novel while he was still on St. Vincent. He was both surprised and pleased. It was heartening to know that Dick wasn't just another bullshitter and it helped confirm Eric's own precarious sense of identity. When sixteen of his paintings were lost on a BOAC flight enroute to Boston, he packed it up, and was back on the streets of Cambridge by the spring of '62.

Dick's correspondence with Eric at this point dealt largely with why he hadn't sent any more chapters of the book. A postcard arrived, sent from Pamplona on July 12, that explained part of the problem. It is hard to write a novel while being chased through the streets by bulls.

Oh madness, musics, & wine. We camp in the country, go to the bullfights in the afternoon, dance, drink, fuck around all night, speak Spanish, piss on Americans, write blues, pass the wineskin, bug the cops.

Bad corrida yesterday but Ordonez fights today. Will start a riot tonight. Almost gored two mornings ago while running. Oh Exhilaration.
                                                    Dick

John Cooke was back in Europe that summer and drove from Paris to Pamplona in his brand new Volvo with Alex Campbell and John and Ian Bennett. They all got together with Dick and Carolyn and whooped it up. It was Hemingway time—Take Two.

Back from St. Vincent, Eric was together with Helen again, and soon another little Von Schmidt was on the way. They lived that summer on Maynard Place, next to Bob and Betsy Siggins, but it didn't last long, and they split up again. Eric was working too hard, drinking heavily, right on the edge. A flurry of letters from Fariña, full of schemes and hustler energy, was about the only thing keeping him afloat.

All that fall Fariña was writing me from France, saying, "You've got to get your ass over here, man. We can hype a book, we can do concerts, we can make a record." He'd arrange this; he'd arrange that. Jesus, I just couldn't cope with it. I just wanted to go somewhere and hibernate — forget everything.

D r. Albert Baez and his family were also in Paris. Baez was working for UNESCO trying to help find ways of teaching science in underdeveloped countries. It must have been a strange time for him. *Time* magazine was in the process of doing a cover story on his daughter Joan. All of it only four years after her unannounced recital in his living room. Only *four* years! A *cover* story! Had the world gone mad? His oldest daughter, Pauline, no longer a Baez, but married to a young, struggling painter. Pauline and Brice Marden? All of a sudden he was a *grandfather*. The only daughter left was Mimi. Poor Al Baez. An honest and honorable man who was quite capable of demonstrating scientific phenomena with far-out examples, but incapable of learning anything from the totally natural reactions of his own daughters. It was King Lear time in the Baez household.

John Cooke was back from Pamplona, caught up in the magic of his new car. Like a mojo, you have to keep your Volvo working. He was in love with Mimi, as was Geno, Todd Stuart, Danny Chevalle, etc.

Some of us were going on a picnic. I picked up Mimi and stopped by and picked up Dick and Carolyn. I said, "Dick, Carolyn, this is Mimi Baez. Mimi, this is Dick and Carolyn," all in the back of my Volvo.

Mimi was originally going to go with Todd Stuart on the back of his bike.

Mother said I couldn't go on a motorcycle, I was fifteen, so I went in the car, in the famous Volvo. I sat next to Dick and it was fun. Carolyn was on the other side. Alex Campbell was in front, and Cookie drove. It was very loud all the way. We drove out to Chartres and there was lots of wine drinking. We had a picnic all set. First, we went to the Cathedral and wandered all around. Dick was very flirtatious, but I didn't know it. I thought he was neat because he was a poet. Todd was somewhere parking his motorcycle — he finally arrived, but Dick was busy telling me all the intricacies of this and that, the demons and so on, in the church. I was fascinated, of course. Carolyn was sort of walking behind with her high heels and her scarf with a cold.

Then we went out to this field and had a picnic. I wasn't used to drinking, and I wasn't supposed to smoke at all, so I chain-smoked all day long and got very drunk, but I didn't realize it. And Dick kept joking and I kept laughing. At one point I spit out a whole sandwich in his face because I was laughing so hard. I was very embarrassed but nothing mattered, and the whole day was a real high. We stopped in a cafe on the way home, and Alex and I danced a jig to some music that was on a television set, and we finally got home. It was pretty late, and I told mother about this wonderful day I had had. I went off to bed around four in the morning. I was throwing up and laughing. In the morning she came in and said, "How are you?" and I said. "The funniest thing happened! I was up all night throwing up, but I was laughing. I mean it wasn't awful at all." She took a look at me, went out, came back with some juice, and said, "I think we're experiencing our first hangover."

Dick was suffering from a malady of more serious consequences: He had fallen madly in love with a fifteen year old girl. Carolyn was scheduled to sing at the Edinburgh Folk Festival, so the two of them left for England. As chance would have it,

This page:
(top) DICK FARIÑA, ALEX CAMPBELL, and company thoroughly enjoying Parisian cafe society. Photographer unknown. Courtesy of Mimi Fariña.

(bottom) MIMI BAEZ as a young schoolgirl by the Seine in Paris. Photographer unknown. Courtesy of Mimi Fariña.

Opposite page:
ALEX CAMPBELL, THE BENNETT BROTHERS, and JOHN COOKE strike a pose beside John's "famous Volvo" on their way to Pamplona. (1962) Courtesy of John Cooke.

Mimi was going to a Quaker work camp near Newcastle. Fariña was not going to let a chance like that go by. He soon had a raft of people involved in a Byzantine scheme — one of them was Mimi.

He kept encouraging me to come with or without Todd. "And the Clancy brothers will be there . . . and there's the festival and you must come." Mother said I could go to the festival because Dick had come up with all kinds of names of families where I was going to stay — the McKuen family — and how he would have people write or call — and the father and the mother — and it all sounded very official. Meanwhile Todd had reserved hotel rooms, which was very naughty of us. So I was picked up in a car from the Quaker work camp and driven down to Edinburgh. We went to the festival and met the Clancy brothers there and Dick, who was singing with them. Carolyn had a terrible cold, and she was in bed most of the time, so that meant he was running around being flirtatious.

By the end of October Von Schmidt was hearing all about it in letters from Fariña, signed Che, Dorticos, King Fucking Montezuma. Winter was settling in, and Eric was in bad shape. Jim Rooney remembers seeing him sing at the 47 in December, looking terrible, like he didn't really seem to be there. He had hoped to hole up on Cape Cod and paint during the winter, but when both house possibilities fell through on the same day, he knew he was coming unglued.

I just fell apart. The next day I went out and bought a ticket to London. I left about a week later on a night flight — December 31. I thought maybe there might be a party or something. Paper hats, noisemakers, or a little taste of champagne. Nothing, man. So I got out my Marine Band Harmonica and gave the bastards a couple of choruses of "Auld Lang Syne."

Ethan Signer of the Charles River Valley Boys had gone from Cambridge, Massachusetts, to Cambridge, England, to do post-graduate work and a little picking whenever possible. He and his wife planned to be at the airport.

Barbara and I came down in a blizzard to meet the plane, and it wasn't there when it was supposed to be. We had no idea where Dick and Eric were, so we went back to Cambridge. I kept calling the Hotel Paris, leaving messages that were never passed on. Finally I got a wire from Eric wondering where *I* was.

The blizzard had so fouled things up that the plane, which was late anyway, taxied around for an hour or so, and they finally had to bring the passengers to the terminal in a bus. Von Schmidt was beginning to wonder if he'd brought his bad luck with him.

ick and I finally got together. He was really broke and was being kicked out of his hotel, but he had managed to con a wealthy painter friend, Rory McKuen, into letting us stay at his town house. It had a heated towel rack and a servant that was never seen. Almost immediately Dylan happened to come to town. He was anxious to do some hanging out. I assumed that Dick and Bob were old buddies because Dick had asked him to play on Carolyn's record for Columbia, and he had. That was when John Hammond first heard Dylan and signed him up.

So when we all got together at Rory's, here were these guys who I assumed were old buddies. So we sat down in this modern palatial room in London, all done in Danish modern, and Dylan claimed he had never seen Dick before in his life! They were sitting side by side, both of them facing me, and neither of them would talk directly to the other. They would talk to me as if I was an interpreter. After a half hour or so things eased up, and Dylan asked if I'd like to hear a song he'd just written, "Don't Think Twice," and since everyone of us was having that kind of problem, that got the party going. It went for a couple of weeks.

Sometime in there we talked to Weidenfeld & Nicolson about Dick's novel in progress. Dick wanted it to be illustrated, but not in the usual sense. I had received a letter in October outlining his concept: "I have in mind that some of the drawings should be about incidents, events, whatnots, that are *not* related in the actual narrative, but which everyone, hopefully, is aware of as having transpired. The pictures would serve to bridge, illuminate, or more precisely aid in the creation of the image. They would cease being just passive illustrations, you see, as I think any kind of accompanying graphic thing should cease being that alone." It was an exciting concept, and that was the kind of guy he was. I had read what he had written and was totally delighted with it, but I had my doubts about his finding an English publisher. In fact, Weidenfeld & Nicolson turned it down while I was there.

They had sent it to six outside readers, the last of them Alexander Trocci. They wanted him to check out the drug aspect of the book, and Trocci was well qualified. He also thought that reading any novel other than his own was a waste of time, so he, of course, panned it. My feeling is that, whatever its literary worth, they felt it was too hot to handle. At that time there was a chapter in it, a pretty funny chapter, where all the college

guys, Gnossos, Heff, Rosenbloom, are all sitting around getting high and Gnossos gets into substituting the word "Cunt" for the noun used in book titles: "Farewell to Cunt," "The Cunt Also Rises," "The Old Man and the Cunt," stuff like that. Sophmoric, but it fit right in, and he pulled it off. He was very afraid that someone else would steal his idea, and he swore everybody to secrecy before he'd let them read that chapter.

It was a time of highs, energy and otherwise. Von Schmidt was making a short film on a folksong theme, "The Young Man Who Wouldn't Hoe Corn," and he and Ethan and Dick got together at Ewan McColl's and Peggy Seeger's and taped a soundtrack with the very pregnant Peggy doing the engineering. Ethan played mandolin,

banjo, and fiddle, Eric played guitar, and Dick played dulcimer and recorder. He had never played the recorder before and learned the tune in one night.

They played in the pubs when they could, and Dylan joined them from time to time. For Eric it was fun again.

We played at a Communist wedding. Everyone was singing Scots-Irish "hey lads, to-me-rum-tum-tum" kind of stuff and we sang "The Cocoa Beach Blues," and "Christian Island," which was a blues, too. We weren't exactly the hit of the party, but we didn't exactly care either.

We played at some folksong club one night and heard a good singer and guitar player, Martin Carthy, do a folksong called "The Franklin." It

DICK FARIÑA and ERIC VON SCHMIDT playing the blues at a Communist wedding (1963).
Photograph by Biran Sheul. Courtesy of Eric von Schmidt.

115

was about a boat that explored Antarctica or something. It was a totally lovely song. Dylan got Martin to show him all the chords and put the melody right in that amazing head of his. Next record he puts out there it is. "As I was riding on a western train…"

Dylan really was amazing back then. He kept changing sizes. He changed shape from day to day. On Tuesday he'd be big and husky; on Wednesday he'd be this frail little wisp of a thing; on Friday he'd be some other size and shape. The trickiest part was that he was always wearing the same clothes.

Fariña and I did a record with Ethan at Doug Dobell's record shop, the same place the Charles River Valley Boys had recorded about a year and a half before. After the last session we all went over to a club that Dick knew about and figured we'd just keep it going. Dylan had sung and played on the record a little and was raring to go. Everybody was drinking gin and smoking some very strong grass. When we got there there was an Israeli chick on the bill, Super-Sabra — the whole bit. Everything but a black eye-patch. She was not about to let us get on the stage. So we all kind of huddled in the back, in a little place partitioned off from the room, and smoked and drank even more.

Between sets Fariña and I got her in a corner, two on one. "Just ten minutes. Just *five* minutes." Her instincts, of course, were totally correct. Maybe an eye patch would have saved her. "All right," she said, looking at her commando watch,

BOB DYLAN (c. 1963). Photograph by Dick Waterman.

(opposite) ERIC VON SCHMIDT and DICK FARIÑA doing the London Waltz. Drawing by Eric von Schmidt.

So we gained the stage, and that was that. We appeared as a five man band, then two would leave and it would be a trio. One would come back and it would be a quartet, three would leave and there would be a solo number. Then reinforcements would arrive, and it was band time again. We were all wacked out, but Dylan was the worst. He was careening around this real small stage jabbering a bunch of dope talk. "Hey, I think we're under water. This some kind of submarine y'got here? Hey, man, where are we?"

It was a tiny little club, and the natives were getting restless. "Sing something or get off the bloody stage!" All the time he was talking he was doing a staggering little ballet. There was a stool on the stage, and he would weave and stumble around doing these little one-foot kicks and then collapse backwards and *always* land on the stool. We were hoping he'd land on the stool, and they were all hoping he'd miss it and fall on his silly little American ass. But he always hit it. He had that Chaplin genius.

About the time he finally got into a song or two, *another* performer came swaggering down the steps of this little basement club, a guy in fucking kilts! A dirk in his argyle socks and everything! It was really getting crazy. Zonked-out Gringos, Scotsmen, Sabras with high-heel boots, it was a circus!

It turned out that the Scots guy had just finished his first big gig down in Trafalgar Square, or someplace, and this was the club where he'd gotten his start. The poor sucker thought this was going to be his night of glory.

He sat down right next to the stage, and every time Bob would say something crazy he'd snap back with a putdown, real loud. I started to think, "We're going to have a battle royal in this place in about two minutes," but everybody was just stunned. The tension was so great. It was like watching a cobra and a mongoose.

Then Dylan did something brilliant. He just went on as if the guy didn't exist. He never looked at the guy and kept talking, more softly, kind of sweet, and totally spaced. The guy was chain-smoking cigarettes by this time, getting nastier with every remark — real mean one-liners. Then the guy realized that he was the one who was being a fool. Dylan kept right on, and finally the guy didn't exist. Didn't *want* to exist. His existence was unacceptable. He took a huge drag on his cigarette, threw it on the floor, ground it out with his shoe, and stalked out of the place.

Eric flew back to Boston on the sixteenth of January. His spirits were soaring. Dick returned to Paris to cope with the surreal details of a Mexican divorce from Carolyn and the bizarre reality of a secret marriage to Mimi.

We did not understand a word. The man opened a huge book. It was the Napoleonic Code. He read down one side of the page, and he looked over the thing at Dick, and Dick looked over at Eve and Tom Costner, who were our witnesses, and Eve said, "Oui," and Dick said, "Oui," and then he read the second page, and I said "Oui," and then we fumbled with the rings. Finally we got the rings on and left. And at the very end of this long hall of an empty church, Eve cracked up. And we said, "What's so funny?" Eve said, "He's waiting for you — he's waiting for a kiss, and you have not made the kiss." Sure enough, he was waiting back at the altar for a kiss. So we gave a big embrace and he closed the book and was satisfied.

MIMA FARIÑA. Photograph by David Gahr.

My baby asked me for a piece of banana,
Said, can I play the blues on your piano?
Just to do that Lindyburg with you.

California to the New York Island

I've roamed and rambled and I followed my footsteps
To the sparkling sands of her diamond deserts;
And all around me a voice was sounding;
This land was made for you and me.

t was time to get out of town. Since Neuwirth had returned from Europe he had been hanging out a lot with Buzz Marten.

I moved in with Buzz, Teddy Bernstein, Jim Kweskin and a kid named Rick who was a theater student and played flamenco guitar. They didn't have gay guys then, just shy people. He was pretty shy. I remember spending one entire winter without sunshine. There was lots of folky-rocky-boom going on.

Neuwirth certainly was a bundle of energy, but he wasn't exactly doing it on the natch. He was kind enough to let Buzzy in on his secret.

When Neuwirth moved in with us he brought a big bottle of dexedrines. That was my first encounter with that stuff. I would sit up all night playing the guitar, and he would strum along on his banjo. He really wanted to learn to play the guitar, so I got him started on that.

Then we went on the road together. We travelled via "Thunderbird." We'd decide to go someplace like Baltimore, and we'd go get two bottles of Thunderbird wine, drink it, and somehow get to Baltimore, usually by bus—drinking Thunderbird wine all the way down on the bus. By this time Fred Basler had left the Golden Vanity and had a coffeehouse in Baltimore where we would hang out. He'd let us play a set a night and pass a coffeecan around, so we had enough to go buy some more Thunderbird. It was a very self-destructive time. Most of it is a blur. We made asses of ourselves in a lot of towns, and I'm not real proud of those days. The Dillmore Brothers, as we called ourselves, were pretty notorious. We really didn't get shit accomplished.

Before I left Cambridge I was doing a lot of speed and it was almost falling-off-the-stage-time. I remember almost hallucinating some nights at the old 47. I had been working some with Sally Schoenfeld from Wellesley College as a duo, and speed probably had as much as anything to do with my splitting up with her.

One day I was walking down Massachusetts Avenue from the Bick, and there was this car full of guys in suits sitting there. Cars of guys in suits had been seen around. As I walked by, I heard one of the guys in the car say, "There he is," and they started getting out of the car and were looking right at me. I ran for it, jumped over this fence and ran up to where Bobby was staying with Betty Stoneman around the corner. We hid out that night. The next day we lit out for Bobby's mother's in Ohio. We stayed there for a while, and then David Piper came through from Cambridge and asked me if I'd like to ride out to California. I might have had a dollar on me, but I was ready to go.

The night he got to Berkeley Buzz wound up singing on KPFA's live folk show. As if by magic, he had found a new home. It wasn't long before Neuwirth arrived.

By that time, Rolf Cahn and Debbie Green were in California and had started the Cabale. And there was a scene at Phil and Midge Huffman's house. It was really great. They were folk aficionados and were social workers who didn't leave the job at five o'clock, and took all sorts of strange people in under their wing. That was a house where you'd wake up, and while you had been asleep, Lightnin' Hopkins and Sonny Terry would have set up shop in the living room and would be drinking whiskey and blowin' blues at 7:30 in the damn morning. So you'd wake up to some strong hangin' out. For anybody into blues, this was the place. K. C. Douglas, Black Ace, T-Bone Walker. All people connected with Arhoolie Records. Chris Strachwitz was in charge there, and he funnelled it through that house. And Rolf Cahn was real tight with the Huffmans, and it sort of went from the club to their house and back. That was Berkeley. A Cambridge/Berkeley axis had formed.

Rolf had been away for nearly three years charging his batteries. It was time to get home.

needed to go back to Berkeley and settle in with Phil Huffman and find a place. Phil and Midge were the Berkeley connection. The Huffman's was an amazing place at that time. 2821 Shattuck. It's a used car lot now. Think of Joan Barry sitting over there and Buzzy Marten sitting over here. They haven't seen each other for a year, and there's four or five other people, and suddenly he's playing, and she's singing, and it's perfect . . . Or Sonny Terry letting loose at two o'clock in the morning with "Great Tall Angel" like only Sonny in his deepest moments could sing it. I

Opposite:
BUZZ MARTEN and BOB NEUWIRTH, THE DILLMORE BROTHERS, plan a trip.
(1961) Photograph by John Cooke.

mean all the way down there, just like that! . . .
Or at one in the morning there's a knock on the
door, and Phil opens the door, and there's this
guy standing there with a pearl tooth, with his
guitar — a real dark, black spade with straight
hair and Phil has never seen him before, and Phil
says "It's T-Bone Walker!" And they went at it all
fucking night.

Through all of this Midge Huffman worked as a
social worker, raised a family, and fed everyone
who happened to be at the table.

Phil was the core as far as I was concerned. We
were both social workers. He wanted to write,
and that's why we came to Berkeley. I continued
to work as a social worker. At some point Phil
became one of the board of directors for Mary
Anne Pollard. She was a close friend of Odetta's,
and put on folk concerts in the Bay area. That's
how we came to know a number of the folk
performers. When they did a concert they would
stay with us. Then Phil started to take flamenco
guitar lessons from Rolf Cahn, and through him
we got acquainted with more folk people, and
our house just became a place where people liked
to come.

When Rolf went east to Cambridge and later
came back, he gave people there our address, and
they just started arriving. A lot of them had left
their own families, so this enabled them to have a
family and yet be independent. For me it was
great to practice on these young kids, because
I had my own children coming up. My whole
commitment for my own kids had been toward
college education and security. But because it
was okay for the kids I found coming to my house
not to go to school and try to do whatever they
found important, I accepted that for my own
kids.

Sonny and Brownie would stay two or three
weeks at a time, and there would be a party every
night. Brownie would stay up all night. Sonny
would go to bed early. About four in the
afternoon they would drift together and start to
play. They'd play very deep, soft blues. Then,
around seven or eight, people would arrive, and it
would become party blues. Every night we'd have
anywhere from ten to one hundred people.

Our bedroom was in the living room, because
Phil's study was in what normally would have
been our bedroom. When the first people came
in, and it started to be a party every night, I used
to go up to the children's room to sleep. Then
when everybody left I would go to bed. I finally
decided I couldn't do that anymore. So I would

MIDGE and PHIL HUFFMAN. Photograph by Charles Frizzell.
(left) SALLY SCHOENFELD and BUZZ MARTEN in a snappy publicity shot. (1960) Courtesy of Buzz Marten.
(right) ROLF CAHN and DEBBIE GREEN (1961). Photograph by Stephen Fenerjian.

put pajamas on, go into the living room, crawl into bed with everybody around, and go to sleep. They didn't tell me not to do it, and they didn't feel that they had to go home. And I could sleep. It was O.K.

With memories of Cambridge and the scene at Club 47 fresh in his memory, Rolf announced the next step to Debbie: "There should be a club!" I just thought, "Well, of course! It's obvious. It can't fail. There's no way it can fail. All you have to do is find some hole in the wall, and we'll do it." So Rolf and one of his students talked some people into putting up some money, and we did it. That was The Cabale. And we became the center of the folk scene in Berkeley for the next two or three years. Perry Lederman, Steve Talbott, Pete Berg, and Toni Brown were all local performers who really got started there. Then people like Tom Paxton and Sandy Bull and Mark Spoelstra would come in, and Chris Strachwitz at Arhoolie Records came around all the time so we had Lightning Hopkins, Mance Lipscomb, and Jesse Fuller. And of course Rolf used it as his showcase, and a lot of people from Cambridge came out here because of him, and they became part of the scene here too. There was a lot of back and forth going on between Cambridge and Berkeley after a while.

There was no question that the Berkeley folk scene had a lot going for it. Fresh from a big bout with Dope Paranoia in Cambridge, Buzz felt like a free man. There was a lot more sunshine in Berkeley, it seemed. Even the police went to college and weren't into hassling people if they looked a little funny or liked to play guitars and sing all night. There were no "townies" looking to beat up on the beatniks. There was the Cabale, the Huffman's, and great weekend parties at Dave and Vera Mae Frederickson's where you might find anyone from Mainer's Mountaineers to K. C. Douglas. So Buzz said to himself, "I want to stay here!" And he did, after first going back east with Neuwirth to face the draft in as terrible shape as liquor and drugs could make him — he failed with flying colors — and getting his girlfriend, Julie. Soon after returning to Berkeley they got married in the Huffman's kitchen right next to the refrigerator.

Buzz was the first of many people to whom Berkeley became a second home for the next few years. For any young folk singer trying to make enough money to live on, it became, with Cambridge, a kingpin of a small, but growing, folk circuit. You could get in a car with your guitar and a friend or two, make it to Ann Arbor, where there was another little folk cell with a paying gig at the Canterbury House and a place to crash, some music and good times, then maybe make it to Denver where Harry Tuft had just established The Denver Folklore Center after Izzy Young's Folklore Center in New York, and then head over the mountains until you found yourself humming a few bars of Jesse Fuller's "San Francisco Bay Blues" and wondering whether to go straight to the Huffman's or check out the Cabale or maybe go by Dave and Vera Mae's. Then there'd come a day when you would give somebody a call in Cambridge, and it would be time to head the other way, to pick up on some more playing and partying all the way back to Cambridge. It was the beginning of a cross-country party that was to last for several years.

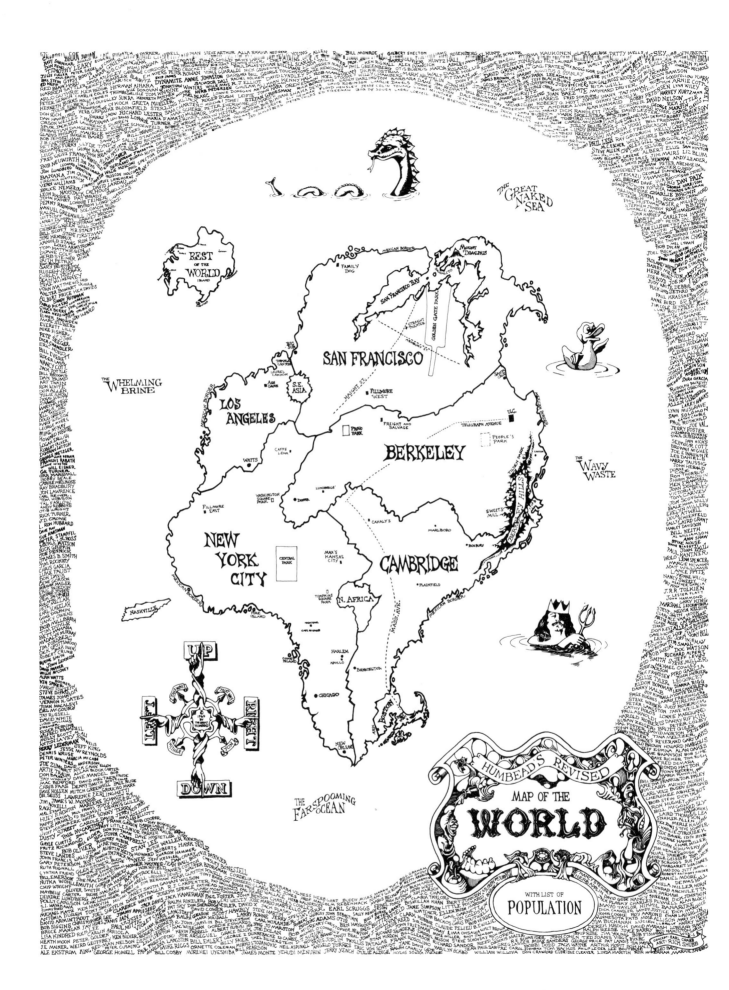

HUMBEAD'S REVISED
MAP OF THE WORLD

EARL CRABB is a citizen of the folk world. He is from Minneapolis and was familiar with the folk scene there that gave us Bob Dylan, John Koerner, Dave Ray, and Tony Glover. He went to Williams College in Massachusetts and soon got caught up in the Cambridge folk scene. He ultimately wound up out in Berkeley where he runs a computer software company, whatever that is. What follows is Earl's account of how the Map of the World came into being.

"I was in Campbell Coe's music store in Berkeley one day. Annie Johnston was behind the counter. Some character was off looking at instruments. Somebody came in and asked, 'Do you know of anybody driving from Kansas City to Boston?' We thought he was kidding, but he said, 'I've got a ride to Kansas City but I need a ride from Kansas City to Boston.' I suggested that it might be easier to put 'Boston' on a sign and go down to the University and try for a straight shot.

"He thought that was a good idea and left. But the other guy who was looking at banjos — who turned out to be Rick Shubb — said, 'You know, that's absolutely right.' I said, 'I know. Berkeley and Cambridge are very close to each other and getting to Boston from Cambridge is easy.' I said, 'Look here. New York and Los Angeles are the same way. People go back and forth between New York and Los Angeles, but did you ever hear of anybody going from Berkeley to New York or from Los Angeles to Cambridge?'

"I drew this little pie with four pieces. Berkeley and Cambridge were on one side. Berkeley to Los Angeles was there, and New York to Cambridge was there. So it was simple. We started rapping and went to my house and spent the next two days talking about all this stuff. Nashville was definitely there, accessible only by airplane from New York. So what is it? It's an island out in the ocean.

"This was a strict metaphysical projection, and it seemed to capture the times. It was early 1967. Southeast Asia looks like a bomb crater."

oing to New York meant going to the "Village," and that meant the area around Bleecker and MacDougal where there were half a dozen coffeehouses and "basket houses" where a folksinger could pick up a couple of dollars singing. After a heavy year of biking, blues, and dope up in Cambridge, David Barry flunked out of Harvard and headed for New York.

In the Village I played with Mark Spoelstra, Fred Neil, Bob Dylan, and Lisa Kindred. We hung out at the "Cafe Wha?" It was a grubby, awful scene there. It was a basket house. We were all treated like shit. The customers were tourists. I slept on floors a lot. It was a desperate struggle there. I guess like a lot of others I was enthralled by the idea of living the Kerouac life — just me and my guitar. I liked playing blues guitar more than anything else in the world, but there was just no money in it there. Although Dylan could neither sing or play the guitar, he clearly had something on stage that none of the rest of us did. He could entertain. The rest of us were doing things that we had studied hard to do — really accurate renditions of Brownie McGhee or Merle Travis — but Dylan had that energy. When he got a job at Gerde's for $90.00 a week it was big news.

Gerde's Folk City was not down there with all the other places. It was over on Lower Broadway in back of Washington Square. The owner's name was Mike Porco. Mike was in the bar business; he liked music, sure, but most of all he liked to see a full bar. In the late fifties the folk community was casting about for a good showcase club, and Izzy Young, who was the proprietor of the Folklore Center, made a deal with Mike to use the club, which they named Gerde's Fifth Peg. Izzy would get the door and Mike would get the bar. Cynthia Gooding arranged to do her WBAI radio show from the club, and the artists rallied around to make it a success — Theo Bikel, Billy Faier, The Greenbriar Boys, Brother John Sellers. It became the place to play and hang out. That was all Mike needed to see, and shortly Izzy was no longer getting the door, and Mike changed the name to Gerde's Folk City.

Compared to the basket houses, Gerde's was a palace. It was a good-sized place with a long mirrored bar which was separated from the performing area by an elbow-high partition. Serious drinkers could sit and watch the performer in the mirror. So could the performer. Folk enthusiasts could spring for the cover and sit at the chromium and formica tables which were held over from its previous incarnation as an Italian restaurant. Wires ran along the long wall in back of the stage on which hung record jackets from the "folk" labels like some kind of permanent New Year's decorations. The stage was small: four people were a crowd. There was one microphone —a chromium banded number that was good for public address announcements. The sound came out of two speakers hung up at either end of the room. There was never a problem hearing, though; it was a good live room. And that was probably why the place worked. Applause always sounded good in Gerde's whether there were twenty people or two hundred. You could have a good time there.

Accommodations for performers were minimal, which is to say there were none. When you came to work you went behind the bar into the kitchen, took a hard right, went down some slightly shaky stairs (watching not to bump your head) and tuned up next to the meat cooler by the beer boxes. When it was time to go on, you went back upstairs and waited in a little area on the far side of the stage until Charlie Rothchild, who booked, promoted, and emceed the shows for fifty bucks a week minus drinks, would muster up his best announcer's voice and bring you on . . . "And now, ladies and gentlemen, Gerde's Folk City proudly presents . . ."

If many of the artists were starving at this time, the audience for folk music wasn't exactly flush either. Robert Shelton, who was reviewing folk music for the *New York Times* and spending a lot of time at the bar, gave Mike the idea of Hoots on Monday for a dollar. It was a winner. Peter Wolf was a young painter just getting into the scene. Peter took full advantage of the opportunity.

I spent a lot of time at Gerde's. Monday night was a dollar. They'd give you a card entitling you to one drink. I was painting and didn't have much money, so I'd bet someone that I could outdrink them on 151 rum straight up. If they lost, they'd buy your card from you for another drink and pay for the rounds. So that was Monday night at Gerde's. I got to see John Lee Hooker. Bob Dylan opened for him. Jack Elliott was in there a lot when he came back from England. Johnny Herald of the Greenbriar Boys had just got back from school in Wisconsin. There was Tom and Jerry which later became Simon and Garfunkel. I can see Judy Collins in her three inch high heels and

black dress. So Gerde's definitely became a place to go all the time. You never knew who was going to get up.

The Gaslight over on MacDougal Street became another haven for young singers and writers. Dave Van Ronk held court there. He and his wife Terri became some sort of parents, advisors, and soul-mates to a lot of young writers and singers starting with Tom Paxton and Bob Dylan, Noel Stookey, Hugh Romney, Len Chandler, and Barry Kornfield. It, too, became a paying gig when it was taken over by Sam Hood. It didn't pay much, but it wasn't a hand-out either.

Everything about it made you want to duck. It was downstairs from the sidewalk. You entered into total darkness. It was always a matter of not hitting your head, not bumping into people, not sitting on someone, or standing in their way. The stage was a small, illuminated area at the far end of the room. The only way to get to it was to walk through the audience into the kitchen which was behind the stage. Unpack your instrument amid the waitresses and dishwashers and go back out through the door, take a right, step up on the stage, taking care not to hit your head on the pipes overhead. Most performers chose to sit down. That was difficult if you happened to be Bill Monroe and the Bluegrass Boys. An "intimate, living room atmosphere" was a kind way to describe the room.

This page: DAVE VAN RONK Publicity shot, courtesy of Manny Greenhill.
Opposite page: MARIA D'AMATO and her fiddle. Photograph by John Cooke.

One of the great things about New York is the incredible number of little specialty shops. A shop is more than a store where you go to buy something. As often as not the business transaction is an excuse to visit or hang out. Conversation is one thing at which most New Yorkers excel. Alan Block had a sandal shop over on West Fourth Street. Alan also loved to play the fiddle, so his shop naturally became a stop for all sorts of people who liked old-timey music. Maria D'Amato was just discovering the folk scene in the Village where she had grown up. She had just been saved by her mother from a fate worse than death — she had almost become a rock and roll singer.

 When I was about twelve or thirteen, Alan Freed hit the airwaves, and I was a stone goner. That was R & B, "Earth Angel," the Platters, the Moonglows — all that harmony, all that *a capella* stuff. So in junior high school I formed a group with three Puerto Rican girls and myself. We called ourselves "The Cameos." We had little matching outfits. We would learn Everly Brothers tunes and stuff like that, and we would sing *a capella* at assemblies.

The next year I went to Hunter High and lost the Puerto Rican girls and found three Jewish girls from the Bronx, and we formed "The Cashmeres." We wore tight, white sweaters and tight, black skirts, seamed stockings, and black flats, and we sewed velvet "C's" for "Cashmeres" on the sweaters. I wrote a whole lot of tunes, which were okay for that sort of "doo-wah" variety. It was like the Chantels stuff:

"Oh, I'm dreamin', dreamin', dreamin', dreamin',

My heart is schemin', schemin', schemin', schemin'. . ."

We'd tell our mothers we were going to the library after school, and we'd go to the Brill Building, look up Irving Whoever in the directory, and go up, walk in the door, and say, "Hi, We're the Cashmeres!", and burst into song. Some of them would give us encouragement, and we slowly made some progress. This guy Marty Katz said he'd manage us. He actually got us a rehearsal hall. On Saturdays the high school would be teeming with groups. You'd open the door of one room and there'd be Frankie Lyman and the Teenagers. Every room had a different group. Marty actually got us a record contract with Don Records. The Chantels were on the label. We were all excited,

and we were supposed to get our parents to sign. Of course, my mother thought I'd been at the library all this time, and she exploded.

"What? They're going to make a white slave out of you!" To this day I'm not really sure what a white slave is, but whatever it was, she was not going for it. She went storming uptown in a taxi and told them, "What do you think you're doing?" The three Jewish mamas didn't think it was such a bad idea, but not Mama "D". It was an abrupt end to my rock and roll career.

Soon after that I started getting into the folkie scene in the Village. Jeremy Steig was a friend of mine, and he turned me on to people like Josh White. I started going to parties and began singing songs like "Jelly, Jelly, Jelly" — very risque. And I got into Odetta and Bessie Smith. And then a big thing was on Saturdays when Alan Block would have people by his sandal shop to play. I was having a pair of sandals made for fifty cents a week, so I'd be in there, and there'd be a whole store full of people. I got to know everyone, and I got totally sucked in. John Cohen and Mike Seeger would be there, and I started singing and picking up on records. The first record I got was by the Kossoy Sisters, and I learned the whole thing — every song. That really got me started into mountain music, which is something I never even knew existed a few months earlier. Alan's sandals were great, too.

For almost everyone connected with the folk scene, the central clearing house and meeting place was Izzy Young's. The sign said the "Folklore Center, Israel G. Young, Prop." Izzy was one of a kind that only New York could have produced. He was loud, energetic, disorganized, petty, big-hearted, and totally dedicated to serving the cause of folk music and folk singers. It was to Izzy's that Jim Rooney went when he first when down to New York to check out the scene with Bill Keith.

Below:
(left) THE GREENBRIAR BOYS (left to right) BOB YELLIN, RALPH RINZLER, and JOHN HERALD. Publicity shot courtesy of Manny Greenhill.
(right) THE NEW LOST CITY RAMBLERS (left to right) TOM PALEY, MIKE SEEGER, and JOHN COHEN. Publicity shot courtesy of Manny Greenhill.

Following page:
BOB DYLAN   Photograph by Dick Waterman.

guess we'd heard about Izzy's from Roger Sprung, who had been showing us around down in Ashville and Galax. At any rate, we went in and it was bedlam. It wasn't a very big place — a couple of narrow rooms strung together. The records and books were out front. There were instruments on the walls, and there were a lot of people generally milling around, some of them apparently trying out instruments. Izzy was on the phone. The word "schmuck" came up frequently. His hair was all over the place. His nose was very big. His shirt was rumpled and coming out of his pants. He had big glasses on. His accent was a caricature of every New York Jew I'd ever dreamed of. I was just sort of browsing around, looking through the records. There was no place like it in Cambridge or Boston. There was nothing there but folk records, folk songbooks, *Sing Out!* magazines, instruction manuals, instruments, picks and strings. I immediately picked up on a Bill Clifton Songbook which had about three-hundred country and bluegrass songs in it. No one but Izzy would have had that in the North at that time.

I don't know how, but we somehow got into conversation, and it turned out that he had heard of Keith. Soon he was grilling us about what was going on up in Cambridge. He'd been getting reports from people like Barry Kornfield and Bob Dylan. As a matter of fact, did we know Dylan? No, we didn't. He said, "Come here. He's back here." With that we went into the back room, and there was Dylan sitting at a cluttered desk, banging away on a typewriter. Izzy told him who we were and where we were from. He immediately handed me a bunch of sheets with songs on them. I mean a bunch. He was writing like a man possessed. His feet were bouncing up and down as he talked. He was on fire.

On our way out who should we run into but John Herald of the Greenbriar Boys. He recognized Bill from some folk get-together. He was on his way to Chinatown to get some food, so we went with him and wound up going over to his place on 10th Street to play and listen to some '78's that he was learning songs off of. That was the first time I heard Riley Puckett, the great blind hillbilly singer who used to sing with Gid Tanner and the Skillet Lickers. He was Johnny's

favorite singer at the time. At some point Ralph Rinzler blew in the door. Ralph was the mandolin player in the Greenbriar Boys and a rising young figure in the New York folk scene along with Mike Seeger. So we all got playing late into the night, and Johnny's little apartment felt like home to us.

The next day was Sunday, and Bill was all primed to get over to Washington Square. Roger Sprung was the king of Washington Square. He was the first person to play Scruggs-style banjo in New York and possibly the north. He was doing it way back in 1954. Somehow or other a tradition had got started of picking in Washington Square on Sundays when the weather got nice. There would be all sorts of groups spread around the big fountain there, some playing bongos, some with guitars playing blues, and always a large folk/bluegrass contingent. Eric Weissberg and Marshall Brickman, Barry Kornfeld, John Herald, Ralph Rinzler, Bob Yellin, Erik Darling, Fred Gerlach, and always in the center of things, taller than anyone else, wearing a Homburg, grinning and bouncing as his fingers picked wildly at the strings, was Roger Sprung.

We were among the early arrivals. Our parking lot chops were in good shape from our trip down south. Roger knew this and brought us into the circle often by asking for songs like "Reuben" and "John Henry" that he knew were our strong ones. That was very generous of him, because there was a lot of competition in that New York bluegrass scene. Notes and speed and hot licks were it, and it could get pretty crazy at times. With guys like Weissberg and Marshall Brickman around, a poor song sometimes didn't have a chance. But it was a gas to be there. We picked for about five solid hours and felt that we had become part of a new scene. We invited everyone to come up and see us in Cambridge, where we promised them we would try to show them as good a time as they'd shown us.

That night as I was wandering around I went by the Bitter End on Bleeker Street. It was where Peter, Paul, and Mary got started, and it was a whole new concept in clubs. It had bare brick walls, a stage large enough for several people to stand on, more than one microphone, speakers hung from the ceiling, stage lights that could go up and down and had different colors. There was even a dressing room in back for the performers. It was definitely "show-business." You had to have an act to play there. There was no announcer who got up, just a godlike voice from the ceiling — "And now, ladies and gentlemen, the Bitter End is proud to present . . ." I didn't have an act, but it was Hoot night. I had my guitar and thought I'd take a look. Theo Bikel was running the Hoot, and the place was jammed — a little too jammed for me. I didn't see any familiar faces, so I went back outside.

There was a good, old, down-and-outers bar next door, and a cold beer seemed like a good idea, so I went in. It was sort of a bowery type place with sawdust on the floor and fifteen cent beer, which was okay with me. I sat down at the bar, and who should be sitting there but Bob Dylan. We remembered each other and started talking. Mostly about what kind of music we liked. It turned out that Hank Williams was someone we both loved. We got into talking about different songs, and after a few beers we started to feel like playing. I mentioned that I'd already been next door, but that it was crowded. He said, "Let's go. They'll let us sing a couple of songs." So we went in and waited until Theo came back where the performers were warming up, and Bob told him that we wanted to play. "I'm sorry, boys, but we're already behind, and we can't put anymore on tonight." So there we were, ready to play, and nowhere to do it. Dylan just sat down, took the guitar, and started to play right there in the middle of this back hall area with people walking around us. Pretty soon we had a good crowd back there. From time to time Bikel would look in with some sort of glare, but everybody liked us, and I guess he figured that he'd do better to just pretend we didn't exist.

It had been an action-packed couple of days. Keith and Rooney had connected with a lot of great people in New York. It was going to become more familiar to them in the years to come—the Square, Izzy's, Gerde's, MacDougal and Bleecker, Chinatown, visits with Ralph and Johnny, craziness with Marshall and Eric, pickin' with Roger. But, as they say, it's a nice place to visit. Maybe it was something about the way Dylan had been jiggling or the pickers had been speeding or Izzy had been shouting, but they felt pretty happy to be heading up to Cambridge and those green fields that Dylan would be talking about on his new record.

This land is your land, this land is my land,
From California to the New York island,
From the redwood forest to the Gulf Stream waters;
This land was made for you and me.

Ocean of Diamonds

I'd give an ocean of diamonds,
A world filled with flowers,
If I could hold you for just a few hours.

It was the kind of cold that makes it hurt to breathe. Ice was forming on the inside of the windows of the Club 47. Mitch Greenhill was onstage picking his guitar for the seven people in the audience. Betsy was in the kitchen. Victor was at the door. They'd sent the waitress home. It was another quiet night. Once in a while someone would open the door, letting in a gust of Arctic air. It was usually somebody's friend just coming by to get out of the cold and have a free cup of coffee. Paying customers were few and far between. It was exam time at Harvard, and no one was out and about. A lot of people didn't even know the Club had reopened. It had been closed for two and a half months, and many had assumed it would never reopen. A lot of them had started to go over to the Unicorn in Boston. Tom Rush had been performing there regularly and was starting to build a following. Since returning from Europe, Tom had been spending more and more time working on his music.

Everybody seemed to have a specialty — bluegrass, blues, Child ballads, Woody Guthrie. I never did develop a specialty. In some ways I was a misfit, because I did a little bit of each of them. But I enjoyed the variety. It kept me happy, and I think the people who came to hear me enjoyed it. It also kept me looking all the time for good songs and not necessarily looking in one particular pigeonhole.

Joe Boyd was a roommate of mine at Harvard. He was a record collector — heavily into 78's. He was into it the way some people are into baseball cards — pressing numbers and all that. But he didn't play his records that much. He just collected them.

If Joe didn't often listen to his records, Tom did. He began digging out songs like Robert Johnson's "Walking Blues" and Washboard Sam's "Orphan Blues." Robert L. Jones was performing a lot at the Unicorn. Jones was becoming known as a masterful singer of Woody Guthrie songs. From him Tom learned songs like "Talking Dust Bowl" and "I Don't Want Your Millions Mister." From Jack Elliott he got Jesse Fuller's "San Francisco Bay Blues" and "Diamond Joe." He immediately recognized the meaningful message in Eric von Schmidt's "Big Fat Woman" and started to include it in his sets. To all of these songs Tom brought a natural sense of ironic understatement which

TOM RUSH in the spotlight (c. 1963). Photograph by Dick Waterman.

contributed to his image as someone who was a bit of a loner. His music was introspective and witty. His pose was of a boy who was bad, but not too bad. He had a mind to ramble, but why not ramble in comfort? Underneath that workshirt was a boy a girl could take home to mother. Soon, a lot of girls started getting interested in folk music, as were some others.

One night this fellow, Dan Flickinger, came in and said, "Do you want to make a record?" So I said okay, and he recorded me live at the Unicorn. That was a very funky record — telephones ringing in the background, waitresses dropping trays. Flickinger told me that editing wasn't hip. That wasn't where it was at. I later found out that he hadn't learned how to do it yet. Byron did the cover and made up the label name — "Lycornu" — the French word for Unicorn or something, and Flickinger distributed the record out of the back seat of his car.

It wasn't exactly a million seller, but the record did make it into the Cambridge and Boston record store windows, and Byron's cover photograph of Tom looking very alone and inward did a lot to establish Tom as a major new face in the "post-Baez" era that had begun in Cambridge.

Opposite:
Club Mt. Auburn 47 Calendar for September 1962. This is the only visual representation that we could find of the outside of the Club. Not surprisingly, it looks like a store. The tone of the flyer is definitely high class. The memory of the court trial lingered on, and it would never have done to admit that folk music was what was really happening. The art work was by Steve Karlsson and Byron Linardos.

As it turned out, the Rush record was one of the last things Byron did at the Unicorn.

think that Jones might have told the people at the 47 that I was having troubles with George, because they approached me two or three times. And things with George kept getting worse. I didn't like it, but I could accept the fact that George wasn't honest when dealing with other people, but if he wasn't honest with me . . . It got really cuckoo. At one point I grabbed a knife. I remember vividly there was this pole, painted by me — it was gold — and I got him up against it, and all I could think of was a gold cross. And he said, "You're going to crucify me!" If he had said anything, I would have killed him. I cooled off to some degree and went back and started making a cup of coffee and just started throwing everything at him.

The offer from the 47 had been made, and each time I had said, "No," but I figured that the only way to save myself would be to leave. It's the strongest thing I've ever done. I walked out. I've thought about it lots of times, but I know that that would have been the end of a lot of things if I'd stayed. There was no way to get rid of him.

Byron's father had warned him about the dangers of a partnership, but what of the Board of Directors of a "non-profit educational institution?" Byron was about to write the book.

I went over to the 47 knowing absolutely nothing about the place. I had a queasy feeling about the lawyer, Fred Greenman, and what connection he had with things. Oppenheimer was the one doing all the talking, and he didn't interest me much. What really interested me was the challenge. They were in debt. Somehow that was a moving thing. But there were no ideas in my head of, "Okay. Here's a great place. Let's create!" It was more like just going in and immediately trying to rub out everything else that existed before — the way things had been run. Automatically saying "no" to something even if it was right. And then letting it come back.

The general thing of running the place was: the house before any one individual. It wasn't against anybody. It was for everybody. But it could get touchy at times.

I used to love the Board meetings. There was so much bullshit going on. I'd get down to the nitty-gritty things like; "Who pays to get in here

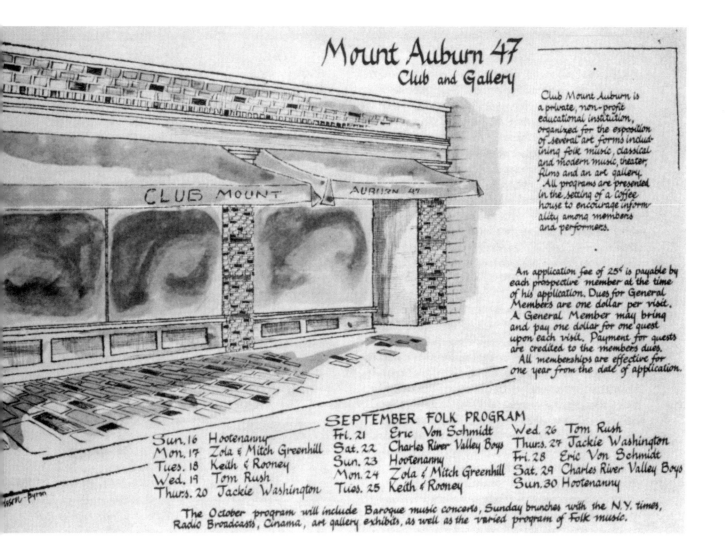

Mount Auburn 47
Club and Gallery

Club Mount Auburn is a private, non-profit educational institution, organized for the exposition of several art forms including folk music, classical and modern music, theater, films and an art gallery. All programs are presented in the setting of a coffee house to encourage informality among members and performers.

An application fee of 25¢ is payable by each prospective member at the time of his application. Dues for General Members are one dollar per visit. A General Member may bring and pay one dollar for one guest upon each visit. Payment for guests are credited to the members dues. All memberships are effective for one year from the date of application.

SEPTEMBER FOLK PROGRAM

Sun. 16 Hootenanny	Fri. 21 Eric Von Schmidt	Wed. 26 Tom Rush
Mon. 17 Zola & Mitch Greenhill	Sat. 22 Charles River Valley Boys	Thurs. 27 Jackie Washington
Tues. 18 Keith & Rooney	Sun. 23 Hootenanny	Fri. 28 Eric Von Schmidt
Wed. 19 Tom Rush	Mon. 24 Zola & Mitch Greenhill	Sat. 29 Charles River Valley Boys
Thurs. 20 Jackie Washington	Tues. 25 Keith & Rooney	Sun. 30 Hootenanny

The October program will include Baroque music concerts, Sunday brunches with the N.Y. times, Radio Broadcasts, Cinema, art gallery exhibits, as well as the varied program of folk music.

and who doesn't? Whoever walks through that door and doesn't pay, there's got to be a good reason why they don't pay. If they have something to do with the house in a positive way, fine. But if they don't, then being friends with the performers or the Directors is not enough. Or having done things in the past. It's got to be current." That really caused an uproar. Tears were shed. There was screaming! People who had never paid before to get in who just *had* to be there for that night.

But it was right. We were making our money off of quarters and dollars. There wasn't anything on the menu that cost a dollar. And the door was a buck. For anyone. No matter who. The Unicorn was starting to charge three bucks a show. We didn't raise it because we didn't think we could get it — it was a whole different idea. Here was a club with no owner! Nobody, no single person, took home all the chips. And I still go for that idea. I started at $100.00 a week, and we made an agreement that if I doubled this or tripled that it would go up twenty-five bucks to

here, twenty-five bucks to there. That seemed fair in relation to the whole picture.

We changed the pay for the performers. It was a formula based on a percentage of the door with a top of $50.00 for a single and $75.00 for a group. That was later raised to $75.00 and $100.00. Rush always used to ask me about that top figure — "What goes?" And I always used to tell him, "What goes is the Club 47 Future Fund." And he'd ask, "What is the Future Fund for?" And I'd say, "For hard times." And I'd tell him, "Do you know how many people you are promoting with all these extra goodies? Up to the point where you've made seventy-five bucks the house has been taken care of in every way, but tomorrow night Tim Hardin is going to play, and we're going to lose money. You're carrying the ball for him." And Rush got into that even though he kept questioning whether or not "The Greek" was taking home all the chips, because I always ended up with a "Byronic" smile that he liked. And he'd think, "Has he been bullshitting me?"

Rush is one of the people who credited me with being a shrewd businessman. I sat around and watched people make me into things that I wasn't. I ran the place as simply as possible. I didn't define everything I was doing on purpose. I defined only when something positive would come out of it, or I needed it, and by defining it something would happen. Otherwise I didn't. This was being called secretive, or as Rush would see me, as shrewd, when basically I was very, very simple. I always had the knack of boiling things down to the clearest form. Like the menu, which was basically coffee, tea, soda drinks, cheese, and pastry — all at a fair price. You can make coffee six different ways. You can make tea six different ways. Hooray for hot water!

Betsy Siggins and I would do the booking together. I would never admit it, because I wanted her to do the programming. I wanted to give her the responsibility, and I wanted to build one figure other than the money man, the boss man, the guy supposedly holding the chips. I didn't want the artists to deal with me directly. So people dealt with her on a friendly basis, and she would check out each figure with me. I actually made up all the figures, and she'd map out the program for a month.

I set three months as the amount of time it would take to get out of debt. Somehow we did it. It was close, so I stayed on for another month, and somehow that extra month turned into forever.

Having Byron around was a shock to a lot of people. From the early days at the Yana, and then at the Vanity, there had always been an "in" crowd whose general attitude was that they were somehow above the poor slobs who paid to come in and paid for their food and drink. The idea was that they contributed so much by their mere presence that they were exempt from such mundane considerations. They would breeze in the door, walk into the kitchen, help themselves to some coffee, hang around in the back area talking to each other and paying scant attention to whatever was going on onstage, unless the performer happened to be a friend, in which case they might call out a request or say something that would make it clear how close a friend they were to whoever it was on stage. Those days were gone, and there was much muttering about "the good old days."

As the weeks passed, however, the change in atmosphere became apparent. For one thing, the audience started to build. It could be that they appreciated being treated fairly. They no longer felt like uninvited guests at a private party. If they wanted something, they could get it. Whatever it was would be good, and the price was fair. The waitress was pretty. Byron saw to that, too. After a while certain artists became associated with certain nights. Keith and Rooney were on Tuesdays. Wednesday was for Rush. Thursday was Jackie Washington's. The Charles River Valley Boys did Saturdays, and Eric von Schmidt got Fridays. That would last for a month, and then the artists would switch around, so that everyone got a crack at the weekends. Byron came up with the idea of printing monthly calendars with good graphics to inform the membership of what was coming up. "Membership" started to mean something. Members and performers were somehow being brought together in a cooperative atmosphere of mutual respect. It became a point of pride to have a 47 membership card; it became a point of pride to be a performer at the 47. "The good new days" at the Club 47 had begun.

here were lines down the sidewalk outside the Club. The people were waiting to get in to see Jackie Washington. He was unique. He was black, but he didn't speak with a drawl. If he had the blues he wasn't telling anyone about it. Not so long ago he knew nothing about folk music and now he was the hottest singer at *the* folk club in Cambridge, running down the same road as Joan Baez. What was the story?

I came tap dancing out of the womb! I was a born performer. It is second nature to me. Somehow I always knew that I was going to go on the stage. That's why I went to Emerson College in Boston. My folks wanted me to go to college. You *had* to go to college. I heard that you could not only get a degree, but that you could get into theater there. so that's what I was doing until this crazy thing happened. I had heard of this place called the Golden Vanity and went over to check it out with a couple of friends. We were sitting there having all this exotic tea and stuff that we'd never had before and then found out how much it was going to cost! We were coming up short, but it was a hoot night, and if you sang you could get your drinks free. So, being a showoff, I got up and sang. I only knew how to play a ukelele, so I got Freddy Basler to accompany me. I did a couple of songs. I remember doing a spiritual, because I knew that would be big — and it was. Everybody said, "Ooh! Wow!" It was me up there instead of

Blind Boy Fiddlestein. Who knows! That's how it started.

After that I met David Greenberg. He worked with my mother who was a record buyer for a store in Boston, and he went to Emerson, too. He was into the folk scene and started to take me around. I heard Joan, and she answered a whole lot of needs. I thought she was incredible. So I fell in love with her, and started to go over to the 47 a lot. I was getting out there and started to meet people and to get a little bit happy for the first time in my life, and I wanted to do it. But I still couldn't play the guitar. For starters, what I did was to take a guitar and take the sixth string off and try to play it like a five-string ukelele. Greenberg said, "This is ridiculous. You've got to learn how to play right." So he took me to Rolf for some lessons.

By this time I was into it. From the beginning I started working regular. I worked once a week at the Vanity. I would work solo or open up for someone like Oscar Brand. Paul and Elaine Wing at The Salamander asked me to play there once a week. Then when Joan Baez left to go to California in 1961 Paula asked me to play at the 47. That was the big time for me. At the same

JACKIE WASHINGTON enjoying himself immensely at the 1961 Indian Neck Folk Festival with MITCH GREENHILL (back to the camera) and JIM KWESKIN. DAVID GREENBERG (far right) seems about to hang it up. Photograph by Stephen Fenerjian.

time, Manny Greenhill had heard me at the Golden Vanity on a night when Mitchell was playing, too. I killed 'em, so he said that he'd start to get me work. The Greenhills became like a family to me. Mitch and I did a lot of gigs together. Manny was some combination of father, advisor, manager. Leona was a real Jewish mother.

For the first time in my life I was part of something. It was called the "folk movement" or the "folk revival" and here were friends. I loved Eric and Rolf and people like Jim Rooney and Bill Keith, and I wanted so to be a part of their world. A lot of the songs that I already knew turned out to be what people called folk songs. I could also do language things. Then I started hearing words like "commercial" or "ethnic" which bothered me all the time I was doing the folksinging thing. I considered myself West Indian, and, because I could do West Indian dialects, I felt that I could sing calypso. Because people liked them didn't make them bad to me. But Belafonte was big at that time, and, because he was popular, he was considered bad. It seemed that commercial was bad, and because I could entertain people and make them laugh I was commercial. So I started feeling ashamed about what I did. I was just too dumb at the time to say, "Well, fuck you!"

So for a long time I tried hard to do "ethnic" material and find tunes that I liked. I liked Appalachian mountain things and learned songs from people like Jean Ritchie and Hobart Smith and Almeda Riddle. I really did a lot of research, none of which I regret, and got to be friends with a lot of those people, which is what I value most out of my folk music experience. But trying to be ethnic I got so far into other people's culture that I wasn't myself. I was trying to make myself into somebody that people would like, and that ultimately was not healthy. I allowed myself to be defined by others. Sometimes it takes you a while to get smart.

Jackie might have been trying hard to be ethnic, but as far as any of his fans were concerned he probably could have sung the phone book. He was a natural, and whatever it was that he did made people happy. None of his humor was malicious; a lot of it was at his own expense. He would glare at his fingers as he tried to make them play some kind of complicated run. He would tell some ridiculous story where he was usually David up against some kind of Goliath. When he did get serious he could come up with gems like his version of Jean Ritchie's *Nottamun Town* or *Maleguena Salerosa*. Probably his best thing was a medley of "Careless Love" blues forms that he called "Sweet Mama." Not one to neglect his singer-songwriter contemporaries, he would close with Eric von Schmidt's tender tribute to teendom, "Acne." By the end of a set, questions of ethnic purity seemed beside the point. Jackie was using folk material to entertain people and somehow enrich their lives. They stood in line to hear him week after week, year after year. It was primarily because of his popularity and that of Tom Rush, another who felt uncomfortable

FRITZ RICHMOND and JACKIE WASHINGTON at the Club 47. (c. 1962) Photograph by John Cooke.

because he wasn't ethnically pure, that the 47 was able to come back so far, so fast, and it ultimately made it possible for the 47 to bring in the "real" folk artists like Hobart Smith and Doc Watson and Jesse Fuller and the Reverend Gary Davis. Popularity seemed like a pretty good thing for everybody in the spring of '62. It felt good to have those lines down the street, to have people becoming members, and to have a good time listening to some good music. If you had a good time one night, it made you want to come back and check out somebody else another night.

That was how a lot of people got to hear Joe Val for the first time. Keith and Rooney had finally gotten on the schedule as regulars and were playing as a duo with Fritz Richmond on the washtub. Fritz was back from the army and immediately had become the "house" bass player at five dollars a night. One night they went into Copley Square to do a little concert for the Community Church. There weren't too many people there, but there was a familiar face in the back row. It was Joe Val. Joe had been on the original "Hayloft Jamboree" as one of the "Radio Rangers" and later had worked off and on with the Lilly Brothers at the Hillbilly Ranch. Joe had definitely paid some dues.

've played some terrible places in my time. The Hillbilly Ranch was the best of them, and we used to call it "The Zoo." But at least they kept it under control. Places like the Novelty Bar were the worst. We'd alternate with a rock and roll band. On a Saturday we'd start at two o'clock in the afternoon and go until midnight every half hour. On Sunday you'd start at one o'clock in the afternoon and go until one in the morning on the half hour. We got eight bucks apiece. There were fights and knives and bottles. We wouldn't even stay in there on our half hour off.

The Mohawk Ranch on the corner of Dartmouth Street and Columbus Avenue was the first place to have hillbilly music even before the Hillbilly Ranch existed. It was the only place in the world where I had a guy stick a gun in my ribs. It took ten years off my life. This turkey came in one night and wanted to exchange coats with me. The other guys — Danny Gillis and Slim Sullivan — were out at the bar drinking. It was last call. I was back where we had played, getting my coat. There was nobody there. This guy walks up to me and says, "Hey, I like your

Mohawk Ranch advertisement in all its glory. (c. 1953) Courtesy of Tex and Peggy Logan.

coat." He had on a beautiful camel's hair coat, about four times as expensive as my gabardine one. So he said, "Hey, would you like to trade?"

"That coat of yours is worth a heck of a lot more than mine."

He started to insist. "I'd like to trade." And he takes his coat off and told me to lift it. So I did.

"It's a nice, heavy coat."

"Do you know why it's so heavy?"

"No."

He goes into the right pocket and pulls out a straight razor. He puts that back in and then says, "But this is the reason it's real heavy." And he reaches into the left-hand pocket and pulls out a .38 and sticks it right in my side. He kept it there for what seemed like an hour. Then he just turned and walked out. I think he thought he was Richard Widmark.

I used to go home at night, and my wife would say, "How'd it go?" and I'd say, "Oh, things were pretty quiet."

Joe had heard of Jim and Bill and brought his friend Herb Applin with whom he had been working as a duo. After the concert they all got to talking, and Jim mentioned that they'd be playing at the 47 that week and would be rehearsing some stuff the night before. Joe and Herb said that they'd drop by. When they did Jim knew that his prayers had been answered.

Working as a duet I had to do all the singing, with an occasional harmony from Bill. It got so I would get tired of the sound of my own voice. When we added Joe and Herb we suddenly had all sorts of possibilities. Joe could sing a strong tenor lead on a lot of Bill Monroe's songs like "Georgia Rose," "Goodbye Old Pal" and "Muleskinner Blues." Herb had a voice like Ralph Stanley's so that opened up all the Stanley Brothers' material. I loved Lester Flatt's singing, and Bill was totally into Earl Scrugg's music. At the time he was transcribing all of Earl's solos note for note. We started getting into harmonies — trios and quartets — with Joe singing falsetto, like on "I Hear A Sweet Voice Calling." It was incredible. We could hardly wait to get down to the Club. It was a week night, and it was sort of slow. I remember someone saying that we were crazy to expand. We'd never make any money that way. They were right, of course, but we could have cared less, because we suddenly had what we dreamed of — a full bluegrass band — and Joe Val to boot. It was great to watch people's faces when he hit those high notes. That was one of the happiest nights of my life.

For Joe it meant the end of working in the bars. After playing for years to a motley assortment of drunks, hustlers and crazies, he was finally in a place where people loved his singing, his playing, and him.

The Club 47 was a whole different thing for me. Even though that first time we played to only a few people and only got paid a couple of dollars, it was a joy to play there. It definitely was a turning point for me. I'd put in thirteen or fourteen years in those other places. Later when I was with The Charles River Valley Boys, John Cooke would sometimes get upset if the audience was talking while we played. Siggins would be laughing about it, and I'd tell John, "Forget it. You ought to come back a few years and play some of the places I've played. This is Heaven compared to those places."

Cooke's determination to learn how to play had paid off.

Sometime after I got back from Europe in the fall of 1961 Bob and Ethan asked me if I'd like to play guitar since Clay wasn't coming back. I became a Charles River Valley boy at last. We had no bass player before Fritz joined up, and the rhythm depended on me and Ethan. Neither of us had very good rhythm, and the tempos of the songs would get totally out of hand. When we finally got Fritz it made us feel very professional, and as the spring progressed we practiced a lot and started playing at the 47 regularly. We were doing some old-timey and some bluegrass. In every set we'd do a gospel song, a frailing song, and one of the Charlie Poole songs like "Frankie and Johnny" or "Leavin' Home." Of course, my big number was "The Auctioneer" which had been a big country hit a few years earlier for Leroy Van Dyke. For a while I began to feel it was my "Over the Rainbow," and if I didn't look out, I'd be performing it when I was eighty. At the time, though, I was just happy to be playing. By the end of that spring the Club seemed to be full all the time, and we were enjoying the applause. Then one night we met Paul Rothchild, and before we knew it we were going to make a record.

Paul and his wife Terry had moved up to Cambridge a few months before they met the River Boys. He had been sent up from New York to open up a branch of a store called The Workbench.

When I got to Cambridge I looked around for two days and called Terry and said, "This is the most incredible town I've been in in my whole life! Not only is it amazingly beautiful, but there is something happening here." I didn't know what it was, but I felt it. So she came up, hadn't been in town more than ten minutes, and said, "Let's live here." A few days later I called my boss and said, "Look, I want to quit as general manager (we had six stores). Why don't you just make me manager of the new store here? I want to live here." He wouldn't go for it, and when it came down to it, I called him up and quit. I was without work for a month and a half. Finally, I got a job at Krey's Record Shop in Boston. I started just as a schlep — ground floor asshole. After about three months, I became the store manager. Then Dumont Record Distributors offered me a job as salesman for the New England territory, and I said, "Sure." I'd never done anything like that before in my life. I went out and became the number one salesman in the territory. I sold a lot of Elektra Records. Oscar Brand, Theo Bikel, Cynthia Gooding, Susan Reed. I remembered Jac Holzman from when I had worked at a small record shop in the Village, and he would deliver his own records on the back of his motor scooter. So I really went out and hustled a lot of Elektra records because there was a contest. They gave you Green Stamps, and we got our refrigerator.

During this time, we didn't know anybody. It was just Terry and me driving around town, going to art galleries. Then one night, we said, "Let's go to a coffeeshop." We had been living in Greenwich Village and going to coffeehouses there. Somebody sent us to the Cafe Yana. There was a girl singing Joan Baez songs. We had a great time and went back the next night.

Then we discovered the Golden Vanity, and later the same week we went to the Club 47. We got over there, walked in the door, and heard bluegrass for the first time in my entire life. The Charles River Valley Boys were on stage. At one point in my life, I had been a serious student of Bach, and now I heard bluegrass. It was country Bach! It had contrapuntal arrangements, all the fugal stuff. I just completely went insane. We both fell apart. We stayed the whole night. At the end, I went up to Bob Siggins and said, "Hey, listen. I'm a record distributor, and I'd like to know if you have a record, because I'll push it. I'll get it in all the shops." He said, "No, we don't have a record or anything like that." The next night, I said, "Hey, let's go hear some more of that music." So we went, and I said, "These guys have never made a record, and I'm going to ask them if they want to." I didn't know shit from Shinola about making a record. So I went up to Siggins and Ethan Signer after the set and said, "How'd you guys like to make a record?" and they said they were interested, so we all went over to my house and talked about it. I had never seen a recording contract, so I made one up. I went to the phone book and looked under "Recording." I called one place, and they just did disc recording. Then I called Steve Fassett, and he said, "Oh yeah, I record all kinds of music." I mentioned that it was "folk music," and he said, "Sure, I can do that. I've got a place we can do it." So we set up a date about two weeks later.

The more Paul came to the Club, the more he realized that his instincts were right. Every night there would be lines down the street. Every night after the Club closed, the picking would continue at somebody's house until the wee hours. The energy was there waiting to be tapped. He approached the Board of Directors of the Club and offered to start a record label — MTA 47. Paul would produce and distribute the records "nationwide." The Club would get a percentage of the profits plus the glory of having its own record label. At that point it sounded pretty good. No one else was around with a better offer, so Paul became a director and set about producing his first record.

All I knew about production was what I had imagined in my mind. I had read liner notes. In those days, Mercury Records would say what kind of microphones they used and where they were placed. So I had an inkling of what some of the technical things were about. What I *did* know was what I heard with my ears.

So we all showed up. The place he had was the Harvard Music Association Library on Beacon Hill. Fassett was a bit taken back by The Charles River Valley Boys at first. He had recorded "folk music," which was a singer with a guitar — Joan Baez and Ted Alevizos — but definitely not The Charles River Valley Boys with "What'll We Do With the Baby-O" and Fritz's washtub.

We went into this room. It was a beautiful room with lots of wood and parquet floors and lots of bookcases with glass doors in it. We opened up all the glass doors so that the books would act as dampers. I figured that out myself. He ran his mike cables from that room out to the coat room where we set up an Ampex mono tape recorder. We used two mikes. We used one for Fritz's washtub bass, and one for everything else.

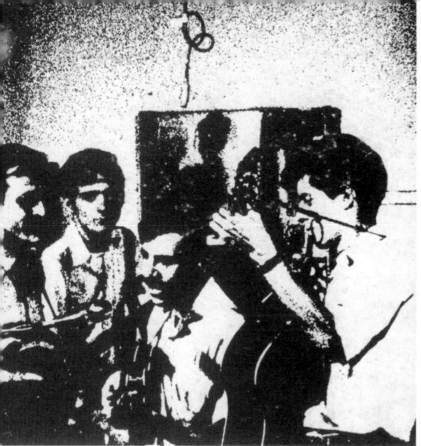

RALPH RINZLER and JOHN HERALD (1962). Photographer unknown.

We had a little two-channel mixer and headphones for both of us. I'd say to him, "No that doesn't sound close enough. It's got to feel closer." I didn't even know the word "presence." We just screwed around until we got everybody standing in the right places. I even got Eric von Schmidt and some other people to come in for the second session to be a mini-audience so that we'd get a live feel. We did only two or three takes of each tune and did it all in two days.

Then I discovered editing. I went into Steve's little shop in the basement of his house on Beacon Hill, and he taught me how to edit. I had studied conducting, and editing was another aspect of conducting. I knew the structure of music and understood how it worked. He spent about an hour doing it. Then I started — picking out the good takes and sticking them together. We did the whole thing in a day. I had made my first record. Now all we had to do was sell it. In the meantime I made plans to do another record with Keith and Rooney.

The cold winds of January were but a dim memory as spring blossomed into summer. The Club was becoming a focal point in many people's lives. Whether they were playing that night or not, performers came by to see what was happening or to sit in. It got so that people were afraid to miss a night in case they might miss a great jam. The Siggins' house had music around the clock. If it wasn't there it would be at Cooke and Ethan's on Columbia Street or at Keith and Rooney's on Dana Street. Roger Sprung had brought a contingent up from New York for a three-day St. Patrick's Day party. Eric Weissberg and Marshall Brickman came to party at Owen and Jane DeLong's. Johnny Herald and Ralph Rinzler played at the Club and all night long afterwards. The word was out in New York that the Club 47 was the place to go if you wanted to have a good time. Ralph Rinzler, for one, came away totally refreshed.

Cambridge was a real high. I remember the first time we played at Mt. Auburn Street. It was a great scene. Bill Keith was on his way to becoming a great banjo player. Jim Rooney was a sensitive singer and had a wonderful sense of humor. Bob Siggins was the perfect embodiment of the zaniness of old-time music, and Betsy — Betsy was just something else. I loved her spirit, and she became someone I could talk to later when I started trying to bring traditional musicians like Doc Watson to the north. It was just a totally different group of people compared to what you had in New York.

Many of the best parties of the summer took place at Billy Burke's place on the corner of River Street and Putnam Avenue. Billy's outlook on life had changed considerably since his parting with Elaine.

Until I got involved with all these people, I saw film as a way to make money. It was like being a plumber. You go in and make films because they pay you, not because there's some ideal film that you are striving to attain. Being in the Cambridge scene made me aware of a whole lot more than I had thought about. There was a group of people who impressed me as being into things for the experience. I didn't play music myself, and I guess one way I felt I could give something back for what I was getting out of all this was to be the party giver; and the summer of '62 was almost a continual party at my house.

It was Friday, July 14th, and Billy was ready for a good one. It was a beautiful warm evening. The next day was Bastille Day, and he was ready to raise a toast to the ideals of the French Revolution: Liberty, Equality, and Fraternity. Down at the Club, Eric von Schmidt was already rocking. He, too, was ready to celebrate. Eight years ago he had received his final discharge from the Army. *Vive la liberte!*

Maria D'Amato's friend Marlena had been telling her about Cambridge and the 47 and they had finally made it up from New York.

We were outside the Club. We didn't have the money to get in. Betsy and her friend Ruthie Buxton were sitting outside in their DR dresses, really putting on the dog. There I was in my little Goodwill denim skirt. I just thought Betsy was class personified.

Inside, Eric von Schmidt was singing, and he was doing one of those great prison songs off of the Alan Lomax Southern Prison record. Somehow I slipped in, and I went up to Eric and asked him if he knew "Rosie" or something like that. We started singing, and the next thing I knew he said, "Come along to this party," and we went over to Billy Burke's. Paul Arnoldi was there, and Geoffrey was there, all looking very blue-eyed and preppy. Betsy was there, flirting a lot with Byron and Tom Rush. And pretty soon everyone started to get into singing. Rooney and

Eric and Betsy did "Green Corn, Green Corn" and "Lost John" just singing and clapping their hands. It was fantastic. I got into it totally, and we all just sang all night long. That was my introduction to Cambridge.

That was also Cambridge's introduction to Maria, and no one forgot her. She sang a lot of country songs that night, and her voice had a beautiful sadness to it that went right to your heart. That voice was not lost on Geoff Muldaur. Geoffrey knew a good voice when he heard one. He had one himself.

When I sang, I knew I had some twists that had never been heard, because I had a quality in my voice that was really different — that vibrato. Nobody ever sang that way. I was born with it.

Geoff had grown up in Princeton, New Jersey, with Joe and Warwick Boyd. He first started listening to jazz at home.

y brother was a record collecting nut, and I listened to them a lot. I knew every soloist on every record. If I didn't he would slam me across the room. Then I went to Loomis School in Connecticut and got interested in the blues. Warwick and I started sneaking out of school into Hartford to collect records. This one place had about two-hundred and fifty thousand records — old '78's — which we would go through and get maybe fifteen records a day and come out totally black with dirt from crawling around in the stacks of records. And then one day Warwick found, next to a Patti Page record, Blind Willie Johnson's "The Rain Don't Fall On Me No More," and that was it! That was it for being totally in love with the blues. That was a spiritual moment and all that shit, and it was the best thing I had ever heard in my life, and it still is. To me, Blind Willie Johnson is still the greatest, and his "Dark Was The Night, Cold Was The Ground" is the finest musical

(left) GEOFF MULDAUR strikes a pose with BETSY SIGGINS in the basement of the Club 47 while DAVE VAN RONK calls up for more cough syrup. (c. 1962) Photograph by Byron Linardos.

(middle) Another basement shot. GEOFF MULDAUR has his back to the camera. ERIC VON SCHMIDT and ROBERT L. JONES form the rest of the trio. MITCH GREENHILL is in the background. We can tell that forehead anywhere. (c. 1963) Photograph by Byron Linardos.

(right) PAUL ARNOLDI right at home in the grass on a western hillside. Photographer unknown.

piece I have ever heard.

Then Joe Boyd and I did some things together. The first thing we did was wonder where Lonnie Johnson was. We found him in Philadelphia washing dishes in a hotel. We got him up to a party in Princeton. Joe also turned me on to Eric von Schmidt. He played me a tape he had made up in Cambridge where he was going to Harvard, I went nuts. "You mean there's another human being on earth who cares about this stuff?" That might have helped me decide to go to school in Boston. I finished low enough in my class so that I couldn't go to any of the schools where my parents would want me to go, and I went to Boston University, which was the best thing that ever happened to me.

When Geoff came around to the Club 47 he made a definite impression on everybody. Eric von Schmidt had just finished a set.
Geoff came up to me and said, "Hi, Rolf." Then when he realized his mistake he immediately quizzed me about some Jim Jackson record. I was talking to someone else, and I guess I didn't answer him right away, because I overheard Geoffrey say to somebody, "See! He doesn't know." When I was through I turned around and answered the quiz, and he just exploded, "He knows! He knows!"

Dayle Stanley was starting to sing at the Club, too. She had a voice not unlike Joan Baez except when she spoke, which was pure Boston, but she was gaining a following at the Club and heard Geoff sing somewhere and brought him in to Betsy to audition. She said, "My God, there's an angel singing in here."
I knew Blind Willie Johnson was going to kill them when they heard it. It did. They died! I mean I didn't think that much of myself. I just wanted to be a part of it all.

The summer was drawing to a close. Paul Arnoldi was getting ready to leave to go to Berkeley to study architecture. He had spent the summer filling in for John Cooke and playing adopted son to Bob and Betsy Siggins.
I was a green kid from Wyoming when I hit Cambridge. I was real shy and naive. I lived in Quincy House right across from the Club 47. I used to go over to see Joan Baez along with all the other guys, and gradually I learned how to play and got drawn into the folk scene. I could have been eaten up at any moment. I could have been devoured by Cambridge, but I wasn't. I sang songs like "Puff, the Magic Dragon," "Prairie Lullaby," and "Old Paint," which brought out the Wyoming in me. And people liked me for that. Cambridge was as pure a folk music thing as I'll ever have in my life. There's something nice about folk music — a lot of heartfelt stuff. That's what folk music is — people singing and playing simple stuff really straight.

To hear you whisper softly,
That you love me too,
Would turn all my dark clouds
To the bluest of blue.

Ain't Nobody's Business

If I knew you was gonna weep and moan,
I swear to God, I would have left you at home.
Ain't nobody's business but my own.

Dear Editor:

Why is it that coffeehouses employ such a motley bunch of folk singers?...I don't get to Boston very often, but it seems that every time I go to a coffeehouse for some relaxation, music, and coffee, I always find a bunch of dirty, ragged, emaciated people who call themselves singers standing in front of a microphone caterwauling like a dying bull moose. They must have miserable lives, because it seems as though they are always pouring their hearts out in musical form ...these singers stamp their feet so loud that it sounds as if they know they are bad and are trying to drown themselves out. (Or are they just killing some insistent vermin in their shoe?) ...Do these people actually live like they look? Are they representative of folk music and folk singers?

I would appreciate it very much if you print this letter in *Broadside* . . . As a suggestion, why don't you start a forum column where people could really let their hair down? I think that would be a real step forward for your magazine.

Sincerely,
G. Blackstone

ature abhors a vacuum. Few vacuums get filled as rapidly as blank pages that are open to anyone who wants to have his or her writings appear in public. Hardly had David Wilson published the first issue of *The Broadside* when its pages began to swell with the writings of all sorts of people connected to the growing folk scene.

The Broadside had evolved quite naturally from Dave's gradual involvement with the folk scene. He had been hooked by one of Manny Greenhill's "Nightowl" Concerts with Guy Carawan and subsequently started going to the Folksong Society concerts that Manny started at the "Y." When I came back from the Air Force in 1960, my roommate, Paul Burrell, and I got a place at 250 Newbury Street right in back of where the Unicorn was to be. I went back to the Folksong Society. It was their opening meeting of the year and I wound up being program director. I knew next to nothing about what was going on and I got plunged into it almost immediately. My first function was to put together the opening hoot. So I started going around and meeting performers and getting in touch with them.

I met Phil Spiro in the fall of '61 at a Jack Elliott concert. He was doing a couple of radio programs at M.I.T. When the 47 ran into difficulties, Phil and I helped organize hoots at the Yana and the Unicorn. Through working with Phil I started going over to his radio shows and eventually I did one of my own called "Raising a Ruckus." Then I did some live stuff at the 47. I had a run-in with Victor Oppenheimer over doing my show from the stage. I got a lot of flack about it and never really understood why. That began what was always a very tenuous relationship with the 47. I never really understood what was going on down there.

In February of '62 I started *The Broadside.* I kept discovering folk music concerts that had come and gone in the Boston area that I didn't know anything about. I thought that there should be some way to know about them. I decided that a newsletter would be the answer, so I cranked out the first one on a hectograph. I did about 900 of the first issue. Three sheets printed on one side. It was crude, but the energy was there. When I started *The Broadside* I knew absolutely nothing about publishing and had no idea of what the commitment was. All I was trying to do was to let everybody know what was going on.

It was not long before the pages of *The Broadside* were filled with a lot more than schedules and announcements. Mr. Blackstone was far from alone in wanting to express his opinions. One Ian Peerless, who used the *nom de plume* of "Torquemada" was a frequent contributor.

Club 47, kiddies, and it was jammed. Before I get into the meat of the situation, let me compliment the management on getting to actually join, and for maintaining two of the coffeehousiest cats I have ever seen! Divertisement aplenty is the word in Harvard Square!

But I was touched that night, and I did enjoy myself enormously. For one thing, the house has a feel. You feel as if something could happen here, even if it isn't happening right now. There is the smell of art there, and it is a good smell.

Also that night, I met a poet. Not a verse-writer, mind you, but a real, honest-to-goodness poet who performed in poetry and created poetry when he played. His stance was poetry. So was his attitude. His name — all that I know of it is Fritz, and he plays the washtub bass. If he errs, it is on the side of a trifle too much volume. But when he plays softly, well, the only thing I can say is that Mozart would have liked it. He sauntered to the

Torquemada's Dream. FRITZ RICHMOND searching for the perfect tone in the basement of the Club 47. (c.1962) Photograph by Stephen Fenerjian.

stage, flung his long leg onto the tub, and quite simply spoke through his instrument with a communication that I would not have believed possible. He was performing a true artistic rite by taking what was at hand and creating beauty from it. What a crime that such a sound was teamed with the raucous wheezings of Von Schmidt's unsympathetic harmonica playing! This man's subtle and evocative presentation deserves partnership with the most highly refined and acutely linear of guitars alone. He is no accompanist but a virtuoso of first calibre, and the audience knew it. In a final build-up song, it was the gradual controlled crescendo of the bass, together with the spontaneous, gentle audience singing (mostly in thirds) that turned the house into a temple for just one magic moment. Let us have an instrumental program featuring Fritz, for both he and we deserve it.

In earlier times the dictum of Torquemada would have consigned Fritz to Heaven, no doubt, and the wheezing Von Schmidt to Hell. In *The Broadside* the purple prose could be considered some kind of literary achievement and, at least, made Fritz and the author feel good.

For those who had an intense interest in folk music but could not play it, *The Broadside* became the place where they could talk about it, analyze it, categorize it, and, once in a great while, clarify it. Tom Rush's roommate, Joe Boyd, gave it a try every so often.

he anniversary issue of *The Broadside* brings to mind some general thoughts about music in particular. It has been observed often that all this coffee house and guitar business began about twenty years ago when the Lomaxes arrived in town with Leadbelly in tow and Woody Guthrie soon to follow. The music of these two men and others like Big Bill Broonzy, Josh White, and Brownie McGhee was "taken over" by the New York group of folksingers led by the Seeger family.

The post-war atmosphere around this group was full of anti-Nazi and pro-World brotherhood sentiments. It was only natural that these feelings should carry over to the music of these early pioneers of the American Folky Movement. Unfortunately, this spirit was carried to absurd extremes, and it became the fashion to sing blues, hillbilly, Scotch ballads, and African lullabies all in one plunk-a-plunk style just to show everyone

that men are the same the world over. The Weavers, of course, are an outstanding example of this unfortunate concept. Pete Seeger is about the only one who could do this and get away with it. But they were the firstest with the mostest, and the New York style became *the* style and was the dominant force in folk music until the last few years.

A few years ago, as all you chillun know, there was this girl, and she had long black hair, and one day she sang at the Newport Folk Festival, and she signed a record contract, and it sold many copies, and she became a national heroine and bought a house in Big Sur and a sports car. The important thing about this was that her success called attention to a new approach to folk music which had been brewing in Boston for several years and was very different from the approach which has been so popular for so long. It wasn't that she cared any less about peace and integration and things like that. Far from it. But she refused to let her political opinions get in the way of her music. She tried to sing everything the way it was really sung at the headwaters. And ethnic suddenly became a household word.

Slowly but surely the word has spread. Folk music has real potential as music and not just as a platform for liberalism. The music sung

JOE BOYD (in sunglasses) greets GEOFF MULDAUR like a long lost brother at the 1965 Newport Folk Festival. Photograph by Rick Sullo.

by the people of the world is not the same. Just because you sing blues as closely as possible to the way a Southern Negro might sing it and Bluegrass as close as possible to the way Lester Flatt sings, it does not mean that you are a segregationist.

Joan Baez' "Letter to the New Yorkers" ushered in the year of the specialist. Eric von Schmidt doesn't sing "Homestead on the Farm." Jim Rooney doesn't sing "Goin' Down Slow." Don MacSorley doesn't sing "Rag Mama." Jim Kweskin doesn't sing "Wee Cooper o'Fife." The tide has turned. Being ethnic is beginning to sell. Bobby Darrin recorded Blind Lemon's "See That My Grave Is Kept Clean." And it all started here. Ain'tcha proud?

Much of what appeared in *The Broadside* was of a less edifying nature and could probably be classified as insider's chit-chat and gossip. First names abounded. It was always George or Byron or Betsy or Manny who was doing something or other. Perhaps this made the readers at large feel like they were getting a peek backstage, but many felt that it was a little chummier than the reality. *The Broadside* was becoming a little world of its own that was feeding off the energy created by the musical community. For better or worse, the Club 47 had become the central focus of the musical energy of the community. The musicians

existed whether or not there was a *Broadside*. They appreciated the help and the publicity, but often they felt that much of what was written had more to do with the writer than the music or the performer. If there was a fault to be found with the magazine, it was that it was too "nice." Very rarely was anyone except the most commercial hack criticized. Every artist had his positive points. Everyone was worth going to see. Every club had a good lineup. It was as if there were no musical standards by which folk music could be judged. The feeling seemed to be that effort was what really counted. For anyone who took his music seriously, *The Broadside* was not where he could look for informed, musical criticism. Wilson's own approach to folk music was, admittedly, not musical.

I approached folk music from a literary point of view more than anything else. I'm a word freak. It was always the words that had a meaning for me for a long, long time. Somewhere along the way the music snuck up on me. But the lyrics were what really grabbed me. Jack Elliott knocked me out with his version of the "1913 Massacre." I also loved Robert L. Jones' singing of ballads and Guthrie songs. I listened to Woody and Cisco Huston a lot.

It was probably because of this point of view that he did feel out of place at the 47 and why the

people at the 47 never really supported *The Broadside*. For them, the music was the thing, and as far as they were concerned, they were the center of the musical scene in Cambridge and Boston. As a result, despite his good intentions, Wilson always remained apart from the 47 and felt that his efforts to promote the Boston/Cambridge scene were unappreciated by many of those who he felt were most benefited.

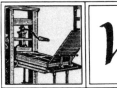hen I asked the people at the 47 to sell *The Broadside* for 10¢ a copy they refused, saying it would jeopardize their non-profit status. So I went next door and put them in Cahaly's, but that always left me feeling that there was something wrong there. If they had said that they didn't want to sell it because they didn't like it for specific reasons I could have accepted it. My intuition was that some of the people involved in the 47 at that time were very protective of their positions as taste-makers and wanted to be the main focus of the attention given this evolving folk scene. They either saw us as competition or possible dilution of that focus.

Gradually we expanded the focus of the magazine beyond just informing people about what was going on. We found that we had an audience outside Boston. In a sense, people outside Boston had more respect for *The Broadside* than people in Boston. A lot of the performers in town either were not interested in writing for us or disdained us. Performers outside of Boston said, "Sure, we like what you're doing. We'll write for you."

As far as the general readership of *The Broadside* was concerned, all of this was beside the point. They were getting information about the folk scene which they could use as they would. They could find out who was playing in all the coffee houses in Boston and Cambridge, as well as coffee houses that had opened at various colleges and in outlying areas like Worcester, Ipswich, and Martha's Vineyard. They could get some idea of what was going on in New York and Philadelphia; concerts anywhere in the New England area were publicized. By reading advertisements they could find out where to buy records, books, and instruments, where they could find folk music on the radio, and where to get lessons on various instruments. None of this had existed three years previous, and the existence of *The Broadside* made it possible for the "folk market" to be reached by

those who had products and services relating to folk music. The very fact of the paper meant that folk music was becoming a business.

Business was certainly what was on Paul Rothchild's mind in the fall of '62 — the record business.

I had become a director of the Club 47, and the label was theirs. MTA Records and I had dreams of the Club becoming an entertainment empire. Part of the sales were through the Club. The Club got a piece of those sales, and I think we sold a third of our 1,000 Charles River Valley Boys records there. Then, of course, I took them with me in my regular route, telling the shop owners about this hot new record.

In the meantime, Paul went ahead with his plans to record Keith and Rooney. Once again the sessions were done in the Marsh Room of the Harvard Music Association Library on Beacon Hill. In addition to Joe Val, Herb Applin, and Fritz, Jim and Bill got Herb Hooven to play fiddle. Herb had recorded with Jimmy Martin and the Sunny Mountain Boys and had been working with the Lilly Brothers. Herb was going to get fifty dollars for his efforts, which was little enough considering what he added to the performances. The sessions went very well. For the first time in his career Joe was recorded, and he rose to the occasion on "Muleskinner Blues." Jim got a chance to do "One Morning In May" and "Moonshiner," which were his two favorite songs to sing at the time. But the unquestionable highlight of the recording was Bill Keith's phenomenal banjo playing on a medley of two fiddle tunes — "The Devil's Dream" and "The Sailor's Hornpipe." No one before had been able to play fiddle tunes note for note within the Scruggs' style. Bill had been working on it for months. He did the medley in one take, faster than he had ever played it before. At the end of the take everyone was breathless. They had done it! Or had they? There was one note that was off. What to do? The take was so perfect otherwise that they didn't think they could capture it again. Paul said that he could fix it and not to worry. Steve and Paul took the tapes over to Steve's basement and set to work.

Paul liked editing with me. I remember him remarking that I was the only person in the world he would trust to edit the original tape without making a safety first. He himself was awfully good at editing. On Bill Keith's recording of the "Devil's Dream" there was one clinker on it, and he found the same note somewhere else in the song, recorded it, and put

it in the place of the bad note. He was very clever at superintending something like that, because musically he was very secure. I really enjoyed working with him very much. What I didn't enjoy was that he was a bit of a crook. At least by my morality. He would run up a bill of five or six hundred dollars, and then he would take that money and play with it on the stock market or something instead of paying you on time. It was always a feeling of having to squeeze, and I didn't like that.

Paul might have been secure musically, but financially things were starting to get a bit shakey.
All of this was financed out of an insurance settlement I had got from a totalled Jaguar sedan. I was paying for the recording, jackets, pressing — everything. Although the River Boys record was selling, it wasn't fast enough to recoup the investment. By the time I was in the middle of wrapping up the Keith and Rooney record, I was in a financial bind.

Jim Rooney knew nothing of all this until he got a phone call one day.

erb Hooven called looking for his fifty bucks, which we had promised him six weeks before. Then I found out that Fassett hadn't been paid and wasn't going to finish the tapes. All of this was going on underground. Nobody knew anything about it, and I was getting madder and madder. Paul was

PAUL ROTHCHILD (c.1964) *Photograph by John Cooke.*

out and about looking like a million bucks. He had an Alfa Romeo and big electrostatic speakers at home. Meanwhile, Herbie Hooven was calling me, and Paul kept saying, "Oh, didn't Terry send that out yet?" The check was "in the mail" for three or four weeks, and it went on and on and on. Then, Paul told me that I was meddling in his personal business, that he had the money in the stock market, and that I should butt out. He also mentioned that the real cause of the delay was that Eric von Schmidt hadn't finished the art work for the cover. I called Eric, and he said that he had been waiting for some photographs that Byron had.

That night I went down to the Club to get the photographs. Paul was working the door. I told him I was going to take the photographs over to Eric. Eric was up at his studio on Brattle Street. I went over there and told him my troubles.

We were sitting there having some rum and playing a couple of songs when I heard some little footsteps coming up the stairs. It was Paul.

"Jim, this is the second time today you've meddled in my affairs."

"What do you mean, Paul? All I did was to bring these photographs from Byron over here to try to expedite things. You said that Eric was holding up the works."

"Those are my photographs, Jim. I paid for them."

At this point Eric said, "Hey, Paul. Come on. Sit down and have a drink, and let's talk this over."

"I'm sorry, Eric, I don't want a drink."

"Come on, Paul. Sit down."

Paul was not going for it, and then Eric just took Paul by the collar, picked him up, and threw him across the room into the corner where he had a big pile of turpentine rags and collage scraps! I

PAUL ROTHCHILD talking to BOB DYLAN. BOB DYLAN talking to the photographer. (1964) Photograph by John Cooke.

couldn't believe it! Paul was over there in a heap. Eric was yelling at him. I was yelling at Eric to stop. "There goes our record," was what I was thinking. But it was also funny. Paul picked himself up and went back down the stairs, and Eric and I just sat there laughing and drinking more rum. It was beautiful.

The next day I sent Paul a letter:

Dear Paul:

You can #1 — pay everybody.

or #2 — I'll bring it up before the Board of the Club.

Blah, Blah, Blah.

I think I sent it registered mail. I'd had it.

Paul was home wondering what to do when his phone rang.

I got a call from Manny Greenhill. He said,

"I've got a man in my office who wants to meet you, and I'm going to put him on."

I heard his voice. "Hey, are you da guy who produced the Charles River Valley Boys record?" I said that I was. So he said, "Well, listen, I want to talk to you about that and some other things."

Then Manny got on the phone and asked me if I could come to a meeting right away. I was on my way. I went over there and met Bob Weinstock, the head of Prestige Records. Manny had showed him the Charles River Valley Boys record. He got Steve Fassett to send over the Keith and Rooney tape. He said, "I want to buy the masters of these records, and I want to buy you."

I thought to myself, "Hallelujah! Hallelujah! The door to show business has opened!"

In those days there were about five producers — people who were actually making records. So I said, "Hey, I'm yours. What do you want me to do? Let me start a folk label for you."

They already had a fantastic jazz label, and they had the Bluesville label with Rev. Gary Davis and Dave Van Ronk. Jack Elliott was on the label. It all excited me, and I said, "Yeah, I'll do it," and I was thinking, "Oh boy! Here it comes. Gravy train." Then we started talking about money. He offered me $100.00 per week. I was crushed, really crushed. It meant moving to Bergenfield, New Jersey, one town away from where I was raised, which wasn't my idea of a good time. So we argued for a while in Manny's office, and I got him up to $135.00 per week. But it was one of those times when you decide that it is something you have to do. The money isn't important. A door has opened, and you've got to walk through.

Paul's good fortune turned out to be everybody's. Not only did the Charles River Valley Boys and Keith and Rooney become Prestige recording "artists," but in the next few months Paul recorded "The Folk Blues" with Eric von Schmidt, "Sleepy Man Blues" with Geoff Muldaur, and "Got a Mind to Ramble" with Tom Rush. All of these records captured the fresh energy that was flowing in Cambridge at the time. Everyone was still pretty close to their sources and were still a long way from coming into their own, but the feeling was there, the heart was there, and the music was there. Like Paul, everyone was learning to skate at the same time, and no one was falling down a lot. And once in a while someone would come up with a figure eight that would take your breath away. People were getting good and that made them want to get better.

What Paul didn't get, Maynard Solomon did. Jackie Washington made his first album, and Robert L. Jones did part of a "new folks" album, both for Vanguard Records. What had been purely fun and frolic just a few months ago was becoming a bit more serious. It was beginning to look like a person could even think about making a living out of playing folk music if he wasn't careful.

Ain't nobody's business, kid,
Who in the world I do my business with.
Ain't nobody's business but mine.

Foggy Mountain Top

If I were on some foggy mountain top,
I'd sail away to the west.
I'd sail all around this whole wide world,
To the girl that I love the best.

he Siggins' were having another going-away party for Bill Keith, but this time Bill was really going away. Bill had been trying to leave for some time, but things kept getting in his way, and he could never seem to quite make it out the door. At last, he was really going all the way to Washington, D.C. Jim Rooney, more than anyone else, had mixed feelings about it.

Through our friend Tom Morgan in Washington, Bill got a chance to go play with Red Allen and Frank Wakefield and The Kentuckians. We had seen them in New York, and Frank Wakefield just blew everybody away with his mandolin break on "Little Birdie." Red's records with the Osborne Brothers were incredible, and now they wanted Bill to come and play with them. Bill would be able to stay at Tom's. He was an excellent craftsman who made beautiful banjo necks and mandolins. Bill would be able to use his shop to work on projects of his own, so it looked like a good thing to do.

I talked to Bill about it. He really wanted to do it, but it was a big jump. It meant leaving home and leaving Cambridge where this incredible scene was happening. I think he was feeling bad about leaving me in the lurch, and I was sorry to see our band break up after just having recorded; but I said, "If you don't do it, you're going to regret it for the rest of your life. This is a chance to go with a real band and to get into playing full-time."

So he did it. Plunged right into some hillbilly craziness. He played with them at a bunch of places around Washington and Baltimore. They would drive to Wheeling in a car to play the Jamboree. We'd listened to that show so many times on the radio, and Bill was looking forward to actually playing on it. The reality was pretty funky. They did the show, went back to a hotel room where Red and Frank took turns screwing some whore, and then drove back to Washington. Red hit Bill up for five bucks on the way, which didn't go over too big. Bill's a real Yankee about money.

Bill was rapidly learning about "the pleasures of life in a hillbilly band," but it was an education which would prepare him well for the next step. Playing with Red and Frank was real. It was a little band, unrehearsed, fighting for survival in the bars. I lived in the attic at Tom's. We'd rehearse very occasionally. Red was loaded half the time,

and Frank would be cutting up worse than ever. We played two or three nights a week. The rest of the time I was copying tapes and writing tablature or working in Tom's shop inlaying or shaping or setting up stuff. But it didn't seem permanent to me. I kept coming back to Cambridge for my Air Force meeting every month. It wasn't that far away.

Then Earl Scruggs happened to be playing in Baltimore. Manny Greenhill was booking Flatt and Scruggs some back then, and he introduced me to Earl at the concert. Manny knew that I had written out many of Earl's solos and had me show them to him. He invited me to come to Nashville to do the tablature for his instruction book.

For Bill Keith, receiving an invitation from Earl Scruggs to go to Nashville was like having God ask a preacher if he'd like to go to Heaven. By this time Bill had spent literally thousands of hours listening to and learning to play and writing down Earl's solos and developing a system of notation which would enable anyone who wanted to learn that style to play it exactly and well. Having Earl ask him to come and work on his book said a lot about the quality of his work. At the time Earl didn't know exactly how he was going to publish the book. He offered Bill several hundred dollars for his work, and said that he wished it could be more, but that if the book were successful he hoped that he could pay Bill more in the future. Earl's word was enough for Bill. Some years later Bill noted that the book received an award for selling more than one million dollars' worth of copies. He was still waiting to hear from Earl about that extra money.

At one point during his stay Earl took Bill into Nashville to see the Grand Ole Opry. The Opry was in the old Ryman Auditorium then, and backstage there were a number of funky dressing rooms which were always jammed with musicians warming up and just picking. At some point Bill got his hands on a banjo and started to play. When, at Earl's request, he got into the "Devil's Dream," heads started to turn. Standing on the outskirts of the crowd were Bill Monroe and his fiddler Kenny Baker. When Keith finished playing they went out without saying anything, but later Kenny came back in and started talking to Bill and asked him what he was doing. Bill told him what he had been up to, and Kenny said, "If you want to play with Monroe, you've got a job." Bill was floored. He told Kenny that he'd have to give Red and Frank notice and get back to Cambridge to really pack, but that he'd be back in about a month to begin work.

JIM ROONEY and BILL KEITH (1962) Photograph by Eric von Schmidt.

*I*t was hard for Bill Keith, from Brockton, Massachusetts, whose family was firmly rooted in New England, who had gone to Exeter and Amherst with the expectation that he would go on to the Harvard Business School and ultimately into some respectable business, to believe that he was instead going to announce to his family and friends that he was about to become a Bluegrass Boy. He was going to Nashville to play with Bill Monroe.

It was a funny trip to leave Cambridge; to get in the car with a bunch of stuff and go down there and do it. For me that was a big jump. Washington was still not that far from New York or Boston, but when you got off into Virginia and then Bristol and beyond, you were pretty far away. This was before the Interstate. I remember arriving and staying in the Clarkson Hotel. Hotels began to be a major factor in my lifestyle. Life on the road. Carrying all you need in two hands. All at a pretty funky level, because at that time Monroe was not making much money and barely paid the minimum.

Within two weeks of his joining the band, Bill recorded with Monroe. As it turned out, it was the only recording he would do with him. Monroe was fascinated by Keith's style. He loved fiddle tunes and was impressed that Bill had obviously put so much time into trying to play them right. They did both "The Devil's Dream" and "The Sailor's Hornpipe" and a tune that Monroe called "Santa Claus." It was typical of Monroe to record Bill so early. He liked to throw a person into the water to see if he could swim. Keith played better than he ever had in his life.

My playing got a lot better fast. It had been a waking-hours occupation for a year or more by the time I got there, and now I had the additional factor of the interplay with Monroe which I valued a lot. It was the real thing: live music, not records and a lot of unspoken direction from Bill. There was a kind of permissiveness where he let a lot of things happen in the music rather than have it spelled out beforehand. There was an improvisation thing which he did and which he wanted other people to do. To a great extent the fiddle tunes that I had learned and taken down there were set pieces and didn't allow for much improvisation, so I really had to abandon that way of playing except on fiddle tunes because it just didn't lend itself to improvisation.

If anything epitomized that particular era when I worked with Bill it was the Oldsmobile station wagon that had over three hundred thousand miles on it. I was in it when the steering gear fell out; I was in it at five o'clock in the morning when the transmission hose blew off. Five people and the bass and all our instruments and luggage were in the car at the time.

A lot of people from Cambridge were hitting the road that Spring. John Cooke and Billy Burke drove out to Berkeley in John's Volvo. If Cooke were the hillbilly he said he wanted to be he would have had a back yard filled with the grinning grilles of countless Volvos. Robert L. Jones and Geoff Muldaur were also taking a trip to California in Jones' blue 1956 Ford. The highest praise that Jones could give his car was that it "made it." Jim Rooney convinced Jones that Nashville was on the way to California and hitched a ride. Woody Guthrie would have approved of Jones' driving style: He talked and sang to his car, quietly urging it on, nursing it through various minor water and tire troubles until the Nashville skyline came into view. Rooney was glad to see his old partner Bill.

BILL MONROE. Publicity shot by Dave Gahr.

We arrived on the day that Keith was moving out of the Clarkson Hotel where he'd been staying with Del McCoury. Del was Monroe's lead singer and guitar player at the time. Ralph Rinzler had come down to Nashville to try to be Monroe's manager, and they had just scored a great apartment out off of West End Avenue. It was the upstairs of Anne and Paul Leeper's big old house. Paul was a food broker. He was mostly into fishing and having a good time. He and Anne had a bunch of young kids, and I don't think they'd ever had anything to do with musicians before. That was all to change. Their place came to be known as The Bluegrass Rest Home, and before it was all over they were up to their ears in music and musicians — from Bill and Ralph and Del to Pete Rowan, Richard Green, and Chris Gantry.

The day after we got there, Jones and Muldaur and the rest of us were all sitting around playing when the door flew open and in came Bill Monroe and Bessie Lee, his woman and bass player at the time. Bessie had her arms full of pies and homemade mayonnaise and all sorts of food that she had made, and she went into the kitchen. Bill just sort of stood there grinning at us through his thick glasses. I guess we were sort of startled, and who knows what we looked like to him. I introduced myself, as did Geoffrey and Jones, and we all sat down. Here I was in the presence of the "King of Bluegrass," and I couldn't think of anything to say that seemed to make any sense. He asked us how the trip down had been. Jones started telling him about his car, and gradually we all loosened up.

There was a guitar lying around. He picked it up and started picking on it. I don't know why, but I was amazed that he could play the guitar. I only knew that he could play the mandolin. I could see Geoffrey's jaw drop, as he watched Monroe's fingers dance on that guitar. It was the most natural thing in the world for him to be playing like that, and we were just sitting there with our faces hanging out. Then he just stopped right in the middle of what he was playing and handed the guitar to me. I panicked. I broke out in a sweat. I had to do something. All I remember was that I played something in "D." I felt totally stupid and scared. After what he had just done, my little upside-down, left-handed style seemed really dumb. When I got through he said, "That's good.

You've got your own lick on that. Keep that up. That's good." That meant a lot to me. I'd never really thought of what I did as being "my own" or original, but it was, and he made me aware of that and made me want to keep at it and improve what I was doing instead of being ashamed of it.

Jones and Muldaur got back on the road the next day, and I settled in for a few weeks. I started to get some small idea of what Monroe's life was like and what it meant to suddenly have these boys from Cambridge and New York taking an interest in him. He had been having some lean times. At one time in the mid-forties he had been one of the biggest stars on the Grand Ole Opry. He sold a lot of records and made a lot of money. Flatt and Scruggs got their start with him. Don Reno, Mac Wiseman, Jimmy Martin, Carter Stanley, Sonny Osborne, Don Stover, Vassar Clements, Gordon Terry, and countless others had been Bluegrass Boys and had gone on to successful careers of their own. Then the bottom fell out of country music. Elvis Presley changed everything almost overnight. Ironically, the song he did it with was Bill Monroe's "Blue Moon of Kentucky." In order to survive, country music had to change. Soon, under the direction of Chet Atkins, drums, backup vocalists, and electric guitars were on everything. But they weren't on Bill Monroe's records. He would not change his music, and it cost him. When Bill Keith and I first saw him in 1960 at Watermelon Park in Virginia, he didn't even have a regular band. That's why he still had that Oldsmobile station wagon when Keith joined him. He couldn't afford anything else.

Ralph Rinzler had idolized Monroe for years. As a member of the Greenbriar Boys he had worked with Joan Baez and knew that there was a growing northern market for Monroe's music. Louise Scruggs had realized it from the start and had sent Earl up to Newport in 1959 and again in 1960. Through Manny Greenhill, Flatt and Scruggs had done concerts with Joan Baez and were beginning to play lucrative college dates. They were being hailed as the inventors of bluegrass, which Alan Lomax described as "folk music in overdrive." It pained Ralph to think that all of this was happening and that it was all passing Monroe by. He determined to do something about it. When he discovered that Keith was going to be playing with Monroe, it just reinforced his thinking that the time was right for Monroe to plug into the "folk world."

But Monroe was a hard man to help. One day while I was there Ralph got all dressed up. He was going over to Decca Records to talk to Harry Silverstein about Bill's contract; he was going to see to it that Decca understood that there were some folk labels up north, like Vanguard, who just might like to take someone like Monroe away from Decca if they didn't give him a good new contract. Ralph was ready to give him a good earful. When he got back that afternoon, he was furious. Just as he was getting into his pitch Harry Silverstein told him, "Ralph, I don't know what we're talking about. Bill just signed a five-year contract with us last year." Monroe had told Ralph nothing about it and just let him go in there and make a fool of himself.

I didn't get a chance to go out on the road with them because there wasn't room in the car, but I did get to go up to Beanblossom where Bill had a little country music park. He has a big bluegrass festival up there now, but back then it was pretty pitiful. We left Nashville after Monroe finished playing the Opry. It was a gas to see Keith out there on that historic Opry stage wearing his cowboy hat. Monroe stepped up to the microphone and said, "We've got a fine young banjo picker with us from Brockton, Massachusetts. His name is Brad Keith, and we're going to feature him on a number that I wrote entitled 'Roanoke.'" With that, Monroe lit into it at a terrific clip. When Keith's break came he tore it up. It was brilliant. He got a huge hand from the audience and a bigger one from the pickers backstage. He was a real phenomenon down there. He was turning all the banjo pickers' heads around. Monroe was all smiles.

When Bill got off I asked him, "What's all this 'Brad' stuff?"

He said, "Well, when I came to work with Bill he asked me what my name was. I said, 'Bill Keith.' Then he said, 'Well, what do people call you?' I said, 'Bill.' Then he said, 'What's your real name? Your full name?' I told him, 'William Bradford Keith.' So he said, 'I'll call you Brad,' because there's just one Bill in Bill Monroe's band, and that's Bill Monroe," and Keith just smiled one of his Keith smiles.

I drove up with Del McCoury and Keith. Monroe was ahead of us in the station wagon with Bessie, Kenny Baker, and Del Wood, who was going to split the show with Monroe at Beanblossom. "Miss Del' was a big woman who played the hell out of the piano. She'd had a million-seller on "Down Yonder" a few years back, and the Opry audiences loved her. The old station wagon was riding mighty low with both Bessie and Del in it. The bass fiddle and a couple of fighting cocks were riding on top. Bill liked to fight cocks in his spare time — he was definitely from Kentucky.

Sometime about six in the morning we were on a real flat stretch of road in Indiana. Monroe had stopped somewhere for gas, and we were all alone. Keith had a two-door Chevy coupe with a hot 327 engine, four on the floor, and overdrive. We used to call it the "science teacher's model." He fooled a lot of people with that car. He hadn't had it too long, and he said in that laconic way of his, "I think I'll see what this thing can do." McCoury was asleep in the back seat. He was definitely one of the most laid-back individuals I've ever met. Nothing got him excited. As the speedometer needle hit 120 he sort of woke up, lifted his head, looked around, and said, "What's going on?" I said, "Del, you don't even want to know. Go back to sleep." And he just lay back down. Bill was laughing hysterically.

You could tell you were getting close to Beanblossom when you got to Gnaw Bone. A few more miles down the road we came to the "park." It wasn't much more than a converted horse shed with a field to park in. There was a Coca-Cola sign up on top that said, "BILL MONBOE'S BROWN COUNTY JAMBOREE." The sign man had mistaken the "R" for a "B." Bill put it up anyway; it seemed to go with the place.

Keith immediately crashed on a picnic table, and everyone else did their best to catch a few winks. Everyone but Monroe, that is. He spent the time puttering about with his older brother, Birch, who was running the place. Birch was Mr. Slowmotion. God knows what he did up there all the time, but if the results were any indication, he didn't do much. Inside the shed was a little stage at one end, finished off to look like a log cabin. There was one microphone. Out in front were about a hundred folding chairs and some plank benches. In the back was a little kitchen area with a stove and a refrigerator. The toilets were out back. Way out back.

Sometime after noon a few people began to show up. Monroe was out at the entrance in his shirtsleeves taking the money. Ralph arrived with an English friend, Barry Murphy, who was also staying at the Leeper's, and they took over the gate while Bill went to change into a suit. By two o'clock about a hundred people were there, and the show began. A local bluegrass band kicked it off, then "Miss Del" did her best to coax "Down Yonder" out of what there was of a piano, and finally it was time for Bill Monroe and the Bluegrass Boys. The audience immediately came to life, calling out requests, and applauding breaks. It was a good show, and you never would have known from watching Monroe that the shabbiness of the surroundings or the smallness of the crowd meant anything to him at all. They were there to see him, and he gave them his best. I've thought about that a lot over the years when I'd start to bitch about a bad gig. His music was evidently enough for him, and that's what had kept him going through all those lean years. He was a tough man.

That night Bill did another show. This time there were only about fifty people, but he still did a full show, and it was getting on towards eleven when it was finally over. At Bill's request, Del McCoury and Kenny were going to stay up to do some work on the latrines and the fences. That, too, was part of being a Bluegrass Boy. "Miss Del" was going back with us, as was Barry. Keith was waiting for Monroe to pay him before we left. Monroe and Ralph were over in the shed talking. As we sat there we could hear snatches of the conversation. Ralph had a tendency to huff and puff when he got excited, and he was huffing and puffing a lot.

ROY ACUFF, "The King of Country Music," and BILL MONROE are all smiles as they listen to "BRAD" KEITH play on the Grand Ole Opry. (1963) Photograph courtesy of Bill Keith.

Following Page:
"From Brockton to Beanblossom" (left to right) BESSIE LEE MAULDIN, BILL MONROE, MELISSA MONROE, JOE STUART, BILL KEITH and DEL McCOURY. Photographer unknown. Courtesy of Bob Siggins.

He was talking to Bill about Brother Birch and how slow he was and how the park needed a live wire to run it and build it into something. Ralph was treading on dangerous ground. Before we knew it, Monroe materialized at the car. "Miss Del, you're going to stay up here tonight and go back with Bessie tomorrow. I'm going now." That was that. He didn't ask. He just told her. She was great. She just got out, and he got in. He closed the door and said, "I'm aggravated. Let's go." He didn't say another word until we got to Nashville.

Bill Keith played with Bill Monroe for several months after that. Despite his trials and tribulations, Ralph managed to connect Monroe with the folk world. He played at the Ash Grove in Los Angeles, for the Friends of Old Time Music in New York, and at the Newport Folk Festival. It was the beginning of a whole new career for Monroe. Through Keith he realized that his music had meant as much to others as it did to him, although they might have gone to college and grown up in the suburbs or the city. There was a universality in his music that broke all barriers. Bill Keith had given back as much as he had taken, and then some.

Shortly before Ralph went to Nashville to manage Bill Monroe's affairs, he had gone to North Carolina on a collecting trip. He had located Clarence Ashley, a fine old-time banjo player and singer who had recorded songs such as "The Coo Coo Bird" and "The House Carpenter" back in the twenties. His recordings were among the classics included in Harry Smith's *Anthology of American Folk Music* on Folkways Records. Ashley was very much alive when Ralph found him, and was still actively playing in the Bristol, Tennessee area. Ralph went with Clarence and some others to a place where they were playing. The guitar player along for the ride was a "blind boy" they called "Doc" — Doc Watson. When Ralph heard Doc play he was astonished. He couldn't believe his ears — he was the best he had ever heard. As far as the others were concerned, Doc was a cripple because he was blind, and they were doing him a favor by letting him play with them for a few dollars.

Ralph recorded enough for two Folkways'

DOC WATSON *at Newport '63 with* JOHN COHEN *and* MIKE SEEGER. *Photograph by John Cooke.*

albums which were entitled *Old Time Music at Clarence Ashley's*. Doc's guitar playing became a sensation. Ralph knew immediately that Doc would find an audience in the folk world, but Doc had never travelled before, had never been a professional entertainer, and Ralph wanted to make sure that his first experience performing was a good one. He thought of all the people he knew in Cambridge that already loved this music, and called Betsy Siggins to arrange for Doc to play at the Club 47.

Cambridge was very fertile turf. When I was trying to get Doc Watson started it seemed right to go there as frequently as possible. People there really got into Doc as a person, whereas in New York he was always treated as a phenomenon who played hot licks. You didn't really have any human interchange there. It was like taking a bath in humanity when you'd come up to Cambridge. I really thought that our visits there were an extraordinary experience. And so did Doc.

When Ralph talked to Betsy about Doc's appearance he asked her to find Doc a place to stay. Betsy's house was out of the question: it was total chaos twenty-four hours a day. Keith and Rooney's was available, but awkward since it was two floors, up one flight. Jim asked Nancy Sweezy if Doc could stay at her house. She had a spare bedroom on the main floor and the layout was perfect. Nancy immediately said yes.

I had an empty space waiting for a new experience in the early sixties, for I was then just divorced and caring for three children in mid-growth. My oldest child, Sam, was at the Woodstock School in Vermont and brought visitors home from school, including Carol Langstaff, whose central interest was music. Carol came to live at our home on Agassiz Street after leaving Woodstock, and entranced us with her ballad singing and dulcimer playing. Through her, Sam, Lybess, Moophy, and I were introduced to musicians and the Club 47 where she occasionally performed. Soon we knew many players and many of the supporting cast — the good and faithful listeners. I began dropping in at the 47, and my children did, too. It was the music, of course. One participated by merely listening. It reached in and got you...and there were all those responsive people near you being "gotten" too.

(top) CLARENCE ASHLEY. Photograph by John Cooke.

(bottom)
THE HOUSE OF BEAUTIFUL WOMEN.
(top, l. to r.) CAROL LANGSTAFF, NANCY SWEEZY; (bottom, l. to r.) MOOPHY SWEEZY, LYBESS SWEEZY. Nancy photographed by Charles Tompkins. Others by Charlie Frizzell.

Eventually I began to help out at the Club as a way of giving back some of what I was getting, but my more important contribution was in offering our house for gatherings and for putting up musicians who travelled from afar to play at the Club. My children and I had glimpses into other kinds of lives — and the flavor of the South came in the door.

Once I went shopping in Harvard Square with Libba Cotten who wrote "Freight Train." She needed a sweater. In Corcoran's she found what she wanted by looking through the glass counter and then asked if I would please buy it. She put the money into my hand, and it dawned on me that she did not want to risk dealing with the white woman behind the counter. One can read endless words about discrimination and not learn as much or as fast.

Carol Langstaff had opened up a whole new world for Nancy and her family. They, in turn, opened up themselves and their home for a steady stream of visiting musicians who were a long way from home. The Sweezy house was known to some as the "House of Beautiful Women" (Sam excepted). Moophy was the youngest and took it all in from her special vantage point.

he Club 47 was like a second home for me, and, conversely, my house was like a second home for the Club. Often music adjourned from the stage to my living room after the Club closed for the night. I could doze off around midnight on the couch, listening to the rich guitar and voice of Doc Watson. I was a lucky kid.

I must have been eight or nine when my family was first introduced to the Club by Carol Langstaff, who moved into our house on Agassiz Street. I remember opening the door to find this tall skinny girl loaded down with luggage standing there waiting to come in. I just stood there eyeing her suspiciously until she had to invite herself in. That was Carol, or Sunshine as she was called then. She was a teenager and quite wild and a constant source of fun for me. It seemed when Carol was around there were always picnics by the river or trips to the beach, parties to go to, and, of course, music.

Doc Watson stayed with us when he came to Cambridge. He knew our house so well that he remarked if any of the furniture was changed or moved around. I could find him in the afternoon sitting in the living room by himself, playing softly, and then I would ask for my special favorites. Once I asked him to play "Long Black Veil" for me at the Club that night. It was getting late and I thought he had forgotten, when suddenly he said he was going to sing a song for a little girl that he knew and wondered if she were still there to hear it. I opened my mouth to say, "Yes," but nothing came out until, after what seemed an endless silence, my sister kicked me, and I croaked out with embarrassment that I was still there. At home, in the kitchen in the morning, we would meet over breakfast, and Doc liked to tell stories about the mountains in the South where he lived, and I had never been. I was fascinated — it was another world.

If it was a long way from Brockton to Beanblossom, it was a long way from Deep Gap to Cambridge. At both ends of the line what made all the difference was the way the music brought people together. The young Cambridge pickers and singers were starting to go beyond the records. They were getting out and around the country and meeting the artists whose music meant so much to them. Those artists were, in turn, coming to Cambridge to find that there was a whole new generation of young people who wanted to hear their music, to share their reality. When Doc Watson sang "Amazing Grace" at the 47, everybody sang with him and felt blessed by his presence. When Jim Rooney and Bob Siggins played with the great old-time fiddler and banjo player, Hobart Smith, they felt as if they had finally gotten into the heart and soul of the music that they had been trying to play for so long. And when Hobart died, his wife Brookie wrote them as if they were his sons. When Almeda Riddle came from Arkansas she was taken to see the Atlantic Ocean about which she had sung in ballads for years but had never seen. Bessie Jones blessed many a table with her Georgia Sea Island table grace. Bill Monroe fried steaks for everybody when he finally got to stay at Keith and Rooney's Bluegrass Rest Home #2. No one was left to sit alone in a hotel room when they came to Cambridge; they were made part of the family which had gradually been developing there, and the Cambridge people became a part of their family and were getting ready to pass their tradition on as they received it *personally*. They were moving beyond the notes and the forms into the spirit and the feeling. Folk music was helping them become people. It was creating a home for them anywhere in the world they happened to be.

JIM ROONEY and BOB SIGGINS accompany HOBART SMITH at the Club 47. (1963) Photograph by Byron Linardos.

You caused me to weep,
You caused me to moan,
You caused me to leave my home.
All these lonesome times in this old lonesome town,
I'm on my long journey home.

Storybook Ball

Up in Mother Goose's book up in the nursery,
Simple Simon says, "I'm feeling sad,"
Said Peter Piper's daughter, "So am I, I think we oughta
Do something that will make the kiddies glad."
Smarty-Smarty says, "I think we'll have a party,"
And he called on the Old Woman in the Shoe.
Now the cat he brought his fiddle,
And he played Hi-Diddle-Diddle,
And what happened then, I'm gonna tell to you.

ritz was taking a well-deserved vacation in Berkeley, escaping the snow and cold of February in Cambridge, when he got the message.

I can't remember whether it was a letter or a phone call, but it was Jim Kweskin saying, "We're having a Jug Band, and you're invited." I was in the Cabale — it was Jesse Fuller's sixty-ninth birthday party — and I realized I'd have to go East again. I thought, "But I've only just come to Berkeley. It's warm here; some of my favorite buddies are here; and I'm nightly scoffing terrific meals at Phil and Midge Huffman's."

The Huffman's were very accommodating with their dinners. Most any evening would find Bob Neuwirth, Buzz Marten, Charlie Frizzell, and Teddy Bernstein playing guitar and trying to drink the legendary entire six-pack of Green Death (Rainier Ale) or listening and trying to drink a whole six-pack. I paid Midge ten bucks a week for dinner every night, and in those days I could eat even more than I could smoke — and finish off with a peanut butter sandwich before heading down to the Cabale to hear K.C. Douglas or Lenny Bruce or a bluegrass band.

I was staying in a one-room apartment in a building called The Tenement. Bob Neuwirth had lent me his room. As a charter member of the International Paranoid Front, he was sure the FBI was watching The Tenement and wouldn't go near the place. I wasn't worried about that and spent lots of time there. One sunny afternoon I was cleaning out the closet getting ready to leave when I found two small, square pieces of stained glass. I held them up to the light, and the sun shot through the most amazing blue I never saw. It made me suck in my breath and smile. I wrapped them carefully and put them in my vest pocket.

I made sure that toothbrush and comb were in front pocket of precious, ratty, suede jacket, slung suitcase into washtub for ease of carrying, and walked up to Cy Koch's place to meet my ride to Cambridge. This was going to be my first non-stop-cross-the-whole-country car ride. The driver was John Cooke.

John had a nearly-new Volvo he'd got in Europe the previous summer. He and his roommate, Bill Burke, were also spending Spring vacation in Berkeley. Bill had never been to California before. He had taken one look, and one look back, and never looked back again. He told John to find a new roommate. We arrived in Cambridge three days later still speaking to each other, so we decided I should move in with him at 6 Ellsworth Avenue.

Kweskin had come back from California to Cambridge in the Fall. For a couple of years he had been traveling around the country getting good. In Chicago I worked in a guitar shop for a month and played music with a young harp player named Paul Butterfield. In Greenwich Village I played the Gaslight Cafe with Bob Dylan. In Minneapolis I met Spider John Koerner and he taught me a song he had just written called "Good Time Charlie's Back In Town Again." And in Berkeley, California I met a guy named Steve Talbott, who had adapted an old Blind Boy Fuller tune and I learned it from him. The song was "Rag Mama" and it became my theme song.

One way I learned to become an entertainer was to drop myself off in a city that I'd never been in before in my life like, say, St. Louis, where I didn't know anybody, didn't have any contacts, and had to make a living at singing and playing the guitar. I would go to the nearest guitar shop and find where the places were. Then I'd go and ask if I could play for free. Then, when I got on stage, it was up to me. Could I do it? That was a great education.

In addition to an education, Jim also got himself a wife, Marilyn, and a dog, Agatha. They settled into a funky place on Fulkerson Street in East Cambridge, and Jim started giving guitar lessons and playing around town.

David Simon had also arrived from California with the Kweskins. Fritz had played a few gigs with Jim and David before he left.
David played the harmonica, the kazoo, the exit light, trash can lids, or anything noisy. He sang in a delightfully offhanded, innocent manner, and his harmonica style was really unique. John Sebastian once told me he couldn't imagine how anyone could breathe that way.

He got into Numerology and realized he could never achieve greatness as David Simon, so he changed his name frequently to aid his career. He was known variously as Bruno Wolfe, Joe Flanken, Hugh Bialy, and Rex Rakish. It seemed to actually work. Sometimes his playing was just out of step with the rest of us, but there were many times he made a musical connection that was so spectacular that if it had been an electrical connection, he would have illuminated a city the size of Ahlington.

Geoff Muldaur was singing around town a lot that winter, too, and often he and Jim would split a night at the 47. Although their styles were very

Opposite:
Today Eleventh Avenue. Tomorrow the World! THE KWESKIN JUG BAND coming from the CBS Television Studios in New York. (1964) (left to right) FRITZ RICHMOND, BILL KEITH, MEL LYMAN, JIM KWESKIN, MARIA MULDAUR, GEOFF MULDAUR, and unidentified friend. Photograph by Michael Harvest.

different, they were both deeply involved in searching out and playing material that they found on old records. Geoffrey was more into the blues side, but he also knew a lot about early jazz. He once said that he'd grown up with a be-bop mind. Jim was primarily interested in ragtime and jazz, but he also had a lot of early blues records. Some bright person at the Community Church in Boston decided to put them on together in a little concert called "The Bittersweet Blues of Geoff Muldaur and The Ragtime Blues of Jim Kweskin." Jim had never met Geoffrey and called him to see if he'd like to do a couple of songs together.

Marilyn and I went over to his apartment, stoned as usual, and found Geoffrey to be straight, uptight and surly. He said that he wasn't into reefer and made sure we weren't "holding" in his place. Somehow we managed to work out a few songs together and we gave the concert on February 3 of 1963. Broadside gave us a good review: "The two of them combined talents on the last few numbers and brought the house down with the "Boodle Am Shake."

I was gigging at the Club 47 a lot. Every time I played there, all kinds of musicians would get up on stage with me and jam. The old Club 47 was like that. It had a huge basement where all the musicians would hang out and play music. Many times a bunch of us would play a song for the first time down there and then run upstairs and play it for the audience.

One night I was jamming on stage with about a dozen other musicians: a blind singer named George Leh who would sit and rock back and forth and stomp his feet and sing at the top of his lungs; a harp player named Gordie Edwards; David Simon, my crazy friend who I'd hung out with in Berkeley; and others I don't remember, kazoo players, banjo players, guitar players, the stage was packed. We romped through a whole set of songs like "If I Could Shimmy Like My Sister Kate" and "Stagerlee." I didn't know it at the time, but Maynard Solomon, the president of Vanguard Records, was in the audience and when the set was over he came up to me and said, "How would you like to make a record with that band?" I said, "That's no band, but give me three months and I'll put one together." That was how the Jug Band got started.

So I started looking for the right combination. There were a lot of musicians floating around Cambridge, but most of them didn't play the kind of music I needed. Geoff Muldaur was an obvious choice. We both loved the same kind of music and he was a good slow blues singer, which I wasn't,

and I knew that we'd have a good balance if we shared the vocal responsibilities. I didn't care that he might be hard to get along with, I'd just light up a joint and say "fuck it." All I cared about was getting a good band together. David Simon was a harder choice because he thought he was a great musician and I knew he wasn't. We had been getting high together for years and he practically lived with us. He was crazy and loose and lived in a fantasy world that I kind of admired. He played the harmonica in a harsh, strange, unique but not very reliable style, and he sang in a funky nasal voice. He could be extremely persistent, and when he demanded to be in the band I gave in. I asked Bob Siggins to be our banjo player. He consented to join the band only long enough to make the record. He was very committed to chemistry and bluegrass.

Kweskin had everything he needed for a jug band except a jug player. Jug rhymes with tub, and tub rhymes with Fritz. Get Fritz back here.
So there was the Orange Dude (which is me) at his first Jug Band rehearsal. Shirt with long sleeves and collar, vest, and precious, grungy, suede jacket. "Yes, indeed," said Kweskin, "it's a Jug Band, a democratic band, and you're elected to be the jug player."

Bob Siggins then handed me an antique coal oil jug made of sheet metal. I already knew how to play it; I just couldn't do it very well. I huffed and puffed through a couple of up-tempo blues, then went back to playing the tub. It made a lot of spray to hit the low notes on the jug, and I began to wonder if I would make any less mess if my mouth were dry, and I thought of smoking a little marijuana. So I went into the bathroom and locked the door.

I had a special pipe I got high with. I found that regular pipes weren't good for smoking pot — one big toke could give one fiery mouthful — so I got a thimble and drilled holes in the bottom and slipped it into a short briar pipe. With a stubby pipe I could look right into the bowl and see the glowing grass. Hee, hee! I'm Popeye the Sailor Man. I had filed off the bottom so it would sit upright for loading. I set it on Siggins' sink and

Opposite:
JIM KWESKIN *at the Club 47. (1963) Photograph by Dick Waterman.*

Following Page:
(left) FRITZ RICHMOND, *"The Orange Dude" (c. 1963) Photograph by John Cooke.*

(right) ROBERT L. JONES *(c. 1963) Photograph by Charles Frizzell.*

filled it one-fourth full. Then Jim K., David Simon, and I went outside for a quick puff. Aaaah, it works every time, don't it?

Bob Siggins was not one of Cambridge's notorious vipers. In those days very few people got high. Those who did were not eager to expand their numbers; those who didn't were considered to be not cool, square, unhip. One didn't offer a joint to a casual acquaintance without prior word from a mutual friend who was aware that both parties got high. "Would you like to smoke one of these?" Sometimes it seemed that friendship needed no other basis than grass. So we were discreet over at Siggins' place. Anyway, his wife was no fun at all about drugs. If she'd known we were getting high, there's no telling what might have happened. Our membership in the Club 47 might have been revoked. How awful.

This was the Cambridge Dope Paranoia. It led to an unreasonable fear of the authorities but kept a lot of us from getting busted. We felt like the early Christians in Rome may have felt. We passed along the rumors of imminent city-wide police raids every spring, and God help anyone who lived over in Boston. We practiced flushing vast cargoes of seeds and stems down toilets at a single flush. We heard that when they busted a building with pressure flush toilets they'd turn off the water first so you couldn't flush your stash. But, in a building with tank toilets, you had one good flush.

"Let's go back inside," we said. I don't know what Bob's neighbors must have thought we were doing out there in the alley. But it's music time now, and I feel just fine, where's my jug?

Phoof, honk, tweep, I think I'll sit down and play. I'm getting dizzy and wobbly. That sure is good smoke. I wonder if there's another dime bag of that available.

I found that if I had a microphone in front of me, I could focus my eyes on it and not wobble around when stoned, but anyone looking at me would say I looked cross-eyed and stoned. Well, not wanting to appear cross-eyed, I took to wearing shades when playing the jug, little round blue sunglasses I'd had made from the pieces of stained glass. Now when I played the jug, I merely looked stoned, and that was all right with me.

It was a busy spring. Paul Rothchild was up to do a record with Geoff for Prestige. Kweskin had been talking to Maynard Solomon about making a record for Vanguard, but no contracts had been signed and Paul was doing his best to head Maynard off at the pass.
I remember driving Kweskin around in a rented car and him saying, "I know Vanguard's a bigger company, but we'd probably make a better record with you, because you understand the music." Jim must have told Maynard that he was thinking about going with Prestige, because Maynard came up right away.

Maynard was probably killing two birds with one stone. Joan Baez was in Boston that weekend to do her annual concert, which had become a big event. After the concert the plan was to go with her and Manny Greenhill over to the 47 where her friend Robert L. Jones was running the Sunday Hoot, not the most glorious of roles, but one that he enjoyed. You never knew who was going to be at one of Jones' Hoots.

ob Dylan had been playing at the Yana, so he was around. Joan was in town doing a concert, the Kweskin Jug Band had just been formed but hadn't really played as such in public. It was my Hootenanny night, and it just snowballed. Joan was there, Dylan, the Jug Band, Jack Elliott, Rooney, The Charles River Valley Boys, Eric von Schmidt, Neuwirth, Carolyn Hester. It was an incredible night. Nobody hogged the show. Everybody just did three things. Jack Elliott sang two songs and told his Provincetown faggot joke; Eric and Geoff did "I Love Jesus;" Dylan and Jack and Eric sang together. The Jug Band flipped everyone out, and Joan played kazoo with them as "Miss Blind Ethnic Pygmy" and sang with the Charles River Valley Boys.

When it was all over Maynard Solomon told the Jug Band that he thought they were ready to record, and he took them out to the Bick, of all places, to close the deal! Joan and I went, too, and she asked me how I liked her record. I said that I thought it was great but that the liner notes were all wrong. Of course, Maynard had written them, and he was sitting right there! He didn't seem to mind, though. As a matter of fact, that's when he asked me if I would be interested in doing some recording. I said, "Fine," and eventually I did the *New Folks* album.

IT'S PARTY TIME! Photographs by Rick Stafford.
(top left) JIM KWESKIN accompanies BOB SIGGINS on the jaw harp to the delight of Jack Elliott's wife, Patty.
(top right) JOAN BAEZ fills up on food. MAYNARD SOLOMON is feeling fine. Hostess SALLY SCHOEN-FELD is heading into the other room. OWEN DE LONG (left) and JOE BOYD are listening to the pickers.
(middle left) JOAN BAEZ is still eating and having a good time. Another of the hostesses, SUZIE CAMPBELL, is holding the quart of beer. Joan's sister, PAULINE MARDEN is talking to BOB SIGGINS while JIM KWESKIN, DAVID SIMON, and GEOFF MULDAUR get together in the background. JOE BOYD is taking it all in, as is MAYNARD SOLOMON.
(middle right) MANNY GREENHILL studies BOB DYLAN in the kitchen.
(bottom left) ERIC VON SCHMIDT studies PATTY ELLIOTT in the kitchen.
(bottom right) JOAN BAEZ, her appetite unabated, chomps on a chicken leg and is obviously having a good time, while GEOFF, JIM, and ERIC play that jug band music.

No contracts were signed at the Bick that night. Nobody likes a contract with egg on it, but it seemed that everyone was in agreement — Jim Kweskin and the Jug Band would record for Vanguard as would Jones. Now it was party time! Everyone from the Club had just moved the Hoot over to Sally Schoenfeld's apartment that she shared with her friends Joy Kimball and Susie Campbell. Sally and Joy were pretty good pickers themselves, and Susie put in a lot of time at the 47 working on the door and generally helping out. With Billy Burke gone, they were doing their best to take up the party slack. They had a real one on their hands this night. Fortunately their apartment was over a store, so there was no one to complain, and pretty soon the place was rocking.

The only person who was a little bit down was Paul Rothchild. It looked as though he had lost out on this one. And just in case he had any ideas about giving it one last try, it was now Maynard's turn to head Paul off at the pass.

Maynard came up to me in the kitchen pantry, grabbed me by the arm and said, "Listen, punk, I'm going to tell you something about this business, and you better remember it. When somebody is negotiating with an artist, it's considered very bad form for somebody else to come in and negotiate." Maynard at that time was one of the gods, and I was a punk. And I believed him. I just plain believed that I had violated some sacred taboo. So I said, "I'm sorry. I didn't know. I really want the band, but if that's the case, I'm the last one to do anything like that," and I backed off. I was just a nobody working for Prestige, which was no contest for Vanguard, which was king of the roost in those days with Joan Baez.

Later, when I told the story to Jac Holzman, he said, "You were had, Paul. You can negotiate right up until the minute they sign. You can do anything you want. Tell your story. Sing your song. Hype your hype. Do anything you can do to sign the act." That summer when Holzman and I were at the ferry going to Newport, Maynard was there, sitting on the grass waiting for the ferry, so we walked over, and Maynard said, "Hi, Paul. How're you doing?" I said, "Maynard, you're a lyin' motherfucker." And I ran the whole story down in front of him while he got redder and redder and redder. He never said one single word to me again. But I did learn from it. He taught me a lesson. Don't believe anything you hear from a captain of industry.

Whatever unpleasantries were exchanged in the kitchen pantry that night were of little or no concern to Fritz. He was no longer just everybody's sideman. He was part of a real, live band.

Once you make a band, you have to use it. Bands don't do well just sitting around; they get flat spots like a tomato or an old tire. We played some gigs around Boston and Cambridge and were delighted how people reacted. Record companies got interested and word spread. Folk music was a big business. Hootenanny became a familiar word. The Jug Band was ready to boogie. We went to New York City to make our first record.

Bob Siggins couldn't go on the road with us, being all tied up with laboratories and university schedules. We needed a new banjo player, and they were nearly as scarce as fiddle players but more plentiful than North African kief. We checked out several local pickers first and finally found a likely one, way out in Waltham. His name was Mel Lyman.

Mel had hoboed around the country and knew the roads. He had lived in North Carolina near Obray Ramsay, and his music was of the High and Lonesome sound. He plunked quietly and sang sometimes with harmonica. He didn't command instant attention, for he played his music for one or two or three people sitting around a small fire off in the world somewhere, or in a kitchen in Cambridge. Whatever he sang of, he gave the hint of having been there or done it before. The effect could be chilling, or very comforting.

Jug Band music must have seemed raucous and outrageous to Mel, and the lifestyle a bit odd. Who knew what a Jug Band was supposed to be like? Not me, I behaved any way I could and caused my life to be very involved with being in the band.

Mel seemed to already know what being a traveling musician was going to be like and had resigned himself to it. He tried hard to learn the uptempo jazz tunes but was much more at home on the slow country blues. He and David Simon would play duets on harmonicas on some songs. Often excellent music happened. Mel could become totally involved with his instrument and be drained dry emotionally at the end of a tune. We knew it was hard for him to then jump into a fast one like "Borneo" or "Beedle-Um-Bum."

Below:
JIM KWESKIN and MEL LYMAN share a musical joke. DAVID SIMON plays to himself in the foreground. FRITZ RICHMOND and GEOFF MULDAUR are obliterated by their instruments (1964). Photograph by Michael Harvest.

Opposite:
MEL LYMAN at the Brandeis Folk Festival (1964). Photograph by Charles Frizzell.

Mel was into astrology and the macrobiotic diet and championed them as ways to understand other people better and for self-improvement. He showed us some unexplainable events.

We were in between gigs one day in Cambridge, and Mel said he had gotten a flash. His wife and four children were in Eureka, California, three thousand miles away and were in danger. Mel knew they needed to leave Eureka, so he borrowed a van, and he and Geoffrey went to get them.

"Hey, man, can I use your van for a few days? I'll bring it right back." Seven thousand miles later, Sophie and the kids were safe in Cambridge reading about the tsunami from an Alaskan earthquake that had turned Eureka into U-Wreck-A. We thought about that.

Another time, another year, another van, Geoffrey and Mel on a snowy night, tearing along the dotted line in Utah someplace: Mel said, "Something fantastic is about to happen." They hadn't gone another tankful when they came to a hitchhiker with his frigid digit displayed way away miles from town. "Stop the machine," said Mel. They backed up, and who should it be but Mel's old hanging-out partner, Eben Given, who hadn't seen Mel in years. We thought about that, too.

Soon after joining the band, Mel became part of the Kweskin household at their new apartment at 131 Huron Avenue. Jim discovered that Mel's lifestyle was a bit different than his.

Mel told me that he was being evicted from his place in Waltham and he'd like to move into the little storage room in our attic. Marilyn and I liked him, but we thought he was pretty weird, and we didn't know anything about him. But he really needed a place to live and we needed our banjo player, so around the middle of September, for fifteen dollars a month, I became his landlord. He brought his cat Theodore, a record player, a dresser, an old cat scratcher, a Tiffany lamp, a school-type desk and chair, a double bed, his old radio, a legless chair, cushions, hot plates, pictures, utensils and an old Mexican fertility rug which he hung on the door. All kinds of stuff went up to that tiny attic room. By the end of the day he had somehow managed to get it all neatly arranged and standing in the middle of the room, slowly turning and pointing, said to Marilyn, "This is my bedroom, and this is my study, and this is my kitchen, and this is my music-room..." Everything he needed was there.

Downstairs it was a constant party, beer, music and all the dope freaks who came to hang out. Marilyn and I had our bed in the kitchen with a curtain for privacy. People slept everywhere, anywhere, the big attic room across from Mel's was always full. The record player was going constantly. I was always lighting joints for people and playing them Jimmie Rodgers or Django Reinhardt, jug bands, jazz bands, and fiddle bands. The beer was flowing. Marilyn was always cooking and people were always eating and smoking dope. But Mel never came down and joined the party. We would all go over to the Club 47 to hear whoever was playing, parties at the DeLong's or Fritz's or the Siggins'. Around three a.m. we would all roll into the Red Fez for stuffed grape leaves and houmis and baklava. But Mel would never come with us. I wanted him to, but he stayed up in that little room and listened to Ray Charles, nothing but Ray Charles. I asked him once why he never listened to any other kind of music. He said, "Ray Charles contains all music."

Soon it was going to be time for the Jug Band to test its wings away from home, and Fritz, as usual, was ready to fly.

We had a gig coming up in New York City. Yay! Our new manager, M.A. Greenhill, had called up and told Jim about it — two weeks at The Bitter End (sounds of cheering). We headed for New York. I may have flown. I always used to like to fly and leave the driving to them until we got two cars. Meanwhile, in Greenwich Village there were a couple of other Jug Bands. One of them had a dozen people in it, including two girls. Another, Dave Van Ronk's Ragtime Jug Stompers, played some truly fine fingerpicking on old authentic rags.

The Even Dozen Jug Band was working up songs to make a record. Their producer was our old buddy from Cambridge, Paul Rothchild, who had made the first Charles River Valley Boys record, their first and his first, my first. Anyway, after making a few records in Cambridge, Paul had moved to New York City, switched from Prestige to Elektra, and here he was at a rehearsal of the huge Jug Band. We told them we were in town for a gig, so Paul said they should all try to come see us. That would be nice — get the word out among Jug Band fans. Most of them showed up. After the first set, the girl from the other Jug Band, the one with the long, wavy hair, sat closer.

A few nights later, we learned there might be a party to go to and get high. Aha! A chance to meet some more musicians and smoke some grass (red-headed jug player is seen rubbing hands with glee and putting on little blue glasses). "Geoffrey, remember that girl from the other Jug Band? The one who played the fiddle? Well, she's here."

Geoffrey says, "I know."

Opposite: MARIA MULDAUR Photographer unknown. Courtesy of Eric von Schmidt.

aria D'Amato had managed to pay off her sandals, but she was still going by Alan Block's on Saturdays, Washington Square on Sundays, and Gerde's the rest of the time. She had discovered her true love as well — the fiddle.

At about this time Ralph Rinzler and Mike Seeger and John Cohen started the Friends of Old Time Music, and they started bringing people up from the South for concerts. Ralph Rinzler had just found Doc Watson and brought him up with Clint Howard, Fred Price, and Gaither Carlton. The concert was wonderful, and afterwards I went to a party. I learned how to clog dance that night, and I also got to meet Gaither Carlton. I just fell in love with him. It was crazy. He was fifty years old, but I really did fall in love with him, and I just had to learn to play the fiddle. I went out and borrowed one, and Gaither taught me some tunes before they went away. From then on I just started working on it.

I became friends with Annie Byrd. She was from the South and helped me a lot. And I started going with Walter Gundy. He was very into it. We'd hear that Reno and Smiley were playing in the Bronx, and we'd get on fifty subway trains and go hear them. For about a day Artie Traum and my friend Marlena had a group called the Poolnoods. Then it was Maria and the Washington Square Ramblers — David Grisman, Steve Arkin, Steve Mandel, and Fred Weiss. Finally Josh Rivkin said, "We're forming a jug band, and Victoria Spivey's going to put out a record. Do you want to sing a couple of tunes on it?" Meanwhile, we had all heard of the Kweskin Band on Vanguard; Dave Van Ronk's jug band was on Prestige. Elektra was saying, "Jug Bands are going to sweep the nation!" So they bought us from Victoria Spivey. That band had Dave Grisman, Steve Katz, John Sebastian, Bob Gurland, Josh Rivkin, Peter Siegel, and a girl jug player (Marlena was in the cover photograph in her place). I can't remember who else. There really were a dozen people in that group. It was ridiculous. Paul Rothchild signed us, but Jac Holzman was actually the producer. I remember him telling me, "Maria, sing like you're a fifty year old black woman with piles!" I went off, reduced to tears; that was supposed to be my solo spot on the album.

Paul Rothchild said that if we wanted to hear a *real* jug band, the Kweskin Band was coming to play the Bitter End. They were all good friends of

his, and so we went. John Sebastian and I were just knocked out when we heard Geoffrey Muldaur sing. It was just incredible. You can still hear Geoff in John's singing. He really loved him. One night after the show we were all invited to a party, and I guess I drank a lot. I could never hold my liquor. Fritz and Jim Kweskin later told me I was quite funny, and they spent some time trying to sober me up. At one point, I went over to Geoffrey, and I guess I was trying to tell him how much I liked his singing, but I just threw up in his lap!

The next day, I was totally ashamed, and for a week I would make this big detour around the Bitter End. I didn't want to see anyone, especially Geoffrey, but one day, I was in the back room of Izzy Young's Folklore Center, and in walked Geoff! He was in the front of the store, looking through all the blues records, and I kept waiting for him to leave. But he just stayed and stayed, so I screwed up my courage and came out of the back and went up to him and told him how awful I felt about throwing up on him. He just said, "It was an honor."

After that the Even Dozen Band played at Gerde's, but it wasn't a very together band. Half the kids were still in high school. Their mothers were bringing them to rehearsals and picking them up afterwards. We weren't doing any gigs, and Geoff asked me to come up and visit him on Martha's Vineyard. I spent a week with him there. We weren't doing anything — not even holding hands. We slept in separate sleeping bags in Sarah Chrisman's attic. She was Tom Rush's aunt. And I started thinking, "Maybe he didn't invite me here." It was totally platonic, plus we hardly spoke to each other! There I was, knowing no one but him, and he'd say, "I'm taking you to Gay Head today. This is probably the most beautiful thing you'll ever see." Then we'd come back and I'd pick mushrooms and help Sarah Chrisman make dinner, and I'd be thinking, "I've got to get back to New York. There's an Even Dozen Jug Band rehearsal." But he said, "You ought to come to Cambridge with me. I've got a gig."

Bobby Neuwirth and he were splitting a bill at the Club, so we went back over the ferry to Cambridge. There Byron Lord Linardos had a big bottle of ouzo, and by the second set, things had picked up considerably between Geoff and me. By that time, I was totally blotto. I was wearing an olive-green wrap-around skirt with a blue and olive striped top, and Eric von Schmidt complimented me on my color sense. Geoff said, "That's really a compliment. He's an artist, you know."

Opposite: GEOFF MULDAUR and MEL LYMAN. Photograph by Jim Marshall. Courtesy of the Lyman Family.

Somehow, by the last and loosest set, Bobby Neuwirth was announcing me from the stage, saying, "This good friend of mine from New York is going to come up and sing "I'm A Woman." Here she is, Maria D'Amato." I had no choice but to go up. Only Neuwirth knew I sang it at that point because Teddy Bernstein used to live upstairs from me on Spring Street, and Neuwirth used to hear me through the floor. So I got up, and that was my first performance at the 47. I don't know how I made it through without dropping his guitar. After that, we went to Owen and Jane DeLong's and had a rip-roaring, wonderful party.

That was my first "Cambridge" party where we all sat around and listened to the Swan Silvertones and had the quiz afterwards. And we just danced and carried on all night. The next day, finding that my rehearsal had been cancelled, I was taken to Eric von Schmidt's farm in Henniker, New Hampshire. They were steaming wallpaper off the walls. Geoff knew what he was doing. I was suckered right in — the country, Eric von Schmidt, my first rum drink, real hard work on the farm, the smell of creosote, reading "Stern" out loud at night. I would go outside at night and just roll around — roll around and laugh under the stars by myself for about an hour. It was great!

I just kept calling, and the Even Dozen Jug Band kept cancelling their rehearsals. This went on for a week. Finally, I decided that I had to go home and get a clean tank top. I took the bus back. Everything was pretty loose between Geoff and me. As I rode into New York, I thought, "I don't like it here any more. This is not my home. It's much groovier up there." I walked all the way to the east side from where the bus let me off, walked into where I lived, took a look at Walter took a look at the house, Spring Street. I got my toothbrush, a new tank top, and said, "I'm sorry, Walter, but I'm going back up," and he said, "Well honey, have a good time." He was always a real nice guy. I got right back on the midnight bus, called Geoff, and he came and picked me up, and that was it.

We lived on Rockwell Street with Joe Boyd, Mr. Pigpen, who lived in the living room, which was wall-to-wall Zagnut bars and baseball lists. Geoffrey introduced me to Haymarket Square in Boston and doing a whole week's worth of shopping on about seven or eight dollars. You couldn't resist eight boxes of strawberries for 99¢. You bought them and gave them away to your friends. Stuff was just pouring out of the icebox. Geoffrey was really into having me cook and clean, and I was really into it, too.

I lived with Geoff and Joe Boyd for about eight months, keeping house and going to his gigs. I had a job in a rotten little Italian restaurant on Boylston Street where these penny-pinching little Italians paid me about 99¢ an hour to wash dishes and made me grate cheese down to where there was about an inch of cheese and my knuckles were going into the cheese.

Then the Jug Band got about a month's worth of gigs on the West Coast. So me and Geoff and Mel Lyman went across country together. We had lots of adventures. Mel kept a hundred pound sack of brown rice in his VW bus. He was already on a macrobiotic diet, into astrology, had taken acid, morning glory seeds, and a lot of pot. He'd show us where he rode the rails and we'd camp out. He'd sing Woody Guthrie songs, and we'd all sing in the car and play harmonica.

When we got to the West Coast, they had three Steve Allen gigs and three weeks at the Troubadour. I got a gig as a cashier at the Ash Grove. We lived in our bus in the driveway of Marilyn Kweskin's parents at the top of Wonderland Avenue in Laurel Canyon. Marilyn and I palled out and went to a lot of material shops and made shirts for the guys. I was a jug band old lady. We cooked and sewed a lot. I was not singing with them at all.

THE STEVE ALLEN SHOW PRESENTS . . .
March 4, 1964. Jim Kweskin remembers it well.
"When the show started, they announced Steve Allen, but Johnny Carson walked out. Even Steve Allen was surprised when he looked at the monitor and didn't see himself. They talked and joked for a while, and then it was our turn to go on. We came out and did "Boodle Am Shake."

Then they came over, and we went into this whole patter where he asked Fritz where he got his glasses and where we came from. Just joking around. Then we said, 'We're gonna do this song. Do you want to play it with us?' Steve Allen had his trumpet. He got Johnny Carson a comb, but I knew he wouldn't be able to play the comb, so I dug down in the Jug Band Toy Box and pulled out a kazoo and handed him the kazoo.

Meanwhile there was this whole thing going on where Johnny Carson was deadpanning — What's going on here? We were innocent and were just being ourselves. It was kind of like he was playing a joke on us, but we were also playing a joke on him. Finally, we got to playing "Overseas Stomp," but he couldn't figure out how to play the kazoo. Melvin said, 'Hum into it,' so he hummed into it and we finally played it for a minute or two.

He comes from the world of humor, and it was like two entirely different worlds meeting in front of millions of people — like oil and water. We didn't quite know how to deal with each other."
Photographs courtesy of the Lyman Family.

At that time, Dylan and Victor Maimudes and Neuwirth were also hanging out in L.A. Dylan was doing the college circuit, and we'd meet every night for parties. Every night, some rich L.A. person would invite some of us crazies over to his house. And we'd all sing. I remember Dylan or Neuwirth would ask me to sing "Trix Ain't Walkin'." I had little songs that I sang; but just for parties. I didn't really have any particular aspirations. I was just happy to be part of it.

Later that spring, Dave Simon quit, and the next thing I knew, I'd been asked to join. We did a few rehearsals and made the second record. I did "I'm A Woman." I would play a lot of rhythm instruments, tambourine, wood blocks. It was a fabulous time. I learned to play "Jug Band Waltz" in harmony with Mel on the harmonica.

The whole trip was so innocent. The Jug Band, for those days, was a pretty successful band, but we traveled around in our Volkswagen buses. Say we'd hit Philly and play the first set at the 2nd Fret, then a bunch of young, rich kids would come up and say, "Stay at our place. My mom will cook you organic turkey sandwiches" or whatever. Or we'd score pads to stay in. We never thought of the Holiday Inn. Being on the road was a groove. People came to wherever we were staying and took us on tours of the city.

We got magnetized into music. It was just folk music — nobody ever dreamed that they could pay the rent with it. It wasn't as if people had sat around in their college dorms and said, "How can we make a million?" We just did it like crazies and got up there and sang, and I'm sure we all weren't very good when we started, but there wasn't any self-consciousness about it. It was just a pure love of music and a real community and family feeling.

Meanwhile, Mel was getting a reputation as a guru — someone who knew something. Today you can go to the local Rexall and get "I Ching" books and Tarot cards, but he was one of the first guys to be putting all that together. He was in on one of the first "if-if" experiments — Leary and Alpert's first acid experiments. So people were starting to come to Mel. People who were in trouble would come in and have long raps with him, or he'd throw their changes for them, or give them morning glory seeds. He was our spiritual leader, while Jim was our show-business leader.

I remember when Mel left the Jug Band. We were at Newport for the first time. We did the afternoon concert. The way we did "I'm A Woman" was that I sang three verses, then Mel played a harp solo, then I sang the fourth verse. You can imagine how nervous I was. There must have been seventeen thousand people out there. I had only been with the Jug Band for a couple of

MARIA MULDAUR *does the boogie;* GEOFF MULDAUR *salutes the world; and* JENNY MULDAUR *makes three. Photographs by Rick Sullo.*

months. We'd been playing little coffee houses, and here we were playing the Newport Festival at the height of its thing. Nobody'd ever seen a gig like that at the time. So how was I to know in my basic tremulous condition of facing 17,000 people that Mel Lyman was so into his harp solo that he wanted to blow at least one, if not two, more choruses. I was not musically and cosmically and sensitively aware of this. So after he did a very lovely solo, I came back in and sang the last verse. That was that, and we finished the set, and that so crimped his musical soul, and I guess he felt we were really going show biz to the point that he quit the band at the end of that weekend. It was never said that I had simply not been aware enough, but that's what I was made to feel. So I learned a big lesson in musical sensitivity.

Mel was replaced by Bill Keith, who is an entirely different story than Mel Lyman — very methodical. The best description of him I ever heard was "the world's foremost nuclear banjoist." And he was.

For Keith, the Jug Band was quite a change from being a Bluegrass Boy. After immersing himself totally in the bluegrass banjo for several years, he was ready to broaden his musical horizons.

he Jug Band gave me a chance to get back into the kind of music I had played back in high school. Jim had a whole stack of records, and he had a lot of ideas about material. Geoffrey sort of reserved the ultimate veto on things. It's funny. It was a democratic group where everybody had a veto. Nobody used it but Geoffrey. I was unschooled in the kind of blues that Geoffrey was into, and I was also unaware of the stuff that Kweskin was into, so I went back to listening to records and learning stuff. Then I was able to contribute some to arranging. Geoffrey was good at that, too. I was learning to work with harmony and choral ideas, whereas up until then with Monroe and bluegrass the main concern was with the melody line, usually fast. So being with the Jug Band really helped me — it was what I needed to

develop my technique on the instrument.

Being in the Jug Band and back in Cambridge got me involved in the whole scene there. It was totally unstructured, but it resulted in a broad education in many musical styles — from blue-grass and old-timey to gospel to blues to ragtime to jazz. A certain person might have a specialty but there was little of the competitive kind of feeling which prohibits anyone from learning what they wanted to know. And the word "community" gets that out to me as much as anything. The Jug Band itself was a community. The whole scene around Cambridge and Boston became a community. It had its newspaper, it had its clubs, it had its grapevine, and it had its connections to other communities in other places. Hanging out was a big part of life with the Jug Band. We spent time in Toronto, Berkeley, and L.A., and in each place we had a lot of friends and kept doing what we did when we were home in Cambridge.

Of all the members in the Jug Band, Geoff Muldaur was the leader in ritualizing the fine art of hanging out. He was not alone in this

endeavor. He had a crew, Owen DeLong, a graduate student at Harvard in political science; Bruce Conner, artist and film maker; Zack Weisner, poker player; Fritz, of course; and Mitch Greenhill, the Shepherd of the Highways.

When Geoff Muldaur arrived we struck up a friendship pretty much because he was the youngest in the scene. I first met him at a "Y" get together. He showed up and sang "Mr. Jellyroll Baker." Robert L. Jones thought that the song was in poor taste, but I defended it, and we became friends.

The tag "Shepherd of the Highways" came as a result of an acid trip. I was ripped on acid for the first time in my life, walking along the streets of Martha's Vineyard seeing these cars glide over the asphalt. It seemed miraculous that these creatures were staying on the right road. I felt I was their shepherd. So I became the shepherd of the highways. I actually became known as the person to call for the fastest route to get somewhere. Fritz often called me up for advice when the Jug Band was on the road.

One of the rituals for Geoff, Fritz, Owen

THE KWESKIN JUG BAND at the Newport Folk Festival. (1967) (left to right) FRITZ RICHMOND, JIM KWESKIN, RICHARD GREENE'S bowing hand, GEOFF MULDAUR, MARIA MULDAUR, and BILL KEITH. Photograph by John Cooke.

DeLong and myself was "Last Call" at the Oxford Grille. Jim Kweskin was not into it. He was into macrobiotics. When we finished last call, we'd hit "next call" at Fritz's. He had curtains made out of the pop tops off of Goldies (Schaeffer Beer) and a wall painted Gaulois Blue. He also had a fantastic juke box. Nickel a play. We'd sit around and listen to records — great records like "Sally Go 'Round the Roses" by the Ronettes; "Hit the Road, Jack" by Ray Charles; "Together Again" by Buck Owens. Everybody had a vote in what to put on it or what to take off. Proceeds went into the "Goldie" Fund. Listening to records was a major pastime. There would be an album that someone would get like the first Howlin' Wolf album. That album would be played every night for about three weeks until we knew every note on one of those records.

While I was still in college, Geoff and I got into another ritual. I'd be home working on my school work, and he'd come by for an hour or so in the afternoons with his clarinet. We were trying to learn Duke Ellington and the early New Orleans stuff. We'd work at that for a while, then he'd go on about his rounds and I'd go back to my work. I remember that very fondly.

Whatever else he was, Geoffrey Muldaur was definitely not a dull boy. He wanted it all, and he wanted it now!

We saw Bobby Orr's first exhibition game, played pool all the time. Drank. Hit Fritz's for "Next Call." One year we averaged 17 "Goldies" a night at Fritz's and we were on the road for about two-thirds of the year! Fritz's thing was "Dig Trips." We'd score some anthrax inhalers and from the inside cotton, cut off pill slices. It was the roaringest high, and we'd just carry on. Fritz would say, "It's Thursday and they're making mace at the spice factory in Charlestown. Let's go there." We'd go and smell the mace for a while and then maybe go to the Watertown Waterworks: "Maybe they'll show us around!" And they always would. We'd see the radio stations at three in the morning.

We were also into the gospel scene. We caught every one that came to Boston. The Easter show at the arena was a chance to see all the great groups — the Swan Silvertones, The Staples, James Cleveland. When Claude Jeter hit that high falsetto note, I almost came.

On the road the Jug Band never stopped. We'd go out and have a major shoot-out before the show and, of course, after the show. All day we'd go around looking for markets, find a Greek restaurant, have a gigantic meal, whip on over to the gig, tear everybody up, including ourselves, and go and party all night.

One of the functions of the Jug Band was to turn people on. In every town we went to we'd turn three or four people on. We had our methods down about how to do it. Instead of giving people a little to smoke we thought it was better to risk the occasional freakout and give them a real hit. That avoided all that, "It didn't do a thing. Ha, ha." We just wiped them out.

Out reasons for doing everything were always the finest, the purest, most revolutionary reasons. We were a family, and we were dedicated to presenting a "life experience" and pioneering experiences for people. We were leaders. I think we all felt that. We were trying to get that kid in the fourth row to finally pick up a guitar or take a trip — or just get down.

There were no jive notes, in life or any other way. We were very dedicated people. And there was this overwhelming respect for each other. There were no jive notes . . .

They danced and pranced 'till early in the morning.
They really didn't know just when to stop.
So as the day was dawning, and the kiddies were all yawning,
They found out the mouse had run up in the clock.

Fixin' to Die

I'm looking far in mind, I
b'lieve I'm fixing to die
b'lieve I'm fixing to die
I'm looking far in mind, I
b'lieve I'm fixing to die.
I know I was born to die
but I hate to leave my children crying.

veryone was going to Newport. After a two-year hiatus, the Newport Folk Festival had been revived through the combined efforts of George Wein, Pete Seeger, Manny Greenhill, and many of the members of the New York folk community. The idea was to make the Festival as representative as possible of the many levels of the growing folk music world. It would have the best of the commercial folk groups like Peter, Paul, and Mary and the Tarriers; the best young artists like Joan Baez and Bob Dylan; the best of the traditional artists like Bill Monroe and Jean Ritchie; and, of course, those who considered themselves the "parents" of this whole revival — Pete Seeger, Oscar Brand, and Theo Bikel. Hovering over the Festival was the spirit of Woody Guthrie. It was going to be a celebration of the culmination of the long struggle to bring the people's music back to the people. The songs of the time were "Blowin' in the Wind" and "We Shall Overcome." The song for all time was "This Land Is Your Land."

A lot had happened since the last festival in 1960, and the Cambridge folks were ready to join in the celebration. Betsy Siggins was hanging out with Joan Baez and got to meet Bob Dylan and Jack Elliott's mother and father. Bob Siggins and Jim Rooney were at a bluegrass workshop taking pictures of Bill Keith playing with Bill Monroe. Fritz and Mitch Greenhill backed Jackie Washington on the "New Folks" concert. Robert L. Jones had a friend in Newport who was restoring an old mansion built by some industrialist in the middle of Jamestown Bay on a big rock; the house became party headquarters. The night-time concerts were held in Freebody Park in town, and in the daytime there were music workshops there and next door on the grounds of the New-port Casino, one of the grand old tennis clubs of the world. If he could have been there, Woody Guthrie would have loved it — all these guitar pickers sitting around where the Vanderbilts used to play.

Eric von Schmidt was at the Casino on Saturday afternoon at a workshop on blues. He was listening to Mississippi John Hurt sing "Spike Driver Blues." It was unreal. John Hurt was dead. *Had* to be. All those guys on that Harry Smith Anthology were dead. They'd all recorded back in the twenties and thirties. They'd never been seen or heard from since. But there was no denying that the man singing so sweet and playing so

beautifully was *the* John Hurt. He had a face — and what a face. He had a hat that he wore like a halo. In another place, in another time, Eric might well have got on his knees, but he didn't. After the workshop was over, he went up to Mississippi John Hurt, shook his hand, and said, "Mister Hurt, I just want to tell you how much I enjoy your music. You know, one time I built a boat, and I named it after you." John Hurt smiled, looked at Eric with his Jiminy Cricket eyes, and said, "Oooh? Thass NICE!"

There was nothing quite like Newport at night. It was cool and sometimes the wind blew the fog in off the water. The combination of the fog and the colored stage lights would make the artists look like they were almost illusions. Ralph Rinzler brought Clarence Ashley and Mike Seeger brought Dock Boggs. A blues collector named Tom Hoskins brought John Hurt. They were not ghosts up there. They were absolutely real. Seeing them all on the stage like that was as if someone had suddenly turned the lights on in a room that had been dark for years. There they all were, still singing and playing just as they had over thirty years earlier. It was a minor miracle.

ow did it happen? That was the question that intrigued Phil Spiro as he sat listening to John Hurt. Phil had gradually involved himself in the folk world for the last three years and had a radio show that he shared with Dave Wilson on the M.I.T. radio station WTBS.

Geoff Muldaur is the one who really turned me on to country blues. I heard him play one night at the Turk's Head on Charles Street. He was still at B.U., and afterwards we went back to his dorm. He played some records, including some Blind Willie Johnson — stuff that really turned on something in my head. I guess it had something to do with the simplicity of the music. From that point on, I really got into country blues.

I listened to a lot of records, and I also went to hear some of the young, white blues singers who were around. There were lots of guys who played blues who left me totally cold, and there were some who I thought were fantastic. Geoff was a beautiful singer. Eric von Schmidt is one of the finest blues musicians I've ever heard. To do what he did with "Galveston Flood," "Grizzly Bear," and "He Was a Friend of Mine" showed a mastery of the idiom. He took something from

MISSISSIPPI JOHN HURT at the 1963 Newport Folk Festival afternoon blues workshop. Dave Van Ronk and Brownie McGhee can be seen behind him. Photograph by John Cooke.

BOOKER WHITE *Photograph by Charles Sawyer.*

within the idiom and transformed it in such a way that nobody could tell that it wasn't always that way. Eric set a standard for me by which I judged many others.

Before 1963, the idea that the bluesmen we listened to on old records might still be alive somewhere hadn't really occurred to us. That all changed when Tom Hoskins rediscovered Mississippi John Hurt. The first contact I had with anybody who was involved in looking for these old guys was when I met Hoskins at Newport. I asked him how it had happened, and it turned out that he had just acted on a hunch. One of John's songs was "Avalon Blues" and it had the line, "Avalon's my hometown, always on my mind." So Hoskins went to Avalon, Mississippi, on the off chance that he would still be living there, and he was! It was that simple.

At about the same time I had met Hobart Smith at the Club 47. He did a radio show, and we became good friends, so I visited him in Saltville a couple of times when I was on my way to

Florida to see my parents. Hobart had a friend named John Gallaher who played "St. Louis Tickle" which he had learned from Blind Lemon Jefferson when he was through there one time. They didn't draw a hell of a lot of distinction between black music and white music in their minds. Hobart also played some beautiful stuff on the piano at home. You haven't lived if you haven't heard him play "Pretty Polly" on the piano. The thing about all of this was that I didn't have a tape recorder with me, and there was all this great music happening. It certainly made me think about going out in the field to collect and record the music out there. I remember Hobart saying that Alan Lomax, who had recorded him, was a good man, and that he'd come into your house, and you'd feel right at home with him, and he'd put his feet up and be one of the family — but watch him.

The whole story of the rediscovery of all these bluesmen after so long is pretty weird. I remember Geoff Muldaur telling me that they

AL WILSON   *Photograph by Rick Sullo.*

had found Booker White and how. John Fahey and Ed Denson, who were blues fanatics from California, addressed a card to: "Bukka White — Old Blues Singer, Aberdeen, Mississippi." They were hoping to pull off another John Hurt, because Booker (Bukka was a typo mistake on the old record label) had recorded a song about *his* hometown called "Aberdeen Blues". Booker wasn't living there any more, but somebody carried the card to him up in Memphis. It said: "Hi. If you're alive and well, call us collect. We want you to come out here and make a record." He called; they sent money for him to go to California, and that's how that happened. Geoff couldn't believe it and neither could I. It just electrified me.

When Booker came to Boston to play at the "Y" I saw to it that he stayed with me, pushy kid that I was. I was sharing an apartment on Roberts Road with Al Wilson who later went on to be called "Blind Owl" in Canned Heat. I met Al through

Laurie Forti, who had a very good blues collection. At the time I met him, Al was an accomplished guitarist. He had already gone through Muddy Waters' records and John Lee Hooker's records. He was very melodically oriented. He was already open for country blues. It was a time when everybody was just digging in. The Origins of Jazz Library records were coming out. We'd sit around and listen to those and could hardly wait until the next one came out. Neither of us were collectors though; we were really interested in the music.

Al occasionally worked for his father's construction firm as a bricklayer. The crew thought he was a hippie because he wore glasses! He was very happy to get out of there and somehow make another kind of living. He made a little money teaching, collected some unemployment, and every so often he'd grit his teeth and go back and lay bricks. He had the blues. He had good reason. If you're looking for a persecuted minority, try the minority of one sometime.

When I moved in with Al, I didn't quite know what I was getting into. I'm not the world's neatest person, but he was something else. Al cleaned house twice. Once when Booker came to stay with us; once when Son House came. His method of cleaning was quite simple. He would bring in the three trashcans from outside and start filling them up. He would then take the cans back outside, and the room would be clean. We didn't have a phone. We didn't have any plates. We had a fork. When we decided to eat in, we'd put a hot dog on a fork and cook it over the burner.

While Booker was staying with us, Al talked to him a lot about his music. Al was exceptional in his ability to relate and empathize with older musicians. He was so in tune with whatever spirit there was in blues that they would play with him and talk to him as a fellow musician. He had no ego. He was into music for its own sake, and that's how he was able to communicate so well. He wasn't interested in finding out what someone had for lunch thirty years ago when he recorded such and such; he was more interested in how he felt about his music. They discussed how Booker approached the problem of writing a song; why he preferred certain techniques to others on the guitar; what qualities he admired in other bluesmen; and so on. Naturally, the conversation would get around to musicians that Booker knew and had known in the old days.

(top) BOOKER WHITE
Photograph by Charles Sawyer.

(bottom) AL WILSON
Photograph by John Cooke.

Booker didn't care too much for Robert
Johnson or anyone with a high voice, as I recall,
but he enjoyed listening to the records of one of
his boyhood idols, Charlie Patton. Eventually, Al
played some of Son House's old records. Booker
really took an interest. He didn't recognize Son's
music at first, but when Al identified it as Son
House, Booker went into deep thought. After a
while, he recalled that a friend of his in Memphis
had casually mentioned seeing Son House last
year.

Both Al and I were astonished to hear this, for
blues collectors had been looking for Son House
for over ten years. The only information known
about him was that his first name was Eugene, he
had lived in Robinsonville, Mississippi, was a
part-time preacher, and sometimes wore a white
cowboy hat. He had recorded commercially for
Paramount in 1930 and again for the Library of
Congress in the early forties. No one had seen
him since.

Through Booker, we got in touch with the
woman who had seen Son in Memphis — Ma
Rainey. Not *the* Ma Rainey, but a woman who is
such a fine blues singer that her friends call her
"Ma Rainey" out of respect for her abilities. I
called Ma (her real name is Lillian Glover) and
she said, yes, she had seen Son House last year.
No, she didn't find out where he was living, but
she would be glad to help look for him. Off to
Memphis! I had two weeks vacation beginning
the second week of June, so I was ready. Al was
playing at the Club 47 during that period and
couldn't go. I contacted Nick Perls who was a
blues record collector from New York. He was
into old records and tapes more than living bluesmen who have problems like food and board,
but he had a car and wanted to look for old '78's.
He also had a gigantic tape recorder. It came in
sections, both of which weighed about eighty
pounds. I also talked to Dick Waterman about
going. He was a good photographer and jour-
nalist, and he, too, had been fascinated by the
"rediscovery" phenomenon which started with
John Hurt.

Like so many others who eventually got drawn
into the folk world, Dick Waterman had started
out to do something else.

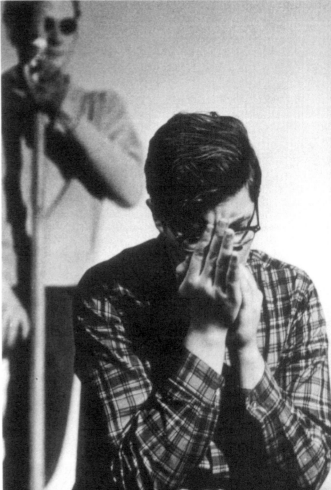

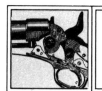 *I* went to Boston University's School of Public Relations and Communications to study journalism. Out the back door of the SPRC was the "Golden Vanity." This was in 1959-60. So I naturally drifted over there and got acquainted with people like Robert L. Jones and got some exposure to folk music.

I worked for newspapers in Bridgeport, Connecticut, and Miami. I was basically a sportswriter and sports photographer. In 1963, I came back from Miami. I was doing some freelance writing for the *National Observer*. By this time, the folk revival was in full swing, and I convinced the *Observer* that this was going to be a major story. So I went to Newport and covered the festival for them. From then on, I started hanging out at the Club 47 all the time.

In February of '64, Mississippi John Hurt needed a place to play in Boston. Dave Wilson and I became partners and rented the Cafe Yana for a week. I had met John briefly at Newport, and he had immediately captivated me. He was a charming, wonderful man, and that's why I wanted to help put him on. So he came in and sold out every night for six nights. We were blessed with good weather; immediately after we closed, there was a blizzard.

A couple of months later Phil Spiro told me that he thought there was a good chance that another of the old bluesmen who everybody thought was dead was somewhere down in Memphis. It was Son House. He wanted to know if I'd be interested in coming along on the trip. I couldn't pass up a story like that, and the next thing we knew we were down in Memphis!

Rev. Robert Wilkins, another rediscovered bluesman, was an old friend of Son's, and he offered to help us look for him down around Lake Commorant, Mississippi, where we heard he had once lived. Without his help we would never have gotten anywhere. We were going around from house to house and farm to farm. We were down in the delta between Highway 61 and the river. We were in there for days, looking for Son and people who knew him. We were four in a Volkswagen with a New York license plate. It was insufferably hot. Spiro and me with our Boston accents, Perls with his New York accent, travelling with a black minister. Wallace was running for President, and the white people in Mississippi were with him all the way. The daily newspapers were full of reports of people being trained to come in to help with voter registration. So people in Mississippi knew who we were and why we were there. We were just not welcome there because of the way we looked and sounded, and when we said what we wanted, they didn't like that either. "What do you want that nigger music for? You come down here with a machine to record..." And we're talking about the Library of Congress and about this music being an art form. They didn't want to hear about it.

One day we were riding along. Perls was driving. Reverend Wilkins was in the front seat. Spiro and I were crushed up in the back seat. We're going down this country dirt road. We needed directions. We pulled up in front of a barn with a fence running alongside of it. There were two young guys — big, heavy, beefy, red-faced guys with their hair cut short, almost to the skull, with big, beefy arms — just standing there.

We stopped the car. They were on the driver's side. Reverend Wilkins opened the door and said over the top of the Volkswagen, "Can you tell us how to get to so and so's house?"

They just looked at him for the longest time and then spat straight down in contempt. Spiro and I looked at each other. We were totally helpless in the back seat. The guys walked over and stood and looked right across the roof of the car at Reverend Wilkins. He had his coat off, was wearing a white shirt, a tie, and steel-rimmed spectacles. If there ever was calm, this man had it. He was so in possession and control of himself. He looked across and said very deliberately, "We're looking for so and so. He's around here somewhere."

They just looked at him, full of loathing and hatred. The air just crackled. They finally said, "Third farm down," and they turned and walked away. As they walked away, Reverend Wilkins said, "Thank you," and got back into the car.

June of '64 in the delta was a serious time. The day we finally talked to Son on the phone from Mississippi to Rochester, New York — June 21, 1964 — was the day that Goodman, Schwerner, and Chaney were killed.

We spoke to people in Indianapolis who put us on to people in Detroit, who put us on to people in Rochester. We called him and asked, "Are you the Son House who recorded for Paramount Records and the Library of Congress?"

He said, "Yeah, that's me."

We said, "Don't go anywhere, we're coming."

We left Memphis the following day and drove

straight to Rochester. When we got there we drove up to a four-story apartment building at 61 Grieg Street. We had sent a telegram so we knew he would be expecting us. He was supposed to be a short, fat man. There was a thin man sitting on the stoop with a woman. Spiro asked him if he knew which apartment Son House lived in.

"This is him," said Son House.

Interestingly enough, on that same day, Tuesday, the 23rd, Bill Barth, Henry Vestine, and John Fahey found Skip James in Tunica, Mississippi, about five miles from where we had been looking for Son. We had been looking for Skip, too, but when you played a record of Skip James for somebody, they'd look at you and say, "Nobody sounds like that." Skip had that high

falsetto and those strange tunings, and he didn't really play into the guitar. He sort of brushed the strings and would play things like "I'm So Glad" incredibly fast. There was simply nobody who played like Skip.

As soon as we found Son, we called Ralph Rinzler at Newport. We made a tape of two or three songs in Rochester and rushed it down to him. Son went to Newport, but he got sick and did not perform that year. The Newport Folk Festival of '64 was the greatest collection of country blues singers except for the '69 Ann Arbor Blues Festival. There was Robert Pete Williams, Sleepy John Estes with Hammy Nixon and Yank Rachel, Mississippi John Hurt, Skip James, Libba Cotten, Reverend Robert Wilkins,

The rediscovery of SON HOUSE, June 25, 1964, Rochester, New York. (left to right) NICK PERLS, DICK WATERMAN, SON HOUSE, and PHIL SPIRO. Photograph by Evie House. Courtesy of Phil Spiro.

SON HOUSE   Photograph by Joseph Sia.

Fred McDowell. It was just incredible. Sam Charters and Dr. Willis James hosted the workshops.

One of the great recollections I have of those workshops is when Skip James came in. He was wearing a hat and a heavy jacket. He had on a badge that said "Kin" (you were either "Performer," "Staff," or "Kin"). No one had heard him play except for the people who had discovered him. They brought him in, and he was sort of a presence on the grounds for the first day or so. People would say, "That's Skip James." He was very quiet, almost mysterious. Finally it came his time on this workshop. There was a little wooden pallet on the grass, and there was a chair on the pallet. Everyone was sitting around on the grass. There were maybe a couple of thousand people gathered around — all very attentive. These were the real folkies — the people who hung out at the 47 in Cambridge, the "Gaslight" in New York, and the "2nd Fret" in Philadelphia.

Skip sat down, and put his guitar on his leg. He set himself, doing a little finger manipulation with his left hand, then he set his fingers by the sound hole, sighed, and hit the first note of "I'd Rather Be The Devil Than Be That Woman's Man." He took that first note up in falsetto all the way, and the hairs on the back of my neck went up, and all up and down my arms, the hairs just went right up. Even now I get a reaction to that note when I listen to the recording of it on "Blues at Newport." It's such an eerie note. It's almost a wail. It's a cry.

There was an audible gasp from the audience. That to me is what it's all about. It was the same with Son when I first brought him to the Club 47 on the way to Newport. I sat him down in a chair on the stage, and handed him the guitar, which he held with the neck down lower than the body. He got himself set, and he lay the slide way down and then just ripped that slide up the neck and quivered it up near the body. Everybody went "AHH!" I looked around, and I could see that he had an ability to communicate powerfully. He could absolutely transfix people. And I said to myself, "What the hell did I get myself into?" I was in it then. I had turned a corner in my life, and there was no looking back from that point.

If Waterman was in it, at least it was as the result of his own choice. Imagine what the phenomenon of rediscovery meant to the rediscovered. That was the other side of the dream — and what a strange dream it was.

Imagine what it must have felt like to be confronted with these young, white, college-educated kids who materialized out of the blue to tell you that something you did thirty years ago on an afternoon had changed their lives, and then to be taken to a place far away where hundreds or even thousands more awaited you and expected you to change their lives, too. On one level it was sheer magic between an artist and those who deeply loved his art. That communication knows no boundaries be they geographical, social, racial — whatever. But what happened the rest of the time? What happened with the rest of the audience to whom you are some kind of curiosity? Peter Guralnick had grown up in the Cambridge area and had gradually become a blues fan. At one point Joe Boyd put together a concert at Eliot House at Harvard with the recently rediscovered bluesman Sleepy John Estes and his partner Hammy Nixon. Peter was in New York when he found out about it.

I had a friend at Harvard, and he called me one day to tell me that Sleepy John Estes was going to play at Eliot House. I said, "That's impossible! He must be one hundred and three years old!" We hadn't heard of anyone being rediscovered at this point. I was in New York going to Columbia, and I came back on the bus just to go to this concert.

Seeing Sleepy John and Hammy Nixon was a thrill for me, but it was very bizarre being in the audience at Eliot House. Estes never said a word. Hammy Nixon hammed it up. Some people in the audience were yelling, "Put it in the alley!" "Let's hear those blues, baby!" Other people were saying, "Shh. Shh." I felt between the two. I'd never had exposure to this kind of thing. I found out later that the best way to hear the music was where it occurred naturally when I went down south or to Chicago. Of course, there I'm an outsider, too. But at least the performer is comfortable, which is probably the better thing.

After that concert Joe Boyd, Geoff Muldaur, Eric von Schmidt, and a bunch of people took Sleepy John and Hammy to a party at Fritz's parents house in Newton. For Geoff it was a thrill just to be with them. For them it was probably strange. Newton is a long way from Brownsville, Tennessee, but everyone managed to have a pretty good time — especially Geoff.

It was a great party. They went to bed late at night with a bottle of Jack Daniels. When they woke up it was gone. They drank it in their sleep! They showed Fritz how to paint his jug. You had to put paint on the jug or it wouldn't have the

SKIP JAMES at the 1964 Newport Folk Festival wearing his "Kin" badge. Photograph by John Cooke.

right tune. At about two in the morning John went into his spiritual trip and started healing everybody. Nancy Wardwell was there and he got hold of her and sang blues to her. His thing was making up blues right on the spot. I went to shake his hand and say goodbye, and he sang:

"Ohhhh Geoff . . . I won't ever see you no more..." I just couldn't stand it.

In the course of the next few years it became clear to Phil Spiro that rediscovering someone was very much of a mixed blessing, and he had some second thoughts about it.

I'm half inclined today to say that if I had to do it all over again, I wouldn't do it. For someone like a Bill Monroe, who is primarily a performer, to drop into obscurity and then be rediscovered — that's life again. But for somebody who maybe recorded four or five records and who sat around with his buddies on the back porch and maybe played once in a while at a local joint, it's a whole other world which has a whole other set of values. To be sure, many of the ones who were found got their rocks off in their old age, at a time when they had no reasonable expectation of anything more exciting than a Social Security check. But what was the price we asked of them? And what did we give them? For the ones who had recorded before, like Son and Skip and Booker, we kept comparing them to their younger selves, and they knew it. How could they help knowing, when perhaps three-quarters of the people that they met were asking them questions about what color shirt they wore on that muggy delta day in 1931 when...Nobody seemed to give a flying fuck that they were *still* living on the wrong side of this poverty line, and that the income from their music was not enough to significantly improve their lot over welfare in most cases.

We also consciously or unconsciously tried to shape the music that they played on stage. The same statement could be made for the guys running Paramount during the thirties, but at least their motive was simple profit, which motive the artist shared. Our motivation was a strange combination of ego, scholasticism, and power. I wonder now what would have happened if we had just left them alone instead of telling them what songs to sing and what instrument to play them on.

The rediscoverers fought over the artists. Spotswood and Hoskins fought Denson and Fahey over Skip James. Hoskins and Waterman were at odds over John Hurt. We ended up embroiling these old guys in a lot of problems.

Money problems, mainly. Most of them wound up feeling they had been cheated. They had no way of assessing what their true worth was. It was something they weren't prepared to deal with, didn't know how to deal with, and, for the most part, didn't deal with well.

Worst of all, aside from a couple of people like Chris Strachwitz and Dick Waterman, the rediscoverers all too often didn't see the old guys as real, breathing, feeling, intelligent people. In general, we were collectors of people, who we tended to treat as if they were the very rarest of records — only one copy known to exist.

Within a year after discovering Son House, Dick Waterman was well aware that he was up to his ears in the story he had set out to cover. If it was too late to put the genie back in the bottle, he could at least try to give it some shape and direction which would benefit the various bluesmen who suddenly found themselves in some form of showbusiness, and at the mercy of some pretty dishonest, coldhearted types.

Nearly a year after the Newport Festival I was at the one and only New York Folk Festival. We were staying at the Henry Hudson Hotel, and I formed Avalon Productions in the bar of the hotel. Until that time, bluesmen were being managed and booked by people who had little record companies. People from Music Research had John Hurt, people from Takoma had Bukka White, people from Delmark had Sleepy John Estes. So I got everyone together and offered to book everyone and to make managerial and booking decisions. I said I would not get into the record business at all; I would route everyone. They would play more dates in more cities. The record people would know where they were playing and would be better able to promote and advertise their records. I was to represent Son, Skip, Bukka, Libba Cotten, Sleepy John, and Babe Stovall.

I said that I would set a minimum price. Then I went to the bluesmen and said that they would have to see to it that no one circumvented me. I knew that people would be calling them at home, telling them that I was asking too much and trying to sweet-talk them into working cheap. Some folkie from Cambridge could work for $50.00/day and come out ahead, but these men were a long way from home — always on the ground, never in planes. They'd spend fifteen hours on a bus, play somewhere for fifty or one hundred dollars, get a place to stay, breakfast, and then they'd be right back on the bus.

So I set up Avalon Productions and started

booking. The people that stood by our agreement did well, and I continued to work with them. Those who repeatedly went around me, I let go. Years later, John Hurt confided in me. He had spoken to Son House and Skip James and the others, and they had said, "Dick is fair. We go in and we get paid. Dick makes sure the money is good, and Dick gives us the money. We always know what we're going to get paid." Then John came to me, and we were moving towards a legal action when John died. Later, Tom Hoskins got a $280,000.00 settlement from Vanguard. He got money, back masters, copyrights, the works. For some people the rediscovery business turned out to be very profitable.

My attitude is that I toil hard for living people. I do the very best that I can for widows and children. However, once the bluesman is gone, I'm depressed by the almost ghoulish grave-robber aspect of it: ne'er-do-well children of former wives — people who never did anything for him in his lifetime — come in after the royalties or the copyrights.

For most of the bluesmen this experience was like the flare of a candle just before it goes out. For those of us who were lucky enough to be there, the light was a blessing and perhaps was enough to enable our own candles to burn a little bit brighter, a little bit longer. For some, like Al Wilson, the experience was what he needed to become himself.

If you talk in a certain way — in my case, like a person who spent the first twenty-two years of his life in a suburb of Boston — you talk in a whole different way — and, if only subconsciously, you attempt to sing the lyrics of a song with an inflection or any other simulation of any dialect you've heard, it creates a situation in which the very sentence, as divorced from music, cannot proceed in a natural, loose, and relaxed way. This is why I think there's an advantage in getting away from the traditional words and using the way you talk yourself — though I definitely would have to agree that the way they talk in Arlington, Mass., is lacking in the poetic quality I hear in the way they talk in Mississippi. Nonetheless, there's nothing gained in attempting to simulate that. You just have to use your own way.

This page:
(top) PHIL SPIRO
Photograph by Rick Sullo.
(bottom) DICK WATERMAN
Photograph by Jerry Jaffe.

Following page:
SKIP JAMES (1964) Photograph by David Gahr.
CANNED HEAT (foreground) LARRY TAYLOR,
FITO DE LA PARRA. (background) AL WILSON,
BOB HITE, HENRY VESTINE. Photograph by
Rick Sullo.

Look over yonder
   on the burying ground
   on the burying ground
Look over yonder
   on the burying ground.
Yonder stand ten thousand
      standing to see them let down.

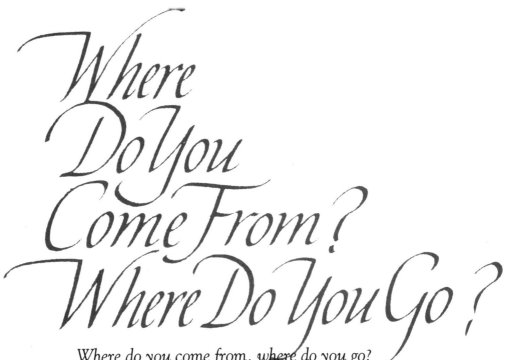

Where Do You Come From? Where Do You Go?

Where do you come from, where do you go?
Where do you come from, Cotton-eye Joe?
Well, I come for to see you, and I come for to sing,
I come for to show you my diamond ring.

t was the year of the Hootenanny, and Jim Rooney was going out of his way to miss it. He was going all the way to Greece on a Fulbright Fellowship — a rare example of the taxpayers' money being well spent.

I guess I could have made a lot of money if I'd stayed home that year. Even though Bill Keith was away with Bill Monroe, I kept playing at the 47 with Joe Val and Herb Applin and Siggins. Robert Shelton from the *New York Times* came up and told me that I had "star quality," whatever that was. The handwriting was definitely on the wall as far as my academic career was concerned. I'd been doing it with mirrors ever since I got into the music scene in Cambridge. I had to teach a Humanities section at Harvard at eight o'clock on Saturday mornings, and at about three in the morning it would get down to whether to shoot through or try to catch some sleep and wake up. My students liked me, though. I was the only

section man who wore cowboy boots and sang hillbilly songs and had office hours in Tommy's Lunch next to the 47. I got a lot done at Tommy's.

I had also been getting more involved in the running of the Club. Byron and I got along real well. We both found each other's boiling point real fast. During one of my first meetings as a Director we got into it over toilet paper — a very important item. My girl friend at the time was working as a waitress, and she used to come home and tell me how mean Byron was and how hard to work for, and so on. It was a little fifth column action. One night she mentioned that she had been shocked to discover that there was no toilet paper in the ladies room, and that this had been true on more than one occasion. Terrible. So I brought it up at this meeting. It might have been my first, I don't know. At any rate, Byron either denied it or ignored it or said something that made me start to get a little bit heavy about it. I wanted to know what he was going to do about it. He came back at me, and before we knew it we were yelling at each other about toilet paper! I think the others were wondering why they'd ever put me on the

Board in the first place. It was ridiculous. The next night I came into the Club and at some point Byron asked me if I'd been downstairs. I said, "Not tonight." He didn't say anything more, so, of course, I had to go down. There was toilet paper forever down there. Boxes of it. Stacks of it. From then on we were together.

The Club that summer was jammed all the time, and it became clear that it would be a good thing if we could find a better place. We'd always had the pretense of being an art gallery and occasionally tried some chamber music, but the place was sort of funky, and those things never had quite jelled there. I'd gotten Nancy Sweezy involved in the Board, because she was pretty together and responsible and smart. Betsy Siggins and Nancy and I started looking around the area for anything that might be available. Over in back of the Harvard Coop was a building in the process of being totally gutted and remodelled inside. It was a great old brick building, one of the oldest in the area. We started poking around. The basement had no floor. It was dirt. Somehow the area looked right to us, and then we discovered that the owner lived right next to Betsy and Bob. Sheldon Dietz. A true Cambridge crazy, but crazy like a fox. He'd burst into opera while he was talking to you about the rent or the rubbish barrels. At any rate, that was it. We could have them do anything we wanted — brick floors, brick and cork and plaster walls, a kitchen area, lights. It was going to look great and be very simple. The rent was over twice what we'd been paying — $750.00/month — but we all thought we could do it because of the increased capacity — about 150 to 175 people — and because we'd accumulated a good-sized nest egg — thanks to Byron's management. So it was decided to move. Naturally, I left everybody else to do the work and pick up the pieces while I sailed off to Greece.

Club 47 Calendar designed by BYRON LORD LINARDOS.

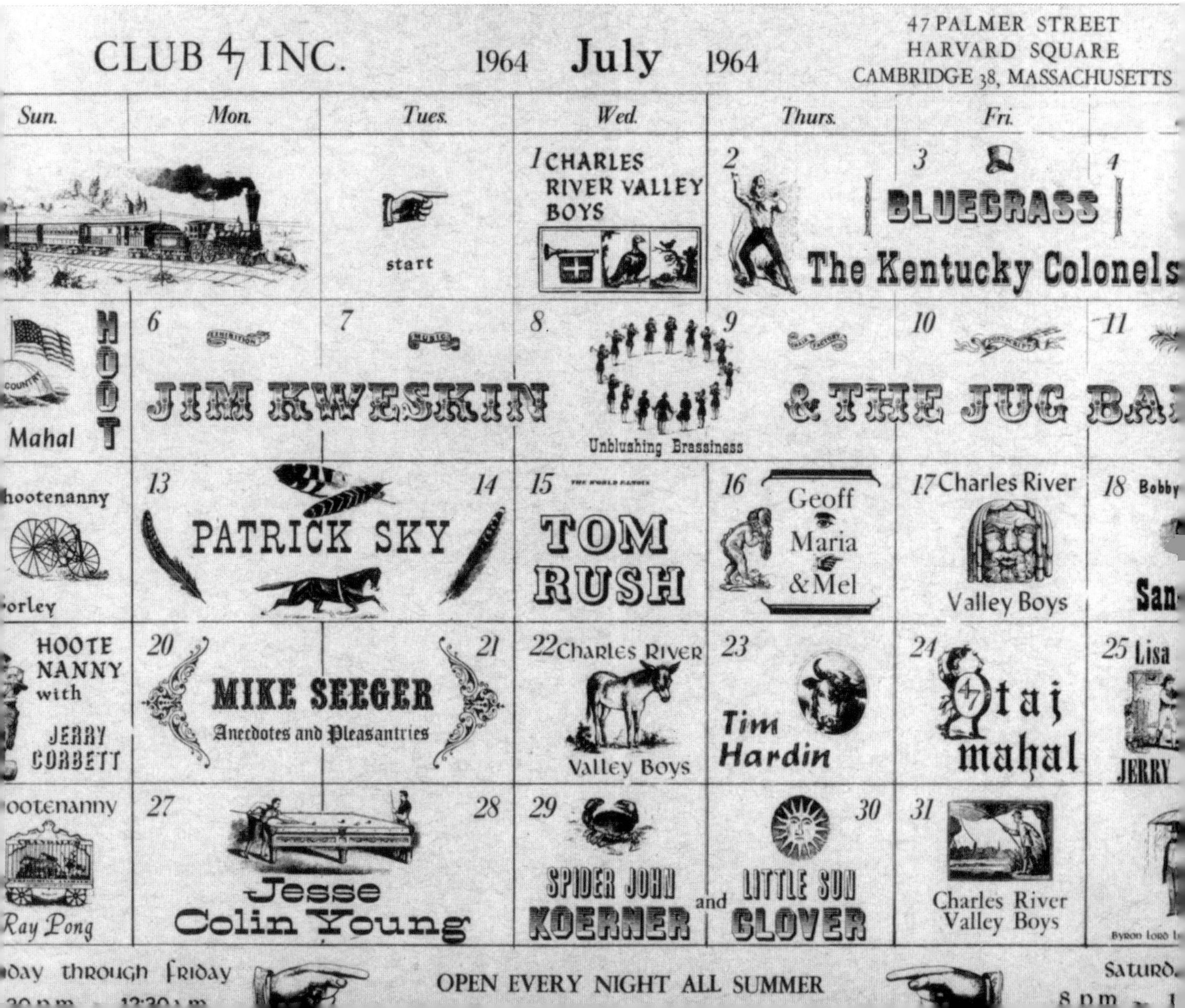

CLUB 47 INC.   1964 **July** 1964

47 PALMER STREET
HARVARD SQUARE
CAMBRIDGE 38, MASSACHUSETTS

In the words of some wise man: "One monkey don't stop no show." Rooney was toasted and serenaded the night before he left to the point that he nearly didn't make the boat. Even as he sailed out of New York harbor the scene up in Cambridge was expanding almost daily and life went on without him. As always, New York was fast becoming the business center of the folk revival. ABC started a "Hootenanny" TV show, which got off to a wonderful start by not allowing Pete Seeger, who was the only person in the world who knew the real meaning of "hootenanny," to appear on the air. Somebody else started *Hootenanny* magazine and hired Robert Shelton to front it. Recording companies started paying attention. Managers became overnight fans of folk music. But on the ground, life was much the same for the singers who began to show up from all over the country to seek their fortune. Many of them came to Cambridge and found that they could make a few dollars, have a good time, get better at what they were trying to do, and get away from the pressure and grind of New York. Mark Spoelstra was one of the first.

 hen I came to New York in the Fall of '59 I hardly knew anyone there. I knew Sonny Terry and Brownie Mc-Ghee from their parties in Los Angeles, and I began to hang out with them. As a matter of fact, I might have perished if it had not been for Sonny slipping me a couple of bucks now and then. Then again, I almost perished from the booze I consumed with them. A friend of mine ran into me on the street one day and said there was a guy he thought I should meet. He was sitting alone in a joint, having just come to town. So I was one of the first acquaintances Bob Dylan met when he came to the big city. We hung out together a lot, because at the time we had a lot in common. One night we were playing at the Cafe Wha?, and John Cohen, who was with the New Lost City Ramblers, came in and was blown away by my John Hurt style guitar and Bob's blues harp — all in the middle of a hundred greasy New Jersey hoods, slick folkie singers, and stand-up comedians. John told Moe Asch at Folkways Records about me, and thus began our two album relationship.

Moe's was the only record company interested in me, and I was elated. I mean I was coming from the bottom — ten cents a glass wine, cold boiled potatoes, and lentils when the basket money was good. When Moe sat across from me at his big desk and said, "I want to make a record," I thought it

represented good times, and I showed my excitement by jumping up and giving a big yaa-hoo! Tears might have come, too. From that time on Moe and I respected each other. I know he did a great deal for me that I guess he wasn't doing for other artists. He really pushed my first single and album. On many occasions, when broke, I would write and ask him for money, or if there was any coming to me I'd mention a figure of what I needed, and that's exactly what the hand-written royalty statement would say.

At that time I simply wanted to change the world and thought that I could. I wasn't interested in politics, but in relationships — in condemning our behavior, through song, and offering the vague banner of love for one another as the answer. But my lifestyle and ability to make peace within the group I hung out with fell far short of my ideal. Thus arose the moral dilemma for me as an artist and person: With no power, how do you love the unlovable — yourself included?

With that sort of turmoil pouring out of my fingertips and mouth it was no wonder that I was restless and somewhat of a rambler. Cambridge seemed like a more relaxed place to live than New York, and I'd heard that there were lots of places to sing, so I moved up there. Until I moved to Cambridge I was singing mostly blues and traditional folk stuff. As I gained confidence up there, I began doing my own songs. So I began to feel as if I was actually finding an outlet for my songs and philosophy. It was much more open up there than it was in New York, and it was a whole lot more fun, with parties all night after the 47 closed. It seemed there were new pickers coming to town all the time. The Newport Festival added to it all, and it definitely was an incredible phenomenon. Maybe some quality was missing, but not the energy. There were so many middle class people looking for some other kind of identity: lovers became clowns; losers became heroes; drunks became saints; poets became comedians; role playing became reality. We had a way of considering everyone but ourselves bizarre, yet we competed for any kind of attention we could get. We created a little world of our own with no absolutes but our ideals.

One of my ideals was that men should not go to war and kill each other. And that's what took me away from Cambridge. Soon after I recorded my second Folkways album at the 47, I headed back to California to work for two years in a semi-migrant black community struggling against the grape vines in West Fresno. That was in lieu of entering the armed forces. That's when my ideals came up against reality, and I had to rethink

everything that I had sung about so easily when I was in Cambridge. It was still a good time, though — low rent, no taxes, and all-out lovin'. And good friends that stuck with me all the way.

Mark was not alone. Many other talented singers started following the trail to Cambridge in the summer and fall of 1963. Tim Hardin, Lisa Kindred, and Jerry Corbett all settled in and began playing not only at the 47 but at the Loft and the Turkshead on Charles Street in Boston. The Cafe Yana was being booked by Dave Wilson, who took a leave of absence from *The Broadside*. The third wave of the Boston/Cambridge folk revival was in full swing.

Boston itself had its own "Hootenanny" show on the largest radio station in town, WBZ. The host was a genial DJ named Jefferson Kaye, and soon Tom Rush, Jackie Washington, and The Charles River Valley Boys found themselves playing in all sorts of places they never expected to be. Bob Siggins didn't mind. He had a great sense of the absurd.

We played a lot of crazy gigs. WBZ had a big free concert at the shell on the Charles River. Twenty-seven thousand people showed up. They had a launch to carry us down the river to the shell. So there we were, on this boat, trying to play for the press and cameras and everything. And the pilot kept flooring it, and we'd fall over, getting covered with spray. Joe was trying to wipe off his mandolin. When we got to the shell, it was just a sea of people, all milling around. "Baby-O" and "Auctioneer" got them up. It was the year of the hootenanny. Everybody would clap along. We made a lot of money.

Over in Greece, Rooney was deep in his research of the native wines. Every so often he would take time out to listen to a tape from home. **Siggins sent me a tape around Christmas time. I was starved for some music from home, and it was great to get caught up on some bluegrass. Then I heard the craziest thing I'd heard since listening to some of the stuff on the *Anthology*. It was "Hangman" by Spider John Koerner. I loved that record. It was the most original thing I'd heard in ages. It was brilliant.**

Just after Rooney had left to go to Greece, Betsy Siggins had gone down to the Philadelphia Folk Festival. It was the first "big time" appearance for the Kweskin Jug Band, and they did great. Then at about two in the morning there was a surprise appearance by three young unknowns from Minnesota: Tony "Little Son" Glover, Dave "Snaker" Ray, and "Spider" John Koerner. Betsy thought Koerner was the funniest person she'd ever heard in her life. Visually he was a treat, too —

(bottom) TIM HARDIN Photograph by Dick Waterman.

skinny as a rail, with his sleeves rolled up, his arms going on a nine-string crazy guitar, his legs really looking like a spider's, long and loose-jointed. It was the beginning of a long romance between Cambridge and Spider John.

1 t's obvious that there was a phenomenon that went on. My own memories of it start in Minnesota with a certain group of people who were listening to folk music. I was at the University of Minnesota studying to be an aeronautical engineer. For about a year and a half I was doing fairly well and then somebody showed me the guitar and other things and school came to be too much drudgery and I started fading. But for eight years I tried to complete school. I quit and came back, quit and came back. Never made it.

Sometime in there, about 1958 or '59, there were these people there. They were a certain kind of type. Some of them were sort of scholarly. There were people who'd know a thousand songs. Who collected records. And they'd gather together and drink wine and play these songs and that was the first I knew of it.

You'd hear the Weavers and Josh White and Burl Ives. It was sort of an underground thing. Then the Kingston Trio came along and — whatever you think of them — the lid was off. Then it was all over the place pretty quick. I took off for a little while, and in the fall of 1959 when I came back, there was a place called "The 10 o'clock Scholar" in an area called Dinkytown in Minneapolis. It was coffee and chess and stuff like that, and sometimes people would play there at night. Bob Dylan was one. He was on the scene at that time. I had learned to play the guitar by then, so I'd play, too.

I learned to play the guitar when I was first at the university. One day some guy comes down — I had no idea about any of that shit — and says, "Would you like to come up to my room and listen to some music?" So I said, "Okay," and I went up there, and he played me some folk records. He had a guitar, and I had never heard about any of it. I didn't know anything had been going on or was coming up or anything like that. So in a sense it's interesting because it's kind of pure. It caught my eye without any previous conditioning. So he loaned me his guitar for a few days and a Burl Ives songbook, and I found out it was pretty easy to learn the chords and to strum. And he was part of this group that used to get together and do all that.

So when I came back to Dinkytown, there was this little scene going. Dave Ray came out of that. He was going to the University High School. All of a sudden there were other places that came up. There was one real funky guy named Mel Leslie who started a coffeehouse on the other side of the river. Some pizza parlor opened up with music Fridays and Saturdays. And it was going.

There was some time then when Dave Ray and I were together. Somehow or another Dave knew Tony Glover. At one point Dave went to New York City. He was working in the garment district and really funking it out. I was back home in Rochester for a while, and I went to visit him and stayed at his place one night, and Tony Glover came around. So we got drunk and played for a couple of days. And that was that. Somehow we all showed up back in Minneapolis once again and started doing it seriously.

One thing I think that happened when we were out in Minnesota was — and I still believe in this process in a sense — we were just enthusiastic. We had no idea what you were supposed to be doing with this material. So we just got into it and went right ahead with it without knowing what anybody else outside our own immediate area thought about it. We were really insular. We didn't know much about what was going on on the East coast at that point, so I think when we came on the larger folk scene, we really surprised some people just because we weren't like the others.

Paul Nelson was out there at the time. They published a little magazine about folk music called *The Little Sandy Review.* They were pretty serious and real opinionated. At any rate, he was interested in our stuff. He thought there was something in it. He knew this guy from Audiophile Records which is located in Milwaukee. It's owned by this guy, Ed Nunn, who has something to do with Nunn-Busch Shoes. We suspect now that the reason he wanted to record us is that he had heard us and was looking for a tax loss. Anyway, he recorded us and after a fair amount of hassling, the record came out, and Nelson sent a copy of it to Elektra Records where it sat in a stack until its turn came up. Jac Holzman listened to it and dug it, called us up, and said he wanted to come right out and sign us up. This was about 1963.

So Holzman signed us. They re-released the Audiophile thing, and the contract also had something to do with recording for them. They cut two songs off of each side of the Audiophile record because we had made a terribly long record. It was pretty funky. He recorded us in some

(top) SPIDER JOHN KOERNER Publicity shot courtesy of Manny Greenhill.
(bottom left) TONY "LITTLE SON" GLOVER and SPIDER JOHN KOERNER. Photograph by Rick Sullo.
(bottom right) "SNAKER" DAVE RAY Photograph by John Cooke.

women's club hall. He would have absolutely no drinking, no swearing. Here we are, the wild boys from Minneapolis, and we've got to sit there and play straightlaced.

They then flew us to New York to record the second record. We were feeling pretty great about it. While we were there, the Philadelphia Folk Festival was coming up, and they took us down there right after the recording sessions. They got us in on the show late at night as an extra, and it worked out just right. It was great. We were surprised that all these people dug it so much.

Siggy was there, and she talked to us and asked us if we'd play at the 47 so we came up. That was the first time I'd ever heard of or saw Cambridge. That was just the beginning. I had a fast life there for a while, starting when I came to Cambridge. The whole scene was going full tilt. There was music and money and women and bars so I stayed. I was out to boogie.

It definitely was phenomenal, and I wonder about that phenomenon — what the hell it was. Like I say, it sort of came out of a very pure thing with no thought of making a killing in folk music. I still feel the old way in a sense. I'm trying to make my living by my music, but I can't see taking advantage of it.

Sometimes you've got an advantage being from another place. Sometimes I find myself in situations, and I say to myself, "Okay, now, just don't forget you're from Minnesota." It gives me a little extra power. Coming from the Hinterlands. It reminds me of a science fiction story about some people who used to live on the asteroid belts. They got real tough because of that. So this guy came from the asteroids to earth to find out who had offed his buddy, and he had to find out all this

shit, and he was always ahead of the game, fighting the mob and everybody. Coming from Minnesota to New York City or Boston, that's sometimes the way I feel.

Koerner was an original. The energy and originality jumped out of Rooney's tape recorder at him all the way over in Athens. Soon he was to hear something else equally as startling.

Bill Keith sent me some great tapes that year. There was one that had Stan Freberg's "New Prince Spaghetti Minstrels" (Gold is the color of my true love's noodles...) and "Dang Me" and "Chug-a-lug" by Roger Miller, complete with barf ending. Music was definitely loosening up at home. But the one that floored me was a tape that Bill had made at his house of him and Clarence White playing fiddle tunes — Bill on the banjo and Clarence on the guitar. The only other person I had heard play the guitar on that level was Doc Watson. I found out later that Clarence was only eighteen. It was hard to believe that someone that young could play so musically, with such taste and sensitivity. It was absolutely beautiful.

larence White had arrived in Cambridge shortly after Rooney had left. He and his brother Roland had a band called The Country Boys with Roger Bush and Billy Ray Latham. As Roland recalls, they took the long way around to get to Cambridge.

We originally came from the state of Maine. My dad played fiddle and banjo. Most of his brothers and some of his sisters played. There were seventeen of them. All French-Canadians. Every

THE COUNTRY BOYS (left to right) ROLAND WHITE, BILLY RAY LATHAM, ROGER BUSH, and CLARENCE WHITE. Courtesy of Betsy Schmidt.

weekend my dad would take us out to Grange halls. We would play and sing country songs — a lot of Roy Acuff and Hank Williams and instrumentals like "Ragtime Annie" and "Rubber Dolly."

We moved to Burbank, California, in 1954. As soon as we got there, we played on a talent show and won it. Out of that we got on a Saturday night TV show every week. We called ourselves "The Country Boys." My brother Eric played tenor banjo, Clarence played guitar, and I played mandolin. An uncle played us some Bill Monroe records, and I started to buy some. I got *Pike County Breakdown* and *Footprints in the Snow.* Then I started ordering from Jimmie Skinner's Music Store in Ohio. If you ordered as much as eight a week, you got a free record. I did that for about eleven years. So from that we started playing bluegrass in about 1956. I played banjo until we met Billy Ray Latham. Eventually we did some Andy Griffith TV shows in 1959 and 1960.

The Ash Grove in L.A. Was the first thing we did in the folk scene. We heard about it from a friend of ours named Walt Pitman, so we talked to the owner, Ed Pearl, and he asked us to come down one night and play a set. We did. We were the first organized bluegrass band in Southern California, and we were the first bluegrass band to play at the Ash Grove. They liked us, and set us up one week to play with the New Lost City Ramblers and another week with the Tarriers. It was all new to us.

I got drafted right after that. Clarence was going to school, and the others just got day jobs. While I was in the Army, the Ash Grove brought in Flatt and Scruggs and Bill Monroe. Doc Watson also played there, and that's when Clarence started to play flat-top guitar. Clarence was still living at home, but sometimes he'd go over to Roger Bush's house. Roger was our bass player. He told me that it was nothing for Clarence to sit all day long by himself in a room and play. When I came out of the Army in September of '63 he was playing the hell out of the guitar. He was listening a lot to Doc Watson, Earl Scruggs, and Josh Graves.

About two weeks after I got out, we left for Cambridge. Ed Pearl had talked to Mike Seeger's wife, Marge, and she set it up with Betsy Siggins for us to play at the Club 47. Marge also booked us into Gerde's Folk City in New York and the Ontario Place in Washington. Then we went back to Boston to play at the Unicorn. The whole trip just about broke even, but it got us out and into the East Coast scene.

Cambridge was an unusual place. Everybody was very friendly to us. The Siggins' house was incredible. We went over there a lot to pick. One night everyone was picking and this girl just went crazy clogging. She went at it all night while we played. It was Maria Muldaur.

Bill Keith was with Monroe at the time, and we took a night off to drive down to Hartford to see them play. Then Keith came down with us to Tracy Schwartz's house in New Jersey. We stayed there for a few days, and Bill and Clarence really picked well together. We played some great music that week.

We left Cambridge December twenty-second, and we were home Christmas Eve! The next summer we were invited to the Newport Folk Festival, so we did the same circuit all over again. We had a new name: The Kentucky Colonels. This time we moved out there. We had had such a good time in Cambridge that it seemed like a good place to make our headquarters. We never got to play to people who listened until we played places like the Ash Grove and the Club 47. It really turned us on to see all those people come out to see us and really sit down and listen. When you did something good they knew it, and that made you want to play better each time. Playing in Cambridge gave us confidence in our own music. It took a long time, but we hung in there, and it made a big difference to us.

Being able to listen to Clarence White made a big difference to a lot of pickers in Cambridge, too. Peter Rowan was in the front row as often as he could be. Peter was another who had given college a try and had come up short.

When I went away to Colgate College in upper New York State, I really got homesick for the scene in Cambridge. I missed that energy. I was attracted to the long ballads on the one hand and the blues of Lightnin' Hopkins on the other, but I couldn't sing either very well. I had heard some bluegrass — the Lilly Brothers and Keith and Rooney — and I thought that bluegrass had both the ballad tradition and a blues tradition that I could get a handle on. So I formed a bluegrass band. I had gotten a D-28 and started to try to flat pick. I'd spend my days reading books and my nights playing in hillbilly bars in the area around Syracuse. It was much more fun than going to school. Without knowing it I was partaking of the creative process I was supposed to be learning about.

As my career in college began to totally disintegrate, I was spending more time in my room playing. I had picked up a mandolin after I saw Joe Val play with Keith and Rooney. I would stand in my room in front of a mirror with a broom taped to the chair. I had watched how people worked a microphone with their acoustic instruments. I'd actually pretend I had a whole band going. I'd step out of the way for the banjo; I'd sing harmony -

all by myself. I was totally engrossed in the magic of holding an instrument up to a microphone and playing with other people.

School seemed to make less and less sense, and I just packed it in and got an apartment in Boston. I'd take the bus to Cambridge and start to hang out. I got to be friends with Joe Val. I started to really meet people. Before, I had really been in awe and hanging on.

I did some gigs with Joe Val as a duet. We played at the opening of a drugstore in Chelsea, among other things. I learned a lot of songs from Joe and the romance of learning songs which another person had sung over the years began to have some meaning for me. I became part of the "Folk Process," learning all those great Louvin Brothers tunes from Joe.

In the summer of '64 I spent some time out on Martha's Vineyard hanging out with Banana and his bunch. They were repairing instruments. Everybody had a different attitude than people had in school. There was a looseness about the scene and if you were into the music, that was all that mattered. It wasn't a star trip. You played bluegrass with other people. If you could play well

enough or sing well enough, that's all that mattered. The White Brothers were a heavy influence on all of us. I remember hearing them at the Unicorn. Night after night I'd listen to Clarence, who was barely eighteen years old. He really inspired me.

"Banana" was in real life a young picker named Lowell Levinger who had come to Boston the year before to study acting at B.U. Like Joan and Debbie and Betsy and Kweskin and who knows how many others, he was soon to founder on the reefs of folk music.

Above:
JOE VAL *and* PETER ROWAN
Photograph by John Cooke.

Opposite:
"BANANA" *and his banjo.*
Photograph by John Cooke.

was raised in Santa Rosa, California. I was at the Robert Louis Stevenson School for Boys in Pebble Beach and getting into the guitar about 1960. I was listening to Sonny and Brownie and Lightnin' Hopkins a lot. My American history teacher and dorm master was a guy named David Litton. He was fresh out of Harvard. He told me about Lester Flatt and Earl Scruggs. I loved the names, but when he put the "Foggy Mountain Banjo" record on for me, my life changed. I just couldn't believe that this was happening. I went right out and got a banjo and learned to play it. That was one of the things that got me to Cambridge eventually. I wanted to study acting. He recommended that I go to B.U., so I went. I lasted a year and a half.

Michael Kane, Rick Turner, and I shared an apartment. I met Michael the first day or orientation at B.U. He played the guitar, too. Rick Turner had an apartment off campus where we spent a lot of time. The next year we all shared the place together. I finally had to leave to play bluegrass. One morning I got up and I wasn't going to school! It felt great. It was the best decision I'd ever made, though it was tough to make it.

So it was "Banana and the Bunch: Bluegrass with A-peel." The Charles River Valley Boys and Keith and Rooney had the bluegrass market cornered in Cambridge, so we played a lot of Bar Mitzvah's and parties. Charles Street in Boston was where a lot of people were playing, because there just wasn't room for everyone to play at the 47. We played at the Loft and the Turkshead and did hootenannies at the 47. Eventually we got in with John and Jane Nagy and formed the "Proper Bostonians." I played banjo, Rick played guitar, Michael played bass, Nagy played guitars, and Jane sang. We had good arrangements of folk material and were pretty good. We got booked all over the place — a lot in the mid-west. By the summer of '64 we'd had it with travelling, and Rick, Michael, and I went to Martha's Vineyard. We opened the Island String Shop in the back of the Mooncusser. We were also the house band. The string shop was sort of a joke. We did some repairs and sold a lot of dope. We managed to stay high most of the time.

Banana and the Bunch weren't the only ones getting high that summer. What had once been a rather exclusive club of vipers was starting to become an open society of "heads." No one noticed the change more than Rooney on his return home. **When I came back from Greece I got together with**

PETER ROWAN, JOE VAL, and TEX LOGAN (1964) Courtesy of Peter Rowan.

some people at the club. We headed off to a party and I gave Bill Keith a ride. As we drove over there we were getting closer and closer and Bill said, "Er, ah, well…" and I think he actually said, "I hope you won't think badly of me but…" — it was that serious. He said that there were going to be a lot of people smoking dope at the party and he was going to be one of them. I said, "Well, frankly, Bill, I myself have learned to smoke dope, too." A very serious conversation. Then he said he had been up at Albert Grossman's with the Jug Band. Dylan and various people were up there, and he finally did it. He stayed up all night and saw all the beautiful colors in the sunrise.

Before I'd left very few people were smoking — mostly Kweskin and Fritz and the people Neuwirth hung out with — and it was definitely out at the Club. Nobody would risk closing the Club for a joint. Byron was adamant about that, and everybody respected that. And I myself was scared to death of acid. My girl friend had been in with Leary and Alpert, and she almost got killed one day riding her bicycle through Harvard Square when the pavement turned to water! That was months after she'd taken anything, so I wanted nothing to do with it.

While I was in Greece, Sally Schoenfeld and Susie Campbell came to visit me, and we drove to Istanbul. We were staying in a fashionable 75¢ a night place, and it happened that there was this American staying there. His name was Lionel, and he was on his way from Afghanistan to Paris. He had a VW bus, and it was full of hash — great big blocks of it. And he had a water pipe with an amber mouthpiece and a brass bowl, and it was too good to pass up. I figured if I was ever going to do it, this was the time — in Istanbul, in a sleazy hotel, with the minarets and everything all around. It was like a Humphrey Bogart movie. So I did it. And nothing happened! I tried some more. Nothing. It was the classic dope joke. It doesn't do…Then it hit, and I was out there for hours. So I was into it after that, but not to the point of buying any. Only if it was offered. When I got back to Cambridge, it was being offered a lot. I don't recall turning any down.

It felt great to be back. I brought Byron a gigantic bottle of ouzo which we did in my first night home. The new club looked terrific. They'd got slat chairs from North Carolina and made tables out of two-inch oak. First class. And I realized how much I'd missed Betsy and Bob and Keith and Joe. I'd had a fantastic year, but I was home, and I knew it. It was worth a year away to find out how much those people meant to me. I was beginning to understand what the *Odyssey* was all about. You had to leave home to find home.

One of the many changes that had taken place while Rooney was away was that Joe Val had become a Charles River Valley Boy, but Joe had a replacement ready for Keith and Rooney. He immediately introduced Jim to Peter Rowan. Joe's recommendation was enough for him and Bill, and Peter no longer had to play alone in front of the mirror.

After I got together with Jim and Bill, I started listening to Bill Monroe more and more. I studied everything I could find at Briggs and Briggs. Then in late October Monroe came up to play in Brattleboro, Vermont. Bill Keith was going to play banjo and he asked me if I'd like to play guitar. I jumped at the chance.

So I finally got to play with Bill Monroe. Here he was — the master — walking fifteen feet off to the left of the band chopping rhythm and watching the band from over there! I couldn't believe it. It was so different from our practiced choreography. His rhythm was so magnetizing you felt there was a direct electrical current running through this man.

Of course, he had never met me in his life. I had learned "Up Along the Ohio River," which was the first duet I ever sang with him. No one ever used to do it. It was an obscure, great, bluesy lament. We sang that, and after the show we were sitting there and he said,

"You pick pretty good. You ought to come to Nashville. I could help you."

I didn't really get the full import of that. He was really asking me to come play with him, but he never said it outright.

But I started talking with Bill Keith. We had endless conversations about Bill Monroe. Finally, we jumped in the car and drove down to the Disc Jockey Convention in Nashville and came back. Then a few weeks later Monroe came to play with Doc Watson at Jordan Hall in Boston. I met Tex Logan that night, and that's when the fiddle began to have meaning for me. That night was also the night that I asked Monroe if I could come to Nashville. He asked me about school and the army. I didn't tell him that I was due to go for a physical. Vietnam was getting hot and I was twenty-one.

I started to get real uptight because I thought the army was going to ruin everything, so I went over to see Banana and Michael Kane and Jerry Corbett and Peter Childs. We had a pioneer encounter group with the help of some wonderful herb. We had a long talk about what was happening, and it was clear that I was making a decision to be a musician. I needed some kind of reinforcement because everyone was sort of taking it for granted that I was going to play, but I felt a lot of pressure — *They* want me to be in school and the army and everything. So we had these long, stoned, philosophical discussions about what they want you to do is *obey* them (whoever "they" are). Grass was a help in that it reinforced the creative urge by giving me that little glow inside which made me want to play music, which made it feel right. So we stayed up for three nights and three days before my army physical discussing the politics of how to be an individual in the twentieth century. When I went to take my physical I was beyond their borders. I had become a full-fledged BEATNIK! I let my freak flag right out there for the army because that was the only way they would not want me.

After twenty-four hours of being in Banana's pad on Hughes Street, it was decided that it was time for "New Pete" to go out in the world and practice. So I went over to Kresge's in Central Square. Dogs barked at me. I went in and went to the pet department and started opening all the doors to the bird cages. I went through all the "No Entrance" doors. Finally they caught up with me. I just walked away. I said nothing. That was to get me ready to ignore the orders at the physical. The idea was not to say "No," but to *be* "No." I was "No," and the army rejected me.

That night I remember Jim and Bill and I had a gig at Marlboro College in Vermont. I was still pretty spaced out, but I was also elated. I was a free man. I had made a commitment to a lifestyle and career that was way beyond any of the considerations I had earlier.

PETER ROWAN Courtesy of Peter Rowan.

BILL MONROE and PETER ROWAN at Newport. (1965) Photograph by John Cooke.

After a few more gigs with Jim and Bill, I drove to Nashville with Keith and started with Bill Monroe. I think it meant a lot to him to have people like Bill Keith or me or Richard Greene go with him. He always told people we were "Good Boys," but he was very reticent about committing himself emotionally.

I got to know him more and more because I could write with him. "The Walls of Time" is a song that I wrote with him, although I'm not given credit for it. We were driving through Kentucky. The sun was just coming up. He was in one car. I was in another. He pulled over and signalled me to stop. I got out and he said, "Listen to this and don't forget it," and he sang the whole melody. I got back in the car singing it over and over, and by the time we got to Beanblossom I had some words for it. We were writing all over napkins in the restaurant where we stopped for breakfast. I think it made him happy to have someone he could do that with.

I tried booking Bill. We played at the Club 47 and at several colleges. When we got back to Cambridge it was still a thriving scene. I was starved for that atmosphere after being in Nashville for a few months. David Grisman was living there then and so was Sandy Getz and Richard Greene. We went up to David's and picked all night. Richard was a non-stop fiddler. At the time he was with the Greenbriar Boys. A little later he called me up and asked me if I'd like to come play with them, but I told Richard he should come play with the man who was the originator. He didn't know about moving to Nashville, but later that year we got Richard to play with us in Montreal and then we played in Cambridge again and Richard came back with us on the bus. That gave me someone to play with, and I taught him everything Bill did. I started getting into writing then, and it began to dawn on me that I really had become a musician. Music had become my life. Which is still a revelation.

Becoming a musician for life was something that hadn't really occurred to many people a few years earlier when they started to pick up guitars or banjos. Music was something you did for fun on the side, but not as a career. Siggins, Sackheim, Ethan Signer, Rooney — even Joe Val — had always kept music on the side. Peter Rowan was one of several who were a little bit younger, who came into the folk scene at a point when a person could make enough money from music so that it became possible to think of music as a way of life. Rooney was impressed by still another of the new faces he saw at the new Club.

One of my first nights back I came into the Club just about closing time to see Byron. I didn't know who had been playing that night, and I was talking to him at the door, but I was hearing some mighty piano playing. It was strong and rockin'. I took a look inside, and it was a big black guy. I didn't register who it was right away, and then he looked up at me and shouted, "Rooney! What are you doing here? I thought you was supposed to be in Greece!" It was Taj! Taj Mahal. He'd come to UMass just as I was leaving Amherst, but I'd met him up there with Bill Keith. So here he was in Cambridge right in the thick of it.

aj Mahal was just at that point in his life when he was testing himself to see how far he wanted to go with his music. He had gone to UMass with the idea of getting into agriculture or veterinary medicine, but music had been pulling him for a long time, and he wanted to give it a try.

I grew up in the city of Springfield, Massachusetts. My mother is from Cheraw, North Carolina. My father was from New York City, but his people were from St. Kitts. So I had the American south on one side and West Indian on the other. I came up in a pretty musical atmosphere. My father had a jazz collection. He had been a jazz pianist, but he gave that up to raise his family. My mother sang a lot of spirituals.

Springfield was an interesting place. There were about 1400 black people from all over the world. We had everything from Holy Rollers to people from Panama who were into Pocomanian music. So there was a lot of music. I tried to sing; I fooled with the piano. But the music that they wanted me to play in school and the music I felt

JESSE LEE KINCAID and TAJ MAHAL at the 47. (1964) Courtesy of Manny Greenhill.

and heard were always in two different places. Eventually my folks gave up on giving me any formal lessons. I tried to work it out for myself. I played a little harmonica but didn't get too far with it. A lot of it was pretty typical of a kid in the city without the input of the teachers.

I was a radio listener, and I began to be able to tell the difference between the pop commercial sound and the sound of music that people played whether they got paid for it or not. I was hearing WCKY in Cincinnati late at night and it occurred to me that you had to make a choice with the type of music you wanted to play. You could play the real fast, hot stuff, or you could learn some real music — but where to learn it? I promised myself I was going to keep my eyes open and if I ever found it, I was going to get involved with it.

By the time I was twelve or thirteen I was really looking for an instrument to play. My own father had been killed and my stepfather was from Jamaica. He had played guitar, but gave it up to go to work, so he gave me the guitar. So I started to work my way around on it. Also about this time some guys came up from North Carolina. One was younger than me and one was older — Linwood and Curtis Perry. They were tobacco sharecroppers, and these guys could play some guitar. Straight blues. Acoustic. John Lee Hooker. I learned a lot of second parts to the real straight blues stuff. I started playing with little rock and rhythm bands. We had some guys from Clarksdale, Mississippi, who lived up the street. They played Clarksdale style — in open tuning with knives. They had electric guitars made out of car speakers and car radio parts.

So that went on for awhile. I kept playing here and there until I got to college. The folk thing was happening by then. The Connecticut Valley Folksong Society had already been started, and I was really surprised that there was an organization dedicated to that kind of music. It was exciting for me because it was exactly what I was looking for. At first I didn't know what "folk music" was. I was asked to join the Folksong Society and I said, "I don't know any folk music."

"Do you play blues?"

"Yeah."

"Well, don't folks listen to blues?"

You didn't have to say any more after that.

Little by little this is what was happening. People were playing. The music was being played. It was exciting and there was an actual market. There was even a coffeehouse — the Salladin Coffeehouse in Amherst, run by Horace Waters. That was the first place I got a chance to sing and I could pick up on the whole folk thing. Buffie St.

Marie was there. Bill Keith was there. I found out that all the people from Boston and Cambridge had it organized. They had clubs and coffeehouses and radio stations so that the music was being piped in real good. So I went over there to check it out.

At college I put together a rhythm and blues band called Taj Mahal and the Electras. We played weekends at the Quonset Club and at mixers. We did the straight stuff — "Do You Love Me" by the Contours, "Twist and Shout," "What'd I Say," "Georgia on My Mind," "Searchin'," "Alley Oop," "Misty" — a pretty good cross-section of the music at that time. We had bass, drums, two guitars, piano, and some horns. We did dances around, and I got a little idea of what the business was about.

One thing I came to realize was that a lot of guys weren't that serious about the music. A lot didn't spend the time doing their homework with their instruments. They'd just go for the surface. But I wanted to really get into it. I started trying to get recordings of the great players and focus in on what they were doing. People like Gary Davis and Jesse Fuller. I had heard "San Francisco Bay Blues," but I had never seen Jesse Fuller. I finally got a chance to see him on a Pete Seeger show that Manny Greenhill put on at UMass. I couldn't believe it. Afterwards I went back to talk to him. When I got to Cambridge I got a chance to see him all night.

I started going over to Cambridge to see different people play and was really getting into it. The fact of it is that it was really the first scene up North that was really trying to nurture the whole thing. I really felt good about that. I spent a lot of nights at the 47. I really appreciated it because it was a place you could go that was dedicated to the music that people wanted to hear. I was so used to the other kind of thing — loud-mouth, crazy clubs — I couldn't believe how it was set up in there and how the people responded to the musicians. There was a total commitment there that you didn't find in a lot of clubs.

The Newport Festivals were exciting and different. It gave me room for personal growth. I also saw that there was a concerted effort to have the true kind of brotherhood situation visible. It inspired me to pay a lot more attention to the music I always could have played and always will play instead of just playing what was popular. This gave me the impetus to play something a little bit deeper and to find out whether or not I had it to be able to play the music as it stood. I also discovered that there was an audience for that music.

I knew guys during those times who wrote a

little bit fast. If they had allowed themselves to grow a little it would have been better. Then they got stuck and constantly had to do that material over and over. I was waiting until the music sounded right and I had absorbed enough things.

My music keeps me inside the instruments — guitars, banjos, mandolins, pianos, upright basses, cellos, fiddles, harmonicas, flutes, and whistles. The longer I'm in it, the deeper I seem to get in it.

Finally, though, I said, "It's about time for me to go off by myself." Mostly I spent time doing my homework with my instrument. Those days in Cambridge had really inspired me to play.

At some point I felt like moving to California. The scene changed in Cambridge. It just didn't have the ring to it that it first had. It just seemed to be time to move on. It wasn't growing any more. I wanted to see about some of the musicians in California. I'd heard about Ry Cooder. Jesse Lee Kincaid just showed up at a hoot once playing incredible twelve-string guitar. So we decided to leave together in early 1965. I was searching, trying to knit something together musically so I could live in my body with those two cultures within me.

It always amazed me that black people never made the connection to the Newport Folk Festival with all of the roots black musicians there. The direction I took was a pretty adventurous direction because there weren't that many young black cats into the music. Now a lot more have started. Back then no one knew about it. It was a wide open field. Maybe I helped open it up. You never know where the arrows you shoot are going to land. All you can hope is that your aim is true.

ecause Taj had gotten into folk music for the music, he was able to think of it in those terms. He was using it to discover his own culture and find out who he was. Jackie Washington, however, had come into it when the Seeger political influence was still a force in the folk movement. The Greenhills had become his second family, and he found himself feeling more and more estranged from the folk "movement," especially as the civil rights struggle began to heat up in the early Sixties.
Manny was part of the left-wing, Jewish, liberal movement which was into unions and all that. You dream of Joe Hill, and let's hold hands with Chinese and Black people and Indians — all dreaming about Joe Hill! "And the banks are made of marble...!" (And today they're damn glad of it!)

So everybody had their own little thing that they wanted you to do. It was an incredible position to be in, but I didn't even know I was in it, asshole that I was.

It started to get foolish, because I started to feel guilty about the money. So I started donating a lot of money to causes, because we had to improve the lot of whoever. I don't mean offense to anybody, but I became white — whiter than I had been. Guilt is a white, American trip. Black people and Puerto Rican people don't have guilt as a group thing. Pain and avoidance of pain is what I see in their music and culture. I didn't have to make up to the Indians! But here I was running around doing all that shit. And I also didn't realize that a lot of people that I thought were special like Eric von Schmidt and Bob Siggins and Jim Rooney and Bill Keith were not on that same soapbox as Seeger and the figureheads of this movement. That was my own blindness.

Then I got involved with the civil rights movement. There was an "army of guitarists" going down south in the summer of '64. So I joined this "army" and quit it when I got to Mississippi. I got in with a group of *niggers,* and we started working *with* the people instead of coming down and singing *at* them. I did one show with the "Freedom Caravan" or whatever it was called. It was in a place that was hot as hell. Phil Ochs got up and started singing about how he wasn't marching and he wasn't this and he wasn't that. And these black kids were sitting there in the heat, bored shitless, listening to this guy who had nothing to do with them. They were being *used.* So I quit and got into the Free Southern Theater.

I realized that the folksingers were talking *at* people. Rhetoric. Joan Baez really started pissing me off. Although she was a goddess to me, I started saying, "This bitch is phony!" She was talking like she wasn't near anyone. What did the people down there need that for? They were singing their asses off! It was the one thing that they had going for them — that got them through the week! They would get together and sing themselves to a fare-thee-well! Who needed Joan Baez or Phil Ochs or me, for that matter? Those people were being used to make the singers look good. They came down to HELP THE NEGRO, but they were helping themselves to all sorts of publicity as humanitarians and then splitting. So I left. I started living with families, and I stayed for several months. It had taken me a long time to begin to figure it all out, but I was starting.

I realized finally that people had an idea of what somebody black was supposed to be. And I wasn't it. I could not do it. I didn't know from gospel or blues. It was inconceivable to people that that was the first time I had had anything to do with that stuff. So I felt that I was letting people down in that I couldn't do, say, what Taj Mahal could do. I finally just decided, "There's a million ways to be black, and I'm going to be black my way. Why am I going around trying to please all these people?" They could always get a hotel room. I'd be traveling around places and not be able to get a cab or a hotel room. It was always shack-up with some white chick who could get you those things. So I said, "What am I doing? I don't need to live my life like this."

When I came back, I did concerts to make money. I had supported myself all the time I was down south. So I started exploiting the civil rights movement. I sang civil rights songs and wore my funny little straw hat that I had gotten down there. I just turned around and exploited the people who had been exploiting me all this time. I got out of debt rapidly. Then I didn't know what to do. There were a lot of offers of money. I could get anywhere from seven hundred to one thousand dollars for two hours work. I was doing about three concerts a week, but it got to the point where I couldn't do it. I couldn't sing "Man of Constant Sorrow" anymore. I loved it, but I couldn't do that material any more, because my head had changed. All I would have been doing it for was the money. I liked the money. I wanted the money. But it turned out that I really didn't. I just had to stop.

So I went back to Manny, which was a big deal. I had always known I was black, but I guess I had never communicated that to him. Because I didn't speak the way people thought a black person should speak. But I knew other black people who spoke like me. As a matter of fact, those black people wouldn't come to see me. I had a friend come to see me once at the 47. He said, "This is nice, Jack, but doesn't it have any beat?" They were going out to lounges where you could get a decent drink. This business of being ethnic and real wasn't for them. They wanted Scotch, not Darjeeling tea.

Manny stopped being my friend then. Without realizing what I was saying, I said I felt I was being made into something that I wasn't going to be. And that at some point I was going to have to put on that sequined jacket and go out and tap dance, because that's what I'm about. Folk music wasn't going to be my vehicle. If I was going to sing popular music, it was going to be a *popular* song. I didn't want to do "folkum" stuff. If I was going to go into show business, I didn't want somebody to manage me who used to do union stuff. I wanted somebody out there with a calculator who really knew how to do it.

So our conversation was about that, and I said,

"I think I have to go and make my way. I'm interested in theater. I can't do this anymore." His reaction was very subtle, but it was like I was a quitter. He was very cold to me. There was that feeling that he had worked to develop me. I didn't feel that way. He was really pimping me off Joan. That's how I got with Vanguard. That's how I got a lot of work. He was answering the phone. People were calling him all the time looking for her, and he'd say, "I've got this kid Jackie Washington. He's great…" But he never went out of his way to really make me aware that I was in some kind of business, or to really give my career direction.

I did six records for Vanguard, but they never cared what I recorded. They put no thought into it at all. I would just go in and sing all the songs I was currently singing in the clubs. They'd say "This one is good. What do you think of that?" And they'd put it out. It turned out that Maynard had done so well with Joan that when he saw that Manny was handling me and that I was playing all over the place, he saw it as another chance to make some money. I was going to be the "male Joan Baez," except that when you came right down to it, unless I had records that were produced, my records were never going to be on the same level as hers. I sing okay and play the guitar okay, but it wasn't anything astounding when you took away all the smiling, the jokes, the making friends with the audience. You had to do something to really make a record and really advertise what was made. Neither Manny nor Maynard had any ideas about that. And I was just letting them call the shots — which turned out to be no shots at all.

I found a song of Jean Ritchie's called "Nottamun Town." It's sung in a minor key against a major, like a lot of these mountain songs. It sounds nice, but I just couldn't do it, so I changed the tune to minor and made sort of a drone sound with the guitar. Dylan *loved* this. I was playing at Gerde's and he would come in every night and ask me to sing it. He went over to Vanguard, and Maynard gave him a copy of my record. The next time I heard my tune — which was *my* tune — it was "Masters of War." I hadn't known I had composed the tune, because it was a simple thing, but it went on to make a lot of money. As far as I was concerned, that was all after the fact, and he was welcome to it. But I felt that my manager should have hipped me to the fact that I was doing something with these songs — that I was making some kind of contribution that was worth money as well as applause. I was coming from a clean place; I was working hard to do the best I could do, but I should have been helped to understand that I should have protected my work. In Cambridge we were used to sharing everything. We were friends, and I think that was beautiful. We really

MANNY GREENHILL. *Photograph by David Gahr.*

JACKIE WASHINGTON. *Photograph by Rick Sullo.*

liked what we were doing, but we didn't realize that we had entered the world of business and that there were those around us who were doing business off of what we did.

When the *Time* article came out on Joan Baez way back in '62, I wondered why Eric von Schmidt hadn't done the cover and why I wasn't even mentioned in the article! We were all Manny's clients, but he made no move to get us a piece of that. I don't know why, but it never seemed to occur to him that he could possibly have done anything about that. At the time I wasn't thinking much that way. I was on a holy quest! But after a couple of years I found that I was thinking about it, and I found myself getting jealous and negative. I was wondering why other artists were getting on Newport and I wasn't. My mother didn't raise me that way. I was feeling like I was being put down for what I did when people didn't even know what I did. I started getting pinched. And it was because things weren't being managed in a right way. I'm my mother's only child. I only got one life. And I wasn't going to throw it away. So I stopped, and at the age of twenty-eight I had to start all over again.

Jackie might have felt that he was unique in his situation, but he wasn't. Once it became clear that folk music had, indeed, become a business, many of the more popular young performers in Cambridge began to reassess their somewhat light-hearted attitude toward what they had been doing. They, too, found Manny's laid-back approach frustrating. Tom Rush was one.

Manny Greenhill's attitude toward me was one of my main stimulants. His attitude was basically, "You're not ready." I wanted him to put me on a co-bill at Jordan Hall with somebody — as opening act — and he said I wasn't ready. So Byron headlined me at Jordan Hall and sold it out.

Geoff Muldaur was best friends with Mitch Greenhill, but he, too, was looking to greener pastures.

We got involved with Albert Grossman at a party at Don and Alice MacSorley's after some Dylan concert. I said to Kweskin, "We might as well ask this guy." Kweskin said, "He'd never do it." Manny wasn't doing a great job, and I got the crazy idea that a big-time manager might. We wanted to go all over the place. We didn't just want to be regional. You'd go to a gig, and he would have forgot to tell them you needed microphones. It was a little too loose. I think he thought of us as a bunch of kids having a good time. He was a great guy, but we were ambitious, and we wanted Big Albert.

Show business was calling, and this time Manny was not answering the phone.

In my case the relationship between folk music and the business side of concerts and management came from my political involvement: the crusade. One was the anti-repression crusade; the other was a crusade for roots-type folk music. Inherent in this approach was sort of an anti-show business mentality. In the early days, my whole involvement in putting on concerts, before getting involved in them financially, was strictly political. If you had a concert, it was always a benefit of some sort: to get somebody out of jail or to get the rent paid for somebody. So in that sense, even the process of making money out of it was a questionable thing.

In a way, I was putting on the big concerts to help pay for the newer, younger artists. Putting on the established professional performers made it lucrative enough for me to tool around with other things and try to help the younger performers come along. I certainly didn't dictate what everybody should do, but I always offered my opinions. Jackie Washington, for instance, on a political level, embodied some of the things you look for. He was black, Puerto Rican. He was very bright, very charming. When I went down to the Village in New York, I would hear guys like Richard Pryor and Bill Cosby doing what I thought Jackie should be doing. My advice to him was to do some of that. Not necessarily be political, but to talk about meaningful things and base his humor on that. He always resented his image as a monologist — probably because it came too easy for him. But I felt that's where his real strength was. I never felt that he could be the male Joan Baez that Vanguard kept insisting he was, which made for a very funny relationship between us. Because I didn't think he was that thing which he really wanted to be, which was a romantic, soulful singer of folk songs. When he went south on some freedom marches and came back with those stories, I thought he was really getting into something.

It seemed that many of the younger performers coming up in Cambridge wanted me to be a "heavy," as opposed to being a "good guy." (Although I always fought that image.) Tom Rush actually said it to me. He said that Arthur Gorson, who he went with, was "lean and hungry," meaning I wasn't. I felt I was very lucky, anyway, and that I was there to give them advice and encouragement.

In the midst of all of this change, the new faces, and the new Club, Rooney found himself riding the waves, trying to get his bearings.

I was thousands of miles away in the middle of Greece when I got the news about John Kennedy being killed. We were in Megalopolis in the middle of the Peloponnesus on an archaeological field trip. I was drinking coffee one morning in a cafe. They were switching the radio dial around and on the Armed Forces Network I heard snatches of something about somebody who'd died — some U.S. Senator. Then I went to buy some chocolate at a kiosk, and the guy started talking to me in Greek, asking me if I was an American and wasn't it awful about Kennedy. I thought he said, "killed," but I thought my Greek was bad. When I got back to the hotel, everybody was listening to the radio. It was true. There was nothing we could do about it. So we just went ahead with the day's activities. That night we were really in the country, in a little village with dirt roads and one well. Everybody was asking us, "Why? Why?" We were totally ignorant. We knew nothing. It was a very strange feeling.

For the next few days I tried to piece it all together, but it just got stranger and stranger. The Greeks had a real cowboys-and-Indians, Chicago-gangster, movie view of American life. Now I was reading about Oswald and Ruby, who had a strip-tease club, and Communists and Dallas and the Mafia. It was too far out. They had to be making it up. When I got back to Athens I started putting it together. It was all true. It took about two weeks for me to get through it. I felt very alone and started to think about what I was doing with my life.

I wrote my family a letter. I told them that I was going to give up my academic career when I got home. I would go to Harvard one more year to give it one more chance — which turned out to be a waste of time except that I did get something out of teaching — but that I no longer wanted to be pretending to do something that my heart was not in. I didn't say what I was going to do. I really didn't know. But I had a feeling that it was probably going to have something to do with music. It was a little late in the ball game, but it was where my heart was. It was what I wanted to do inside.

I had once thought of politics as a life, and had been turned on by Kennedy. A lot of it was the Boston Irish in me, but when he was killed and the Vietnam thing started to get worse and worse, the most important thing seemed to be to do something that was personally satisfying. I started to get selfish. I wanted to save me before I saved the world, and that was a big step.

So I finished out my year, played with Bill Keith, and made no plans for the future. One day I was talking to Byron. He told me very matter of factly that he was going to stop managing the Club. I don't know why, but I wasn't surprised. It had stopped being a challenge for him. It had become a routine. So we both said, "What'll we do?." Then I said, "Well, I guess I'd better do it." And that was that. I had finally come into my own, and I suddenly felt very good.

If I had a needle, and if I could sew,
I'd sew you to my coattail and down the road I'd go.
Where do you come from, where do you go?
Where do you come from, Cotton-eye Joe?

Children of Darkness

Now is the time for your loving, dear,
And the time for your company.
Now when the light of reason fails,
And the fires burn on the sea.
Now in this age of confusion,
I have need for your company.

y 1963 every young girl in America who could possibly get her fingers around a guitar neck and could grow her hair down past her shoulder blades had already been "Joan-Baezed." Because Joan was really damned strong. Mary Travers never would have grown hair like that if it hadn't been for Joan Baez. Joan had the looks, had the presence and the humor, and, of course, an incredible voice. She really was the symbol of the whole era.

Bob Neuwirth's assessment of the Baez phenomenon was close to the mark. Bob knew Joan from the early days, and he had the rare talent to simultaneously participate and observe. He had been a good buddy of Dylan's from their first meeting at Indian Neck and was going to be a strong force in the changes that were to come.

Joan had put down her roots in Carmel, California, but she was one of the exceptions. The next few years were to be a time of great change and movement. Marriages, divorces, children, relationships forming and dissolving, reforming with someone else in some other place. The singers were searching, growing. They were coming of age, and the music itself was about to undergo a similar transformation.

After the London Waltz with Fariña, Von Schmidt, and Signer, Bob Dylan was back in the frozen slush of a New York City winter. Despite the cover of his second album which showed him snuggling down 4th Street with Suze Rotolo, they were having problems. He was also having problems with Columbia Records. He had been scheduled for a spot on the Ed Sullivan show where he had planned to sing the "Talking John Birch Society Blues." The appearance had been cancelled at the last minute when he refused to do something less controversial. Not only that, but Columbia bounced the song off the new album. Dylan and his managers, Albert Grossman and John Court, were furious. They tried unsuccessfully to break his recording contract. It was a frustrating moment.

Manny Greenhill had heard Dylan at the First Indian Neck Folk Festival and was impressed by his humor and his audacity. If Joan had a hole in her concerts it was where the humor ought to be. Her delightfully caustic wit was strictly an off stage affair. Manny had been sent an acetate of a dozen

JOAN BAEZ and BOB DYLAN. Photograph by Norman Vershay.

or so of Bob's songs, and he gave it to Joan with the suggestion she give it a listen. She had met Bob once at Gerde's Folk City and had been taken by his waif image, humor, and style. It took a lot of prodding on Manny's part to get her to listen to the acetate, but when she finally did she began to recognize the power of the lyric content. So when he showed up at the Monterey Folk Festival in May she went out of her way to have others hear him. She also realized that he was writing the songs that she had been searching for.

He wrote songs that hadn't been written yet. There aren't many good protest songs. They're usually overdone. The beauty of Bob's stuff is its understatement. Anything that is brilliant is an understatement like that. You don't have to hit people over the head with it. Even his most blatant stuff, when he was really young, is still clever enough so that it's not dull or heavy.

I just wanted people to hear him. I think we liked each other, and I really loved him. I wanted to take care of him and have him sing. I mean brush his hair and brush his teeth and get him on stage . . .

Dylan stayed with Joan for a few weeks after the festival in her house in Carmel. She was scheduled to do a concert tour after the Newport Folk Festival and asked him if he would come along and be her mystery guest. It appealed to the theatrical in both of them, and Bob said okay. In London he had told Dick and Eric that he thought that she was a fine singer but that she was out of step with the times and should "step out." Now they would be doing a little stepping out together.

Eric von Schmidt returned from England a month before his second daughter, Megan, was born. The child brought Eric and Helen together again and despite the dirty, grey snowdrifts of a Cambridge winter, things were brightening up. He recorded his first solo album for Prestige with Paul Rothchild as producer, using Fritz Richmond, Geoff Muldaur, and his brother-in-law, Bob Jones, as back-up musicians. Maynard Solomon contacted him about illustrating a book of folksongs as sung by Joan Baez. He also sold a book of illustrated folksongs to Houghton Mifflin Co., which was to be released at the same time as a record by Pathways of Sound in Cambridge. Both were called *Come For To Sing*. The singers appearing on the record with Eric were all old friends, Jack Elliott, Rolf Cahn, Jackie Washington, and Carolyn Hester.

During the summer Eric got another call from Rothchild. He had a blues record in the works. It had no title yet, but he wanted Eric to be on it and also to do the jacket. Paul thought the time had come to do an album of white blues singers.

One idea I came up with was when I was working on what came to be called the "Blues Project." I thought as I was making that record, "Here is a great format for the various areas of folk interest around the United States." There was the blues thing, the banjo thing, the old-time string band thing, singer-song-writers. So we did projects based on all these themes. When I did the blues project, which was done in one thirteen-hour session, I did it with Tom Rush, Mark Spoelstra, Dave van Ronk, Eric von Schmidt, Danny Kalb (who used the name of the record for his band, the Blues Project), Dave Ray, and Geno Foreman. He played Gary Davis spirituals on the organ. Didn't make it on to the album. The record took thirteen hours. We gave everybody fifty bucks a cut, and at the end, I called Jac up. He was afraid that this was going to turn into a very expensive record. I said, "Jac, the album cost $963.00." He said, "Great, because it's probably going to sell about a thousand records." I was still operating in my naiveté. That record has probably sold close to 300,000 copies over the years. It is what I had intended it to be, which is a capsulization of white blues singers.

That gave Jac a lot of confidence in the movement and me, and allowed something else to happen about a year later, which was their first move into electric music. That was the Butterfield Band, which was a violent departure for that label.

The taping for the "Blues Project" was done at the Mastertone Studios in New York City. Von Schmidt arrived with a bottle of Bacardi Dark Rum, and the session was soon in fluid drive.

Elektra had Koerner, Ray, and Glover on the label so their stuff was already in the can before we recorded. Paul tried to get Johnny Hammond, but Vanguard wouldn't release him. All of us had recorded by this time except Geno, and both Paul and I figured it was about time. Geoff and me, and I'm pretty sure Mark Spoelstra and Geno recorded the same afternoon. It was very loose. John Sebastian came by, as did Bob Dylan and Robert L. Jones. I think Dave Van Ronk was there, too, but he may have already recorded. It was almost a jam, and everybody was pretty smashed by the end of it. I did one song lying on the floor.

Geno came blasting in about mid-afternoon. He had been leading Gary Davis around then and when he spotted that studio organ it was all over. He sat himself down and whipped out about four spirituals, one right after the other. Rothchild finally said, "Hey Geno, thanks — *Next.*" I couldn't blame him, I was pissed, too. Figured they'd get him another day, but there wasn't another day. It was so obvious he was destroying himself it was heartbreaking. He was treating his talent like he was treating his teeth and his mouth was looking like Buchenwald. We loved him but he was deep into New York, getting out of music and into politics.

"THE BLUES PROJECT" ALBUM COVER
Elektra's art director, William S. Harvey, originally planned the cover as a wrap-around and wanted the guitar player to be shown sitting on a bed with a sexy girl. Elektra was nervous about just how sexy the girl should be. Eric von Schmidt's naked lady seemed a little too sexy to Jac Holzman. Although they had already used a photograph of a nude on one of their jackets, it had been taken through pebbled glass, which gave it the effect of a peeping-Tom out on a rainy day. Harvey explained to Von Schmidt that if the guitar player and the girl were black, total nudity would be okay, but since they were white it was unacceptable. It wouldn't sell in the South. Eric was asked to put a chemise on the female figure, but to "keep it sexy, right?" With great reluctance, he complied. Even draped, the girl was just a little too sexy. When the album finally came out, the cover had lots of notes by Paul Nelson and no nubile companion at all. No wonder so many white guitar players have the blues.

imi had promised her parents that whatever else, she would finish high school. Now that Dick had swept into her life everything else seemed totally unimportant, but she knew how important it was to her father and mother. After the secret marriage ceremony she had dutifully returned home to study her history lessons. It was a difficult time, and at one point the lovers were ready to flee. **Dick was determined and so was I. I was determined to leave home, and Dick was determined to have me go with him. We were going to run away the first day of spring. Then my father went away to the States. He was going to go for two weeks, and I woke up in the middle of the night and decided I had better write him a letter, because I would be gone by the time he got back.**

I handed it to him and he said goodbye. And the next morning at 6 o'clock, a telegram came. The doorbell rang, and I thought, "Ohhh, he came back." I was sure he had returned. It said, "Tell Mimi she has made wrong choice and broken promise." And my mother came in my room completely confused "Mimi, maybe you can explain this..." The broken promise was that I would finish high school and the wrong choice was Dick. So then she begged me and pleaded that I stay and finish school . . . I said, "Okay." So I stayed. Then there was a series of discussions with the family, with Dick trying to grab my hand on the top of the table while my father talked to us, and me trying to pull my hand away, and my father looking at our hands . . . My father was getting very serious and choked up; it was the first time my father said to my mother, "Joan, I need a drink." So after about the third or fourth meeting like this it was decided that indeed it would be better for the kids to get married rather than to live in sin.

Dick and I left by train and then boat back to the states without my father's blessings, but with my mother's blessings, after I had finished my last high school exam, which my father gave to me the night before. He'd written all my book reports. I really did hate school. I did not do well in school and felt very inferior and strange about it. Mother said if I did all the exams they could wait for the results — I could leave town. At two in the morning we finished the last exam, and at six in the morning we got up to take the train. My mother took us and said, "Well kids, what can I do?" I was very torn, because she was very sad.

The *Time* cover article on Joan Baez began: "Anything called a hootenanny ought to be shot on sight, but the whole country is having one."

The Newport Folk Festival was starting up again that year after a two year lapse and this time Manny Greenhill helped with the organization. **George Wein called me and said, "I'd like to try this again, but without Albert." I said, "I'd be very happy to work with you, but it's got to be done on a non-profit basis, and it's got to involve Pete Seeger." He said, "Sure, why not?"**

All performers were to be paid fifty dollars for any day they performed, whether it was in a concert, a workshop, or both, and they were given food and lodging. In addition to the concerts on the large stage, there were workshops in various categories, and the most popular were, in effect, mini concerts, sometimes with huge audiences sitting on the grass. The workshops ran simultaneously and the result was a wonderful musical stew — the cooks didn't spoil the broth at all.

Even at that pay scale big name groups like Peter, Paul and Mary, were happy to get the exposure and knew their presence would draw large crowds to hear the lesser known performers. Dylan's second album included "Blowin' In the Wind," and Peter, Paul and Mary, also managed by Grossman and Court, had a big hit with it. If Bob was still an unknown to many in the audience at the Festival's start, that was certainly not the case when it closed. Both the younger performers and the Old Guard, the more politically oriented folksingers of the forties and fifties, sang his songs and his praise.

The concert ended with Bob singing "Blowin' In The Wind," joined first by Baez, then Seeger, Bikel, the Freedom Singers, and Peter, Paul and Mary. The encore was a linked-arm version of "We Shall Overcome," and the audience sang along. The ovation was deafening.

Bob Dylan had overcome. The tremendous outpouring of recognition, adulation, and even the beginning signs of worship, was threatening to engulf him only two years after standing around the beer barrel singing Woody Guthrie and Hank Williams songs at Indian Neck. After the Festival was over Baez started on her concert tour with Bob as mystery guest. His influence was established, and his fame was building.

(left) "We Shall Overcome" The finale of the 1963 Newport Folk Festival. (left to right) PETER YARROW, MARY TRAVERS, PAUL STOOKEY, JOAN BAEZ, BOB DYLAN, THE FREEDOM SINGERS, PETE SEEGER, and THEO BIKEL. Photograph by John Cooke.

In Carmel, the Baez family's attention was not focused on Joan's most recent triumph, but on Mimi's marriage to Dick which they considered a disaster. After the concert tour with Dylan, Joan and Betsy Siggins headed for California.

I went west with Joanie by train the summer that Dick and Mimi got married. She didn't like to fly and she asked me to travel with her. We had a compartment which we never left — we had all our meals delivered in bed. We did get out at Chicago, because we had to change trains, but we got back in the next compartment and had all our meals delivered and watched the rest of the United States swing by. For some reason we got out in Ogden, Utah, too. Then we arrived in San Francisco. Joan's secretary, Kim Chappell, picked us up and drove me to Monterey. We went to a Festival in Monterey where Joanie confronted the John Birch Society. I thought that was big stuff. We all got rip roaring drunk. It was two days before the wedding.

The day before the wedding we all drove up to the Baez house. Everyone was nervous. There was one side of the ballpark that said, "How can she do this? She's ruining her life." The other side said, "It'll be okay." Chit chat all day and into the night. Pauline and I took off for a party somewhere while the family cried a lot. The father didn't come out of his bedroom for three days or something like that. He was very serious about the wedding.

Joan and Betsy were not big fans of Fariña either, and it was a difficult time for the newlyweds. The couple was beginning to feel like outcasts. A large measure of acceptance finally came, but in the beginning, when they really needed it, there was none.

His and my playing together really developed out of living in a one-room cabin in Carmel Highland. He was writing on a daily basis. He was up at six every morning. My own opinion is that he was taking quite a bit of speed. That's my opinion now — I had no idea then. He wrote hard all day long, worked and worked and worked. And I had no identity — nothing to do. I was very, very lost, and so was completely dedicated to him and Joanie who lived up the hill — which made me double-identityless. There was really nothing for me to hold on to. I took ballet classes, but he had to drive me, because I couldn't drive. I remained a thumbsucker until I was twenty-four, without an image of myself. During that year, he shot a deer, which we ate. We had no money. After the wedding, the whole family wasn't getting along. Joan couldn't stand Dick. My father couldn't stand him to begin with. Nobody liked each other and I was in the middle, not knowing what to do.

MIMI and RICHARD FARIÑA cut the cake. Photographer unknown. Courtesy of Mimi Fariña.

I n the fall of '63 Geno Foreman had become a member of the Dylan entourage. Dylan had become worried about crowds, and Geno, Albert Maher, and Victor Maimudes were his bodyguards, or "thought guards," and general hang-out-buddies. They could be counted on to handle various situations. The times did seem to be changing for Geno. Clay Jackson knew him as well as any of the Cambridge group.

When I came back to the states, I'd never heard of revolution or Bob Dylan — "You mean the kid from Minnesota that keeps doing all those old songs and changing the words?"

What Geno did, two months after he came back, was to get himself into a position where he and Albert Maher were working. They were being paid. They had jobs as Dylan's bodyguards. I was in New York briefly about that time and got in touch with him and he showed me his shillelagh. He carried a shillelagh that he hand carved out of a tree root. It was one of the most ferocious looking weapons you've ever seen in your life.

So it appears from that that Geno had readjusted to the culture just like that. He was in Cambridge for a little while, and he used to come over. It was a strange, sad thing because he'd try to convert me and Bob Siggins to the cause, the leftist movement, and I don't think there were ever two less political people in the world than me and Bob Siggins.

So we'd either try to ignore him, or make bad jokes. He'd show us his newspapers and stuff like that. I felt he'd just gone too crazy.

Then, on November twenty-second, President Kennedy was shot and killed in Dallas. It was a traumatic time for the nation. For Dylan, who had just stepped into the glare of the unblinking spotlight, it must have been nerve-wracking.

In January of '64, Dylan headed out to California by station wagon to smoke a lot of grass, pick up on the grassroots, and play a few concerts along the way. It was a pretty heavy-duty tour, and when they finally reached San Francisco, Dylan was flying. He gave a concert there that seemed to transcend anything he had done before. A young, hip crowd was there, including Mimi and Dick, and Bob Neuwirth. For a switch, it was Bob Dylan who introduced a mystery guest — Joan Baez.

Over in Berkeley, Rolf Cahn and Debbie Green had been running the Cabale. It was a combination of the Blind Lemon and a Club 47 West, and, as usual, there were problems. Rolf, the Ramblin' Rabbi, remembers it like this:

GENO FOREMAN with his wife, Marcy, and their child. Geno died in England in 1965. Clay Jackson recalls it. "He went to the Public Health Service a few times and they said, 'You're not feeling too good. Lay off the dope and lay off the booze.' And then one day he walked over and lay down on the couch and he said, 'Marcy, I feel bad,' and he died." Photograph courtesy of Betsy Schmidt.

I opened the Cabale and that started to break up certain aspects of the friendship with Debbie Green. You learn these things with hindsight, but the priests will always love each other until they open the temple. So here are these priests, and the moment they open the temple, they each are convinced that the other priests are tearing the temple down out of sheer stupidity.

Debbie's account is less metaphorical:

Well, we were supposed to put in our time equally because we were co-owners. Rolf used to just use it as a showcase for his whole thing, and he didn't work. And we said, "Uhn, uhn — you don't get any say-so, you gotta work just like everyone else, or we run the place and tell you when to work." We were just pissed off, it wasn't fair, and he would take all the credit, you know.

By the fall of '63, Debbie had about had it with the Cabale.

I was working my ass off doing everything. I knew my time was drawing to an end. I had met Eric Andersen, and he was cute. He went back to New York, and I stayed at the Cabale. All of a sudden he was sending me clippings from the *New York Times*. Bob Shelton said that he was America's answer to the Beatles!

I came East, and Eric and I ended up in New York. He started making a record for Vanguard in the ballroom of the Manhattan Towers. It was the weirdest thing, I couldn't imagine making a record myself. That's when Maynard Solomon was really curious about the origin of all of Joanie's tunes. By that time I'd stopped singing because Eric was jealous, and he didn't like it when I played guitar. So I stopped, and from then on, I just played behind him. Also, Joanie had taken my whole trip, and by her second record, I was a Joan Baez imitator. I hadn't naturally evolved to a place that was more distinctive than that. I was struggling to find something that was individual.

We were living on East 10th Street. It was too crazy. I just couldn't live in the city. We had to make money; it was hard; it was dangerous; so I said, "Listen, kid, I'm going to Cambridge." I went by myself. Eric wound up there for a brief period. We had separate apartments.

Von Schmidt was back in Cambridge that spring after living with his family on the beach in Florida for the winter. Geoff Muldaur and Maria D'Amato had been down, raving about a group called the Beatles they had been hearing on their Volkswagen bus radio. Mitch Greenhill was down. Jack Elliott was down in his destructible Land Rover. It was the last month of the Year of the Hoot. Eric played a benefit for Muscular Dystrophy at the Sarasota Civic Auditorium, met

Below:
ERIC and DEBBIE ANDERSEN getting into a serious conversation. Photograph by N.C. Pei.

a lady named Kay Paul, and found himself in a similar postion to Dick Fariña's a year earlier.

Dylan was back in Cambridge, on a high from the western trip and staying with Betsy and Bob Siggins. John Cooke was on hand for some of the field trips.

'64 was the year of the greatest Dylan concerts. It was just Bob and Victor Maimudes in a blue Ford station wagon with perpetual bottles of Beaujolais. We all were really friendly, and we went to a number of concerts that spring. We went to UMass in Amherst. Possibly the greatest concert was at Providence. Charlie Frizzell, Paul Rothchild, Bob and Betsy Siggins, and I went to these concerts for about a week. We suspended other activities and drank a lot of wine and hung out with Bob and Victor.

That fall, when Neuwirth and I were driving across the country, we knew that Dylan was playing in Kenyon, Ohio. We drove all night, got into town around eight in the morning, got a motel room, slept all day, and went out to the university at night and looked in at the concert. It was just the same. All that year, he had crystallized the extension of that one-man, one-harmonica, one-guitar, how-far-out-can-these-songs-get. He was doing "The Gates of Eden," "It's All Right, Ma," "Mister Tambourine Man," and the concerts were just killers. You wondered how one little kid from New York could do all this stuff. Inevitably, there would be people from the English department there, talking about what it all meant — the imagery and the poetry. They were all going nuts.

The imagery of his lyrics sparkled, and by the time an English Department could get together on what it all meant, Bob would have written six more songs. Neuwirth was in tune with Dylan the man as well as Dylan the artist.

A Dylan Fieldtrip. (left to right) CHARLIE FRIZZELL, someone's friend, VICTOR MAIMUDES, PAUL ROTHCHILD, BOB DYLAN, and JOHN SEBASTIAN (1964). Photograph by John Cooke.

ob has one of those personalities that causes people to react one way or another. A lot of people don't react as positively as other people do to that personality. I find him a really amusing and funny cat, very intelligent and totally human. I've always thought of him as totally capable of fucking up, very fallible. But I accept Bob as a contemporary, and I accept him as an artist. There ain't a whole bunch of people that I can call artists — of any age. An artist is a non-compromising person. You can't compromise very much at all and be an artist. Bob has earned my respect that way. I don't think he's a great poet, but he knows how to have so much fun with words. He loves words! He loves the little permutations and the twistings and the playing. He instinctively falls into alliteration and onomatopoeia. He really loves language.

The same kind of thing had come across loud and clear to Eric von Schmidt in London.

Dylan has a calypso mind. He can tie one thought or one phrase to something totally different and make it work, with each illuminating the other, and kick it around in a way that really floored me when I got together with him and Fariña on that trip. No one was a match for Bob. We all tried to keep up, but he did it in a way that I had never seen anyone do it. He always brought it back. And it wasn't planned. He did it on his feet and was brilliant.

Eric and Kay had a small house on Gerry Street that summer, and while Kay's two young girls were exploring the mysteries of Harvard Square, they were pondering the amazement of two hearts that beat as one.

Joan and Bob and Paul Clayton came by sometime after Newport. Joan was doing a concert at the Boston Arts Festival and got Dylan out in the second act. By that time everybody knew she was going to bring him out, so the crowds were really big. After the concert, when we were walking back to the parking lot, she picked up Gigi, Kay's eight-year-old, and carried her. She figured that she wouldn't get mobbed carrying a sleepy little kid. I was driving a green Volkswagen bus, and Dick Fariña, his buddy Alfredo, and a couple of other people were beating out Cuban rhythms on the floor and the sides and the whole thing was like being right inside a percussion instrument. We all got to the 47 just as it was about to close, and started to play. Joan was pretty beat, but we kept it going for a couple of hours—Joan, Dylan, Mel Lyman, and Dick. It got real sweet.

JOAN BAEZ, MEL LYMAN, BOB DYLAN, and ERIC VON SCHMIDT at the Club 47. Photograph by Dick Waterman.

I remember something Joan said right around that time. It was lovely the way she put it — "Eric, he doesn't jiggle like that when he's asleep." I think she wanted to let me know that they were lovers, and that was nice.

That was a good summer at the Club. I did my second Prestige album at the end of it with Geoffrey and Mel. Kay had driven back down to Florida with her kids. I had met Mel through Geoff. We jammed together some at the Club. He was there the night that "Kay is the Month of May" happened to me onstage — singing the song in one key and playing it in another. Mel did something on the harmonica which, characteristically, was the best thing in the song. He wouldn't do it when we tried to record it shortly after that. That's the one song on the record with no harmonica and it was the best harmonica he had played with me.

I was staying with Don Reed across the street from where Mel was living on Huron Avenue. One morning I came down and found a note that said, "Eric, I love you — Mel." I think I was being courted in a way. Dick Fariña wrote the liner notes after I got back down to Florida.

(top) DICK FARIÑA and BYRON LINARDOS at the Club 47 (1964). Photographer unknown. Courtesy of Eric von Schmidt.

Dick and Mimi had wound up in Cambridge after spending their first year together in Carmel. It was hard not to be accepted by the family, but their feeling of isolation eased some when they got to know some of their neighbors, others like themselves, living in small cabins scattered in the woods.

People got to know each other and we knew several families where we would go and have dinner and often Dick would cook. And it was always a party feeling, musical instruments and singing.

And then Nancy Carlin decided to put on a Big Sur Folk Festival and Malvina Reynolds was around, Mark Spoelstra, Joanie, and she said "Why don't you guys come and play?" Pauline played, I can't remember who else was on that first bill. She played herself, Nancy Carlin did. Both Elektra and Vanguard representatives were there, and a smaller label, too. All of them approached us right after the thing. We then began being professionals. We came east the next year with the intention of going to Europe, but, again, ran out of funds and stayed in Cambridge.

That was the fall of the Muldaur/D'Amato nuptials which was the occasion for a splendid bash at the House of the Beautiful Women. Nancy Sweezy's daughter Moophy has a lovely memory of the party.

Maria and Geoff Muldaur's wedding party was huge and quite wild. Maria was four or five months pregnant, doing the lindy hop in her white dress, dancing up a storm — I was favorably impressed by that. As it got late, I was getting pretty sleepy and wandered into my room to find my bed covered with coats and little kids, snoring away happily. So I sat down on the piano bench, the piano being in my room. I sat down with a sigh and patted my dog, who was feeling cross because there were so many people in the house. It was easy, I found, to feel a little lost at the end of a big party, when all the grown-ups were high and dancing and bubbling to each other, and I was mostly just sleepy.

As I sat there Dick Fariña walked by and noticed me and stopped to chat. He came and sat down next to me on the bench and patted Nemo and started telling me stories about his dog, a shepherd, who was out in California. I had watched Dick and Mimi arrive at the party earlier that night — Mimi had on a red dress and a red hat. She looked striking, and a bit glacial despite all that red. I had associated this with Dick, too, and so was surprised when he stopped to talk to me — pleasantly surprised that he

wasn't patronizing or condescending as adults can be with kids. He just sat down and really enjoyed talking with me.

For some of the old-timers the Club 47 might have seemed as mellow as always, but that was not necessarily the case with the newer performers. Von Schmidt heard about some of this in a letter from Dick that December.

Cambridge. Still don't know what to make it. Byron and I got straight very quickly and he turns out to be a lovely guy. But the relationship with Betsy (never very good) has deteriorated to the point where she fails to say hello to either Mimi or me, either on the street or in the Club. Which we don't go to very often unless we're working there. The girl has a kind of class-celebrity consciousness which precludes more profound associations with people. And as such, she fails to see certain critical qualities in the people she's (afraid of) down on. How much of Mimi's day is spent at the Boston Conservatory, for instance, or mine at the machine, or anybody's, anywhere? It's all a drag because the tension generated among so many otherwise friends, and probably lovers, portends disaster. Of a form that is still taking shape.

etsy Siggins rubbed a lot of people the wrong way. When Dick wrote, she was in the last weeks of her pregnancy with their daughter, Leah, but pregnant or not she was capable of giving certain people a hard time. As Dick realized, part of it was "the best defense is a good offense" approach. Betsy was doing the booking at a club where she very well could have been performing if she had not been too timid to develop that part of her potential. She was smart, beautiful, and had a good voice, but others — not her — were up there on the stage.

Dick Waterman rankles and sputters to this day about one of Betsy's less attractive qualities. **There is nothing quite like standing in a line outside the Club 47 in the snow or the rain. You'd be huddled up against the wall to see Doc Watson or somebody you really wanted to see. Then here would come Her Majesty, the Queen! Queen Betsy would come in with an entourage. They would come to the top of the steps, and she would lead her entourage down through the people. She would knock on the door, and they would sweep in.**

(bottom) BOB DYLAN and BETSY SIGGINS backstage at Boston's Symphony Hall (1964). Photographer unknown. Courtesy of Betsy Siggins.

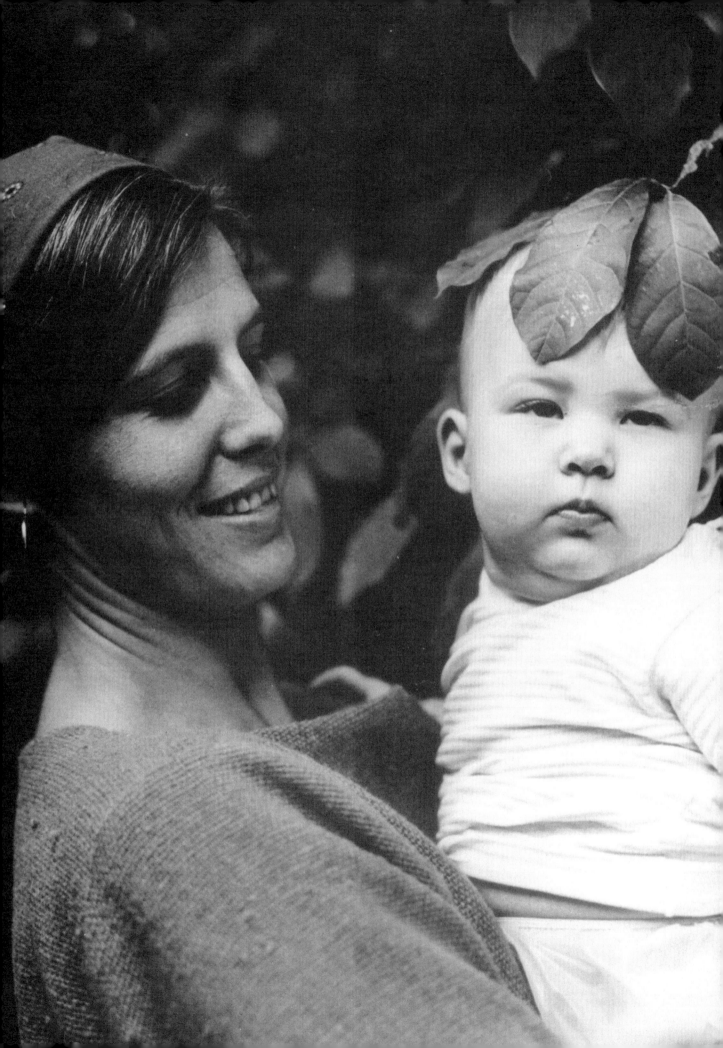

You never get over the smouldering resentment you feel from that. You never forget that you're an "out." There's "ins" and there's "outs," "haves" and "have nots," and you're a "have not." I never forgot that. It was a real motivator for me, and it made me work harder. The years have not dimmed the intensity of the distaste I had for that. I loathe it. I will not walk by a line to go to a door. I know what it's like to be in that line and see somebody sweep on by with royal contempt.

Eric Andersen and Debbie Green didn't feel at home either. Debbie was particularly annoyed both because she had been one of the very first performers at the 47 and because she had been running the Cabale for over two years herself. **When I got back there, Cambridge had really changed. Betsy had taken up the hip, put-down trip. I had just owned a club myself. I could own a club and not be snotty, and I didn't respect that attitude. Dick and Mimi and John Cooke and I were outcasts. I came back to Cambridge, and I was not about to do their little dance. Everybody got chomped on.**

Eric Andersen felt the pressure, too.
Bob Siggins was always great to me. Betsy was sort of terrifying. She ruled the roost. I just stayed clear of her. I liked her and she booked me in. I just didn't mess with her.

Betsy was not unaware of the problem.
I think my reputation was that of an ice-cold bitch. I deserved it. I think if you asked me what I did in those five years, it was practice being a bitch. I had a lot of good role models. There was Byron. You never could please him. There was that desperate, desperate search to make one-hundred bucks in the kitchen. I took it seriously, and you had to be real nasty to keep everybody hopping. If you got a hundred bucks, Byron would smile at you. The waitresses got five bucks a night plus tips, which weren't very much.

It wasn't hard to get on each other's nerves during those cold Cambridge winters. During the Christmas vacations performers were pretty much playing to the walls. One group that stared at a lot of seats that December was the Unicorn Jook Band, which consisted of Eric Andersen, Debbie Green, David Cohen, and Paul Arnoldi. Since nobody could play the jug, Paul huffed and puffed on a tuba. The band disbanded immediately after their three week engagement at the Unicorn.

Opposite:
BETSY SIGGINS and her daughter LEAH. Which goes to show that Betsy did have her warmer side. Joe Val is another who got through the tough exterior.

"Everybody was terrified of her. I'd walk in their house to practice and she'd be mad about something, so I'd say, 'Betsy?' She'd say, 'Oh, what now, Joe.' 'Jesus Christ, I love ya.' 'Goddammit, Joe, I can't get mad at you!'" And people would say to me that Betsy was a real terror. But all I can say is that I was around her enough to know that as soon as anyone from anywhere in the country hit Cambridge with no place to stay and no place to eat, Betsy would put them up and feed them. She was a lot harder on the outside than she was inside."
Photograph by Charles Frizzell.

Below:
The Unicorn Jook Band was a brilliant example of how not to cash in on a musical trend. Actually, with the exception of the Kweskin Jug Band, which happened to be very good, forming a jug or jook band seemed to be a one-way ticket to oblivion. This particular band might have set the record in that department. Fortunately, all concerned survived to move on to bigger and better things. (left to right) DAVID COHEN, ERIC ANDERSEN, DEBBIE ANDERSEN, and PAUL ARNOLDI. Photographer unknown.
Courtesy of Paul Arnoldi.

The Baez/Dylan surprise concerts had done somewhat better than the Unicorn Jook Band even though neither Bob nor Joan could play the jug either. They had done so well that their managers, Greenhill and Grossman, figured why keep giving the fans two stars for the price of one? Why not have a Baez/Dylan tour? Or would it be a Dylan/Baez tour? Ladies before gentlemen? Even that old softy Spencer Tracy had insisted that his name be listed before that of his beloved, Katharine Hepburn. "It's a theater marquee, not a damned lifeboat," he said. It was getting to be showbiz time in the Dylan/Baez, Baez/Dylan camp.

Manny Greenhill thought that it would be difficult to attempt as a joint effort.

By late '64, both Bob Dylan and Joan wanted to do a tour. Albert Grossman suggested that we do it together. I said, "I'll either sell her to you or you sell him to me, but only one of us will do it." So he decided to sell Bob to me.

Charlie Rothchild was working at the Grossman office at that time after barely surviving his stint as the P.R. man at Gerde's Folk City.

Albert wanted to produce the tour of Dylan and Baez. Manny was convinced that Albert was trying to take advantage of him, so he took the offer that Albert had made him and offered it to Albert. It turned out that in several situations Dylan had walked away with more money than Joan Baez. Albert was always an astute businessman.

Once it was decided who was running the tour, Greenhill called Von Schmidt in Florida about doing a poster.

t one stage of the game I had quit doing work for Manny altogether. I had been doing his graphics from the start — from when "Manny Greenhill" became "M. A. Greenhill presents." The "S. Hurok" trip. Back in '62 I got a call from a reporter from *Time* magazine who wanted to talk to me about a story they were doing on Joan. She came up to my studio, and we talked. About half way through the interview, I realized that this was going to be a *cover* story, and I said, "Wait a minute! Who's going to do the cover?" I threw the gears into hustle overdrive and said, "I'll do you one on speculation. I mean, how many people are there around who are friends of Joan, painters, and folksingers, all at once? It's a natural." And bless that girl, she said, "It sounds like a good idea to me," and picked up the phone right there and called *Time* magazine. Just like that. It turned out that a cover *painting* of Joan had been done, accepted, the whole bit. *Shit!*

About five minutes after she'd left, it hit me. *Son of a bitch!* Manny's known all about this for *months*, and I'm talking to him on the phone every damn day about two-bit flyers, and he's never mentioned it once? So I called him up. Man, I was livid by this time, and I said, *"Why did you not tell me about this?"* and he said, "I don't know. I guess I didn't think you'd be interested. Don't they use photographs on the cover of *Time* magazine?"

Opposite:
JOAN BAEZ and BOB DYLAN at the Club 47 after Joan's appearance at the Boston Arts Festival (1964). Photograph by Dick Waterman. For Eric von Schmidt's version, turn the page.

Below:
GOOD TIMES. Newport '64. Photograph by Mary Stafford.

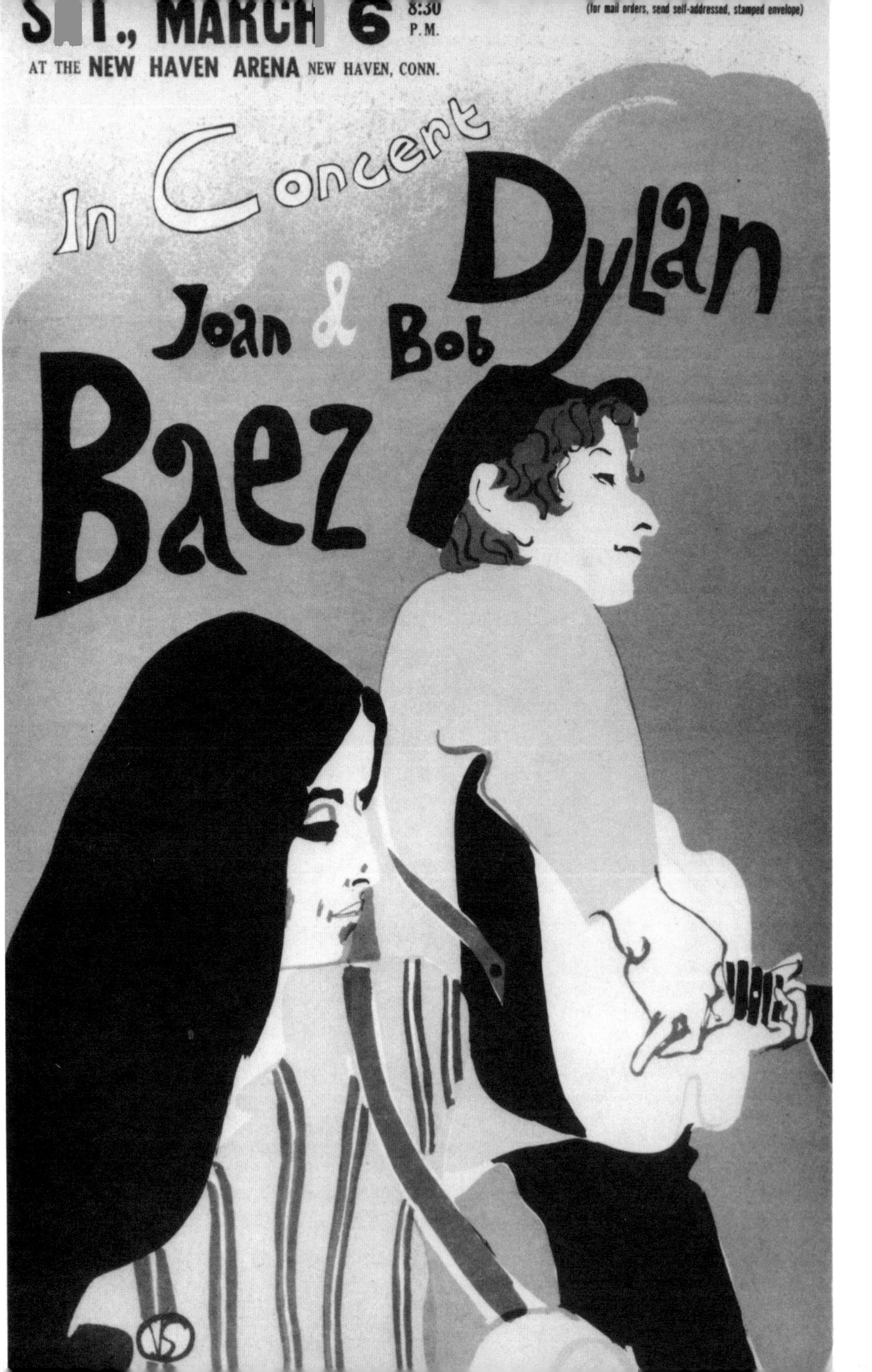
SAT., MARCH 6
8:30 P.M.
(for mail orders, send self-addressed, stamped envelope)
AT THE NEW HAVEN ARENA NEW HAVEN, CONN.
In Concert
Joan & Bob
Baez
Dylan

Anyway, we got through that. He had helped me get started playing in Cambridge and had lent me money for a guitar, you know. So when he called about the Dylan/Baez thing, I said, "Sure." I did a Toulouse-Lautrec kind of thing, trying to give equal importance to both Joan and Bob, because I liked them both a lot, and they were equally important as far as I was concerned.

Dick Waterman brought the poster down to Dylan thinking he'd like it.

In early '65, I was doing a little work for Manny Greenhill. The Dylan/Baez tour was coming up, and the posters, which Eric had done, came into the office. Dylan was doing a concert at Bridgewater State, so I took one down. Dylan looked at it. He asked if he could keep it and went out and did the show. On Monday morning, I went into the office and Manny said, "What the hell happened over the weekend? I came in this morning, and Albert had been calling me, telling me that Bob wanted to kill the poster." Evidently, Bob felt that his nose looked too semitic. Who knows. At any rate, that's the birth and death of a poster.

Eric's version of the story was that *nobody* liked the poster.

I couldn't believe it. Everybody was worried about their noses: Albert thought Joan's name was too big; Manny thought Dylan was too prominent. I thought, "Did Lautrec have to put up with this shit?" Then I thought, "Yeah, he probably did."

Mimi Fariña recalls a time when she had had enough of the bullshit that was going down, and remembers with keen pleasure having the guts to do something about it.

This moment of glory, it made me so high . . . It was an evening in Woodstock before it was "Woodstock." We were having dinner at Bernard Paturel's restaurant. Joanie was leaving the next day, or it was her birthday — it was some celebration on her behalf. And Dylan was ignoring her — talking to other people. Finally, there was a very unappealing girl who was staring at Dylan, and he said, "Come and join us." So she came over. She was genuinely moronic, and Dylan started making fun of her. She was eating and dribbling food, and he kept making fun of it. Finally, Joanie tersely said something like "Won't you cut that out — stop picking on a fan," but he did it all the more. Then he was rude to Alfredo, who couldn't stand to be insulted. Alfredo took about three cuts — I don't know what they were or where they came from — and finally took his napkin, threw it down on the table and said, "I can't take this any longer!" and got up and split — just left the restaurant. And I thought, "Ooh, how interesting!" No one does

MIMI FARIÑA and CAP'N BOB
Photograph by John Cooke.

that to Dylan — what fun!" Minutes later, Dick said, "I think I'm gonna go find Alfredo." And then minutes later he was still insulting Joanie, and Joanie said, "Fuck it," and she, too, got up and left.

So I was sitting there. He hadn't hurt me yet. He was carrying on and Victor Maimudes was watching it all. So he said something unpleasant to me and I thought, "I don't have to sit here, my company is outside." So I just got up slowly. I made no exit, I just split, and he went on talking to this poor girl. I found them all down the road, sitting on a bench. It was a long walk, about a mile, and I said, "What's everybody doing?" And they were discussing how could he have been so rude. Alfredo: "How could he do that to me?" and Joanie said, "Oh, he does it to everybody" — trying to stick up for him and at the same time being upset herself. Joanie's party was ruined, so I marched back to the restaurant, went in, and sat down next to him. And I said, "Do you know what you're doing?!" And he kind of laughed . . . and because he was laughing and would not pay attention, I took his hair and pulled his head back. And Victor burst out with some laughter, which I had never seen from Victor. I said, "Don't you do that to my sister!" This little burst of identity came screeching out of me. And Dylan thought that was very funny. I think he was quite shocked, because I made his eyes tear, which later delighted me, but at the time kind of scared me. And that was that. But there were many moments like that, when I thought, "He's so mean! Why does she like that?" Well, there was something in her that liked that — so what could I do about that?

Up to this point, Dylan's record jackets had illuminated his rapidly changing image more accurately than the hordes of retainers, explainers, and complainers; the rafts of rightists and leftists; the brown-nosers and purple prosers, the amused perusals of the confused and the bemused; the workers of words, blind and confined, usually one, if not two, steps behind.

If Dylan's lyrics were often rambling and elliptical, his album covers were right on target.

The first album, "Bob Dylan": Sullen waif who ain't gonna drink that chicken soup no mo', no mo'. The second album, "The Freewheelin' Bob Dylan": Spunky kid, chick on arm, Little Davey, gonna play on yo' harp or kick some bad ass Goliath? Third album, "The Times They Are A-Changin'": Prophet of Pellagra, the dust bowl revisited, skinny-neck and all. The fourth album, "Another Side of Bob Dylan": Ethnic funkpunk, anotha motha, mean streets and bloody sheets.

By the time the fifth album came out in March of '65, it's surprising that Pete Seeger and Company couldn't decipher the graffiti on the latrine wall, or at least look at the message on the jacket.

"Bringing It All Back Home" pictures Dylan in the lap of outrageous luxury. Albert Grossman's wife, Sally, desirable, elegant, aloof, in flame-red, reclines behind Bob who fondles a grey kitten and slouches over a magazine emblazoned with the name "Jean Harlow." Behind him, resting on an opulent overmantle is a Lord Buckley album. Beneath it is his own most recent album, *Another Side of Bob Dylan*. On the couch are record albums by The Impressions, Robert Johnson, Ravi Shankar, and Eric von Schmidt. Dylan's attire is early English mod: French cuffs, button collar, no tie. We can't see his leather boots with their tiny heels, but we know they are there. Under Sally's right arm is a glowering picture of Lyndon Johnson (*Time*'s "Man of The Year" Cover) and a blurry fallout shelter sign. It was an optical celebration of opulence and disdain. A visual open letter to the Old Folk Guard: Kiss off.

Bob Neuwirth was on the Dylan/Baez tour.

Publicity shot of BOB DYLAN by Dan Kramer.

Opposite:
BOB NEUWIRTH *creating. Photograph by Charles Frizzell.*

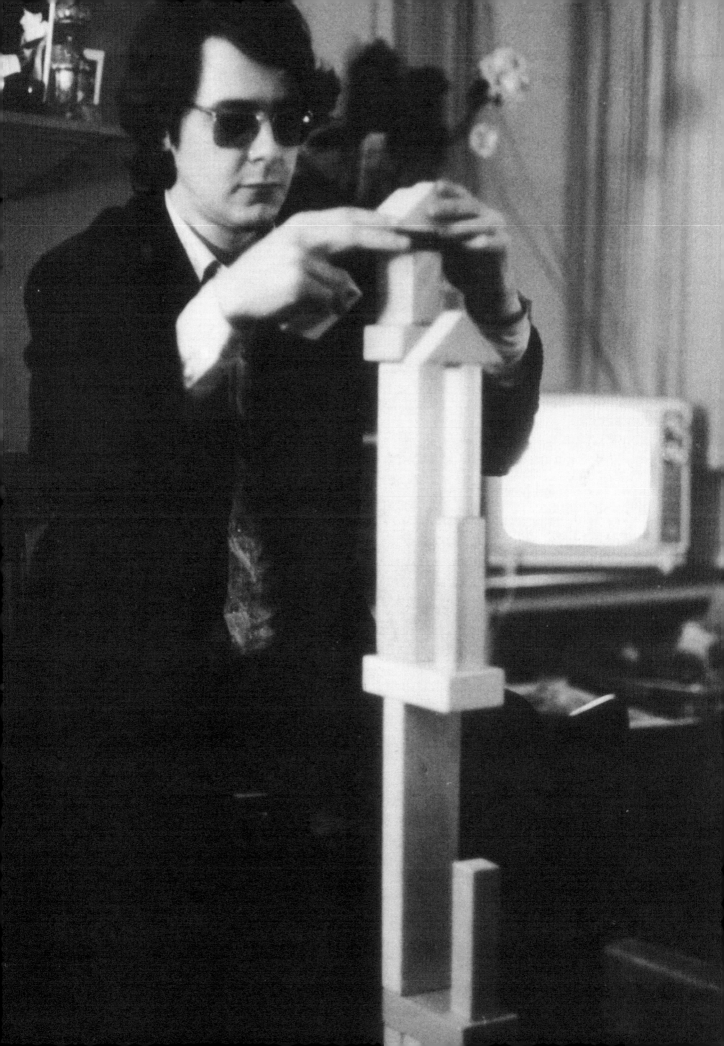

*T*he Dylan/Baez tour would never have happened if Joan hadn't already been a star. She was already selling lots of records. It's not that Joan *made* Bob particularly, but she certainly didn't hamper his career at all. She introduced Bob. Bob didn't introduce her.

The feeling around that tour was pretty good. The only one who was in a sweat about it was Manny. As far as Bob was concerned, Albert was the guy who took care of all that shit. If there was anything he didn't want to talk to Albert about, he would try to find someone between Albert and himself, like me. And that was mostly just trivial stuff and almost never. Mostly they'd discuss whatever it was they had to discuss about business. Albert would ask him if he wanted to do something, and he'd say yes or no. There was never any of the evil shit that a lot of people imagined.

The music was fantastic. The audiences were estatic. It really was goosebump time. There is a fantastic picture taken during that time. It was taken from behind. There's just the light flare. The two of them are on stage together with acoustic guitars. I remember that very shot in my own particular mental movie. The song was "Purple Heather." It was a goosebump, and that's how commercial it was. And the warmup tune that they played to get themselves loose before they went on stage was "You've Lost That Lovin' Feeling." If their intentions were evil and commercial, they would have opened with that and forgotten the folk music. But it wasn't evil. At that point, those two peole owned it, and they didn't sell it out to "show business."

When that tour was over they all headed for England with a film crew, Leacock-Pennebaker. The situation was reversed. Dylan had been over in late '64, had hung out with the Beatles and Eric Burden and the Animals. He was already a star there, and Joan Baez had never been to England. I should never have gone on that tour. It was sick. You see, originally I was going to go to England and have a concert tour, and in the middle of that Bobby's rise to fame came so fast that a few months later, we thought we'd go together and do split concerts. By the time it got around to England, Bobby was much more famous there than I was, and so Bobby just took England. I mean I didn't even bother with a tour. But, you see, I thought he would do what I had done with him, would introduce me, and it would be very nice for me because I'd never sung

JOAN BAEZ presents BOB DYLAN. Photographs by Stephen Fenerjian.

(top) *JOAN BAEZ. Photograph by Berkeley Folk Festival Staff.* (bottom) *BOB DYLAN. Photograph by John Cooke.*

in England before. That's what I had in my mind. And by the time we got to England, whatever had happened in Bobby's mind — I'd never seen him less healthy than he was in England — he was a wreck and he wouldn't ask me on the stage to sing. And I was really surprised. I was very, very hurt. I was miserable. I was a complete ass; I should have left. I mean, I should have left after the first concert. But there's something about situations like that — you hang around. I stayed two weeks, and then I walked out the door, I never came back after that. I went to France and stayed with my parents. They lived in France then. But it was one of the really most painful weeks in my life because I couldn't understand really what the hell was going on.

> *It's once I was free to go roving in*
> *The wind of a springtime, mine.*
> *And once the clouds I sailed upon*
> *Were sweet as lilac wine.*
> *Why have the breezes of summer, dear.*
> *Been laced with a grim design?*

It's All Over Now, Baby Blue

Leave your stepping stones behind, there's something that calls for you.
Forget the dirt you've left, they will not follow you.
The vagabond that's rapping on your door,
Is standing in the clothes that you once wore.
Strike another match, go start anew,
And it's all over now, Baby Blue.

 oc Watson was up in Bill Keith's room listening to a new record, *Rubber Soul* by the Beatles. When the record was finished he said, "Man! Those boys have been doing their homework!" Doc knew a trend in popular music when he heard it; he'd been listening carefully for over thirty years. From Bing Crosby to Frank Sinatra to Elvis to Ray Charles to the Beatles. He knew that there was no way to escape something like that any more than you could get out of the way of a hurricane. What you could do is to live through it and possibly use some of that energy to advantage. There was no point in sticking your fingers in your ears. Doc knew too much about blindness for that.

Electricity was definitely in the air as a result of the British rock explosion. Down in the Village, Maria Muldaur's old friend John Sebastian was thinking of getting back to his roots.
I'm talking about Gene Vincent and the Blue Caps! That was the point at which I went crazy and said, "Oh, my God! That's what I want to do!" Then I started singing in a "shoo-bop" group in prep school. Then I found out what was going on

down at the bottom of the buiding we lived in at Washington Square West. That's when I started getting into the blues and playing harmonica as much as possible. I was going to Gerde's almost every night until they finally started to let me in for free. I met John Herald there. I met Dylan in Washington Square and hung out with him in the basement of Gerde's and over at Izzy Young's Folklore Center.

I was very much on MacDougal Street playing with as many different people as I could. I'd have to switch styles as I went from club to club. I was going straight from Tim Hardin over to Doc Watson to Mississippi John Hurt to Freddy Neil to the Modern Folk Quartet. Then I was also playing with the occasional jug band that would form up like the Even Dozen Jug Band — which gave me great respect for the Kweskin Jug Band and especially Geoff Muldaur and Fritz Richmond.

It was as a result of recording with the Even Dozen Jug Band that I met Paul Rothchild. At some point in the session he made some remark that had to do with reefer that nobody else picked up. Afterwards I went over to him and very quietly asked him if maybe he might have a little something, and we immediately started hanging out together. I was an absolute appendage of

BOB DYLAN. Photograph by John Cooke.

244

Paul's for about a year. He gave me all sorts of work as a harmonica player, and I learned a lot about making records from watching Paul work.

One of the great records from that time was the Blues Project album. I was there for every minute of that one. The cut I did with Eric von Schmidt was just wonderful right away. The whole record went that way. There was so much of that music being played at that time, and it was so undocumented, that the minute you got it into a studio, everybody was so stoked to be there that it all worked. It was real, but it wasn't too nervous. You could smoke pot in the bathroom or drink rum in the control room. Take your pick.

Around that time I met Zal Yanovsky who had been traveling around as guitar accompanist to a lot of different, small, modern folk groups, as opposed to your traditional groups. He'd started out as a rock and roller, too, and he hit me at a time when I was starting to come out of my intense traditionalist phase. It seemed to me that a lot of what the whole traditional scene was based on was prejudice against the music I had come from before I got into the folk scene — good old rock and roll!

So Zally and I hung out together a lot, wandering around the Village looking for a drummer and a bass player. We wanted what we had both experienced to be the combination of music that should go into this group. Which was all of it — folk *and* rock and roll. Which *nobody* at that time was interested in. Which was interesting, because it was a major part of American music!

At that point the Beatles were inspirational. I remember walking into the Playhouse Cafe with Freddy Neil and seeing a Beatles poster on the wall. It was a novelty. Everybody was saying, "Wow! What's this?"

"It's the Beatles! They're this new group from England. They're really great!"

Then one day I was talking to Fritz Richmond, who was instrumental in turning me on to funny, little, round glasses, and I said, "This is going to be a rock and roll group which sounds like Mississippi John Hurt!" At that point he said, "Why not call it the Lovin' Spoonful?" Fritz Richmond, cultural hero *enormé* of the period!

That was the point where it really turned around. In the beginning both Zally and I had been rock and rollers, and then had really embraced folk music. When we got together we said, "Wait! Let's go to the Night Owl and blast out the folkies with two super-reverbs!" We really relished what we would be putting all those traditional guys through. There was a point at which we really wanted to blow it all over — with the natural excitement of the moment.

JOHN SEBASTIAN (1964) Photograph by John Cooke.

ews of the Lovin' Spoonful traveled to Cambridge immediately via the Jug Band. Half their material was either from the Jug Band or the Holy Modal Rounders — songs like "Fishin' Blues,""Blues in the Bottle," and "Wild About My Lovin'." Sebastian wrote most of the rest of the tunes like "Do You Believe in Magic," and "Younger Girls," but even there he was coming right out of traditional material — prison walls became younger girls in John's fertile imagination. A definite improvement.

The Jug Band's recommendation was enough for Byron and Betsy. The Spoonful were booked into the 47. It was music to Sebastian's ears.

Did we want to KILL in that room! We came to kill! When the possibility of that gig came up Zally and I looked at each other, and our eyes lit up. We were going to be face to face with the folkies at last. And it turned out great. Everybody who was moving with the times loved it. Everybody who was becoming a period piece hated it. **They put their fingers in their ears. Zally would see them and go over and turn his amp up! It was the beginning of the end.**

As it happened the end was beginning in several places that year, starting virtually at the stroke of midnight, December 31, 1964. Once again, Fritz was the man of the hour, and Paul Rothchild was about to walk through another door.

There was a New Year's Eve party at Cooke's in Cambridge, and I got a call from Fritz. "We're in Chicago, and we just heard Paul Butterfield's new band, and it's the greatest thing you've ever heard. Get on a plane right now and go to Chicago." I had met Paul earlier that year at the Cabale Creamery in Berkeley. I was staying at Jim and Suzie West's with Neuwirth and Fritz. We went down to the club because Neuwirth would be doing an odd little set every once in a while. Butterfield came in and sat in. I had never heard him. I had never heard harmonica played that way except on old records. I told him, "You're great!" Are you ever going to put a band together?" He said, "I don't know."

THE LOVIN' SPOONFUL (1965) (left to right) JOE BUTLER, JOHN SEBASTIAN, ZAL YANOVSKY, and STEVE BOONE. Photograph by Henry Diltz.

So I left Cooke's party and flew to Chicago and caught the last set. I walked into Big John's and heard the most amazing thing I'd ever heard in my life. It was the same rush I'd had the first time I heard bluegrass. I said to myself, "Here is the beginning of another era. This is another turning point in American music's direction." We went next door to the pizza joint; I talked to him, told him I wanted him to record for Elektra. He was going for it. He was totally, magnificently jive. Beautiful. I loved him. Chicago street hustler. Here's this hot shot from New York telling him he wants to make records. I'd shined up my act a little bit, so I was pretty good at it by that time — talking to artists about making records.

After I finished talking with Paul and the band, which was Elvin Bishop, Jerome Arnold, and Sam Lay, somebody said, "Let's go over and catch this other band at an after hours joint." So I heard Mike Bloomfield's band for the first time. When they came off, I leaned over to Paul and said, "Hey, Paul, let's get this guy into your band." He said, "No. He's got his band, and I've got mine. He'll never leave his band. Anyway, I've already got a guitar player." I said, "Can you imagine two guitars in your band!" He said, "Well, you can ask him." So I leaned over to Bloomfield and said, "How would you like to join the Butterfield Band. We're making a record. Blah. Blah. Blah." We talked for about twenty minutes, and he finally said, "Yeah!" and he leaned across the table and said to his band, "I quit!" And we were off.

I played manager for them for a little while. I got them gigs at the Philadelphia Folk Festival, the Newport Folk Festival, and the Club 47. First, we cut a whole album in New York at Mastertone. They played the Cafe Au Go Go in New York. They all looked really shoddy. And at that time, the British bands were all wearing suits. So we went down to the lower East side to one of those really sleazy suit places and got them all brown suits except for Butterfield, who got a green one.

One of the cuts on the album we recorded was "Born in Chicago." Jac had come up with the idea of putting out samplers for $1.98. On this sampler were a number of the new acts which I had brought up to the label. Rush was on it. And Dick Rosmini and Judy Collins and one by Butterfield. Up until this point, he had sold maybe twenty or thirty thousand copies of these samplers, which was great for then. This sampler sold 200,000 copies! In a three month period. Jac said, "What's going on?" And I kept saying to him, "This tune is going on. *Born in Chicago.* **Jac, we have a hit band on our hands.**"

We finished the entire album. Edited it, which took a month. It was very complicated cutting. I was engineering. I was doing it all at that time. I finally completed it, lacquered it, pressed it, jacketed it. It was sitting in boxes in the pressing plant, ready to be shipped when Jac and I flew up to Martha's Vineyard to visit Tom Rush for a few days and eat zucchini. While I had him up in the plane, I said, "Jac, I want to scrap the Butterfield album." I thought we were going into the sea and that he was going to have a cardiac arrest right then and there. He wanted to know why. I said, "Because I haven't captured the band. "Born in Chicago" is the only good cut. The rest of it sucks." And he got really upset. "What do you want to do? You've made this album, and we've spent more on it than we ever have, and you want to scrap it? What do you want to do?" And I said, "I want to record them live. I want to capture that live feeling." By the time we landed, he agreed, and that's when we set up the gig at the Cafe Au Go Go. We brought a recording truck in, and we discovered how much it cost to record at union rates in New York City. We recorded four nights, took out miles of tape. I listened to the tapes back for two weeks with Paul, and we didn't have a note. Nothing. I went into Jac's office and said, "Jac, we don't have a record." He did ten minutes of high velocity vocalization at me and said, "I don't care what you do, just get me that record." Because by then he knew that they were going to happen. So I re-recorded the album back at Mastertone. I set it up differently to get a live feel, and by that time everybody had more studio chops, and I knew what I wanted to go for and was able to give them better direction. We edited it — about 263 splices. I wanted it to be great. My ass was on the line. My personal feelings about myself in a creative way were on the line, too. If I couldn't pull this off, I had blown a really major opportunity for me to prove something to the world about whites playing black music, about me making good records, about Elektra being able to make the conversion to electric music. All of those things.

During that time, I called George Wein and asked him to put them on Newport. I called Albert Grossman and told him I had a band that was way beyond my capabilities and asked if he would consider managing them. He came down and heard them and said, "I'll see them at Newport."

C oming to the Newport Festival as a performer for the first time could be a strange and exciting experience. First of all, there was the aura of the town. The heart of town was made up of very old wooden houses packed together on a hill overlooking the harbor. The waterfront area was a mixture of shops catering to the international yachting set and honky tonks for sailors from the Navy base and kids from the surrounding towns. But the main attraction in Newport was the splendor of the age of millionaires. As you drove out along Bellevue Avenue past the mansions with their beautiful grounds and handsome trees you could not help but marvel at the extravagance of it all. To turn into one of those driveways and actually stay in one of those houses while you performed at the Festival was more than you would have dreamed of. To be sure, by Newport standards the houses owned by Vernon Court Junior College were modest — only fifteen or twenty rooms — but to folks coming to the festival they were all right.

This was the first time that the Charles River Valley Boys had been invited to the Newport Festival, but John, Bob, and Joe had all been to Festivals before and knew what to expect. For their bass player, Everett Alan Lilly, it was a totally new and exciting experience. He was the son of Everett Lilly, Sr., of Hayloft Jamboree and Hillbilly Ranch fame, and had grown up with true folk music all his life. He had been raised by his grandparents in West Virginia and had only been in Boston for a couple of years.

I came up from West Virginia in 1963 to go to school. To make extra money I played with Dad and Bea at the Hillbilly Ranch, and played in the country bars with my brother Tennis and my cousin Monte. I knew that folk music was happening nationally from watching the Hootenanny TV show, but that wasn't very country or very anything, really. Then I went over with Dad and Bea once when they played at the 47. Bill Keith and Jim Rooney and Joe Val played a set, too, and that was the first time I had an idea that something more was going on.

Through Joe Val, Bob Siggins got in touch with me to play a job with the River Boys. Fritz was getting really busy with the Jug Band and couldn't do it any more. I had only been playing

the bass for a year. I had an aluminum bass, so it wasn't far advanced from Fritz's washtub. Soon I started playing with them regularly, and that was what I needed to get me out of the country bars.

The great thing about the Cambridge scene was that it was very spontaneous. It was not cut and dried. Siggins was as spontaneous a banjo player as I've ever seen. If he missed something, it was because he got so enthusiastic, and he was just doing what he felt like doing. That gave the music a lot of energy, and the people reacted to that.

In 1965 we went to Newport for the first time, and I thought that was an incredible event. It was like taking an alcoholic to a picnic. Over in one field you had genuine Southern Comfort; over here you had Ballantine Ale; over there you had Seagram's; then you had very fine, old wine somewhere else — maybe too many people wouldn't go over there, but the ones who did really understood it. I was tireless. I didn't want to miss anything. Whenever we weren't playing, I was out in the field going to hear Maybelle Carter or Doc Watson or Bill Monroe or Bob

THE CHARLES RIVER VALLEY BOYS (left to right) JOHN COOKE, BOB SIGGINS, JOE VAL, and EVERETT ALAN LILLY. Photograph by Julie Snow.

Dylan or Joan Baez. As young as I was, I was impressed by the range of music and styles and also by the quality of the music. And then there were the parties in those mansions! Where else could you go and walk among so many truly great musicians?

George Wein's wife, Joyce, was in charge of taking care of the two-hundred or so performers, and every year a corps of volunteers from the folk communities of Cambridge and New York would take their vacations or arrange their lives so that they could be at Newport at Festival time. It was an enormous task to see that everyone's needs were taken care of. Unlike the Jazz Festival, many of the performers at the Folk Festival were not professional entertainers, used to being away from home, sleeping in a strange bed, eating strange food, being with people they had never met in their life. One of the joys of working at the Festival was to see all these people come together in the course of the week, bound by their common love of music and people. Every day the performers would participate in workshops at the field, be taken to the houses for dinner, driven back to the field for the evening concert, and then either taken home to bed or to one of the mansions or hotels where a big party would be in full swing with non-stop music until three or so in the morning when a halt would be called to insure that everyone would have the strength to do it all over again the next day.

Jill Henderson was one of many volunteers who had come down from Cambridge.

Joyce Wein had asked me to be a house mother. I saw this lanky, tall dude sitting on the steps of the house next to Paul Butterfield. Butterfield was smoking a joint. I told them to do it somewhere else. The lanky dude asked me who I was. He was the biggest, tallest, black dude I'd ever met in my life. I said, "I'm your housemother." He cracked up and said, "You're too little." I asked him who he was, and he told me he was George Chambers. So we talked and carried on, and he said, "There's some other people you've got to meet." I met the Brothers right away. They were great. We had supper together. Then we went back to the house. They were sitting around, and Joe said, "What are the words to such and such?" George sang him the line, and all three of them sang in harmony, and I fell totally in love with the four of them.

Joe Chambers and his brothers, Willie, George, and Lester were relatively new to the folk scene, and they had never dreamed of going to Newport.

ur family moved to L.A. in 1954 from Carthage, Mississippi. We had been a gospel group there and played around locally as far away as Louisiana. The main concern when we got to Los Angeles was schooling. Music had always been such a big part of our family that we never thought of it as a career. After a couple of years we found a church and joined up, and we started singing again as a gospel group. We did that straight through until 1961 — churches on Sunday and concerts in churches on Sunday evening. It wasn't really for a career. It was just that being Baptists, if you go to church, you sing. You sing as much as you can. The collection plate would have a few dollars which we'd split up, and that would be that.

We had a friend from Texas named Long Gone Miles. I had got into hair processing as a hobby, and I had done Long Gone's hair. Lightnin' Hopkins was playing at the Ash Grove, and Long Gone wanted me to go over there and do Lightnin's hair. So I did, and that's how I met Ed Pearl, who ran the club. He drove me to the drug store to get the stuff for Lightnin's hair, and as we drove he started telling me about the club and what kind of place it was. At that time we had this strict rule that we wouldn't sing our music in nightclubs where there was wine or anything like that, because we had been brought up really strict Baptists.

After we had talked about it for a long time, Ed said, "Come out to the club one night and sing. If you like it we'll give you a contract, and you can make some money." It was a coffeehouse and they'd already had the Clara Ward Singers, so we decided to do it.

We went in there and were so nervous the first time. We could hardly sing a note, but Ed saw the potential, and he just told us to relax and to come back when we felt a little more ready for it. So after a while we went back, and he put us on with Barbara Dane and Sonny and Brownie and Doc Watson for a New Year's show. We were booked in for three weeks after that. As a result of that we became good friends with Barbara Dane, and she helped us a lot.

At first we did straight gospel. After the shows every night people would invite us over to house parties, and we'd lay a little blues on them. It kind of got around then that we did blues also, so then we started doing a set of blues and a set of

THE CHAMBERS
BROTHERS QUARTET.
*(left to right) GEORGE,
LESTER, JOE and WILLIE
Photograph courtesy of
Festival Productions.*

below:
*JILL HENDERSON and
GEORGE "POPS"
CHAMBERS Photograph
by Rick Sullo.*

gospel. Soon we started getting jobs in other places — The Insomniac in Hermosa Beach and the Xanadu in Los Angeles where you could jam all night.

Until then we'd never been into the folk scene. We knew who Josh White and Jimmy Reed and Lightnin' Hopkins were, but we had no real knowledge of what folk music was all about. Meeting Sonny Terry was a big influence on us because he turned us on to the harmonica. Sonny gave us a whole set of his old harmonicas, which was a big step in helping us develop our sound. At first, it was just Willie and his guitar. The rest of us would just sing.

After playing at the Ash Grove everything started to snowball. We had never thought that it would be so easy to get into show business. At that time nobody thought of folk music as show business or as a way to get into it. After our introduction to it we knew that that was the way we had to go to achieve anything in our career.

So we went from there to San Diego and San Francisco, and eventually we bought into the Cabale Creamery in Berkeley. Rolf Cahn owned it then with Carol Perry, and we bought her share. We met Rolf then. His ex-old lady, Barbara Dane, kept encouraging us to go on with it, and it was Barbara who set it up for us to go to Newport in 1965. By that time our musical style had begun to take on a little more form. We all started to learn to play guitars and the bass and harmonica.

Simply hearing the Brothers sing was it for Jill, and that was it for everyone who heard them that weekend — or almost everyone. Before the weekend was over, they, too, were to get caught up in the controversy over electricity and folk music.

Paul Rothchild was pleased with the line-up that year. The Elektra sampler with "Born in Chicago" was still cooking right along, and if it was cooking on an electric range that was all right with him. He was happy to ride with the future and had a feeling that big things would be happening for the group at Newport.

The Butterfield Band was given the opportunity to open the first night's show. That meant that they played while everybody was walking in. They were a mild sensation. The next day, there was a blues workshop in the afternoon. Alan Lomax and Eric von Schmidt were the hosts.

Von Schmidt arrived on Friday in his Volkswagen bus jammed with wife, their four daughters (one with a boyfriend in tow), and a black Labrador Retriever named Tar Baby. They were all shoehorned into one room and in the ensuing logistical confusion, missed the Butterfield Band's opening set. The Blues Workshop was called "Bluesville" that year and was scheduled for Saturday afternoon in two sections. Alan Lomax was hosting the Black traditional bluesmen, and Eric was doing the same for the predominantly white, urban blues singers, although when Dick Waterman arrived late with Skip James he was happy and honored to include him. However, there was one name on the list that was unfamiliar to Eric.

"Who the hell is Mike Bloomfield?" Geoff Muldaur said to me, "Man, you ought to hear this guy. He's a great guitarist." He was going to be on last. By that time, I was pretty juiced. And I don't know why Lomax did it, because I had introduced everybody else and had played a little bit myself, but I probably said, "Next is going to be Mike Bloomfield from Chicago," and I got off the stage and about forty-five minutes went by with people setting up all sorts of mikes and amplifiers.

As the band set up Rothchild took in the whole scene. He had the feeling once again that his instincts were about to be proven right.

The thing that stunned me while this was going on was the size of the audience. At workshops they only expected a few hundred people to show up, and *thousands* of people showed up. The whole area was packed. The wind was blowing dust and sand everywhere. Then Alan Lomax got up on stage and went into a five or ten minute introduction — like, "Used to be a time when a farmer would take a box, glue an axe handle to it, put some strings on it, sit down in the shade of a tree and play some blues for himself and his friends. Now here we've got these guys, and they need all of this fancy hardware to play the blues. Today you've heard some of the greatest blues musicians in the world playing their simple music on simple instruments. Let's find out if these guys can play at all."

With that, the Butterfield Band hit and hit hard. Whatever Lomax had said was totally blown away — far away. The music went right through Maria Muldaur.

I was sitting with Fariña and Mimi, Mitch and Louise Greenhill, Geoff, and Eric von Schmidt and Kay and the kids all on our shoulders. We were boogying and totally blown out by the Butterfield Band. I had heard a lot of blues, but I had never heard the like. I'd never heard real Chicago electric blues like this, and we loved it.

(top) THE CHAMBERS BROTHERS at the Sunday morning concert. (left to right) JOE, LESTER, WILLIE, and GEORGE. Photograph by John Cooke.

(bottom) THE CHAMBERS BROTHERS on the Sunday afternoon "New Folks" concert. What a difference a few hours and a change of clothes makes. (left to right) JOE, LESTER, WILLIE, and GEORGE. Photograph by Rick Sullo.

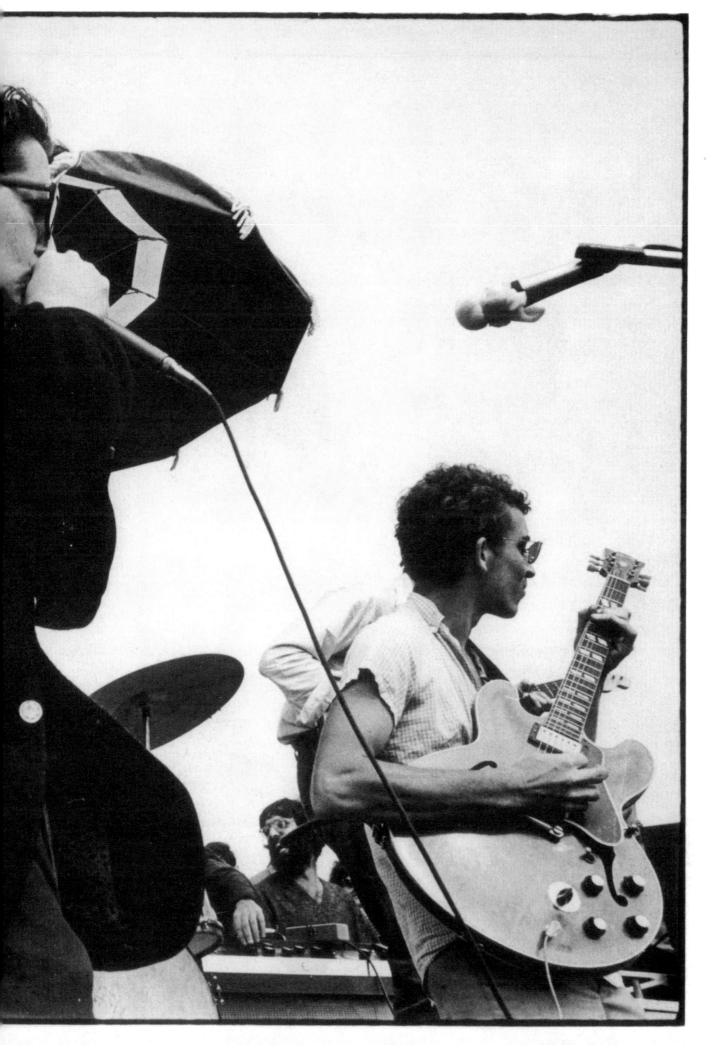

Previous Page:
"BUTTERFIELD BLOWING IT AWAY" (left to right) JEROME ARNOLD, PAUL BUTTERFIELD, and ELVIN
BISHOP. ERIC VON SCHMIDT *is behind Elvin loving it. Photograph by David Gahr.*

Opposite Page:
(top) "THE CAMBRIDGE MAFIA" (left to right) KITTY, KAY, and ERIC VON SCHMIDT; SPIDER JOHN
KOERNER; MITCH and LOUISE GREENHILL; OWEN DE LONG; MARIA MULDAUR; MIMI FARIÑA; GEOFF
MULDAUR; and RICHARD FARIÑA. *Photograph by Rick Sullo.*

(bottom) *A long shot of a "workshop" crowd. Photograph by Rick Sullo.*

This Page:
THE BUTTERFIELD BAND (left to right) SAMMY LAY, ELVIN BISHOP, MIKE BLOOMFIELD, and
JEROME ARNOLD. *Photograph by Rick Sullo.*

lectricity! That's what it was. It was taking the old music up to another level. It was reaching way beyond the back porch. It had to. And it had finally caught up with the folk world. Woody Guthrie had said it:

> Don't like dictators not much, myself,
> But I think the whole country ought to be run
> By e-lec-tri-ci-ty!

Woody evidently hadn't checked with Alan Lomax before he wrote such heresy. Alan's afternoon had been ruined, and injury was soon to be added to insult. Rothchild couldn't believe his eyes.

Lomax walked down off stage. And Albert Grossman, who the evening before had decided that he definitely wanted to manage the band, walked up to him and said, "What kind of a fuckin' introduction was that?" and Lomax said, "What do you know about blues?" and Albert said, "I don't have to know anything about blues to know that that was a terrible introduction," and Lomax said, "Oh, yeah? What are you going to do about it?" and before anyone knew what was happening there were these two giants, both physically and in the business, wrestling around in the dust!

It *was* incredible. Butterfield's drummer, Sammy Lay, no lightweight himself, and no stranger to barroom brawling, cooled it out, but it was only a preliminary for the main bout to be held Sunday night. Joe Chambers and his brothers took it all in. **Standing there watching that fight between Grossman and Lomax was when we learned our first lesson about competition in the music world. When we discovered that we could play music and make a living doing what we loved, we thought we weren't going to have any hard times after that. We were innocent. That fight that day was the beginning of a struggle. People were bringing in amplification and electric guitars, and we really didn't care about the politics of it all. The performers were all happy and into their music — Joan Baez, Dick and Mimi Fariña, Dylan, us. We were just happy we had become part of that family.**

The Saturday night concert that year was an exciting occasion for another musical family, the Jim Kweskin Jug Band. Mel Lyman was at Newport but not as part of the Jug Band. Maria Muldaur and Bill Keith were by this time kicking the gong. The Band had played the year before on the Sunday afternoon show, but this was the big leagues. They had gained a large following, and

ALBERT and SALLY GROSSMAN. Photograph by Rick Sullo.

other performers participating — Jean Ritchie, Roscoe Holcomb, the Moving Star Hall Singers, and Bill Monroe. It was powerful music and made a good beginning to the last day of the Festival.

The Brothers stayed out at the field after the religious workshop was over because they were also scheduled to perform on the afternoon "New Folks" concert as were Mark Spoelstra, Kathy and Carol, Hamilton Camp, Pat Sky, the Charles River Valley Boys, fiddler Byron Berline and his father Lou Berline, Gordon Lightfoot, and Dick and Mimi Fariña. Peter Yarrow was organizing the concert, and if you weren't confused or on edge when you got there, he'd help you out. Jim Rooney and Bill Keith had met the Berlines at the beginning of the weekend and had been jamming with them whenever they could. At the party the night before, Byron asked them if they'd back him and his father up on the concert. Jim was delighted.

Byron had grown up right near the Kansas/Oklahoma border and was a big, raw-boned, football-playing country boy. This was his first time at anything like a folk festival, and he was just having a great time. His dad, Lou, was a reaper and drove one of those big combines for a living. He was a champion fiddler and so was Byron. Lou was a crusty old son of a bitch. He had a gravel voice and about every other word was "goddam." Bill Monroe was there that year. Pete Rowan was playing with him by then. The Charles River Valley Boys were there, too, so we really had some great jams. Monroe really liked Byron's fiddling, and he liked Byron's old man a lot, too. Shortly after that, Byron went to work for Monroe.

Keith and I were very pleased that they had asked us to back them up. We even came up with matching shirts so we'd look like a band. We went over with them to the field in the afternoon. Peter Yarrow was in charge, and we reported to him. Peter was always very serious and officious. He introduced himself to Byron and Lou and introduced them to Jerry White, who was the emcee: "Mr. Berline, this is Jerry White, who will be introducing you this afternoon. It would be a big help to Mr. White if you could give him some information which would help him communicate meaningfully to the audience about the style of music you play and where you come from and so forth." All I could think of that Lou might choose to "meaningfully communicate" was, "I'm from goddam Kansas and drive a goddam reaper and play the goddam fiddle and this here is my goddam son Byron!" As far as Lou Berline was concerned, Peter might as well have been from the moon, Lou was definitely from earth.

they were ready to boogie their woogies away. Everyone was high on the excitement created by the Butterfield Band that afternoon and the battle of the titans that followed. The audience picked up on all of the energy and went wild. They didn't want to let them off and started chanting, "We want more! We want more!" The one encore allowed was not enough to satisfy the crowd, and they were not happy at all. Time was always a problem on the evening concerts. There always seemed to be too many performers, and the problem was compounded by the tendency of the emcees to ramble on as they introduced the performers. If the audience and the Jug Band were having a love feast that night, Theo Bikel was not invited to it.

Throughout the evening people met who had been at the Bluesville workshop and talked about how great the Butterfield Band had been and how funny it had been to see Alan Lomax and Albert Grossman wrestling each other on the ground. For those who missed the fight of the century, Von Schmidt was ready with a replay. Jim Rooney ran into Eric over by the beer tent.

I had my white Irish sweater on. Eric started telling me the story of Albert and Alan and illustrated it with a shadow show on my sweater — "You jerk!" Boom! "You asshole!" Bam! I'm sure it was more entertaining than the real thing. It was ridiculous.

The next day was Sunday. The Chambers Brothers got up early to participate in the late morning program of gospel and religious music. They did not feel that they were newcomers on *this* program. It was what they did best and loved most. They also got to share fellowship with many of the

A s is often the case in Newport in July, the morning had been overcast. The breezes blown in from the sea had bathed the gospel singers in pearly grey light. By midday, the hope of resurrection gone, the sun boils down. It gets plain old New England hot. Perhaps that's why God made T-shirts, beer stands, and graced it all with New Folks Concerts.

As the afternoon wore on, the heat and moisture began to combine and the clouds began to gather. Mimi and Dick Fariña looked particularly fragile under the building thunderheads. Delicate and small, they carried with them a stunning grace, a painful insecurity.

They started their set with "Birmingham Sunday." Eric had said, "Why don't you do Birmingham Sunday?" and Dick did, his voice a bit strident, the pitch a touch unsure, but bravely, *bravely,* and then, suddenly, the skys opened up, and a summer shower was pelting down. Mimi was so intent on the music she simply didn't know what was happening.

I thought people were getting up to leave . . . I thought, "Oh, no we can't be that awful — my pessimistic point of view — and I was looking at him to see if we should stop because I thought people were splitting 'cause we weren't doing that well. 'Cause we were the newcomers and so on. But he went on playing, and then he went on introducing another song — and I thought, "How could he do this? They're fed up!" And then people

started taking their clothes off and I realized it was raining and the people were *dancing.*

Dancing! Blue jeans sopping, T-shirts dripping, Dick ripping into "Hard Loving Loser," "Reno, Nevada," anything that cooked, and then Bruce Langhorn was out there, and Fritz Richmond was out there, and everybody was *dancing!* God had stopped by Newport after all.

Bob Dylan was not out at the field that afternoon. He had gotten together with Mike Bloomfield and Sammy Lay and with Al Kooper and Harvey Brooks, who had come up from New York. Harvey and Al had already recorded with Dylan on his most recent album *Bringin' It All Back Home,* which was half electric, half acoustic.

Like Geoff and Maria, Dylan had first heard the Beatles on a car radio, and it made an equally big impression on him.

But I just kept it to myself and I really dug them. Everybody else thought they were for the teenboppers, that they were gonna pass right away. But it was obvious to me that they had staying power. I knew they were pointing the direction of where music had to go. I was not about to put up with other musicians, but in my head the Beatles were it. In Colorado, I started thinking it was so far out that I couldn't deal with it — eight in the top ten. It seemed to me a definite line was being drawn. This was something that never happened before. It was outrageous and I kept it in my mind. You see, there was a lot of hypocrisy all around, people saying it had to be either folk or rock. But I knew it didn't have to be like that. I dug what the Beatles were doing, and I always kept it

in mind.

They were doing things nobody was doing. Their chords were outrageous, just outrageous, and their harmonies made it all valid. You could only do that with other musicians. Even if you're playing your own chords you had to have other people playing with you. That was obvious. And it started me thinking about other people.

Not only had Dylan heard the Beatles, he had hung out with them during a concert tour in England in May of 1964. The Beatles, the Stones, Eric Burdon and the Animals. They'd smoked some reefer, had a ball. Dylan was particularly excited about a song he himself had sung on his first album.

My God, ya oughta hear what's going down over there! Eric Burdon and the Animals, ya know? Well, he's doing "House of the Rising Sun" in rock. *Rock!* It's fuckin' *wild!* Blew my mind!

He knew electricity was definitely the direction and he was going with that flow. When he heard the Butterfield Band the day before and saw the reaction of the crowd, it seemed that the time might be right to try to work up two or three songs to play on the evening concert. Bob left it to Albert Grossman to make any necessary arrangements with the stage crew and the sound and lighting people, Terry Hanley and Chip Monck.

In the aftermath of the afternoon raindance inspired by the Fariñas, everybody was in a good mood and up for the closing of the festival. Pete Seeger opened the concert and instead of singing, played a tape recording of a baby crying. It was the first cries of John and Penny Cohen's child, and Pete dedicated the program to this new citizen of the world, asking what kind of world that baby would grow up in and what the singers that night would sing to that baby about. Seeger's own view seemed to be that they would sing that it was a world of pollution, bombs, hunger and injustice, but that PEOPLE would OVERCOME. And that theme was taken up by Seeger's old friend from the Weaver's days, Ronnie Gilbert, who sang Dylan's "Masters of War" and a Phil Ochs song about freedom. Theo Bikel had also sung the same Ochs song the night before. It would appear that Seeger's program to the new baby was working out as he had hoped. The old guard was singing to it in the words of the younger writers, but the message was the same.

It was Eric von Schmidt's first appearance at Newport, and he was neither part of the old group nor part of the young group. He remained his own furry self and treated the whole thing as if it was some vast party.

Yeah, I was very excited to be there. Happy and thrilled to be there. My big song, my *theme* song was "Grizzly Bear." I had heard it on a southern prison recording by Lomax and Pete Seeger. It was a work song, but I put a guitar part behind it and it just drove along. I was walking around the Festival grounds and I heard this voice just floating in the air, "Tell you 'little story 'bout a griz-*zully* bear, great big griz-zully, griz-*zully* bear." It was the same damn guy that I'd heard on the record! Newport was just great like that. There the guy would be and you'd meet him. Incredible!

So I sang that on the evening concert, and I sang "My Love Comes Rolling Down," and let go, and took the chance of making up a verse on stage. I might have sung "Joshua Gone Barbados," too, and then I got the message to get off the stage, but the crowd was yelling for more, so I did "Out On the Rolling Sea" with Geoff and Maria, and Fritz singing Bahamian bass. So we were a little late getting off.

If Von Schmidt had loosened things up a little, the peace and harmony of the evening was soon to be shattered altogether. Paul Rothchild went backstage with Albert Grossman, Dylan, and the musicians. It took a few minutes to get everyone set up. Peter Yarrow was going to introduce Dylan, and, as usual, he was pacing around nervously. He brought Bob on with his most reverential, "We are now approaching the genius," tones, and the band hit. Once again, Rothchild observed an incredible scene.

I was on the left side of the stage. Albert was there. Theo Bikel was there. Pete Seeger was there. George Wein was there. The band got on stage and started to play. All of the old folk mafia were saying, "Get them off stage! This is a violation of what this festival is all about! This is pop music! This can't happen!" And Albert was saying, "Hey, you can't do that. They're really great. Look at the audience." Pete Seeger was livid. He ran back somewhere and came back with an axe, and he said, "I am going to chop the power cables if you don't take them off the stage right now!" Theodore Bikel, who was on the board of directors, said, "You can't do that! Pete, you can't stop the future. Look at those people! They are going to learn the music we want them to know through these young musicians. Leave them alone. It's okay." I was surprised, but Theo was choosing to blow with the winds of change, whereas the others were trying to hold on to their sanctuary.

DICK and MIMI FARIÑA catching fire in the rain. Photograph by Rick Sullo.

Peter Yarrow came to me and asked me to mix the sound, so I ran out to the board, which was in the box seat area, and started to mix it. But by then, there was a fight going on at the board with people trying to turn the knobs down, and me bringing them up. People were shouting, "Turn it up!" "Turn it down!" Half the audience was going, "Yea," and half were going, "Boo." It was the great split.

Eric von Schmidt was one of the "Yea" sayers. I was in about the twelfth row, and during the first song, which was "Maggie's Farm," you couldn't hear Dylan even from where I was. And immediately several people, including me, started to holler, "We can't hear Dylan! Turn up the mike!"

Maria Muldaur was holding on for dear life. I was sitting next to Betsy Siggins. It was God awful loud, but to me it was exciting. It was interesting and new. But lots of people just freaked out. They just couldn't stand it. Me and Betsy were just clutching each other. We couldn't believe it. He was getting booed!

Rick Stafford, who was there to photograph the concert, was so caught up in the event he just stared through his viewfinder without snapping the shutter.

I don't care what Bob Dylan says, he was shaken. I had a telephoto lens on his face, and he was shaken.

Almost as soon as it got to the point where you could begin to hear Dylan's voice over the band, he stopped and left the stage. The audience was in a total uproar by this time. Some thought he had gone for good; most didn't know what was going on. In fact, he had only intended to do the two songs they had rehearsed — "Maggie's Farm" and "Like A Rolling Stone" — and had gone to get his acoustic guitar and pull himself together for the rest of the set. Peter Yarrow didn't help matters any when he said, "Want to hear more? Bob's gone to get his *acoustic* guitar, if you want to hear more." The way Peter put it made it look as if Dylan was somehow giving in to the crowd. Things got even more confused because Bob had trouble finding his guitar and took about five minutes to get back on stage. Many cheered, thinking that they had forced him to give in and play acoustic. But acoustic or electric, the message remained the same as "Maggie's Farm" and "Like a Rolling Stone," because he immediately went into "It's All Over Now, Baby Blue," and followed it with "Mr. Tambourine Man." Bob was definitely not going along with the Seeger program. The tone of the evening had been shattered.

BOB DYLAN sheds a tear. Photographs by Rick Sullo.

"THE FOLK MAFIA" (left to right) JAC HOLZMAN, President of Elektra Records; THEO BIKEL; PETE and TOSHI SEEGER; Pete's manager, HAROLD LEVENTHAL; former Weaver, FRED HELLERMAN; and MAYNARD SOLOMON, President of Vanguard Records. (1965) Photograph by David Gahr.

Many of the old-guard felt betrayed by Dylan's performance. They had embraced him as an heir to the Woody Guthrie tradition — one of his first major appearances in New York was on Pete Seeger's annual fall Hootenanny in 1962. But he evidently was choosing to turn his back on all that and was taking a new direction. He was no longer writing songs about "causes," about peace and civil rights. He was no longer traveling the same highway as those who had bummed around during the Depression. He was starting to travel by plane and was wearing high-heeled shoes and high-fashion clothes from Europe. He was showing himself to be a true child of the atomic generation. In the face of nuclear violence he was choosing to preserve himself alone, and he was challenging the audience to be on their own. He was no longer going to tell them what to think or

solve their problems for them with a song. Pete Seeger's banjo had borne a little hand-written message for years: "This banjo fights Fascism." Dylan was no longer fighting any "isms." If that meant that he was no longer a folk singer, so be it. He had chosen himself over "the people" — after all, he was people, too.

Many of the younger performers at the Festival agreed with Dylan. The politics of the folk movement weren't necessarily their politics. They were really in it for the music, which they dearly loved. One of them, Mel Lyman, made an attempt to heal the wound of the evening with his own powerful brand of folk mysticism. He had seen the split coming even before Dylan went on and talked to him, trying to get him to see that he had a responsibility to the folk movement, that he could help it with his music, if only he would accept that responsibility. When Mel saw the chaos and confusion and rage which followed Dylan's performance, he was moved to do something to bring everyone back together as a family. He asked Pete Seeger and George Wein to let him go and play "Rock of Ages" on his harmonica. Neither of them thought it was a good idea, and told him that neither of them had the authority to tell him to do it. That was up to the Board of Directors. So Mel did it anyway. The concert was over, but the sound system was still on, and soon the sound of his harmonica floated out over the field. Everybody was just in the process of leaving the park emotionally drained after the events of the night. The first to stop and listen were the other musicians backstage and those sitting down front. Mel kept playing. Then others heard and stopped where they were. Mel kept playing. "Rock of Ages" washed over everyone again and again until they finally were satisfied and slowly left the park. It was pure music — folk music — and it said it all with no words.

The "party" that night widened the split between the generations. The Chambers Brothers were set up to play. No sooner had they started when Jean Ritchie put her hands over her ears to shut out the hated electricity. Theo Bikel was glum. Ronnie Gilbert left early. Dylan was over in a corner engaged in a long discussion with John Cohen about the meaning of all this. Maria Muldaur came in with the Fariñas.

At the party afterwards, everyone was still talking about the concert. The Chambers Brothers started to play. Dylan was off sitting in a corner buried, and Fariña told me to go over and ask Dylan to dance because Fariña was always into starting some rhythm going and starting to boogie and dance and stuff. So I went over to him and said, "Do you want to dance?" and he looked up at me and said, "I would, but my hands are on fire."

You must leave now, take what you need, you think will last.
But whatever you wish to keep, you better grab it fast.
Yonder stands your orphan with his gun,
Crying like a fire in the sun.
Look out, the saints are coming through,
And it's all over now, Baby Blue.

Got My Mojo Workin'

Got a gypsy woman, givin' me advice,
Got a gypsy woman, givin' me advice,
Got a whole lot of tricks, I'm keepin' 'em here on ice.

he Mohawk Ranch, scene of Joe Val's encounter with the wrong end of a .38, was no more. It had become The Bavarian Hofbrau House, and nightly you could hear the sounds of drinking songs and accordians emerging from the doors. Upstairs, however, the sounds were anything but Teutonic. The place was crawling with jazzsters and rockers, and Peter Wolf was in the middle of the action.

We had a loft on Columbus Avenue on the corner of Dartmouth Street. It was an incredible building. The Bavarian Hofbrau House was on the ground floor. Frankie O'Day's bar across the street had the greatest juke box in the world—early Wilson Pickett, Sarah Vaughan, Aretha Franklin, Jack McDuff. So we spent time in there.

There were painters and writers and musicians living in this building. It would be like: "There's a party on the second floor — Coltrane's coming down after his gig." There were a lot of dubious things going on after hours. People whose creative juices were on the darker side of midnight hung out there. Mostly jazz cats. We were sort of weird because we were getting into rock and roll. The Beatles and the Stones were getting real popular. And we were into blues. But we all became friends. People didn't use the staircases. You used the fire escapes to get up to different places. That building never slept. It was intense.

Ever since his days in the Village, Peter had been hearing about Boston.

Boston had this aura about it. "Joan Baez got her start in Boston." "Bob Dylan got his start in Boston." "When Ramblin' Jack Elliott rambles around, he rambles to Boston." It was like that. And everyone seemed to be ready to tune up a guitar. Boston seemed to be the breeding place — the school. You trained there and went down to New York to compete. You'd get there Sunday and hit Washington Square. Somebody'd ask, "Foggy Mountain Breakdown?"

"Yeah, what key?"

And the capo would come on.

Or, "Do you know 'You Win Again'?"

"Do you know any 'Luke, the Drifter' Stuff?"

It was like seeing who knew more. It was always a little competitive.

I grew up in New York City and went to the High School of Music and Art for painting. My father was an old vaudevillian with the

PETER WOLF (right) receives a special award for sartorial elegance from his friend, TOM SWAN.
Photograph courtesy of Peter Wolf.

Schuberts. He was a chorus boy in shows like "The Merry Widow" and "The Student Prince." They played all the Shubert theaters. Later on, he became a classical music D.J. He was into light opera. His brother used to manage a wrestler and a dance team. His office was the automat.

My old man used to frequent the Village in the days before it was commercialized, and Izzy Young's place was interesting because there were always a lot of young musicians around. My father knew Izzy from his political days. He liked Leadbelly, The Almanac Singers, and Woody Guthrie, and the first music I connected with as a kid was "Songs To Grow On" by Woody Guthrie. I used to put my hand in the air and make sounds like a car and all that stuff.

So there was a lot of classical music and what today you'd call folk music in the house, and I was also just turning the dial and picking up what was on the air. I got into Jocko "The Magnificent" Henderson — "Ooh Bop Be Doo and How De Doo Time! It's eleven-fifteen and you're listening to Jocko's rocket ship machine! 10 - 9 - 8 - 7 . . ."

Music was something I enjoyed. It was inspirational. But I was a serious art student at the time. When I was at Music and Art, I had my own studio in a building at 89th Street and Columbus and Amsterdam. On the top floor was a hat factory. At five o'clock that all stopped and all these people came out of the woodwork. You'd hear John Lewis downstairs from the MJQ. And there were lots of painters around.

At that time I'd go down to Birdland to hear some jazz or go to Symphony Sid's midnight shows at the Apollo. Then me and my friends would go down to the Village for parties. There were lots of clubs. The Bitter End was going. Gerde's was hot. The Gaslight was very big and so was the Kettle of Fish next door. That microcosm was just starting to happen. People were just starting to filter in. There were very traditional kinds of music being played.

There was sort of a group of people you got to know who spoke your language, and it was real easy to get together. People would come by with guitars and tune up and start playing. We all had sort of a fever or passion and we shared it among ourselves. It was before the press or the "Alternative Media" knew anything about it. We didn't know we were an "Alternative." And it was not just music — it was books and art, too.

There was always the feeling you had. Say if you were a young writer, you'd have this feeling about Paris in the Twenties. There was always this feeling — "Boston. Oh yeah. There's a lot of people up in Boston." It's like, where do you go? People in the mid-60's would take off to California. In New York at that time, the place you really wanted to end up in was Boston. There were a lot of things going on. A lot of coffee houses, a lot of painters, a lot of artists. A lot of people from the Rhode Island School of Design — a lot of interaction going on. So you got the feeling that Boston was an interesting place. People would come down and say, "I just had a great time in Boston. Spent the week up there, and it was fantastic."

I hitched out to see friends in Chicago and Madison, Wisconsin, at that time. I met Danny Kalb out there. Eric Weissberg and John Herald were out there. They had a great little folksong society at the University of Wisconsin, and they would have concerts. Big Joe Williams was popular there. John Koerner and Dave Ray and Tony Glover were coming along, too. What I'd do as I traveled around was to sell portraits.

Finally, I headed to the University of Chicago to study painting. I got connected into the Blues scene there. You'd go across the street to some bar and there'd be this band, and it would turn out to be Junior Wells or J. B. Hutto and the Nighthawks or Otis Rush. Then one night this guy was driving from Chicago to stay with his friend from Harvard, and he asked me if I wanted to go along. So we drove over. I took some paintings with me and stayed with someone I knew at Harvard. I went over to the Museum School and checked it out and wound up getting a scholarship to go there, so I stayed around.

I got connected with the music scene and there was a lot of interaction between the painters and the pickers. I got to know Betsy Siggins and Bob Neuwirth and Jon Shahn. I caught some people at the 47 before it moved. *The Broadside Magazine* was going. I lived in Boston up on Mission Hill in Roxbury. There was a lot of music on Charles Street. This was before drugs hit the street. There were drugs going around but it was very personal and you kept it real cool. Speed was very big then, but I was already hyper and couldn't use that, and grass sort of made me loco, so I just stuck to the old ways — the old juice.

 was working real hard at the Museum School so I was just feeling the music in the air. But we had our own little clique. Once a week or so somebody would have a party in some loft. I had a tuxedo jacket I'd bought at Goodwill, and I'd wear that to these parties. So one night I went to this party. I'm walking by, and I can't find the loft, but I hear this music. There was an electric band playing, so I said, "This must be the place."

There were these four guys playing. One guy had an old Gibson electric guitar and another guy was singing, but he couldn't remember the words. I always carried a harmonica. My father played the harmonica. I could play a mean "Red River Valley" as a kid. One thing I would do to get attention was to draw somebody's portrait and paint and hold the harmonica in my mouth at the same time! So this night I started playing with these guys. Paul Shapiro was the singer, and that was the start of "The Hallucinations" and the end of my painting career.

I played harmonica and sang. I'd never really sung before, but I knew the words to a lot of songs. We did Jimmy Reed stuff, Little Walter stuff. We had Steven Bladd, who is still with the Geils Band, on drums. Doug Slade on guitar. Joe Clark on bass. Four of us went to the Museum School. Paul Shapiro was really into the real definitive Rhythm and Blues stuff. He had a stack of old 78's. He and I started hanging out together over at the loft up above the Hofbrau House where Doug and Joe lived. We frequented places like Louie's Lounge and the Jazz Workshop. Louie's brought in people like Junior Parker and Bobby Bland. Otis Redding played there. B.B. King, Little Milton, T-Bone Walker, Jimmy Witherspoon, Gatemouth Brown. Slim Harpo was there a lot.

Our first gig was at the Putney School in Vermont. I knew a girl there. We only knew three songs, but we were ready. Our equipment was a Silvertone amp, a drum kit consisting of a snare drum, a bass drum, and a cymbal, and a mike stand with a tape recorder mike taped to it with masking tape for me. I had my tuxedo jacket, and that was it. We did the longest versions of songs like "Bright Lights, Big City." That would go on for twenty minutes. So we got going and never stopped. We started playing at B.U. and on Beacon Street. We played fraternities and parties and then hit the clubs in Revere and the North Shore.

One day we read in *The Broadside* that John Lee Hooker was going to be playing at the Odyssey Coffeeshop. We couldn't wait to go. I had never met him, but I had all his records, and we must have done every one of his songs. We got to the club about 5:30 so that we would be sure to get some seats. We were sure it would be packed. When they opened the doors, we went into the place and sat down. We got some coffee. And some more coffee. There were only about five people in the place when Hooker went on. He was sensational. After the show, we went back and knocked on his door and he asked us in. So I got the idea that what we should do is get the band to back him up. The full band could open for him, then just Paul, Steve and Joe would play with him, and

Doug and I would sit out. I could do the emceeing. So he said okay. Dave Wilson, who was booking the club, said okay. By the next day we had handwritten posters all over the place, and the place was packed the next night with all the kids who'd become our fans. We got real friendly with John. He was staying at the Lenox Hotel, so in the daytime we'd get together and show him around Boston.

Then what started to happen was that the folk scene started to be swept up into this electric blues thing. That's when Butterfield hit town. I had heard about them through the grapevine. When I heard them in person it was incredible. Then the Chambers Brothers came to town, so everything was changing real fast. It seemed that all the Chicago bands started coming to town.

JOHN LEE HOOKER. Photograph by Charles Sawyer.

Over in Harvard Square, Officer Guida thought he heard music — loud music. Which was strange, because there weren't any bars that had music around the square. The only place that had music was the Club 47, and that was folk music. This was rock and roll. But as he followed his ears up Palmer Street the music kept getting louder and louder. Guida got madder and madder. What the hell was Rooney putting on in there? Rooney had already met Officer Guida on his first night as official manager of the 47.

The day I started running the Club we had a big picnic for Byron down at my folk's place near the beach. We had lots of ouzo, Pendeli wine, grape leaves, hoomus, Greek salad, and lamb. Everyone got very mellow and sentimental, and we all told each other how much we loved each other. Then I drove to Cambridge and opened the Club. It was a Sunday, and Don Macsorley was going to run the Hoot. It was going to be a quiet night.

At some point in the evening these three guys came through the door, walked past the desk, and stood looking into the room. I was standing not too far away. They looked like trouble — probably drunk. I went over and stood beside one of them and said, "If you're going to come in, pay the girl at the desk." Smasho! He decked me and jumped on me screaming. "Pay at the desk? Pay at the desk?" Macsorley came off the stage and got cut to the cheek bone for his efforts. Nobody else in the place made a move. Folkies believe in peace and love. Finally he got tired of beating on me, and they all went out. The guy was a maniac. I ran down to Harvard Square and got Tony Guida, the cop on the Square. Tony's neck is only slightly thicker than his head, but this guy took *him* on when we caught up with them. It took three cops to finally pin him down. So that was my first day of running the Club. At least it made me friends with the cops right away. Every so often they would come in handy.

This was one night when Rooney was glad that he already knew Guida. It was Muddy Water's first night at the Club, and he didn't want anything to go wrong.

ight after the '65 Newport Festival the Butterfield Band came up and played three nights at the Club for $100.00 a night. Some of them were staying at my house, and Paul and I got into hanging out a lot, listening to music and singing Hank Williams songs together. He was telling me how hard it was to be working for so little money, and I was telling him how hard it was to pay him what we were paying him because we were still only charging a dollar at the door. But he really liked playing at the Club, and he told me that I should get some of the other bands from Chicago, starting with Muddy Waters. I found out early on in running the Club to always trust the judgement of other musicians and never listen to agents.

So I took Paul's advice and got hold of Bob Messinger at Shaw Artists, who was booking Muddy, and I did it — for twice what we had ever paid anyone before. At the same time, I met with the Board of Directors and told them about what I thought were becoming the new economic realities. Our audience wanted this music. We wanted it. We also wanted artists like Flatt and Scruggs and Bill Monroe. If we wanted to be able to present them, we would have to be able to pay them without going broke. At that point, none of us were aware of the "youth market." Since most of us managed to live on air, we assumed that our audience did the same. We reluctantly raised the admission to $1.50. It was still an incredible bargain, when you stop to consider the quality of the talent.

So Muddy was my first venture into this new world — the world of Chicago blues. I didn't know what to expect. I didn't know how many people would come. I didn't know what he was going to be like. I mean, I was thinking about knives and guns and trouble. The Club 47 coffeehouse wasn't exactly a whole lot like a Southside Chicago bar.

Muddy got into town, and I called him up at the Hotel Diplomat. I introduced myself as the manager of the Club and gave him directions to get to the Club, and told him what time the shows were and everything. I told him that the Club was a coffeehouse, but that you didn't have to drink coffee. I said, "What kind of coffee would you like?", and he said, "TSIVAS."

I said, "What?"
"TSIVAS!"
"What?"
"TSIVAS! Tsivas Regal!"
And I said, "You've got it."

That night he got a bottle of Chivas Regal and everything was straight. The place was packed and here was this young, white audience treating him like a king. At that point Guida came through

Opposite:
(top left) OTIS SPANN and WILLIE DIXON. Photograph courtesy of Manny Greenhill. (top right) MUDDY WATERS Photograph by Charles Sawyer. (bottom left) PAUL BUTTERFIELD Photograph by Rick Sullo. (bottom right) MUDDY WATERS. PETER WOLF, and MOJO BUFORD at the Club 47. Photograph by Juke Joint Jimmy.

the door ready to kill. Fortunately, I was standing right there, and I herded him into my office.

"What's with this rock and roll? That ain't folk music out there! You can't have that in here. You ain't got a license for that! You gotta have folk music!"

I let him blow off for a minute, and then I gave him a little lecture on folk music and how Muddy was one of the greats and how he'd met the Queen in England. I just started making stuff up. Then, who should come back in there but Muddy! Dressed in a beautiful suit, smiling, gracious. He'd just finished a set, but looked totally cool. He didn't know I was busy and excused himself, but I said, "Muddy, I'd like you to meet one of Cambridge's finest. Tony Guida. Tony saved my life here not too long ago." Muddy said, "Is that so? Well, you must be a good man. Jim here is my buddy! If Jim says you're all right, that's good enough for me." Muddy went out, and Guida was speechless. He gave me a look and mumbled something about "keeping it down" and left. It was almost worth getting beat up for that little encounter.

For a young bluesman like Peter Wolf, being able to see Muddy Waters and his band in a place like the 47 was an opportunity to connect personally with the musicians he loved.

I remember Muddy Water's first appearance at the Club. It was incredible. I had seen him over at the Jazz Workshop, but it wasn't the same. There it was sort of routine, like another job. But at the "47" it was sensational. Every nuance that he did was picked up. And the band was the greatest. James Cotton on harmonica, Otis Spann on piano, Sammy Lawhorn on guitar, S.P. Leary on drums. But when Muddy hit, it was sensational.

What was great about that band was that everybody would have his favorites. Muddy was the star, and then there were these individual personalities. Otis had his spot. Cotton had his. Then when Muddy hit, they would bring it up to another level. No matter how many times they might have played it, they always kept the intensity up.

Between shows I walked into the men's room of the 47, and there was Cotton, Spann, and S.P. Leary all gathered around a pint. They're all passing it around. They are my idols, so I picked up my cue real good and ran out and scored a couple of pints, and after the next show they were all over me, and my apartment by then was only four blocks away. I was living over Cronin's.

Otis Spann became sort of a superhero. He got friendly with the guys who became "The Cloud" and they would pick him up after the show and he'd play and jam. Dave Maxwell would organize jams over at M.I.T. and all the piano players would come around to listen to Otis and play with him. Otis' and my birthdays were like a day or two apart, so we would either write or call and keep in touch.

We became like family. When Muddy or Junior Wells or Buddy Guy or any of those guys hit town it was nonstop. There would be interviews for college newspapers, radio and T.V. shows. Lee Tanner and Dave Wilson had a show on Channel 2; Channel 5 had a show; and there were jams and parties all the time.

The Chicago/Cambridge combination was a volatile one. In the course of the next two years the Club 47 brought in Howlin' Wolf, Junior Wells, Buddy Guy, Otis Rush, Willie Dixon, Sam Lay, James Cotton, the Staples Singers, and the Siegel/Schwall Band as well as Muddy Waters, Otis Spann, and the Butterfield Band. At the same time, through Dick Waterman, the Club was presenting Skip James, Son House, Booker White, and Robert Pete Williams. Peter Guralnick realized that it was the opportunity of a lifetime for a writer.

It was like the realization of all my dreams. It was beyond my wildest expectations.

The first interview I ever did was with Skip James. I bullshitted my way in there, saying I was from *Blues Unlimited*. They said, "That's funny, *Blues Unlimited* just did a series on Skip." This was when he was at Waterman's house. I had made a commitment to myself to do it. I said to myself, "This is one of the people I most admire in life, and I must interview him." I forced myself to do it, because I really felt that greatness like this wasn't going to pass my way again. So I did it.

Up until this point, I was strictly a fan, subscribing to *Blues Unlimited*, corresponding with people in England. Then when Howlin' Wolf played at the 47 in '66, Paul Williams and I interviewed him for *Crawdaddy*. I had known Paul for quite a while. He said that he was going to interview Wolf but that he didn't know anything about him. So he asked me if I'd go back with him. I jumped at the chance, and he talked to us about Elvis Presley and how Little Walter was doing himself in. I showed it to Wolf, and it really delighted him to hear one of his own lines quoted back to him. He'd shake his head and say, "Where'd you get that? That's really something."

I started writing for *Crawdaddy* about Robert Pete Williams and Skip James. Then *Boston After Dark* started, and I was writing previews for them about Buddy Guy, Wolf, J. B. Hutto. I'd write about any bluesman who I liked who was coming to town in *Boston After Dark*. I also wrote for *Blues World* in England.

So I went from being totally an outsider to being 3/4 an outsider. I did it strictly as a hobby. I had always wanted to be a writer, and I was writing novels, which was my main work. I also published two collections of stories in '63 and '65. I wrote fiction every day, but I thought of my writing about music as a way of giving something back for what I had received. It was a way of calling the attention of people to something that I thought was vital and exciting and important.

Cambridge became like a second home for the Butterfield band, and before long both Paul and Elvin Bishop had found the girls who would eventually become their wives. The Chambers Brothers moved to Cambridge. Jill Henderson tried to help them with their business. Joe Chambers couldn't get over the way it all happened.

When we came east to play at Newport, we had only planned to be there three days. Then Jill Henderson got us into the Unicorn and the 47, and we just went back and forth between the two clubs. We met so many friends and had such a good time in Cambridge that it didn't make any sense to go anywhere else. We felt all these warm vibrations. A lot of other artists were coming through to play at the same time. Music was becoming a family. Everybody knew each other and jammed together and partied together. We got a lot of inspiration out of being in that scene. We learned how to appreciate good, down-home music and good, down-home vibes. Even after we started to play big concerts, we always tried to come back to the 47 or the Unicorn just to keep that intimate feeling we grew up with. You lose all that when you get out on those monster stages. That's what gave us strength and helped us to grow during those years.

This influx of energy had its effect on the local scene. The folk world was starting to merge with the world of electric blues and rock and roll. Harvey Brooks became a familiar face as he backed up Tom Rush and Eric Andersen on electric bass when they played at the Club. Jackie Washington put a band together with Mitch Greenhill, John Nagy, and Steve Ambush. Banana and the Bunch became the Trols. Jerry Corbett and Joe Bauer joined Jesse Colin Young as the Youngbloods. Banana followed shortly. The Hallucinations made it onto the Club schedule. Young performers like Peter Rowan's brothers, Chris and Loren, and J. Geils started bringing amplifiers to Hootenannies. Somewhere in town Gram Parsons and John Neuisse were getting together the International Submarine Band. Even the Charles River Valley Boys did an entire album of Beatles songs. John Cooke had gone to California again, and Mitch Greenhill's ex-roommate at Harvard, Jim Field, took his place and got the idea.

 had gone to Andover Academy. While I was there, I got myself a real cheap Danelectro guitar and got together a little rock and roll band called "The Invictas." I was a screamer and shouter. We did stuff like the "Hully Gully." I listened to a lot of rock and roll. Fats Domino. I bought all of Elvis' early stuff and used to sing "That's All Right, Mama." While I was at Andover, I started listening to WWVA. I kept it a secret.

When I got to Harvard, I went to the Club 47 and saw Bill Keith and Jim Rooney playing, and it was instant "ga ga." Keith was doing a number with the tuners, and I just couldn't believe that. So I used to hang around the Club a lot. I swept up. Mitchell introduced me to everyone, and soon I got an acoustic guitar.

After my freshman year at Harvard, I was dismissed. I went out to California where my girlfriend, Barbara, was going to Occidental College. I worked for an insurance company and heard a lot of music. That was the high point of the Ash Grove. I saw Maybelle Carter, the Dillards, the Kentucky Colonels, the Country Gentlemen. There were also some great parties — bigger than those in Cambridge, with three bands going in different rooms. By osmosis, I learned a lot of songs. I drove Doc Watson and Fred Price and Clint Howard from Monterey to Los Angeles for Ralph Rinzler. I took my only guitar lesson from Clarence White. I remember seeing Ry Cooder on the sidewalk outside McCabes, and people were just standing there agape. He was only sixteen, but he was great. I came back to Harvard and got married in '63. That responsibility probably kept me in school.

In the summer of '64, I was down in New York. I knew the New York Ramblers needed a lead singer because Eric Thompson had just left them. So I went down, and it worked out. It was funny. When I went down to join, they thought they had finally found a WASP player. When I told them I was Jewish, they went, "Aw, shit!" The band was Winnie Winston, David Grisman, Gene Lowinger, Fred Weiss, and me. We mostly played pass-the-hat places. Played and played and played. The highlight was playing at Gerde's. We actually got pretty good. Peter Siegel made some tapes of us. It was real whiny, slick bluegrass. Fast and sharp. Real aggressive. We even played Newport that summer. We also went to Union Grove. The band had won the contest there the year before, and we should have known that you don't get to win two years in a row. It was really phenomenal. We also went to Ashville, which was a great parking lot scene and where I first saw clogging, which was great. The kids had clogging teams, and it was really strong and rhythmic.

In the fall of '65, I came back to Cambridge to go back to school. John Cooke had gone to California, and Siggins knew I was around and asked me to join. We started to do "I've Just Seen Her Face, " and we played for the "Winterfest" at the War Memorial Auditorium.

Joe Val had done a lot of things in his musical career, but he had a few doubts about doing Beatles material until that concert.

We were on right before Muddy Waters. We did our show, and the people liked it, but when we hit that song, they went crazy. Paul Rothchild was there and told us to learn some more of those. About a week later, I saw Muddy Waters at the 47, and he said, "You guys stole the show."

Being an old traditionalist, I wasn't too keen on doing a whole record of Beatles songs, but the more they talked to me, the more interested I got. So we learned some more and made a demo tape in some basement. The next thing we knew, Paul called and said that Jac Holzman liked the Beatles stuff, but that we'd have to get a whole album's worth. He didn't want to mix it in with straight bluegrass. We really put our noses to the grindstone then. Fields really worked on the arrangements. "Norwegian Wood" is the only song I recorded that my wife liked. The only one.

One thing the Beatles did was make people more aware of contemporary songs. A song didn't necessarily have to be traditional to be good. Tom Rush had always had a good ear for material, and he was about to hear something which would make a big difference in his life and the life of a lot of other people.

THE CHARLES RIVER VALLEY BOYS at the 1966 Boston Winterfest. (left to right) BOB SIGGINS, JOE VAL, and JIM FIELD. Photograph by Rick Sullo.

I met Joni Mitchell in Detroit. She was already married — she was no longer Joni Anderson. She'd been up in Toronto trying to get something going. She'd hit Bernie Fiedler at the "Riverboat" for a job, and he said, "I already have a dishwasher" — that Germanic touch! But she was swept off her feet, moved to Detroit, and married Chuck Mitchell who was a local folksinger. I was playing there at the Chessmate. The owner there — Murray Weidenbaum — asked me if it was okay if she did a guest set, and I was really impressed by her. So I started doing the "Urge for Going," and I started telling everybody about her and got Jim Rooney to book her and Chuck into the 47. I tried to get Judy Collins to do one of her tunes. At the Siggins' house one night, I sang "Urge for Going" and "Circle Game" for Judy who just wandered off. It was frustrating. Then I played Jac Holzman at Elektra a tape of Joni, and he said that she sounded too much like Judy. She did at the time — but still and all, the songs were so strong.

At any rate, I cut a tape in a demo studio of "Urge for Going" with Bruce Langhorne playing guitar, and Jefferson Kaye started playing it over WBZ in Boston. At that time you could walk into 'BZ — a 50,000 watt clear channel station — and put out whatever you wanted on the air for an hour. Those days are gone. The tape really became a sensation. They said they had never received more calls for any record. In retrospect, I think it was partly because it was a tape. You couldn't buy it in a store. There was no record. I couldn't get Elektra to release it. For a year and a half it was driving me nuts. When they finally did release it, it was too late. It had become so strongly identified with 'BZ that although it was number one on 'BZ's chart, it didn't appear on anyone else's. It's a shame, because if they had moved at first, I think it would have gone big.

Then, two years after this episode, "Circle Game" came out. She had sung me a bunch of tunes and threw it in as an afterthought. Later, after Judy Collins finally had a big hit with "Both Sides Now," I asked Joni why she hadn't shown it to me. She said, "You know, it's a funny thing! When I wrote that, I thought of you." Yeah! That's the Joni Mitchell story.

Joni Mitchell was one of several young performers who started to come to the Club on a regular basis who were to become major artists in a relatively short time. Jesse Colin Young, Richie Havens, and Arlo Guthrie came three or four times before they were "discovered" and became too big to have back. Tom Rush and the Kweskin Jug Band had to be booked through their agents in New York, but still managed to make several appearances a year. The rest of the Club's calendar was taken up with Blues bands from Chicago, Bluegrass bands from Nashville, some of the older traditional performers like Doc Watson and Maybelle Carter and the older bluesmen, and the established 47 performers like Eric von Schmidt, the Charles River Valley Boys, and Keith and Rooney. For a young folk singer like Chris Smither, who had come to Cambridge with hopes of breaking into the folk world there, it could be rough.

CHRIS SMITHER sings at a Newport Folk Festival Workshop while TAJ MAHAL listens. (1967) Photograph by Rick Sullo.

I came to Cambridge because of Eric von Schmidt. I had grown up in New Orleans, but my folks weren't from there. My dad taught Spanish literature at Tulane. I grew up listening to my folks' records of Burl Ives and Susan Reed. My uncle had a ukelele and showed me enough chords so that I could play the Burl Ives' tunes. Then I got a guitar from my father. I went through a Kingston Trio phase, but the first time I really found out what one guitar could really do was when I heard a Lightnin' Hopkins record, "Blues in the Bottle." That was something else. I started working on that. Bob Dylan really excited me and so did Eric von Schmidt. I had the Folkways album that he did with Rolf Cahn, and I also had the "Blues Project" album.

I was visiting a friend in Sarasota, Florida, and he mentioned that Eric lived over there, so I just called him up. He invited me over to the house. We picked a little, and he said lots of nice things to me which were really encouraging. I was a senior at Tulane, and I was thinking of trying to be a singer, but there was no folk scene to speak of happening in New Orleans.

I went back to Florida and saw Eric again, and he said, "If you want to play, no one down here is going to listen to you. You should go up to Boston and Cambridge and places like that." I took him at his word. One day I just got in a car with a girl I knew named Sam, and we drove up there. All I knew about was the Club 47. So I went there and looked at the calendar and, by God, Eric was playing there that very night! Jim Rooney was standing at the door. I introduced myself and said I was looking for Eric. We connected, and that night he had me do a guest set. I couldn't believe it. My very first night in Cambridge and I was playing at the Club 47! It felt right to me. I found someplace to crash that night and never left. That was the end of my career as an anthropologist, which was what I had been studying. Since then I have managed to support myself by singing.

After a couple of weeks, though, it began to dawn on me that I just wasn't going to jump into a place like the 47, so I started looking in *The Broadside* to see where all the other places were. I went down to Charles Street in Boston and ran into a girl I had met who was a waitress at the Turk's Head, which was run by Arnold Cummings. I was sitting out on the steps talking to this girl when Arnold came out. She said, "Arnold, you've got to hire this guy." He said, "Okay, he can work tonight." Somebody had just cancelled on him. He really liked me, so he started putting me on two nights a week.

The Loft, the Sword in Stone, and the Turk's Head formed an equilateral triangle on Charles Street. That's where all the people who were in the same situation I was in were surviving. Bill Staines, Paul Geremia, Paul McNeil, Leonda, Nancy Michaels, and some others were the regulars. Everybody was trying to figure out how long they were going to last. Those clubs paid ten or fifteen dollars a night. Gradually I got enough work to keep me going. It was sort of hand to mouth, but I didn't mind that in those days.

Come the end of summer, I didn't know what I was going to do. I was supposed to go back to school. In a *Broadside* poll I placed first in the "new performer" category. My picture was on the cover, and I thought, "All right! Here we go!" I don't think I really believed it, but what kept me from going back to school was the fact that I actually had a place to live, I had enough to eat, and I hadn't had to get a job. I had made some good friends, I was getting better with my music and was getting to hear and meet a lot of the people I loved and had learned from. And it was the first time I had done what I wanted to do instead of something that somebody told me I was supposed to do.

People kept telling me that folk was "out" and that I should get a band. Rock was really booming. But I was happy doing what I was doing. My material came from the old bluesmen, some of Eric von Schmidt's songs, some of John Koerner's stuff, and eventually I started to write some of my own tunes. I built a following in Cambridge and Boston and in Philadelphia and, by God, I started making a living at it. I had money in my pocket.

I'm going down to Louisiana, get me a mojo han',
I'm going down to Louisiana, get me a mojo han',
I'm gonna have all you pretty women stretched under my command.

Wet Birds Fly at Night

IS is just for an instant,
Then instantly, it's WAS.
Makes you want to grab a rock,
And smash the clock,
For the beastly harm that it does.

T
he Sunday afternoon Dance in the Deluge at the '65 Festival was not the only triumph for the Fariñas that year. After a hard winter in Cambridge, Dick finally had his novel, by this time called "Been Down So Long It Looks Like Up To Me," accepted by Random House in April. Von Schmidt had insisted that Dick not make illustrations a prerequisite for publication. He felt that it would hurt Dick's chances of getting the novel published, which was the most important thing. He felt that Dick had a vast potential, but that he must establish his position as a writer from a critical standpoint, and a money-making standpoint, before he could get the rest of it to happen.

As it turned out, his editor at Random House turned down the illustrated concept from a purely economic standpoint and suggested that Eric design the jacket. The first sketches included a mob scene including the whole cast of characters, and involved a flurry of letters between author and illustrator. Of the main character, Gnossos Pappadopoulis, Dick wrote:

Paps has this preoccupation, you might call it, with exemption from the macrocosm. Immunity. No Valence and like that. Can't touch me, I'm Invisible, he says somewhere. Also digs allatropic forms, disguises, Plasticman. The microcosm, Inside, Wigville, Private, all are potential alternatives to externalized dimensions.

Since it all sounded to Von Schmidt like a pretty good description of Fariña, he opted for the externalized dimension and made Gnossos look a lot like Dick. The mob scene dwindled to the girl,

MIMI FARIÑA, JOAN BAEZ, and DICK FARIÑA singing in the rain. Photograph by Dick Waterman.

Kristen, and the Monkey Demon. Fariña had often spoken to Eric about the Monkey Demon. Its dreadful and unaccountable presence was connected with the smell of camphor. It was the embodiment of evil, and, more specifically, violent death. The sense of its presence filled Dick with dread and there had been a few moments in his life when he almost caught sight of it, a terrifying blur just at the edge of vision, a movement too fast to register on the retina, but lodged for a madly howling instant deep in his heart.

Fariña was a juggler. It was sometimes hard for him to remember how many balls were in the air. He was a young man in a hurry. He and Mimi were originally to have been managed by Manny Greenhill, who seemed to have all the time in the world. Mimi recalls the switch:

Manny and Dick had a discussion wherein we verbally agreed that he would manage us. Then Dick, in some of his scheming — I think during the time when Dick was taking the Vanguard contracts over to Grossman and saying, "Do these look good to you?" — had some discussion about whether we would like to be managed by Grossman. And Dick in his own way probably said, "Yes," probably didn't say much about Manny, probably was vague. At any rate, there was suddenly an ad in the paper — "Albert Grossman presents" — and we were on the list. Manny called us up and said, "What's going on?" And Dick acted very innocent. And I asked, "How did that happen?" "I don't know!" "What is this?" Dick was definitely upwardly mobile, and I think at that time Albert represented, except for Joan, all the real big money-making folk acts.

As far as Bob Neuwirth was concerned, Dick made the right move.

The next step up the ladder was that if you do get paid for performing, you should get as much money as you can. That's the show business principle that disturbed everybody. So they turned to someone like Manny. He became a manager because everybody was afraid to ask for their money. And he was an amateur manager. He was still at the level of not wanting to ask for the money and feeling that it's a dirty, nasty job. But if you wanted to get somewhere and improve your pay scale, he wasn't the guy to call. Because he had Joan, he didn't have to do anything to be a manager except pick up the phone.

Albert, however, *invented* Peter, Paul and Mary. He *invented* Bob Dylan. Bob Dylan could not get arrested before Albert came along! We both sat on the curb and counted up to see if we had enough money to buy a bottle of Thunderbird. Albert made it possible to have a $50.00 a week allowance to have enough money to pay the rent.

After her '63 and '64 triumphs, the '65 Newport Festival was a comedown for Joan Baez. She sang at the opening concert on Thursday night but, except for workshops, that was about it. She had been shunted aside by Dylan on his tour in England and arrived at Newport with Donovan who wore a Dylan look-alike outfit. Since Dylan showed up wearing English mod, well, maybe a poor joke was better than no joke at all.

By the time Sunday came, she must have been ready to blast off to the moon, so it was no surprise that she was on hand for Dick and Mimi's debut. To have her backstage ready to help out would be an ace in the hole for any performer, and, as nervous as they were, they welcomed her presence, and hoped to end up with a little family jam, just in case.

When the rain hit and Mimi and Dick carried it off with a graceful display of musical delight that was echoed back and forth between audience and performer, perhaps it would have been asking too much of the Queen of Up-stagers to have stayed off the stage all together and let her younger sister and her not-so-favorite brother-in-law have the hard-earned moment of glory they had struggled towards for two years. It didn't matter. As always, the crowd loved it, and Dick and Mimi were so high on the euphoria of the moment that they wouldn't have cared if the Marine Corps Band had come on stage as long as they could swing right into "Hard Lovin' Loser."

And, too, nothing succeeds like success. Joan had sometimes taken their side in family hassles, and had helped them financially, and could understand Dick on one important level — the concept of "Making It."

ick and I knew when we talked how stupid the whole concept was — that a public image was based upon some truths, some half-truths, some innocent rumors, and a few nasty lies. It meant general overexposure and self-consciousness (as opposed to self-awareness) and the constant danger of accepting someone else's evaluation of you in place of your own — your own being practically impossible to make already. Money meant power, an irresistible prestige value, and lots of extra attention — all of which could be used, almost in spite of themselves, for good things if you kept your head. We also knew the meaning of the word temptation, and what a smart thing it was for Jesus to say, "Lead us not into temptation," because He knew well that once we got there we were all so very weak.

For some time Joan had been trying to find a way to put her ideals into some form of action. She decided to create the Institute for the Study of Nonviolence, and asked Dick and Mimi to be a part of it.

We got a letter from Joanie saying she was starting a school and would we like to participate. We had a choice of trying to make it to Europe on not much money, or returning to California where my heart was. I was born in California, and part of my family was there, part of my identity, so I was all for going back to where I was comfortable, and not out into the big European world that I was not sure of. And I think Dick was infatuated with Joanie's fame and if he was being requested to come and be near her, that was something special. So we went back west and started helping her with the Institute. It turned out there were no official titles, no roles, and on top of that — what about salary? Where was the salary going to come from? Was there going to be one? So, what had looked like a job with a title with some official name didn't exist, and I think he was terribly disappointed. But he threw himself into it at last and would come to sessions and would either cook lunch or participate in some way. I taught exercise classes. They would sit and meditate and then they would have classes. When it would be time to move around, I would teach an exercise class, which gave me something to do. It didn't mean a whole lot to me.

John Cooke remembers this time in California and the mixed feeling he had about it all.
Dick liked to turn small events into theater — into ceremony — and I liked that. At the same

MIMI and DICK FARIÑA on the beach at Carmel (1966). Photograph by John Cooke.

time, I was a little standoffish about Dick, because he was so intense and so pushy. I was a very judgmental fellow in those days, in a very defensive way. His thing about making a ceremony was augmented a lot with Joan around, because Joan had such a highly developed sense of ham or theater.

One night, we went to dinner in Carmel, and they both pretended to be blind, not for five minutes or ten minutes, but throughout the entire dinner! Both of them. With their eyes open. And doing a great job of it. But after a while, the other patrons and the management were driven nuts by this trip.

Another time, Dick and Kimmy Chappel and I took an acid trip. We went to Point Lobos in Carmel, a beautiful, beautiful place. We went in the middle of the day, and what we had taken was really good. We went through the woods, through the pine forest, then we came up to the top of a ridge, and the sun was about half an hour from going down, and it was Christmas time, and the air was absolutely pure and fresh. It was an extraordinary experience we shared together. We got back to the house and ever since this evening I've harbored certain reservations about Dick Fariña — because Dick and Kimmy vanished. I don't mean physically. They were sitting in the same room with me. But they disappeared. There was *no* contact. The sun had gone down. Mimi was not there. There was no fire, no dinner. And either Dick or Kimmy put on a very lugubrious record, which made it even

worse. They were sitting on opposite ends of the couch, and a couple of times I tried to make contact but got nothing. I thought he was making me the object of a game. Finally Mimi came home, and we got a fire going and food, and it all passed.

Later, after I'd taken care of their house for a couple of months, and Kim was in a psychiatric hospital, and Joan was on the road, Dick and Mimi came back, and we became pretty close. It was a special time in many ways. Dick was starting to encourage Mimi in certain ways, encouraging her to grow up, encouraging her to leave the network of Mama and Joan and the family. He was encouraging her to learn how to drive and was putting her into situations where she could take more responsibility. It was out of character for him because he was so assertive, but I think he was becoming aware that she had to be free if their relationship was to get stronger and grow. It was for his own benefit and hers, too.

I remember most clearly nights when we'd eat at their house, open the paper and pick a movie, get in the car, and go. When you live in the country and like things like movies, going to the movies can become a ceremony, too. You get your popcorn, an ice cream sandwich, a Dr. Pepper.

We'd be piling out of the dark wilds of Carmel over the hill to Monterey. And Dick was at his most comfortable in this scene. It was his house, his car, and he'd be driving — playing pilot in the fog on the road.

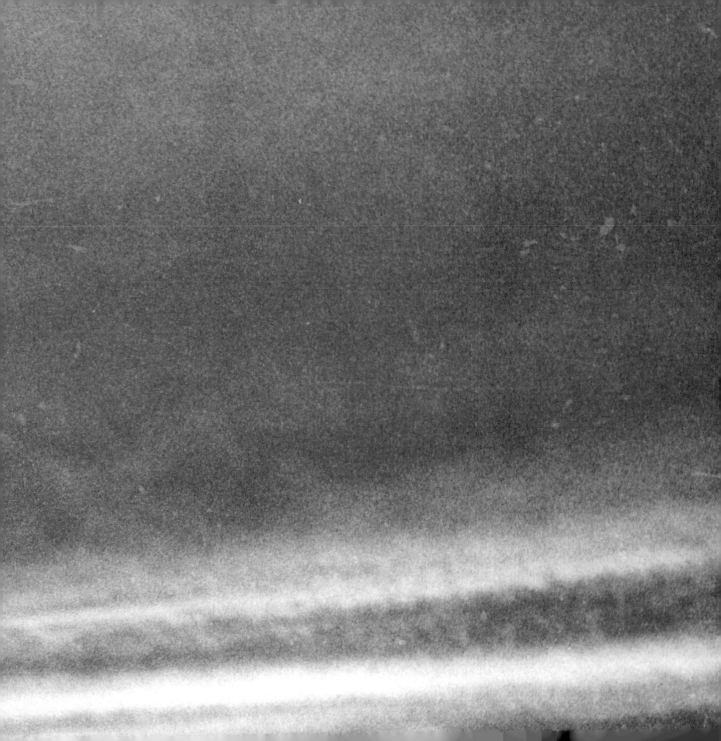

It was April of 1966. Eric von Schmidt remembers that it was a beautiful, spring day.
I picked up the phone and it was Mitch Greenhill calling from California. He just said, "Dick has been killed; I know you'd want to know." He didn't know much more than something about a motorcycle accident. I hung up the phone and it just kept flashing through my head, "There's been a mistake. It can't be true. It's a mistake. It can't be. This can't be true." And then I started bawling. I grabbed the rum bottle out of the closet and was cursing and swearing and crying for about fifteen minutes. Half a fifth in fifteen minutes. I was so furious at him. I was cursing at him, you know. You stupid son of a bitch! I staggered outside and threw up and crawled up under some trees and passed out. I loved the bastard, and he was gone.

The word spread. Dick, so full of life, was suddenly gone. No one could quite believe it or cope with it. Geoffrey Muldaur heard it in New York.

When we got the news about Fariña we were at Mary Travers' house taking group pictures. We had a gig that night in the Village. Mel sat all night in the Dugout crying. I cried most of the night, too. He said to me, "I didn't know him well, but I feel this incredible loss."

Before his death, Dick had written many letters to Von Schmidt about his relationship with his inlaws.
I've never understood the Baez family's attitude towards Dick. Joan dug him near the end, because he could make her laugh. But he sure took a lot of shit early on. People who loved him loved him for himself not for any connection to the Baez Dynasty. People love Mimi because she's Mimi. I think the family is a little snobbish, you know. They were pretty upwardly mobile themselves. Maybe Dick's Cuban/Irish hustler trip was bringing it all a little close to home.

Maria Muldaur:
Who were they? The Queens of France? He was a fantastic dude. And she was a totally gorgeous

girl. The thing about him was that he was a
writer, which is a much more lonely art. He had
this whole awareness that was on a deeper level
than the others who were writing protest songs
at the time. His songs — "The Simple Joys of
Brotherhood" and "The Raven" — are haunting
even to this day. They went beyond the level of
"put the Negroes at the front of the bus." He was
at another level of political consciousness. He
knew about literature and politics, and most of
us were just totally immersed in music. And
musically he had that rhythmic thing from being
Cuban. He had this whole Cuban-Irish trip
going.

Fariña knew how to throw a party. They were
living on a shoestring, and we'd go to
Haymarket, and he'd do it all with chicken
gizzards, rice and some yellow burgundy.
There'd be olives, the right spices, hot French
bread — gourmet food or nothing at all! And
after dinner, we'd all sit around and play. He'd
play congas and really get us into these rhythmic
trips.

My fondest memories of Cambridge center
around Richard Fariña, who I dearly loved and
miss to this day. I realize now that he was years
ahead of his time.

*Preceding Page: MIMI and DICK FARIÑA
and LUSH in the dusk.
Photograph by Charles Frizzell.*

*Opposite:
The last photograph taken of
RICHARD FARIÑA with MIMI at
his book signing party in California.
A symbolist to the end. Taurus is
behind him, and the Monkey Demon is
reflected in his sunglasses from
Eric von Schmidt's cover drawing.
Photographer unknown. Courtesy
of Mimi Fariña.*

*Right:
MIMI FARIÑA (1966)
Photograph by John Cooke.*

*Following Page:
THE CHARLES RIVER VALLEY
BOYS go "mod." (left to right)
BOB SIGGINS, JOE VAL,
EVERETT ALAN LILLY, and
JIM FIELD. Photograph by N.C. Pei.
Courtesy of Bob Siggins.
JOHN COOKE and BOB
NEUWIRTH in California.
Photographer unknown. Courtesy
of Betsy Schmidt.*

_W_hen John Cooke came back to Cambridge in the fall of '66 he dutifully set about learning all the Beatles songs which the Charles River Valley Boys had recorded in his absence. But the days of the Hootenanny craze were over. It was a mod, mod world, and calls for bluegrass bands — even those that did Beatles songs — were getting fewer and farther between. Betsy Siggins and Jill Henderson organized a Mod Ball, complete with fashion show and psychedelic lights, and Bob Siggins even got himself a Nehru jacket, but John began to realize that if he was going to count on bluegrass for a living he was going to wind up thinner than he already was. He began to give more serious thought to his other love: film.

By the summer of '67, I had been going up and down to New York. I'd been shooting this bizarre movie with Charlie Frizzell and Joan Oppenheim and Doug Goldman. It was called "Get Fat at the Watertown Federal." Neuwirth was in New York at the time, hanging out at Leacock-

Pennebaker, cadging film equipment from them. Come June, we began to get word from California that there was going to be one hell of a music festival, and that it was going to be done nonprofit, which appealed to me. Pennebaker made a few phone calls, and they said, "Sure, you can come film it." So I made sure I got a job on that.

The Monterey Pop Festival was the first union of the various elements of what was becoming the New American Pop Music. In the course of two years, America had finally overtaken the British rock explosion with the Soul sound of people like Otis Redding, Joe Tex, Sam and Dave, Wilson Pickett, and James Brown; with the L.A. sound of the Doors and the Mamas and the Papas; the Folk Rock sound of The Byrds and the Lovin' Spoonful; the Electric Blues sound of the Butterfield Blues Band, The Blues Project, and Canned Heat; and the psychedelic sound of Jimi Hendrix, the Grateful Dead, the Jefferson Airplane with Grace Slick, Quicksilver Messenger Service, and Big Brother and the Holding Company with Janis Joplin.

San Francisco was becoming the center of

another musical culture, and already California was in the process of being psychedelicized. With the assistance of the ubiquitous Neuwirth, Cooke led the River Boys into this new world.

After the pop festival, Siggins and Joe Val flew out, and we played for Joan Baez at the Big Sur Festival. Then we did the Berkeley Folk Festival, and we played the Jabberwock in Berkeley for a week, and then we played the Ash Grove in L.A. Peter Berg from Berkeley was our bass player for these gigs, and he decided to assume an alias for a time. He dressed in an entirely purple outfit, including a purple cape, jeans that were dyed purple, purple sneakers, and a great purple cowboy shirt. He was called "Purple Man," and became an instant legend.

We stayed at Peter's folks place, drinking their Jack Daniels and smoking this dope that Neuwirth had scored. It was called "icebag" because it came in plastic ice bags. It was the strongest dope any of us had smoked. Joe Val, however, was real leery of the crazo hippie scene that was coming on so strong at that point. When Bob and I started wearing psychedelic shirts on stage, Joe didn't know what to make of it. He was real wary that we were going to get him in a scene where he could get arrested. So he stayed somewhere else, while we stayed at the beach and gooned out listening to "Sgt. Pepper's Lonely Hearts Club Band."

Joe had to go home the last night, so David Grisman played mandolin with us, and we did the first painted-face, bluegrass opera. Neuwirth and his girl, Tonto, painted our faces, and we played the Ash Grove. We started the set, introduced the first song with a story, then the next guy would have to pick up the story and lead it into the next song. Things were so loose that summer of '67 that the audience just accepted all of this.

After that summer it was clear to me that whatever was happening musically was happening in California, and that it was time to leave Cambridge. By this time I knew Albert Grossman a little from our encounters when Neuwirth had been road managing Dylan. When a chance came up through Albert to become the road manager for Big Brother, I took it. Big Brother was an early rock band. Those early San Francisco people had something going like what we had had in the early days of Cambridge. They were bright, they came out of an academic background. They were into drugs, but for exploratory reasons. Their music was very personal. They hadn't come out of the Berkeley folk scene, which I knew well and loved, but which had remained a very pure little folk music cell. Many of the San Francisco people came from Palo Alto. They had been folkies who played bluegrass and blues and all kinds of stuff. Jerry Garcia was one of them. When the scene became less productive for folk, the Palo Alto people sort of migrated to San Francisco and the whole psychedelic scene started to evolve. The Berkeley people just turned to other things for their living and kept music as an avocation so they could continue to play whatever kind of music they wanted to with no commercial pressures.

I really liked the people in Big Brother, and I grew to love Janis. That job was an opportunity to see what I wanted to do, to get me out to California, to make some money, to meet some people, and see what the possibilities were for me to get into the movie business. Before Janis died, Neuwirth and I were hard at work getting a movie together called "The Fool of Paris," which was going to have Michael J. Pollard and Janis in it. We couldn't get the money together, but I did write my first script out of a bunch of notes that Neuwirth had accumulated. So at least I had done that, and it occurred to me, "Well, I wrote a script out of somebody else's idea. Suppose I wrote one out of an idea of my own." That ultimately led me to where I am today: writing screenplays in Hollywood and still trying to get one to the silver screen.

JANIS JOPLIN at the 1968 Newport Folk Festival. Contact shots by Ali Sullo. Photograph by Rick Sullo.

el Lyman and Jim Kweskin wound up out in Hollywood, too, but they took a different route. After the 1965 Newport Folk Festival, Mel journeyed up to Woodstock hoping somehow to connect with Dylan and talk to him about the direction his music was taking. He never got to see him. The next Spring, after Richard Fariña died, and before the next Newport Festival, he called Mimi Fariña and Joan Baez, among others, to try to get people back into the spirit of folk music. At that Festival Mel and Jim joined with Pete Seeger on the Sunday night program to emphasize their commitment to the Guthrie/Seeger tradition, but even as they did, the commercial world of the music business was tugging at their sleeves. The first page of the Newport program book had a big picture of Mel selling the Hohner Blues Harp. The ad read, "Until now, harmonicas just weren't made for blues. For one thing, they didn't last. After two or three blues sessions it was tough even for a musician like Mel to get a good sound. The punishment of blues wailing often caused the reeds to lose pitch and flat out. Now you've got the Blues Harp . . . Mel said the Blues Harp was the best harmonica he'd ever played. See if you don't agree."

The Kweskin Band was involved more than ever in show business. Albert Grossman had provided them with a road manager, Jon Tapplin; a full concert and club schedule; and television appearances on the Roger Miller Show, the Al Hirt Show, and others. He also introduced them to Mo Ostin at Reprise Records and was in the process of extricating them from their Vanguard contract and negotiating a new deal with Reprise. Bill Keith was learning the pedal steel guitar, Richard Greene was soon to join the band on fiddle, and Geoff was looking to get into a more arranged style of music. A wonderful seamstress in L.A. was making them some pretty far-out stage outfits. The Jug Band was moving out.

Right after the '66 Festival Mel met Jesse Benton through David Gude, who had started out as a singer, but had been working for several years for Vanguard as an engineer. Davy's family had known Lee Hays and the rest of the Weavers, so he was firmly in the Guthrie tradition. His family spent summers out on Martha's Vineyard, which was where he had a group called the Islanders that had done some concerts on the Vineyard with Bill Keith and Jim Rooney and Tom Rush back in the early sixties. Jesse was the daughter of the well-known American populist painter, Thomas Hart Benton. The Bentons also had a place on the Vineyard as well as one in Kansas, where he was from. Jesse was a beautiful, striking girl, with a voice to match. She had appeared on one of Manny Greenhill's "Night Owl" concerts back in the late fifties, and anyone who ever heard her sing never forgot her.

Soon after meeting Jesse, Mel acquired some property in a run-down area of Boston called Fort Hill. The hill was actually one of the oldest parts of Boston, and the Fort was part of the fortifications during the revolutionary struggle with the British. A tower stands there from which you can see the entire city. It is a powerful location, which is possibly why it appealed to Mel. Mel, Jesse, Davy, and some others started what came to be called the Fort Hill Community. Soon,

THE KWESKIN JUG BAND (1967) (left to right) RICHARD GREENE, FRITZ RICHMOND, JIM KWESKIN, GEOFF MULDAUR, MARIA MULDAUR, and BILL KEITH. *Photograph by Charles Frizzell.*

Jim and Marilyn Kweskin moved from Huron Avenue to the Hill.

Kweskin began to find that his life as the leader of the Jug Band and his life as a member of the Community were pulling him in two different directions.

For a while I was very enthralled with the idea of entertaining people and having them applaud and love me. I would eat it right up. But it was through learning things from Melvin that I came to a different realization. You learn something from someone because you realize when they say something it is the truth. After a while that experience became very unsatisfying. What I really wanted to do was to be *with* people, to share something, to communicate something and have something communicated back and have a relationship — and not be an entertainer.

When Jim tried to put his new ideas into practice, Geoff Muldaur found himself in an awkward position.

Mel left because the music wasn't honest enough. I guess it meant that we didn't see God every minute or some bullshit. But from Kweskin's point of view it was true. He had to sing all the jive shit. Kweskin had to go "Deet Deedly Dum" and he wanted to sing "You Are My Sunshine." I got to pour my heart out.

The last few months were the dumbest. We'd sit on the edge of the stage, me and him. Some poor guy would have called out for "Rag Mama." I'd have to say, "Okay, Jim, why don't you want to do 'Rag Mama?' We're being paid to be here. What do you think?" Then he'd say what he thought, and the guy in the audience and Kweskin would have a conversation. Sometimes I'd say, "Jim, you're so into this frame of mind that I don't think you should play this set," and he'd leave, and I'd try to do some of his songs. He was struggling. Mel had left, but he was very much there as far as Jim was concerned.

Finally, Kweskin announced to the rest of the band that he was going to disband at the end of the series of gigs they had lined up. Bill Keith accepted the news with his usual reserve.

Towards the end things got a little strange. One gig we played was at some Catholic girls' school. On the way up, Jim talked about wanting to swear and use dirty words on stage. That was later carried through by the Lyman Family when they got into provoking reactions from the audience. It was not enjoyable for me to be involved in those later gigs. On the very last gig, Jim very ceremoniously shaved off his mustache, which signified the end of the band. He told us that he would be doing it, so we all grew them. I have had mine since then.

After the Jug Band broke up, I stayed around. Dan Bump and I had the Beacon Banjo Company and were making banjo tuners and pewter pieces. I was getting into the steel guitar more and more, and at one point I had to decide between devoting my full time to the company or being a full-time musician. I finally decided for good when I went with Ian and Sylvia in 1968.

In a way, my commitment to music was made

MEL LYMAN, JIM KWESKIN, and PETE SEEGER at the 1966 Newport Folk Festival. *Photograph by Ed Fox. Courtesy of the Lyman Family.*

before I knew it. It was almost a decision by default, because it started when I first went to Washington, and it involved an acceptance of what I learned about the lifestyle. Most people don't like living out of a suitcase or in hotels for the rest of their life, but it's only if you say, "I will never do that," or, "I can't ride in the car that long," that you definitely exclude music as a way of life.

For each person there is one thing or a combination of things which make one subject which he may have been exposed to something which he must learn and know. It happened to me, and it happened through a specific kind of music — Bluegrass music. That is a kind of self-feeding energy. The more you learn, the more you want to learn. The same thing happened to Geoffrey with blues and Kweskin with ragtime. And within the Cambridge community there was an open-mindedness which included all of those kinds of music. When I finally left Cambridge, I didn't feel like I was leaving a scene behind. Music has kept our associations together over the years. Playing music is a great life. If you can make ends meet doing that, why do something else?

The breakup of the Jug Band forced Geoff Muldaur to make a decision, too.

It was like the bottom of our lives. Fritz Richmond was in shock; I was in shock; I couldn't believe it. Jim wouldn't allow us to continue without him, and I don't respect him for that. But Jim was a great leader, and without him we were nothing. He cared more about us than he did about himself until the last few months of the band, and you don't find that quality anymore. The guy was a true-heart beyond belief.

So after the band broke up we played a lot of pool, drank a lot of booze, and tried to figure out what to do next. I realized then that I would have to start relating to musicians on a non-family level. I was going to have to learn the language of music, which meant learning to read. That was a wilful act on my part. One day I heard "The Rites of Spring" by Stravinsky and went nuts and started studying. I would play that record every day and read along with the score. The first day I could only follow the first few bars, and the next day I went a little further. I did that every day for a year and learned to read music.

Fritz might have been shocked and saddened to see the Jug Band finally come to an end, but he wasn't unprepared. Paul Rothchild had been helping him get ready for a change.

Every time Fritz came to New York, he'd do what John Sebastian had done for two years. He'd sit and watch everything I did in the studio for hours on end. One day he called me from the road. He told me about the rumblings in the band. "I'm not sure how long this gig is going to last, and I'm not sure what I want to do next. I was wondering, if the band does break up, is there some job I could get working with you?" I said, "Any time you want, you could be my assistant or an engineer. I'll teach you how to be a producer." He said, "That's not my psychological style. I don't think I could do that. I'm a cautious, shy New Englander, and I don't think I could deal with artists on the level that you have to deal with them and be creative at it. But I'm great with machines, and I could probably be a really good engineer." I said, "You just say when." A number of months after that, he called me and said, "The band just had its final meeting. I'm done."

At that point, Elektra was in the very last stages of building its studio in California. John Haney was chief engineer. I went to John and asked him if there was a spot for Fritz to come in, and he said, "It he wants to come in and sweep the floors and carry coffee, that's fine with me. We'll put him on the payroll at $75.00 a week." I said, "Fritz will take the job."

I was living at Sebastian's house in the canyon on Ridpath Lane. Fritz came off the road and moved into the same room with me at Sebastian's.

John Haney liked him immediately. About a week later, Sebastian was moving out of his house, so Fritz and I took it over. It gave me a chance to have a California house, to be with someone that I liked, someone that I could room with. It would keep us together a lot of the time, so that there would be a constant flow of information. For a solid year we'd go home, and, besides hustling every chick in town and getting as loaded as we could, we'd be talking records. "How do you do this?" "Could this be done?" We continually evolved new things to do.

During that time, Fritz learned from John Haney and Bruce Botnick and me. He had three wonderful instructors in engineering. At the end of a year, he was a capable engineer. At the end of

another year, he was a superb engineer. We made some really excellent records together. He introduced me to a whole lot of the inner meaning of the world in the off-handed sidewise way that he does things. He was a great teacher for me, as were Eric von Schmidt and Geoffrey Muldaur. They taught me where to look for music. That whole period was a great education, which keeps me in focus still today. What is a good song? What is honest musically? What is dishonest? What are the limits? Granted, I have become part of the "pop" world. But as John Lennon said, "Grow with music, or it'll grow without you."

One of the influential books to appear in the late sixties was Marshall McLuhan's *The Medium is the Massage*. It wasn't long before Dave Wilson was being approached by people from the Fort Hill Community who were looking for a medium for Mel's message.

Eventually, I got involved in the media. I got together "Folk Music, U.S.A." for Channel 2, the Boston PBS station. Later I worked on their production of "What's Happening, Mr. Silver?" I did the music section of "Artists Look at the Sixties." We even did a few editions of *The Broadside* on video tape. It was a little ahead of the times.

At some point, Wayne Hansen came to me from the Fort Hill Community and told me that he'd been thinking that Boston should have an "underground" newspaper. I'd been thinking of that, too. Out in California the *Berkeley Barb* and *The Los Angeles Free Press* had already started. Within the next two weeks several other people, including Bud Burns, Ed Beardsley, and Gunther Weill, all talked to me about the same idea, so I brought everyone together at a think-tank on Mt. Auburn Street called "Crazy Eights," and we decided to do it.

There were long and heavy discussions about a name — a couple of suggestions were *The Mystic River Bridge* and *The Boston Anvil*. The people from Fort Hill suggested *Avatar,* which is a Hindu term for the embodiment of God's spirit. I wasn't totally enthusiastic about the name, but it did get the message across that the paper was going to be something other than news. It would be a forum for the "underground community," with a spiritual direction. That direction was not going to be limited to the spiritual values of the people from Fort Hill, although they would be well represented. We weren't thinking of it as "Mel Lyman's newpaper." The people from Fort Hill

didn't tell us that. They talked a lot about Mel, but the rest of us saw them as contributing individuals not as spokesmen for Mel. That was beyond our concept.

What was very difficult about working with *Avatar* was that you were always dealing with Mel *in absentia.* How do you deal with three persons who have a vote who say, "Mel says . . ." I'd say, "I can't argue with Mel. He's not here." So we'd go 'round and 'round. About the fourth issue we voted them out. They got very penitent and came back, saying that they understood better what it was all about, and in our ebullient brotherhood and camaraderie we not only welcomed them back, but gave them an additional vote! After that it really became "Mel" oriented.

At some point in the Spring of '68 the people on Fort Hill started withdrawing, and they decided to take *Avatar* away from all the people who were working on it — to take it up to the Hill. At that point the rest of us hired a lawyer. I was still president of the corporation on paper. They had never voted in another president and they hadn't filed any of the necessary corporate forms with the state so it was very easy to have a corporate meeting and vote to take it all away from them. But this all took time, and in between came the famous issue that was confiscated by Fort Hill. They came in the middle of the night and confiscated thirty thousand issues and stored them in the tower on the Hill! Craziness! I put out five more issues of *Avatar.* Then the Fort Hill people regained control. I resigned along with Sandy Mandeville, and we walked out free, never to be tempted again.

At the same time a splinter group had broken from *Avatar* just to cover the Spock trial which was going on in Boston. They called themselves the *Free Press.* Somewhere in all of this *The Phoenix* started as well. We were doing *The Broadside* the whole while. It was a killer time.

The Broadside finally stopped in 1970 as a result of all that was going on. The competition on the newsstand had become ferocious. There was *Avatar, The Mole, Boston After Dark,* and *The Phoenix.* Street vendors were the only means we had to keep going. Because we had a second-class mailing permit we were not allowed to sell to vendors for less than half of the cover price of the magazine — 12½¢. *The Phoenix* and *Boston After Dark* got into a circulation war. They were charging vendors between 2¢ and 5¢ apiece, which put us out of the ball game.

MEL LYMAN Photograph by Michael Harvest.

294

Whatever the controversies surrounding the publication of *Avatar*, it certainly succeeded in getting Mel's message to the world. One person who responded to the message was Owen DeLong, one of the charter members of Geoff Muldaur's "last call" gang.

he country followed Dylan off into rock music and others followed Mel off into Fort Hill in the end of '66. I went in '68. In '68 I was still in my apartment in Harvard Square, but it was absolutely dead. I knew that if I stayed there one more year I was going to die myself. Martin Luther King getting killed and Bobby Kennedy getting killed was like the end of it. People came from all over the country in response to Mel's message. There were ten people from Michigan who read an *Avatar*, took a train, wound up on Fort Hill, and are still there. I was a Ph.D. candidate in government and I was reading everyone in the world, and no one was making as much sense as he was. It was very clear to me. The spirit had gone there. He's the kind of person who forces you to make a choice. If you are looking for what he is doing, and you see that he is really doing it, you either join, or you find a lot of reasons why not to join.

What I learned from Mel was that the whole revival of folk music and what happened around it was a gift from God and that, once having received it, you then had to work hard to do something with it. I was just a student at Harvard. The whole thing was a gift for me. It gave me all this music and all these people and all this life. Then, when it went away and I was still sitting there in my apartment, I realized that what he'd been telling me for five years was true and that I had to go out and do something. I had been going to work for Bobby Kennedy. Now, where was I going to do it? With Melvin and what he was doing. That was it for me, anyway. It was time to get together with other people who wanted to have personal relationships and build and to have the faith that if we build honestly enough and long enough that we would at least create a life together. Everyone of us has had opportunities to do other things and yet everybody has stayed in the community, brought together by the music — which still binds us together. Music — folk music, especially — is the binding force.

For many of Mel's friends and admirers it was not his simple philosophy that presented a problem, it was the "us/them" mentality which was encouraged among his followers. It seemed that unquestioning devotion was becoming a prerequisite for sharing Mel's company. Simple love was not enough. Maria Muldaur found it more and more difficult to penetrate the barriers that were being placed between her and her friend and teacher.

We'd go visit, because Mel really had taught us a lot and we loved him. And I know that Mel loved singing with me and Geoff. But the people who started surrounding Mel were too rigid and just on too many trips. After the Jug Band broke up, we were still living in Cambridge. We did the *Pottery Pie* album, and at that time, they really made a pitch for us to join. They invited Geoff to play on a session for their *Avatar* record and at a certain point he said, "Hey, I love Mel because he's a great guy, not because he's God." I wasn't there, but apparently a deadly hush fell over the thing, and the next thing he knew he was "out."

Then they called me and made a play for me to get hooked into their trip, and I went down. It was the day of the first moon landing. I'll never forget that. We were all at the Petrucci and Atwell studio doing this cosmic session. Meanwhile, the moonwalk was happening on the television in the other room. We kept going in and out. There was this whole trip about how portentiously cosmic this all was. That night, we did "People Get Ready," and it was really beautiful, and Mel had tears in his eyes. But

OWEN DE LONG taking a dive. Photograph by John Cooke.

shortly after that, the party line got so complicated with Geoff and me that we just said, "We think we'll pass, thank you."

I think that Mel started out as a guy who was truly looking for the truth and thought he had found some answers and that people gravitated to him. There's a lot of people who are too chicken to write their own life story, who are kind of your weak, not-too-together people, and I think the whole trip corrupted him. I think he was truly right on at first, but the trip of him being worshipped corrupted his best intentions.

Jesse Benton found a guy important enough to protect from others, as her mother had protected Tom Benton. Mel had many old ladies in his life, but it was when she was with him that it really

started being the "inner circle" and the "outer peons," and you couldn't get in to see Mel, and things got more and more mysterious, and there were more and more slaves on the periphery actually drilling with arms and so on. I think she was a corrupting influence on the whole trip.

Some people say that you can judge a religious leader by his ability to get other people to give their lives and their worldly goods to him. By those standards Mel must be judged a success. His

MARIA MULDAUR. Photograph by Charles Frizzell.

community has properties across the country from Martha's Vineyard to Hollywood. His followers listen to Woody Guthrie on the tapedeck while they are wisked from place to place in a curtained limousine. Their collection of Thomas Hart Benton's paintings would be the envy of any museum. They entertain guests generously and gather 'round to sing songs on beautiful oriental rugs. They grow most of their food themselves on a farm in Kansas. They cruise on a yacht which would make Jay Gatsby's eyes light up. Everyone in the community works or contributes in some way to the common good. They have an ambitious project underway which involves collecting, cataloguing, and taping as much of American popular, jazz, and folk music as they can in their quest to preserve for posterity what they consider to be true tradition of America, the music of its people, uncontaminated by crass commercialism. By choosing to live this way their gaze is more inward than outward, their view is more to the past than the future, and they are committed to an insular way of life, apart from their former companions on the quest. As far as Jim Kweskin is concerned, though, he's a better man than he was.

I was a dope smokin' , beer drinkin', sex fiend until I met Mel Lyman! Now I'm a record collector, I don't drink beer, and I have very little sex! But that's not it, of course. My whole relationship with other people has changed. I never realized how shallow I was when I was in Cambridge. However, I did learn a lot there from people like Rolf and Eric and then Mel. It was a beginning. It was a whole lot more than where I came from, which was Stamford, Connecticut.

JIM KWESKIN. Photograph by John Cooke.

FUN IN THE SUN

JOAN BAEZ, Vanguard recording artist, and MAYNARD SOLOMON, Vanguard Recording Society President. (1964) All in fun, of course, but the Cambridge group didn't have much luck with their New York record companies. The Kweskin Jug Band had a particularly hard time with Vanguard when they wanted to leave the label. Maynard Solomon, whose business it is to make records, steadfastly remains off the record when it comes to discussing most of the events that concern many of the people in this book. Maynard, who won Joan Baez over with his liberal attitudes and proletarian decor, proved that signing a contract is more than an exercise in penmanship. Photograph by Rick Stafford.

ISLANDS IN THE RAIN. NEWPORT '67.
JOAN BAEZ was still the queen, but there was competition in the wings. JONI MITCHELL is wearing the pretty stockings and LEONARD COHEN is wearing an extremely heavy guitar. MANNY GREENHILL is wearing his sneakers, and JOAN is wearing her beautiful feet. Photograph by David Gahr.

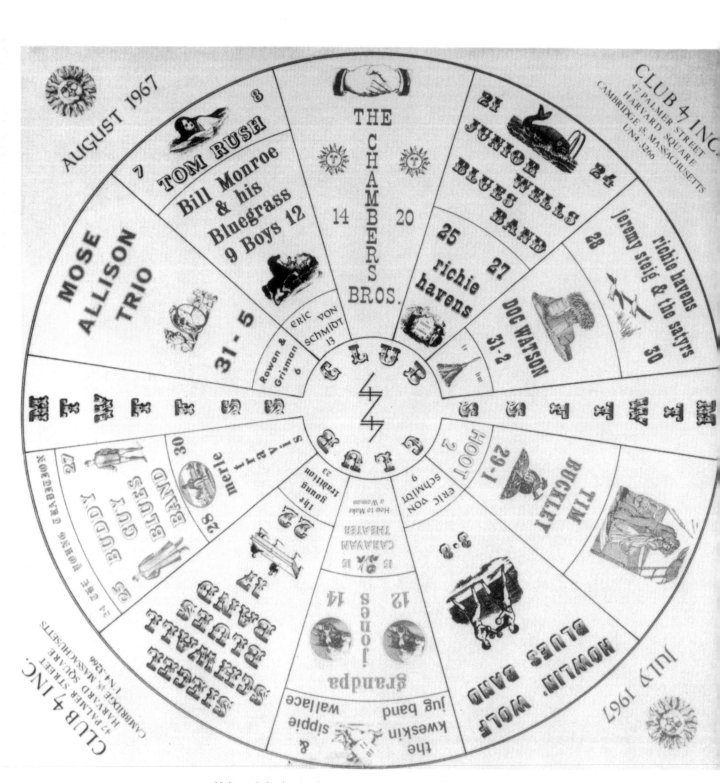

Club 47 Calendar for the summer of '67. Designed by Jim Rooney.

JIM ROONEY *living the life of a millionaire at Newport (1967). Photograph by Charles Frizzell.*

 he disbanding of the Kweskin Jug Band was the most obvious sign that the Cambridge/ Boston musical community was breaking up. For someone in the middle of everything like Jim Rooney, the obvious took a while to sink in.

One of the problems about running the Club 47 was that it was impossible to spend any time thinking about anything. Just getting the daily show on the road was a feat. With children's programs on Saturday afternoons and chamber music programs on Sunday afternoons and a concert series that we were doing with Byron, it was like a ten-day week. I was doing the booking, laying out the calendar, going to the printer's, mailing the calendar, getting the kitchen together, scheduling waitresses, putting the show on every night, and still finding time to party and play, but not as much as I used to.

What kept me going was the quality of the music we were presenting. The feeling in that room when the Chambers Brothers or Muddy Waters or Bill Monroe or the Butterfield Band or Mose Allison or whoever was on made me forget that we were slowly but surely going broke. And

the people who worked for us were great. The Club survived as long as it did because a lot of people who loved the music put in their time for nothing or next to nothing because they wanted to give something back for the music they received. We were all totally dedicated to the music and the musicians and really believed that we were the best music club any of us had ever seen.

By sometime in the fall of 1966 I started to become aware of what was going on in San Francisco and New York. My friends Charlie Rothchild and Peter Edmiston had opened up a place in New York on St. Mark's Place called the Balloon Farm. It was the first psychedelic dance hall in New York. They had the Fugs and various other groups with a mixed media film and light show. Charlie asked me if I knew a place they could open in Boston. There had been a coffee house called the Moondial which had a brief life in what long ago had been a synagogue on Berkeley Street in Boston. It was a big ballroom with a balcony. Charlie came up and looked at it and it looked right. The owner was a commercial filmmaker, and he had already made arrangements to lease the place out to a Boston branch of the Filmmakers' Cinematheque, which was run by George Pepper and some people from the Fort Hill community. Charlie had been burned in dealing with the New York branch of the Cinematheque, and didn't want to share the lease, so it never happened. If it had, I probably would have left the 47 to do it.

A little while later this guy named Ray Riepen came over to see me at the Club. Ray was a friend of Peter Edmiston's from Kansas City. He had been an Assistant D.A. there and was taking some graduate law courses at Harvard. On weekends he'd been going down to New York to visit his buddy Peter and had seen the business they were doing at The Balloon Farm. When he heard that Peter and Charlie were passing on the place in Boston, he decided to check it out. So he was asking me a lot of questions about booking acts and this and that. He liked to come on like he was just a little ol' country lawyer from Kansas, but Ray's head was screwed on tight. He had the know-how to deal with the politics of licenses and so on, which was a big problem in a city like Boston, where everyone was on the take. Of course, I discouraged him as much as I could and told him he'd never make money at it. He opened it up in the middle of the winter. I told him that was the worst possible time of year to do anything new. I would guess that he had to have made about one-hundred thousand dollars clear in the first year. Before he was through he also bought a couple of FM radio stations. WBCN in Boston became on of the top underground radio stations in the country. Ray did pretty good for an ol' country boy. He couldn't believe that none of us had done it. He saw right away that Boston was ripe for the plucking and went right in and plucked it clean. We were still apologizing for charging $1.50 at the door.

The opening of Riepen's club, cleverly named The Boston Tea Party, signaled the arrival of the psychedelic culture in Boston. Soon tie-die and flowered prints were all the rage. Drugs were to be had anywhere around the Boston Common. One fine spring day John Nagy found himself going to a "love-in" at Franklin Park.

It must have been one of the first "love-ins" in Boston, complete with kids rolling around in the mud. And who do I bump into there but Peter Rowan! He told me that he and David Grisman were getting a group together. When I heard what Peter was writing and what David was playing, it was like when you're in love. You don't ask; you know. This was the first musical experience that I had with other people that was uniformly agreeable to me. I jumped into it with all my heart and played with them for two years.

After two years in Nashville, the electric atmosphere in Cambridge was a total change for Peter, and he was ready for it.

 came back to Cambridge in 1967, not knowing what in the world I was going to do. All I knew was that I had written fifteen songs and that I wanted to play them. David Grisman had been to California and had just got back. We got together over at Jim Rooney's and Bill Keith's and picked some. We were all a bit played out on Bluegrass because the closer you got you realized that end of the tunnel there was Bill Monroe saying, "This is my music, not yours." So at that time we were really up to play some new music.

My tunes were almost anti-Bluegrass, although in fact they were Bluegrass slowed down. I was into hearing the notes ring on the instruments. I was into arpeggios instead of strumming. David played mandocello and I played guitar. If we hadn't been growing so fast we could have held onto that and matured the concept, but we were really getting caught up in the idea of forming a band. The 47 was having more and more bands. The Boston Tea Party started up. So the spirit of the times was definitely to take your folk music and make a band out of it, which we did with John Nagy and Paul Dillon. It was called Earth Opera. It was also when John Coltrane was creating magnificent music. I heard his records and bought a saxophone. We were trying to play everything from sweet bluegrass-oriented stuff to total free, dissonant music. Eventually we recorded for Elektra and toured with the Doors. The Vietnam war became a cancer which affected everyone. Our music became very socially oriented — almost apocalyptic. We took some of the social messages from the folk days and added the energy of rock and roll.

It's been ten years since then and I am finally able to feel at one with my music. It's like an arrow that you work on for years, and that arrow is going to fly true. Back then I had a lot of weird arrows, and I put them all in the air at the same time.

However much Boston tried to act as if the psychedelic culture was at home there, it was not the source of that energy. It was all coming from California. An attempt by MGM records to create the "Boss Town Sound" with groups like the Ultimate Spinach and the Beacon Street Union

PETER ROWAN. Photographer unknown. Courtesy of Peter Rowan.

was a failure. Like many others, Mitch Greenhill decided to move west. On the way he got a sad confirmation that he was moving in the right direction.

I had left Cambridge for California, had picked up Louise and Matty (who was a year old at the time, what a trip!) at her parents' place in Florida, and were almost through Texas when the transmission died a groaning, agonizing death.

So there we stayed on the outskirts of El Paso while we took care of this nonsense — bored, drinking beer, shooting pool, went to Juarez once — when, on the third day, there comes this phone call. It actually came through a phone booth outside the motel office; how they traced me I can only guess. It was Geoff and Fritz from "next call" at the apartment on Green Street. They were letting me know that the Oxford Grille, our traditional "last call," was gone. Or, as Memphis Minnie might have put it, "What's the matter with the Grille? Done burned down!"

MITCH GREENHILL at the Berkeley Folk Festival. Photograph by Manny Greenhill.

As Jim Rooney looked out the door of the Club at the flames and smoke, he took it as another sign that the party was over.

*T*he Grille had always been a place where I could go to get out of the Club even if it was only for a quick beer. A coffee house was never my idea of heaven. I don't even drink the stuff, it makes me too nervous. With the Grille gone, the Club was starting to feel a little bit like prison to me. The pressures of trying to compete with the Tea Party and the Unicorn were giving me a headache that never went away. That summer we had probably done more business than we ever had, but our expenses for talent went out of sight. The days of the Tom Rush/Jackie Washington cushion were long gone. I really broke the bank when I paid the Butterfield Band two thousand dollars for six nights. That was purely out of pride. I was bidding against George Papadopoulos at the Unicorn, and I was damned if I'd let him take Paul away from us. But that obviously couldn't go on. My one hope to get ahead of the game had been the concert series, but we discovered that anything short of total sellouts could get you in the hole faster and deeper than ever. Finally, I just had to give in. I was exhausted. I'd been in that room every day for two years, and I just didn't have anything more to give.

It was clear that the Club was going to have to move in one of two directions. It either had to find the capital to finance a move to a larger location which could perhaps have room in it for a gallery, a restaurant, or a cinema, or it had to close. Byron Linardos offered to give it a try.

I don't know whether I was trying to save it or close it. I wanted to try and save some people we owed money — printers, people like that. I remember feeling a lot of casualness among people who had been involved for a long time. It was just at a point. It was over. I think it went as far as it could without becoming something else.

Talk about idealism, at one point, I remember being asked what I would like to see the 47 become. And I loved what we came up with. I don't know where it came from. I wanted to buy a building, and in it house and consider all the arts. And have whatever you could sell — you could sell the music — have that take care of the paints for the painter. It all boiled down to stuff like paints — to being able to buy paints for a painter who couldn't buy paint; having a room for him to paint in, if he needed that. Or whatever. And to have whatever he did become a part of the place — not belong to the place — but be a part of it. And I could see all of this — from dance to everything. If someone needed an instrument, or lessons, and couldn't afford them, we'd provide it. And this all had to do with a master organizer, a god of the place, saying, "Yes, you're worth it." But that was a dream.

The Club 47 finally closed in April of 1968. Jim Rooney wasn't there. He was in New Orleans working on the production of a jazz festival and getting ready to work for the Newport Folk Foundation as talent coordinator for the Folk Festival and with Robert L. Jones as a road manager of jazz shows for George Wein's Newport Jazz Festival. He was gone. That spring Bob Siggins became "Dr. Bob." He got his Ph.D. in biochemistry from B.U., and that summer he and Betsy moved to Washington where he went to work at the National Institute of Health.

Even as all this was happening, and everybody started going in all directions at once, the life of the Cambridge community was being perpetuated by many young pickers and singers who had heard the music on records and had dreamed of the day when they could be a part of this world. Bonnie Raitt was just in time to be too late, but, as it turned out, it didn't matter.

  had been waiting to come to Cambridge since I was fourteen. I used to come east from California to a camp in the Adirondacks — Camp Regis. It was run by Quakers, but most of the people there were Jewish and progressive. The counselors went to colleges like Antioch and Brandeis and Swarthmore and were into the civil rights, peace movement thing. I went there every summer from '58 until about '65. It counteracted the whole

DR. BOB SIGGINS with his inflatable party duck. Photograph by John Cooke.

BONNIE RAITT Photograph by Dick Waterman.

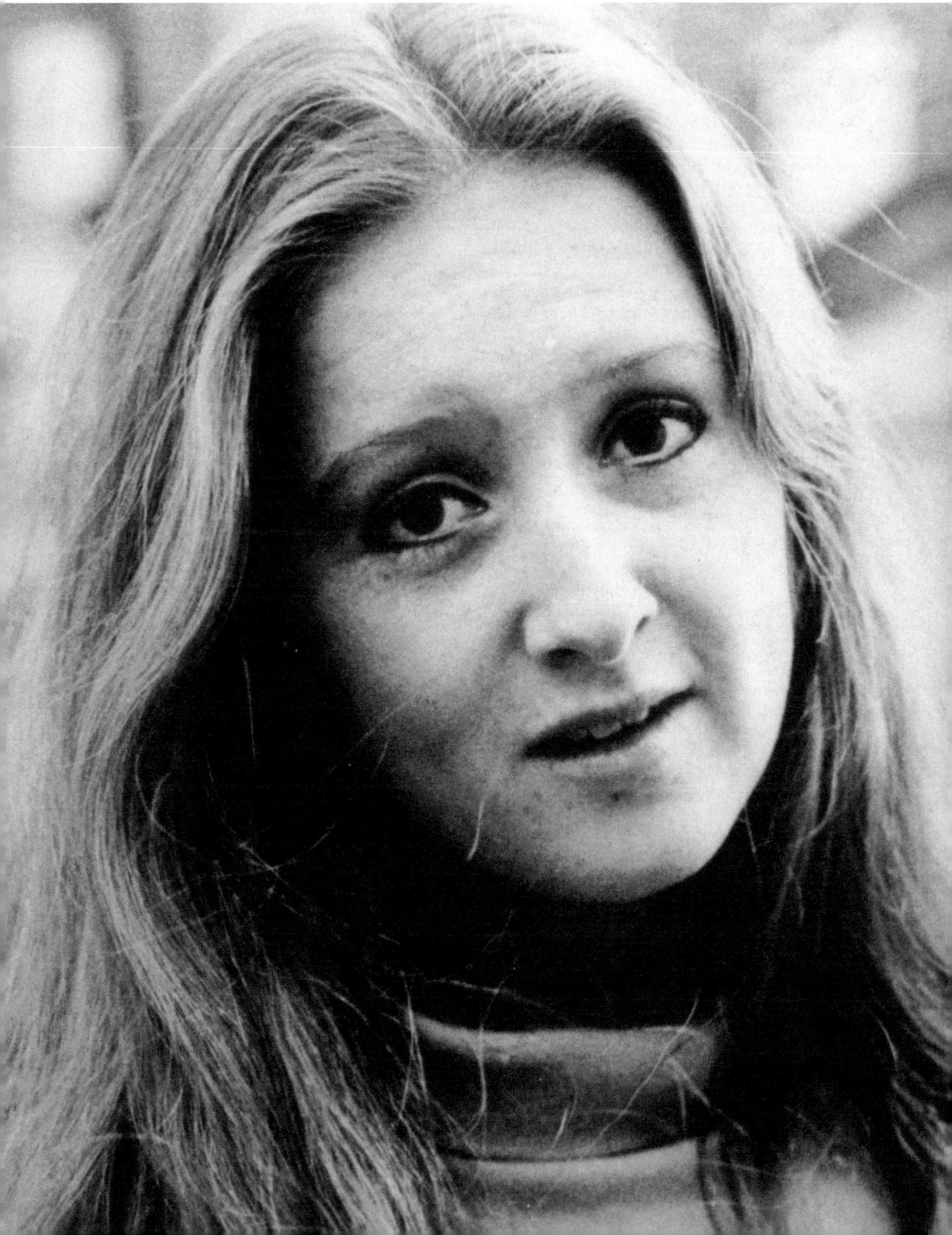

beach boy scene in California which I couldn't stand.

I started wearing peace symbols around my neck and listened to an Odetta record that one of the counselors had brought up in '59, and I learned to play guitar from that. Then I heard Joan Baez and fell in love. I wanted to pierce my ears and grow thin cheekbones. When I heard the *Blues at Newport '63* album, I wanted to get away from camp and go to the folk festival, but I was "too young." I was thirteen.

When I heard "Candy Man" by Mississippi John Hurt on that album, I went, "What is that?" I'd been doing a lot of Odetta and Joan Baez stuff, but when I heard that I went — "I don't know what that stuff is, but this guy is so cute, his voice is so cute, and his guitar is so pretty..." I just had to learn about it. I couldn't figure out the tuning because I just wasn't versed in guitar. I didn't ever look at a guitar book, and I didn't know anybody who played that stuff. I found out later that Taj Mahal and Ry Cooder were all in L.A. at the time and that there was a little burgeoning folk scene going on at the Ash Grove, but I was living on top of Cold Water Canyon and was still only thirteen or fourteen.

By the time I was in the last two years of high school, I went to a Quaker school in Poughkeepsie, New York, and that's where I started to hear about the Club 47. I just couldn't wait. I was playing guitar, and I was a real folkie. It wasn't that I wanted to play music so much, it's just that I wanted to be around it. So I chose Radcliffe because of Cambridge and the Club 47 and went there in the fall of '67. I was a regular little freshman, wearing my tights, but I soon started listening to the Harvard radio station, WHRB, and found out that some of the guys like David Gessner and Jack Fertell were connected with the folk and blues circuit.

Jack started taking me to the Club 47. The first person I saw there was Spider John Koerner, who I fell in love with and since have never stopped being in love with. I saw Canned Heat. Jack wouldn't let me see Taj Mahal because he figured I'd jump the stage! I saw Joni Mitchell, wearing that little, red satin, pleated mini-skirt with her hair rolled up. That was it! Then at some point Jack called me up and said, "How'd you like to come and meet a friend of mine?" — knowing full well I'd fall over when I found out who it was — and I showed up at Dick Waterman's house, and Son House was sitting there! By this time I was hanging out with the blues freaks at the radio station, trading Charlie Patton licks and Son House licks and trying to see who had the most esoteric licks. So here was Son House in the flesh, and we actually sat with him all afternoon because Dick had to go out and do something, and he didn't want to leave Son House alone. That was the beginning, boy! After that I really started getting proficient on the guitar.

I guess Dick was sort of interested in me because he likes redheads or something. There's nothing worse than meeting someone and finding out that the last five women they went out with were all redheads — makes you feel really special. The next time I saw him was when Buddy Guy and Junior Wells played at the 47. Being Dick's friends, we came in, and that's when Dick and I started hanging out. He took me with Buddy Guy over to "Uncle T's" radio show at WTBS at M.I.T. We went there and made out in the car in the parking lot across the street. That was great. Buddy did an interview that night, and that was the first time I'd ever been behind the scenes and actually meeting the people. I wasn't trying to be a groupie. It was just that Dick was really trying to put the make on me, and I wasn't going out with anybody. I thought he was real neat. You know, he was Walking God! I was real affected by John Hurt, and he had just died before I met Dick, and just talking with Dick about him and all the other people he knew was a trip, and there was no way I wasn't going to hang out with him.

I went to Europe for the summer, and when I got back things had changed. The 47 was gone. About the best you could do for music was the Ultimate Spinach at the Tea Party or Canned Heat at the Psychedelic Supermarket with Al Wilson wearing that hat with his earplugs in. Waterman had moved to Philadelphia because Skip James lived there. I took the Spring semester off and went down to live with Dick. Skip was ailing, so we used to go out every Sunday and have dinner with him until the time he died. The Second Fret and the Mainpoint were still going, which sort of filled Dick's nostalgia for the old 47 scene.

One night I was in this club and I saw this girl doing "500 Miles," and I said, "This is 1969. There's better music around than this to be doing. If she can get twenty bucks, so can I." By then I had met Fred McDowell, too, and I was doing a lot of blues stuff, some Judy Collins, some James Taylor. So Dick helped me get a job at the Second Fret, and it was well received.

I went back to school in the Fall, and about the only thing I did in Cambridge was to hang out at Jack's Bar on Massachusetts Avenue every Monday night, when Koerner moved back from Minnesota or Denmark or whatever planet he had been living on and started playing there Monday nights. Chris Smither, Paul Geremia, Peter Bell, a couple of journalists from *The Phoenix* and I would go and get completely piefaced. Cambridge to me is drinking endless beers at Jack's watching Koerner and having peanuts, going out in back, smoking a joint, and coming back. It was a good time.

I never did get into working the places on Charles Street for money. I worked once at the Sword in Stone and only made eight bucks. My friends in Worcester said you could make twenty bucks a night up there, so I'd go there on the Trailways bus with my dog. I had a dog I traveled with and my guitar. I'd take my clothes on the bottom of the kennel which I trusted the dog on, and I'd go hang out on the Clark University campus with my friend Paul Pena and play any number of seven or eight coffee houses there every other weekend while I was in school.

Bonnie was on her way down the same road that the others had discovered ten years earlier. Cambridge was no longer *the* place to be. The energy created there had been transferred to people all over the country. Bob Neuwirth, no stranger to buses himself, is one who helped to spread it around and can see the results.

Cambridge was one of the navels of the cultural period, and a lot of influence came out of it. It put a lot of intelligence into the guitar movement, and the guitar movement was the forerunner of the peace movement. It made people aware enough to allow the peace movement to enter people's consciousness. Between Elvis Presley and the folksingers, the guitar movement enabled kids to believe in youth and the correctness of their own thinking. So when the peace movement started, they didn't buckle under at the first signs of parental authority — the people who said, "You're Communists. Shut up and crawl under a rock."

It's great to know that as long as you have the basic skills of being able to play the guitar and write, you'll never not be able to get a burger and a beer and a blow job. The three "b's." We definitely learned to survive and have a good time with or without money.

There are some who've got the patina, but there's a gap between the soul and the patina. The true enjoyment of being an existentialist is not available to them. It's scary, but if we hadn't gotten loose, we'd be ciphers. It's a party that's still going on, as far as I can tell.

NOW is just for a moment,
Then in a moment, it's THEN.
FOREVER is WAS, NOW, and WILL BE,
While THE END comes again and again.

AFTERWORD

This story is like a long narrative ballad. It is still being made up and has no end. As a result of our life together we each found ourselves charting our own course and abandoning the one that had been set for us by our parents or by society at large. Spontaneity replaced security as something to be desired. The quest became as important as what it was we were questing after. We redefined ourselves as people through the music we chose to sing and play and listen to. Our school had no structure. We made up our curriculum and shared between us. Our progress was marked by the level of our performance onstage, on recordings, and among ourselves.

There were always more questions than answers, and the questions concerned things other than music. What were the limits — the limits of life? What are the bounds of freedom? What is the cost? All are questions which have been asked before and will be asked again, but which had been put aside or ignored by the generation before to save us the pain of trying to find the answers for ourselves. As it turned out, we didn't want that. We were willing to take our music and our life raw and make of it what we would. If it takes a lifetime, what of it? What else is a lifetime for but to create yourself in some way — as yourself, not what somebody else thinks you are or should be?

For most of us, music has been the way we got to where we wanted to go, and music, we discovered, is a very important thing in many people's lives, whether they play it or not. It is a basic form of communication. The energy created by the rediscovery of the *living* root forms of American folk music and their recombination through electricity, chemistry, and technology into the music of today and tomorrow is what changed our lives. We allowed that reality to enter our lives, and we, in turn, are using it to create something of our own that we can hand on to those who are to follow. As many of us as are still alive are still playing, singing, photographing, painting, acting, recording, dancing, potting, inventing, quilting, writing, cooking, carpenting, loving, producing, sculpting, learning, building, teaching, praying, growing, and trying to get to the bottom of it all. We invite anybody who wants to do so to follow us down.

The voices in this book, the people who have joined with us on our journey, are set in **demi-bold type.** We wanted to celebrate their words. A lot of us are pickers and singers and are still on our long journey home, wherever home may be. The following is a partial list of the record companies who have issued our records, starting with our most recent affiliations and working back. It is a way to set the voices free.

Eric Andersen:	solo on Arista, Columbia, and Vanguard Records; with the Woodstock Mountains Revue on Rounder Records.
Joan Baez:	solo on Portrait, A & M, and Vanguard Records.
Paul Butterfield:	solo on Bearsville; with Better Days on Bearsville; with the Butterfield Blues Band on Elektra Records.
Rolf Cahn:	solo on Folkways; with Eric von Schmidt on Folkways Records.
The Chambers Brothers:	on Columbia Records.
The Charles River Valley Boys:	on Elektra and Prestige Records.
Bob Dylan:	solo on Columbia and Elektra/Asylum Records; with The Band on Elektra/Asylum Records.
Mimi Fariña:	solo on A&M Records; with Tom Jans on A&M Records; with Dick Fariña on Vanguard Records.
Mitch Greenhill:	with Mayne Smith on Bay Records; with Rosalie Sorrels on Folk Legacy; solo on Prestige Records.
John Herald:	solo on Bay and Paramount Records; with the Woodstock Mountains Revue on Rounder; with Mud Acres on Rounder; with the Greenbriar Boys on Vanguard.
Bill Keith:	solo on Rounder; with the Woodstock Mountains Revue on Rounder; with Mud Acres on Rounder; with Geoff and Maria Muldaur on Reprise; with Muleskinner on Elektra/Asylum; with the Blue Velvet Band on Warner Brothers; with the Kweskin Jug Band on Reprise and Vanguard; with Jim Rooney on Prestige Records.
Spider John Koerner:	solo on Sweet Jane; with Willie Murphy on Elektra; with Tony Glover and Dave Ray on Elektra Records.
Jim Kweskin:	solo on Mountain Railroad; Reprise, and Vanguard Records; with the Lyman Family on Reprise Records; with the Kweskin Jug Band on Reprise and Vanguard Records.
"Banana" Levinger:	with the Youngbloods on RCA Records.
Taj Mahal:	solo on Columbia Records.
Bill Monroe:	solo on MCA Records.
Geoff Muldaur:	with Amos Garrett on Flying Fish Records; solo on Reprise Records; with Better Days on Bearsville; with Maria Muldaur on Reprise; with the Kweskin Jug Band on Reprise and Vanguard; solo on Prestige Records.
Maria Muldaur:	solo on Reprise Records; with Geoff Muldaur on Reprise; with the Kweskin Jug Band on Reprise and Vanguard; with the Even Dozen Jug Band on Elektra Records.
Bob Neuwirth:	solo on Elektra/Asylum Records.
Bonnie Raitt:	solo on Warner Brothers Records.
Jim Rooney:	with the Woodstock Mountains Revue on Rounder; solo on Rounder; with Bill Keith on Rounder; with Borderline on UA/Avalanche; with Mud Acres on Rounder; with the Blue Velvet Band on Warner Brothers; with Bill Keith on Prestige records.
Peter Rowan:	solo on Flying Fish Records; with the Rowan Brothers on Elektra; with Old and In The Way on Rounder; with Muleskinner on Elektra/Asylum; with Sea Train on Capitol; with Earth Opera on Elektra Records.
Tom Rush:	solo on Columbia, Elektra, and Prestige Records.
John Sebastian:	solo on Warner Brothers Records; with the Lovin' Spoonful on Kama Sutra; with the Even Dozen Jug Band on Elektra.
Chris Smither:	solo on Poppy Records.
Mark Spoelstra:	solo on Columbia, Elektra, and Folkways Records.
Joe Val:	with the New England Bluegrass Boys on Rounder Records; with the Charles River Valley Boys on Elektra and Prestige; with Keith and Rooney on Prestige Records.
Eric von Schmidt:	solo on Philo, Poppy, Mercury, and Prestige Records; with Rolf Cahn on Folkways Records.
Jackie Washington:	solo on Vanguard Records.
Muddy Waters:	solo on Blue Thumb and Chess Records.
Doc Watson:	solo on United Artists, Poppy, and Vanguard Records; with Clarence Ashley and others on Folkway Records.
Roland White:	solo on Ridge Runner; with Country Gazette on United Artists; with Clarence White and the Kentucky Colonels on United Artists.
Peter Wolf:	with the Geils Band on Atlantic Records.

Cover Key

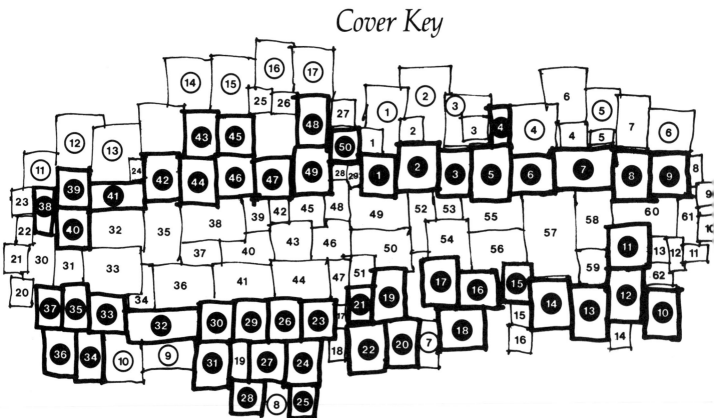

COLOR SHOTS (black circled numbers) clockwise from center top

1 / Rolf Cahn
2 / Eric von Schmidt
3 / Jim Rooney
4 / Betsy Schmidt
5 / Taj Mahal
6 / Jim Kweskin
7 / Tom Rush
8 / Bob Dylan
9 / Peter Wolf
0 / Peter Rowan
1 / Geoff Muldaur
2 / Debbie Green
3 / Fritz Richmond

14 / Bonnie Raitt
15 / Richard Fariña
16 / Maria Muldaur
17 / John Cooke
18 / Bill Keith
19 / Bob Neuwirth
20 / Joan Baez
21 / Steve Fassett
22 / Jack Landron
23 / Dick Waterman
24 / Paul Rothchild
25 / Mitch Greenhill
26 / Tony Saletan

27 / Joe Val
28 / Earl Crabb
29 / Chris Smither
30 / Tex Logan
31 / Joyce Chopra
32 / The Hillbilly Ranch
33 / "Banana" Levinger
34 / Barry Kornfeld
35 / Buzz Marten
36 / Ethan Signer
37 / John Nagy
38 / Mark Spoelstra
39 / Joe Chambers

40 / Manny Greenhill
41 / Brian Sinclair & Lynn Joiner
42 / Clay Jackson
43 / Bob Siggins
44 / Byron Linardos
45 / Dave Wilson
46 / Robert L. Jones
47 / Paul Arnoldi
48 / Eric Andersen
49 / Spider John Koerner
50 / Phil Spiro

SOURCES (circled numbers) clockwise from center top

1 / Sonny Terry
2 / Woody Guthrie
3 / Jimmie Rodgers
4 / Muddy Waters
5 / Elvis Presley
6 / Mississippi John Hurt
7 / Pete Seeger
8 / Uncle Dave Macon
9 / The Confederate Mountaineers

10 / The Carter Family
11 / Bill Monroe
12 / Leadbelly
13 / Burl Ives
14 / Hank Williams
15 / Josh White
16 / Lester Flatt & Earl Scruggs
17 / Jesse Fuller

*The Everly Brothers and The Beatles should be on this list, too.
We love ya madly.

MEMORABILIA clockwise from center top

1 / "Living on the Mountain" Keith & Rooney '63
2 / "Rolf Cahn & Eric von Schmidt" '61
3 / "The Blues Project" '64
4 / "Joan Baez" '61
5 / 1968 Newport Folk Festival "Kin" tag
6 / Woodcut by Peter Schumann, "Bread and Puppet Theater" '65
7 / Baez/Dylan concert poster by Eric von Schmidt '65
8 / Club 47 flyer for John Hammond '63
9 / "The Natch'l Blues" Taj Mahal '65
0 / "Mother Bay State Entertainers" '66
1 / Club 47 membership card '62
2 / Ash Grove Poster, Maybelle Carter & The New Lost City Ramblers
3 / Newport Folk Festival Program '68
4 / "See Reverse Side For Title" Jim Kweskin Jug Band '65
5 / Newport Folk Festival Program '64
6 / "Folk Singers 'Round Harvard Square'" '59
7 / "Little Wheel Spin and Spin" Buffy Ste. Marie '65
8 / Poster, "Joan Baez and Progressive Jazz" '59
9 / Humbead's Revised Map of the World / Earl Crabb & Rick Shubb
20 / "Richard Fariña & Eric von Schmidt" (England) '63
21 / "Dave Van Ronk, Folksinger" '63
22 / Newport Folk Festival Program '66
23 / "Doc Watson" '64
24 / "Sing Out!" '63
25 / "Charles River Valley Boys" '62
26 / Concert flyer, Folksong Society of Greater Boston
27 / "Judy Collins #3" '64
28 / 1965 Newport Folk Festival "Kin" tag
29 / Concert flyer, N.Y. Friends of Old Time Music

PHOTOGRAPHS (black & white) left to right

30 / Fritz Richmond circa '64
31 / Odetta '65
32 / The Chambers Brothers with Joan Baez '65
33 / Eric von Schmidt, Geoff Muldaur, and Robert L. Jones '63
34 / Rolf Cahn '60
35 / Bob Dylan at 1964 Newport Folk Festival
36 / Jim Rooney and Joe Val '67
37 / Charles River Valley Boys '60
38 / Nick Perls, Dick Waterman, Son House, and Phil Spiro.
39 / Dave Van Ronk circa '63
40 / Bill Monroe and Doc Watson circa '64
41 / Newport Folk Festival workshop audience '65
42 / Boston "Broadside" cover '63
43 / Mimi Baez and Dick Fariña wedding photo '63
44 / Jackie Washington (Jack Landron) circa '64
45 / Debbie Green circa '58
46 / Rev. Gary Davis circa '65
47 / Clay Jackson in Tangiers '62
48 / Geno Foreman circa '63
49 / Mimi and Dick Fariña with Joan Baez at Newport '65
50 / Fritz Richmond and Jim Kweskin circa '66
51 / Eric Andersen circa '63
52 / Mel Lyman at the Brandeis Folk Festival '64
53 / John Hammond circa '63
54 / Taj Mahal circa '64
55 / "We Shall Overcome" Newport Folk Festival finale '63
56 / Paul Butterfield, Newport Folk Festival blues workshop '65
57 / Maria Muldaur circa '64
58 / Joan Baez and Bob Dylan circa '64
59 / Tom Rush circa '63
60 / Cambridge mafia watching Butterfield at Newport '65
61 / Debbie Green and Mimi Fariña gone to California circa '68
62 / Ramblin' Jack Elliott '66

ERIC VON SCHMIDT *has been active in the fields of music and the graphic arts for thirty years. He has written four children's books and has illustrated many others, including the* JOAN BAEZ SONGBOOK. *He has had numerous one-man shows and his mural-size painting,* HERE FELL CUSTER, *can be seen at the Ulrich Museum in Wichita, Kansas. His musical aggregation is a loosely knit group known as The Cruel Family. He lives in Henniker, New Hampshire.*

JIM ROONEY *is also the author of* BOSSMEN: BILL MONROE & MUDDY WATERS *(Dial Press, 1970; Hayden Publishing, 1972). After leaving Cambridge, he lived in Newport and New York and was the talent coordinator for the Newport Folk Festival and road-managed Jazz concert tours for George Wein's Festival Productions. In 1970 he moved to Woodstock, New York, where he supervised the construction and operation of the Bearsville Sound Studios for Albert Grossman. He maintains his connection with the Woodstock musical community as a member of the Woodstock Mountains Revue. Currently, he lives in Nashville, Tennessee, where he writes songs and is a member of Jack Clement's musical family, singing and playing rhythm guitar in Cowboy's Ragtime Band.*

JIM ROONEY *and* ERIC VON SCHMIDT
Photograph by Brad McCourtney